Forging a Socio-Legal Approach to Environmental Harms

Environmental harms exert a significant toll and pose substantial economic costs on societies around the world. Although such harms have been studied from both legal and social science perspectives, these disciplinary-specific approaches are not, on their own, fully able to address the complexity of these environmental challenges. Many legal approaches, for example, are limited by their inattention to the motivations behind environmental offences, whereas many social science approaches are hindered by an insufficient grounding in current legislative frameworks.

This edited collection constitutes a pioneering attempt to overcome these limitations by uniting legal and social science perspectives. Together, the book's contributors forge an innovative socio-legal approach to more effectively respond to, and to prevent, environmental harms around the world. Integrating theoretical and empirical work, the book presents carefully selected illustrations of how legal and social science scholarship can be brought together to improve policies. The various chapters examine how a socio-legal approach can ultimately lead to a more comprehensive understanding of environmental harms, as well as to innovative and effective responses to such environmental offences.

Tiffany Bergin is Assistant Professor in the Department of Sociology at Kent State University, USA. Previously, she was Sutasoma Trust Research Fellow and Director of Studies in Politics, Psychology and Sociology at Lucy Cavendish College, University of Cambridge.

Emanuela Orlando is Lecturer in Environmental Law at the School of Law, Politics and Sociology of the University of Sussex. Her main research interests lie in the area of EU and international environmental law. Prior to fully engaging in an academic career, she worked for major international law firms and the European Commission, and served as legal adviser for the Italian Ministry of Environment, Land and Sea (IMELS) in the framework of its bilateral cooperation activities in the Balkan countries.

Law, Justice and Ecology
Series editor: Anna Grear, Cardiff Law School, Cardiff University, UK

In an age of climate change, scarcity of resources, and the deployment of new technologies that put into question the very idea of the 'natural', this book series offers a cross-disciplinary, novel engagement with the connections between law and ecology. The fundamental challenge taken up by the series concerns the pressing need to interrogate and to re-imagine prevailing conceptions of legal responsibility, legal community and legal subjectivity, by embracing the wider recognition that human existence is materially embedded in living systems and shared with multiple networks of non-humans.

Encouraging cross-disciplinary engagement and reflection upon relevant empirical, policy and theoretical issues, the series pursues a thoroughgoing, radical and timely exploration of the multiple relationships between law, justice and ecology.

Titles in the series:

Law and the Question of the Animal/
Edited by Yoriko Otomo and Edward Mussawir

Wild Law – In Practice
Edited by Michelle Maloney and Peter Burdon

Earth Jurisprudence
Peter Burdon

Contributions to Law, Philosophy and Ecology: Exploring Re-Embodiments
Edited by Ruth Thomas-Pellicer, Vito De Lucia and Sian Sullivan

Law as if Earth Really Mattered
The Wild Law Judgment Project
Edited by Nicole Rogers and Michelle Maloney

Forging a Socio-Legal Approach to Environmental Harms
Global Perspectives
Edited by Tiffany Bergin and Emanuela Orlando

The Global Emergence of Constitutional Environmental Rights
Joshua C. Gellars

Forging a Socio-Legal Approach to Environmental Harms

Global Perspectives

Edited by
Tiffany Bergin and Emanuela Orlando

Routledge
Taylor & Francis Group
a GlassHouse Book

First published 2017
by Routledge
2 Park Square, Milton Park, Abingdon, Oxon OX14 4RN

and by Routledge
711 Third Avenue, New York, NY 10017

a GlassHouse book

Routledge is an imprint of the Taylor & Francis Group, an informa business

© 2017 selection and editorial matter, Tiffany Bergin and Emanuela Orlando; individual chapters, the contributors

The right of Tiffany Bergin and Emanuela Orlando to be identified as editors of this work has been asserted by them in accordance with sections 77 and 78 of the Copyright, Designs and Patents Act 1988.

All rights reserved. No part of this book may be reprinted or reproduced or utilised in any form or by any electronic, mechanical, or other means, now known or hereafter invented, including photocopying and recording, or in any information storage or retrieval system, without permission in writing from the publishers.

Trademark notice: Product or corporate names may be trademarks or registered trademarks, and are used only for identification and explanation without intent to infringe.

British Library Cataloguing in Publication Data
A catalogue record for this book is available from the British Library

Library of Congress Cataloging in Publication Data
A catalog record for this book has been requested

ISBN: 978-1-138-93663-8 (hbk)
ISBN: 978-1-315-67671-5 (ebk)

Typeset in Baskerville
by Taylor & Francis Books

Printed and bound by CPI Group (UK) Ltd, Croydon, CR0 4YY

Contents

List of illustrations   vii
List of contributors   viii
Acknowledgments   xii

PART I
Conceptualising a socio-legal approach to environmental harms   1

1 Forging a socio-legal approach to environmental harms   3
   EMANUELA ORLANDO AND TIFFANY BERGIN

2 Environmental crimes and harms: a green criminology approach and socio-legal challenges   20
   NIGEL SOUTH

3 Green criminology and the prevention of ecological destruction   38
   RUTH E. MCKIE, PAUL B. STRETESKY, MICHAEL J. LYNCH AND MICHAEL A. LONG

4 The EU and the protection of the environment through criminal law   58
   LUDWIG KRAMER

5 A law and economics approach to environmental crime   78
   MICHAEL G. FAURE

PART II
Assessing the limitations of current approaches to environmental harms   107

6 International financial institutions as facilitators of environmental crimes   109
   DAWN L. ROTHE AND VICTORIA E. COLLINS

7 Learning lessons from deepwater disasters: common ground in oil exploration in Brazil and the United States 132
DANIEL JACOBS AND MARCELO VARELLA

8 Toxic ships, environmental crimes, and the North–South discourse 154
JONA RAZZAQUE

PART III
Forging socio-legal solutions to environmental harms: lessons from around the world 183

9 Determining the public interest in environmental enforcement, sanctioning and prosecution 185
ANNE BROSNAN

10 The legal and social context of wildlife trafficking 205
TANYA WYATT

11 Eco-crime and green activism 220
REECE WALTERS

12 The criminalisation of the intentional destruction of cultural heritage 237
ANA FILIPA VRDOLJAK

13 Concluding thoughts: towards a socio-legal research and policy agenda on environmental crimes 267
TIFFANY BERGIN AND EMANUELA ORLANDO

Index 279

Illustrations

Figures

3.1	United States trends in criminal prosecutions, toxic releases and carbon dioxide emissions, 1995–2012	49
12.1	Arch of Titus, Rome, Italy	238
12.2	The Temple of Baal Shamin, Palmyra, Syria	260

Tables

3.1	Major multi-lateral environmental agreements (n=18)	43
6.1	Subscriptions to capital stock of the International Finance Corporation	119
6.2	Countries included in the World Bank extraction industry transparency initiative reports	127

Contributors

Tiffany Bergin is Assistant Professor in the Department of Sociology at Kent State University, USA. Previously, she was Sutasoma Trust Research Fellow and Director of Studies in Politics, Psychology and Sociology at Lucy Cavendish College, University of Cambridge. She is the author of *The Evidence Enigma* (Ashgate, 2013) and *Regulating Alcohol around the World: Policy Cocktails* (Ashgate, 2013).

Anne Brosnan is Chief Prosecutor with the Environment Agency, England. She is qualified to practise as a solicitor in both England and Australia where she has worked at the Department of Environment and Conservation, in Sydney. She has a Master's degree (MSc) in Environmental Quality Management. Anne established the Agency's Serious Casework Group in 2007 and was instrumental in the introduction of the English environmental civil sanctions regime in 2010. Anne is the President of the European Network of Prosecutors for the Environment (ENPE).

Victoria E. Collins is an Associate Professor in the School of Justice Studies at Eastern Kentucky University. Victoria's research and teaching interests include state crime, victimology, white collar crime, transnational crime and violence against women. Victoria has recently published a book with Routledge titled *State Crime, Women and Gender*. Some of Victoria's articles have appeared in journals such as *Social Justice, International Journal of Law, Crime and Justice, International Criminal Law Review, Critical Criminology, Contemporary Justice Review*, and *Australian and New Zealand Journal of Criminology*.

Michael G. Faure is Professor of International and Comparative Environmental Law and Director of the Maastricht European Institute for Transnational Legal Research (METRO), Maastricht University, and Professor of Comparative Private Law and Economics at Erasmus School of Law, Erasmus University Rotterdam, the Netherlands.

Daniel Jacobs is currently Visiting Associate Professor in the Management Department at Loyola Marymount University. Previously, following award-winning service at the Justice and State Departments in Washington, DC, he was the founding director of the first interdisciplinary graduate program in sustainability management in a US business school (which he led to a #1 sustainability specialty ranking by Bloomberg Businessweek). The author of *BP Blowout: Inside the Gulf Oil Disaster* (Brookings Institution, 2016), he lectures, consults and speaks about sustainability (including CSR), compliance and risk management in the US and abroad.

Ludwig Kramer served as Judge at the Landgericht Kiel (1969–2004) and as Official of the European Commission Environmental Department (1972–2004). He has written extensively in the field of environmental law, authoring some 20 books and more than 250 articles on that subject. He is visiting professor at University College London, and has lectured in more than 50 universities in Europe and North America. He is currently running the environmental law consultancy "Derecho y Medio Ambniente" in Madrid.

Michael A. Long is a Senior Lecturer in the Department of Social Sciences at Northumbria University. He conducts research on environmental issues, political economy and alternative agriculture and food systems. He has published two books and more than 40 peer-reviewed journal articles and book chapters. Some of his recent articles appear in *Deviant Behavior, Research in the Sociology of Work* and *Justice System Journal*.

Michael J. Lynch is a Professor of Criminology and Associate Faculty in the Patel School of Global Sustainability at the University of South Florida. He has been engaged in research related to environmental/green crime since the mid-1980s. His recent books include *Exploring Green Criminology* (Routledge, 2014, with P.B. Stretesky), *The Treadmill of Crime: Political Economy and Green Crime* (Routledge, 2014, with P.B. Stretesky and M.A. Long) and *Environmental Law, Crime and Justice* (LFB Scholarly, 2014, with R.G. Burns and P.B. Stretesky). Some of his recent work has appeared in *Critical Sociology, British Journal of Criminology* and *Capitalism Nature Socialism*.

Ruth E. McKie is a PhD student and research assistant at the Department of Social Sciences at Northumbria University. Her research interests include green criminology, environmental sociology, social movements and extreme energy. Her current research focuses on potential relationships between resistance to climate change mitigation, crime and deviancy, and political economic theory. She has recently published in the journals *Environmental Research Letters* (with P.B. Stretesky) and *Critical Criminology* (with P.B. Stretesky and M.A. Long).

Emanuela Orlando is Lecturer in Environmental Law at the School of Law, Politics and Sociology at the University of Sussex. She was formerly at the University of Cambridge, as Isaac Newton–Dorothy Emmet Research Fellow at Lucy Cavendish College and affiliated lecturer at the Faculty of Law. Her main specialisation and research interests lie in the area of EU and international environmental law, with a special focus on the relationship between EU and public international law. Prior to fully engaging in an academic career, Dr Orlando practised law in major international law firms in Rome, worked for the European Commission, and served for several years as consultant and legal adviser for the Italian Ministry of Environment, Land and Sea (IMELS) in the framework of its bilateral cooperation activities in the Balkan countries.

Jona Razzaque is Professor of Environmental Law at the University of the West of England, where she specializes in the intersection of human rights and the environment. Her most recent publications are *Globalisation and Natural Resources Law* (Edward Elgar, 2011) and *Environmental Governance in Europe and Asia* (Routledge, 2012). Her co-edited books include *Natural Resources and the Green Economy* (Brill, 2012) and *International Environmental Law and the Global South* (Cambridge University Press, 2015).

Dawn L. Rothe is a Professor of Criminology at Eastern Kentucky University and Chair of the School of Justice Studies. She is the author or co-author of eight books and more than 80 peer-reviewed articles and book chapters, all related to the harms and crimes of the powerful. She has formerly served as Chair of the American Society of Criminology, Division on Critical Criminology.

Nigel South is Professor in the Department of Sociology and Director of the Centre for Criminology at the University of Essex, England. He is an Adjunct Professor in the School of Justice at Queensland University of Technology, Brisbane, and a Fellow of the Academy of Social Sciences, and in 2013 received a Lifetime Achievement Award from the American Society of Criminology, Division on Critical Criminology. With Avi Brisman, he is co-editor of the *Routledge International Handbook of Green Criminology* (2013), co-author of *Green Cultural Criminology* (Routledge, 2014), and both are co-editors (with Rob White) of *Environmental Crime and Social Conflict: Contemporary and Emerging Issues* (Routledge, 2015).

Paul B. Stretesky is Professor in the Department of Social Sciences at Northumbria University. He researches issues related to environmental crime and justice. His recent books include *Exploring Green Criminology* (Routledge, 2014, with M.J. Lynch) and *The Treadmill of Crime: Green Crime and Political Economy* (Routledge, 2014, with M.J. Lynch and M.A. Long). His most recent work has appeared in *Symbolic Interaction*, *Health and Human Rights Journal*, and *Urban Geography*.

Marcelo Dias Varella is the Dean of the Graduate School of Law at University Center of Brasilia. He received his PhD from the University of Paris. He is also CNPQ Researcher. He has published many books, including *Internationalization of Law: Globalization, International Law and Complexity* (Springer,

2015), and has co-edited *Global Change, Energy Issues and Regulation Policies* (Springer, 2013).

Ana Filipa Vrdoljak is Professor of Law, Faculty of Law, University of Technology Sydney. She is the author of *International Law, Museums and the Return of Cultural Objects* (Cambridge University Press, 2006) and editor of *Culture and Human Rights* (Oxford University Press, 2013) and *International Law for Common Goods: Normative Perspectives in Human Rights, Culture and Nature* (Hart Publishing, 2014, with F. Lenzerini). She is co-General Editor, with Francesco Francioni, of the new Oxford University Press book series entitled *Cultural Heritage Law and Policy* and member of the Advisory Board of the *International Journal of Cultural Property*. She is a secretary of the International Cultural Property Society (US).

Reece Walters is Professor of Criminology in the Centre for Crime and Justice Research and Assistant Dean Research in the Faculty of Law at Queensland University of Technology, Brisbane, Australia. He has published widely on crimes of the powerful and the sociology of criminological knowledge. His current research focuses on state and corporate eco crimes against the essentials of life, namely food, air and water. He is the author of *Deviant Knowledge* (Willan, 2003) and *Eco Crime and Genetically Modified Food* (Routledge-Cavendish, 2012), and is co-editor-in-chief of the *International Journal for Crime, Justice and Social Democracy*.

Tanya Wyatt is a Reader in Criminology at Northumbria University in Newcastle, UK. Her expertise is in wildlife trafficking and green criminology. She has conducted research in Russia and Mexico and supervised projects in Vietnam. Tanya explores the role of corruption, organised crime and terrorism in the trafficking of wildlife. She was the rapporteur for the UK FCO, DEFRA, OECD and US State Department conference at Wilton Park about strengthening law enforcement to stop wildlife crime, and is a consultant to the USAID Wildlife Crime Technology Challenge.

Acknowledgments

As editors of this volume, we would like to thank the *Modern Law Review* for its support in funding the two-day seminar 'Linking Green Criminology with Law: A Socio-Legal Approach to Environmental Crimes', where different versions of several of the chapters included in this book were initially presented. The seminar, which was held at Lucy Cavendish College, University of Cambridge, in September 2012, brought together legal scholars, practitioners, criminologists and other social scientists to share their expertise and disciplinary perspectives on how to best prevent and respond to environmental crimes. Therefore, we would like to thank also the participants in the seminar and the other contributors to the book (who subsequently joined this publication initiative) for their collaboration, enthusiasm and commitment to this project. We also owe a special thanks to the editorial team at Routledge, and particularly to Colin Perrin, Sarahjayne Smith and Laura Muir, for their helpful advice, support and patience throughout the stages of the publication process. Finally, on a personal level, we would like to express our sincere gratitude for the Sutasoma Trust Fellowship and the Isaac Newton–Dorothy Emmet Fellowship, which we respectively held at Lucy Cavendish College. The fellowships and the supportive environment of the College made it possible for us to originate this interdisciplinary research project back in 2012.

Emanuela Orlando and Tiffany Bergin

Part I

Conceptualising a socio-legal approach to environmental harms

Chapter 1

Forging a socio-legal approach to environmental harms

Emanuela Orlando and Tiffany Bergin

1 Legal and social science perspectives on environmental harms

In recent decades environmental harms and crimes have received increased attention from governments and societies around the world. Examples of such harms include illegal dumping of waste, illegal trade in wildlife, and illegal logging. The harms produced by such crimes are vast; for example, the UN Environment Programme and INTERPOL estimate that the illegal logging trade alone is worth some $30–100 billion each year.[1] The magnitude of the harms that can result from environmental crimes means that the question of how to design better legal strategies to prevent these offences needs greater attention from researchers.

Although such offences have been extensively studied from both legal and social science perspectives, these discipline-specific approaches are not, on their own, fully able to address the diverse causes and potential remedies for these environmental harms. Legal approaches to environmental crimes have traditionally focused on the role of criminal law in promoting the effective enforcement of environmental legislation, but tend to overlook the wider range of *motivations* – both intrinsic and extrinsic – behind environmental offences, as well as the potential added value of non-legal strategies. In particular, by focusing on individuals' behaviour, legal analyses of environmental crimes are limited by their inattention to the broader social and economic processes that trigger or facilitate global environmental harms and crimes. On the other hand, many social science analyses are hindered by an insufficient grounding in current legislative frameworks, leaving a gap between social science *knowledge* about the motivations and facilitators of such crimes and current *laws* and *policies* to address such crimes.

The increasingly complex and transnational nature of many environmental concerns means that a combination of both legal and social science expertise is needed to comprehensively understand this topic. An interdisciplinary approach that combines legal expertise with findings from social science disciplines could offer significant

---

1 UN Environment Programme and Interpol, *Green Carbon: Black Trade* (UNEP/GRID-Arendal 2012) 6.

insight into the drivers of environmental crimes,[2] as well as the legal loopholes that have allowed environmental criminality to expand so widely. Within social science, the *green criminology* theoretical perspective – which considers environmental crimes to be by-products of societies' cultures, economies, and inequalities in resource distribution – can offer particular insight, and fruitfully complement legal scholarship by envisaging new methods and approaches to effectively address environmental crimes.[3]

There has been so far surprisingly little exploration of the potential for productive collaboration and cross-fertilisation among legal scholars and social scientists in this area of research. The present collection aims to fill this gap. It illuminates new convergences between the fields of law and social science and aims to provide an innovative platform from which to explore cross-disciplinary interactions and foster further research on environmental harms. Specifically, this book envisages a socio-legal approach to these offences that draws upon the strengths of both legal and social science frameworks. Thus, this book's conception of a socio-legal approach differs from the more specific '*critical, socio-legal approach*' defined in South's chapter as a perspective that 'examin[es] environmental harms that are not statutorily prohibited but regarded as equally or more damaging than some actions that are legal offences'.[4] Instead, we use the term *socio-legal* to advance an epistemological and methodological approach that involves the merging of both legal and social science knowledge to improve our responses to these harmful offences. Our definition thus draws upon the idea that 'socio-legal theory…involves theoretically informed social science applied to law theoretically informed'.[5] Overall, this volume aims to spur a more comprehensive and indepth dialogue among lawyers, criminologists, and other social science experts; such dialogue will help stakeholders find points of contact, learn from each other, and ultimately forge a coherent and useful socio-legal approach to more effectively respond to – and prevent – environmental crimes and harms.

2 Defining the scope and object of the study: environmental harms and environmental crimes

A major challenge that must be faced when crafting an interdisciplinary approach to environmental harms and crimes is how to identify and define the subjects of

---

2 For a discussion of definitional issues surrounding the term 'environmental crime', see K. Eman, G. Meško and C.B. Fields, 'Crimes against the environment: Green criminology and research challenges in Slovenia', *Journal of Criminal Justice and Security (Varstvoslovje)* (2009) Vol. 11, Issue 4, 574.
3 S. Farrall, 'Where *might* we be headed? some of the possible consequences of climate change for the criminological research agenda', in S. Farrall, T. Ahmed and D. French (eds), *Criminological and Legal Consequences of Climate Change* (Hart Publishing 2012), 8.
4 See Chapter 2 by South in this volume.
5 B.Z. Tamanaha, *Realistic Socio-Legal Theory: Pragmatism and a Social Theory of Law* (Oxford University Press, 1997), 7.

analysis. Depending on context and academic discipline, different terms have, in fact, been used to describe the environmental concerns that form the subject of the present study. The actions we are referring to are very diverse in their composition, motivations, scale, and perpetrators, and such diversity complicates any effort to establish a general definition of these behaviours. In particular, the question of whether environmental 'harms' or 'crimes' is the most appropriate term to use reflects different disciplinary perspectives to the problem and encompasses a much broader debate about how to define our subject of interest.

On the one hand, legal approaches to the problem tend to employ the term *environmental crimes* and emphasise the *illegality* of the acts, omissions, and conducts which cause or are likely to cause harm to the environment.[6] In this perspective, environmental crimes generally refer to environmentally harmful actions which are proscribed by domestic law or international regulations and conventions,[7] and, as such, are subject to sanctions. This conception is exemplified by Situ and Emmonds who describe environmental crime as

> an unauthorised act or omission that violates the law and is therefore subject to criminal prosecution and criminal sanctions. This offence harms or endangers people's physical safety or health as well as the environment itself. It serves the interests of either organisations – typically corporations – or individuals.[8]

In practice, the specific elements which constitute an environmental crime (such as the mental status of the offender, or the seriousness of a given conduct) are defined by applicable legislation. Consequently, in the absence of a harmonised legal framework at the international or regional level, the definition of environmental crime will be necessarily subject to geographical and jurisdictional limitations according to the different legal systems and legislative contexts.

On the other hand, and in contrast to these legalistic definitions of environmental crimes, some criminologists tend to use a broader conception of the subject of interest that extends beyond just those acts that are criminalised in law to also encompass harmful (but not necessarily criminalised) acts.[9] Although not all criminologists have adopted this broader definition – with some adhering to the traditional, legal definition of environmental crimes as those acts proscribed by

---

6 Environmental Investigation Agency (EIA), *Environmental Crimes: A Threat to Our Future* (2008).
7 UNEP and Interpol identify the following conducts as crimes of international law relevance: illegal transport and dumping of hazardous waste, illegal transfer of hazardous materials and controlled chemicals (including ozone-depleting substances), illegal trade of wildlife, illegal logging and associated timber trade, illegal, unreported, and unregulated fishing.
8 Y. Situ and D. Emmonds, *Environmental Crime: The Criminal Justice System's Role in Protecting the Environment* (Sage Publications, 2000), 3.
9 R. White, *Transnational Environmental Crime: Toward an Eco-Global Criminology* (Routledge, 2011), 5–6.

law – recent trends in critical green criminology have expanded the spectrum of analysis to encompass any conduct that, although *per se* not illegal, is unsustainable or environmentally harmful.[10] These new approaches argue for wider definitions of environmental harms, and highlight the limitations of the conventional law-based definitions to properly address the range of human acts, behaviours, and social processes which cannot be encapsulated into the strict boundaries of criminal law; nevertheless, such acts undoubtedly exert a negative impact on the environment and trigger serious environmental damage at the domestic and global level.[11] A further argument often raised by criminologists is that governments, which control how environmental crimes are defined in their legal codes, may be perpetrators of environmental harms and therefore 'shape official definitions of environmental crime in ways that allow or condone environmentally harmful practices'.[12] Given this conflict of interest, existing legal definitions may not capture many of the most significant environmental harms.[13]

By widening the scope of analysis to include a more comprehensive and holistic notion of environmental harm, green criminologists and other social scientists working in this area can make an important contribution to traditional legal approaches to the problem. Extending the focus of analysis beyond just non-compliance with environmental legislation or regulatory frameworks enables scholars to also give attention to acts and conducts (such as governmental environmental crime, individual car emissions, and unsustainable consumption choices and behaviours) which negatively impact on the environment but would normally fall outside regulatory frameworks. It also facilitates a better understanding of the diversity of causes and motivations behind environmental harms/crimes. For example, economic profit is normally considered to be the motive behind violations of pollution control laws; however, such violations may instead simply be the result of a lack of knowledge or understanding of the applicable law, or even the offender's belief that current regulatory demands are unreasonable or illegitimate.[14] Other forms

---

10 R. White, 'The criminalisation of environmental harm', *Criminal Justice Matters* (2008), Vol. 74, Issue 1, 35–37. For a discussion of green criminology and how scholars working in this area define their subjects of interest, see: McKie *et al.*, this volume; South, this volume.
11 See A. Brisman, 'Crime–environment relationships and environmental justice', *Seattle Journal for Social Justice* (2008), Vol. 6, Issue 2, 727, 731. The author refers to a range of activities and practices that may be legal, but are nonetheless environmentally destructive such as: using animals in tests and experiments; vivisection; the sale of dangerous pesticides; unsustainable agricultural production processes, with significant harm to biodiversity; but also automobile emissions deriving from driving sport utility vehicles (SUVs).
12 R. White and D. Heckenberg, *Green Criminology: An Introduction to the Study of Environmental* Harm (Routledge, 2014), 11.
13 R. White, n. 9 above.
14 R. Kagan and J.T. Scholz, 'The "Criminology of the Corporation" and Regulatory Enforcement Strategies', in K. Hawkins and J.M. Thomas (eds), *Enforcing Regulation* (Kluwer-Nijhoff Publishing, 1984), 67–86.

of environmental crimes, such as illegal trafficking of endangered species, of timber, or of precious minerals such as diamonds may be encouraged and alimented by other types of incentives related to the global economy and overall consumer demand. Finally, whereas the majority of existing legal scholarship tends to focus on business violations of pollution control laws, a broader approach to environmental crimes allows us to consider other situational contexts and actors – such as governments, international organisations, criminal bands, terrorist forces, and even private individuals.

However, the manifold benefits of an interdisciplinary approach to environmental harms are also accompanied by important challenges. From a legal perspective, criminal behaviour is typically defined as behaviour subject to criminal sanctions; thus, an overly broad definition of the problem might be over-encompassing and could clash with legal guarantees and the principle of legal certainty. Furthermore, over-extending the concept of environmental crimes could hamper the adoption and implementation of specific legal and regulatory frameworks. It is therefore important for social scientists to engage with legal scholarship and appreciate legal approaches to defining concepts of 'environmental harm' and 'environmental crime', as illustrated in the legal chapters in this volume. Greater familiarity with legal analysis and with legal conceptualisations of environmental harms and crimes could help criminologists and other social science scholars properly appraise existing legal and regulatory frameworks, and contribute more fully to the development of appropriate policy and legal strategies to respond to such harms and crimes.

This difference between strictly legalistic and broader social science conceptualisations of environmental harms is fundamental, and presents a promising launching point for greater dialogue among lawyers, criminologists, and other social scientists. Both legalistic perspectives and broader, harmed-based perspectives retain significant value for defining the subject matter of interest, but bringing together these approaches could yield a richer understanding of the phenomena, and help researchers move beyond discipline-specific perspectives on these offences. Ultimately, it is contended in this volume that greater interaction and collaboration between law and social science approaches could be particularly useful for identifying the most appropriate response strategies to cope with the breadth and variety of environmentally harmful behaviours.

3 Framing the appropriate responses to environmental crimes: exploring potential intersections between law and social sciences

Determining the types of strategies to respond to, and prevent, environmental harms and crimes has become a central issue in interdisciplinary discussions between law and social science scholars. In focusing mostly on violations of environmental norms, legal responses to environmental crimes have mostly relied on the application of criminal penalties as the strategy of choice. Comparative studies conducted in Europe as well as studies concerning developments in Australia and the US show that criminal law and the application of criminal sanctions have represented an important means of enforcing environmental legislation and promoting compliance with environmental standards.[15] This increased interest in the role of criminal law to address environmental law violations has primarily emphasised the deterrent effect of criminal sanctions. In the European Union, for example, Directive 2008/99 on the protection of the environment through criminal law underlines the need for dissuasive criminal penalties to improve compliance.[16] In addition to the deterrent rationale, criminal liability's expressive function also supports its use over other mechanisms of law enforcement, such as civil or administrative penalties.[17] Reflecting on the enforcement of environmental statutes in the United States, Shroeder observed that the use of criminal sanctions is particularly supported by those who see environmental statutes as setting fundamental ground rules of societal behaviour; according to Shroeder, 'compliance… constitutes an obligation, not a business decision, and violations are greeted with outrage'.[18] The symbolic role of criminal sanctions in reaffirming the importance of environmental values has also been explored by other scholars, with Adler and Lord commenting that 'Environmental laws are designed to prevent death and serious illness from exposure to toxic and other pollutants or the destruction or waste of valuable or irreplaceable natural resources'.[19]

Despite the central role of criminal law in addressing violations of environmental statutes and enforcing environmental legislation in many domestic legal systems,[20] insights from other social science disciplines – such as economics, criminology, and sociology – reveal how an absolute reliance on criminal sanctions is not always the best strategy to secure compliance with environmental norms and enhance the protection of the environment. For example, a seminal study by Ogus and Abbott used Gary Becker's economic approach to legal

15 See, in Europe, M. G. Faure and G. Heine (eds), *Criminal Enforcement of Environmental Law in the European Union* (Kluwer Law International, 2005); for evidence of the increasing provision of criminal sanctions for environmental offences in United States legislation, see R. Lazarus, R. 'Assimilating environmental protection into legal rules and the problem with environmental crime', *Loyola Los Angeles Law Review* (1993), Vol. 27, 867–891; for Australia, see S. Bricknell, *Environmental Crime in Australia*, Australian Institute of Criminology Report, Research and Public Policy Series, No. 109, Canberra 2010.
16 Directive 2008/99/EC of 19 November 2008 on the protection of the environment through criminal law, OJ L 328, 6.12.2008.
17 As Hart observed, 'what distinguishes a criminal from a civil sanction is the judgment of community condemnation which accompanies and justifies its imposition'; see H.M. Hart, 'The aims of the criminal law', *Law and Contemporary Problems* (1958) Vol. 23, 401, 404.
18 C.H. Schroeder, 'Cool analysis versus moral outrage in the development of federal environmental criminal law', *William & Mary Law Review*, (1993–1994) Vol. 35, 251, 257.
19 R.H. Adler and C. Lord, 'Environmental crimes: Raising the stakes', *George Washington Law Review*, (1990–1991) Vol. 59, 781–861, 787.
20 J. Di Mento, 'criminal enforcement of environmental law', *Annals of the American Academy of Political and Social Sciences*, (1993) Vol. 525, 134, 136–137.

compliance to critically assess the UK Environment Agency's enforcement strategy.[21] According to this approach, compliance would mainly depend on the outcome of a cost–benefit calculation whereby individuals and firms comply with regulatory obligations only if the benefits derived from contravention are exceeded by the costs.[22] Thus central to the law-and-economic theory of deterrence is the assumption that offenders rationally consider the costs and benefits of committing an offence.[23] (In criminology, this theory of lawbreaking is often referred to as 'rational-choice theory'.[24]) Such theories often endorse the use of harsher penalties and effective monitoring or inspections to ensure offences are detected. Applying this assumption to the empirical data concerning the rate of prosecution and imposition of fines for environmental violations, Ogus and Abbott concluded that the Agency's cautious approach to the prosecution of criminal offences and the low level of fines imposed by the courts significantly diminished the deterrent effect of criminal law and ultimately undermined its preventive function.[25]

Some sociological expertise supports the above conclusions and can help identify the specific contexts and categories of subjects for which a law and economics approach to deterrence would be most appropriate. For example, Du Rées has suggested that a crime prevention strategy based on cost–benefit analysis is most suited to address environmental offences committed by corporate actors.[26] This is because 'environmental crimes committed in the context of various types of enterprise are assumed, unlike many other forms of criminalized behavior, to be determined by rational calculation and are generally the result of a premeditated decision'.[27] In supporting these arguments, Du Rées referred to the additional social and reputational costs that criminal prosecution can bring. An important consideration is that criminal sanctions – and their resultant reputational damage – can impact offenders differently depending upon their social status.[28] Translated into the environmental context, Du Rées has affirmed that 'the threat

21 G. Becker, 'Crime and punishment: An economic approach', *Journal of Political Economy*, (1968) Vol. 76, Issue 2, 169–217. Essentially, he proposes a theory on a cost–benefit approach, which assumes that individuals and firms comply with regulatory obligations if the benefits derived from contravention are exceeded by the costs.
22 For an analysis of how the law and economics approach can aid in identifying effective legal responses to environmental crime, see: Faure, this volume.
23 For a discussion of deterrence theory, see: R.L. Akers, 'Rational choice, deterrence, and social learning theory in criminology: The path not taken', *The Journal of Criminal Law & Criminology* (1990) Vol. 81, Issue 3, 654.
24 See, for example: I. Piliavin, C. Thornton, R. Gartner, and R. L. Matsueda, 'Crime, deterrence, and rational choice', *American Sociological Review* (1986) Vol. 51, 101–119.
25 A. Ogus and C. Abbott, 'Sanctions for pollution: Do we have the right regime?' *Journal of Environmental Law* (2002), Vol. 14, Issue 3, 283.
26 H. Du Rées, 'Can criminal law protect the environment?' *Journal of Scandinavian Studies in Criminology and Crime Prevention* (2010), Vol. 11, Issue 2, 109–126, 111.
27 Ibid. 111.
28 R.A. Berk, A. Campbell, R. Klap, and B. Western, 'The deterrent effect of arrest in incidents of domestic violence: A Bayesian analysis of four field experiments', *American Sociological Review* (1992), Vol. 57, Issue 5, 698.

of sanctions [in this field] is directed at groups of people of high social standing who feel considerable loyalty towards the legal system at the general level'.[29] Due to rising awareness about the importance of protecting the environment, a criminal conviction for the commission of serious environmental crimes can significantly affect a firm's reputation, and therefore act as a 'mutual enforcement' tool.[30] Specifically, there is emerging evidence that the adverse reputational consequences of criminal conviction for a company may have substantial financial implications, such as a decrease in the price of the company's stock price or an increase in insurance premiums.[31]

However, social science research also suggests that environmental offenders do not always behave rationally and seek financial profit – a finding that undermines principles of deterrence theory and hints at the broader limitations of criminal law. Specifically, a study of individuals convicted of conservation and wildlife offences in one US state found that some cited excitement or fun as their reason for offending; others denied responsibility and said their actions were simply an innocent mistake or oversight (such as failing to provide proper paperwork).[32] The complexity of environmental legislation means that individuals are not always aware of what the laws are – and thus do not realise that they have violated the law.[33] Such empirical findings raise a fundamental question: Would offenders who find crimes exciting or offenders who claim simply to have made innocent mistakes be deterred by tougher sanctions? Can such offenders be said to have acted *rationally*?

Another example that shows how difficult it can be to generalise about offenders' motivations for committing environmental crimes is that of small-scale fly-tippers who are rarely motivated by profit considerations; instead, much 'non-commercial fly-tipping occurs largely because individuals wish to avoid the inconvenience of travelling to licensed waste disposal sites'.[34] In other words, some fly-tippers might be motivated by financial gain, but others are simply lazy. Would the same kinds of penalties – such as fines – deter both groups equally? Is it possible to create penalties that could deter all potential environmental offenders, regardless of their specific motivation?

Interestingly, historical research suggests that even the most extreme punishments have not always been effective in deterring environmental crimes. For example, one social scientist has examined whether the passage of the so-called

---

29 H. Du Rées, n. 26 above, 111.
30 P. de Prez, 'Beyond judicial sanctions: The negative impact of conviction for environmental offences', *Environmental Law Review* (2000), Vol. 2, Issue 1, 11–22.
31 Ibid. 13.
32 S.L. Eliason, 'Illegal hunting and angling: The neutralization of wildlife law violations', *Society & Animals* (2003) Vol. 11, Issue 3, 225.
33 C. Locke, 'Environmental crimes: The absence of "intent" and the complexities of compliance', *Columbia Journal of Environmental Law* (1991), Vol. 16, 311, 318.
34 M. Watson, "The enforcement of environmental law: Civil or criminal penalties?" *Environmental Law & Management* (2005), Vol. 17, 4.

Black Act in England in 1723 had a deterrent effect.[35] The Act prescribed the death penalty for offenders who illegally killed deer under certain circumstances. Yet, according to this analysis, 'A month after the passage of the Black Act the old offenses were being committed as freely as ever',[36] In this example, therefore, the most severe sanction there is – the death penalty – had little deterrent or preventive effect on committing this wildlife crime. Such a finding casts doubt on whether a simple, consistent relationship exists between the severity of sanctions and the level of resulting deterrence.

Therefore, a criminal law-based deterrence approach may not always be the optimal strategy to prevent environmental offences. Indeed, when a company's non-compliance with environmental norms is due to a misunderstanding of the complex technicalities of environmental regulation, rather than intentional action based on a rational profit calculation, recourse to criminal prosecution could even be counterproductive.[37] In particular, a generalised application of strict criminal liability, regardless of whether intentionality or even serious negligence is present, could lead to indignation on the part of businesses found guilty of offences.[38] Such a scenario would ultimately risk undermining relationships between regulated firms and competent authorities. Social psychologists who have studied this problem have emphasised the importance of promoting trust between regulators and potential offenders in order to encourage compliance with the law.[39] Additionally, some scholars have expressed concern that the broad use of criminal sanctions in the environmental field in the UK and in the US (particularly for strict liability offences) might diminish such sanctions' symbolic and stigmatising effects.[40] Accordingly, it has been argued that criminal penalties should be used selectively for the most serious offences.[41]

The previous paragraphs presented a variety of examples showing how social science theories and research findings can offer insight into the motivations behind environmental offences as well as suggest potentially effective regulatory

---

35 M. Stockdale, 'English and American wildlife law: Lessons from the past', *Proceedings of the Annual Conference of the Southeastern Association of Fish and Wildlife Agencies* (1993), Vol. 47, 732.
36 Ibid. 735.
37 P. Grabosky and F. Gant, *Improving Environmental Performance, Preventing Environmental Crime*, Australian Institute of Criminology, Research and Public Policy Series, No. 27 (Australian Institute of Criminology, Canberra: 2000), available at www.aic.gov.au/media_library/publications/rpp/27/rpp027.pdf (accessed 22 January 2017).
38 M. Woods and R. Macrory, *Environmental Civil Penalties: A More Proportionate Response to Regulatory Breach* (Centre for Law and the Environment University College London, 2003).
39 See e.g. T.R. Tyler, 'Trust and law-abidingness: A proactive model of social regulation', *Boston University Law Review* (2001), Vol. 81, 361–406.
40 M. Cohen, 'Environmental crime and punishment: Legal/economic theory and empirical evidence on enforcement of federal environmental statutes', *The Journal of Criminal Law and Criminology* (1992), Vol. 82, No. 4, 1054, 1104.
41 M. Woods and R. Macrory, n. 38 above, 9.

and enforcement approaches for these offences. Empirical evidence on the limitations of traditional enforcement and compliance tactics has contributed to the recent emergence of intense scholarly interest and debate regarding socio-legal approaches to environmental regulation; such debate has, in turn, spurred the elaboration of several increasingly influential regulatory theories. For example, in the UK, the responsive regulation approach advanced by Ayres and Braithwaite has exerted a powerful influence in the reviews of the regulatory enforcement strategy outlined first by Hampton[42] and then by Macrory.[43] The responsive regulation approach combines elements of the 'deterrence approach' (and its emphasis on sanctions and criminalisation of environmental offences) with elements of the so-called 'compliance approach' (and its focus on dialogue and persuasion between the regulator and the regulated industry). By bringing together these two regulatory approaches to compliance, responsive regulation introduces greater flexibility into enforcement; coercive sanctions are only used when other, less intrusive, enforcement tools (such as warning letters or persuasion) have proven unsuccessful.[44]

The idea of a diversified *mix* of compliance and enforcement tools has been further pursued by other scholars interested in overcoming the limitations of criminal law's essentially reactive nature.[45] From this perspective, an effective strategy should primarily focus on changing behaviour and promoting a culture of respect for the environment through education, awareness-raising, and the internalisation of values that respect the environment. For example, Hedman has observed that one cannot simply expect the imposition of sanctions on its own to completely deter environmental crimes; instead, 'the success of efforts to protect the environment will depend upon the extent to which all of society, including the business sector, internalizes environmental values'.[46]

Scholars who focus on prevention and on alternative environmental governance and compliance acknowledge the limits of solely relying on traditional legal

---

42 The Hampton Review (2005). *Reducing Administrative Burdens: Effective Inspection and Enforcement*, HM Treasury. Available at http://webarchive.nationalarchives.gov.uk/20130129110402/http://www.hm-treasury.gov.uk/bud_bud05_hampton.htm (accessed 22 January 2017).
43 The Macrory Review (2006). *Regulatory Justice: Making Sanctions Effective*, London: Cabinet Office. Available at http://webarchive.nationalarchives.gov.uk/20090609003228/http://www.berr.gov.uk/files/file44593.pdf (accessed 22 January 2017).
44 I. Ayres and J. Braithwaite, *Responsive Regulation: Transcending the Deregulation Debate* (Oxford University Press, 1992).
45 Studies on the effectiveness of criminal law have identified some of the deficiencies of reactive strategies including their focus on centralised enforcement of the law rather than the facilitation of compliance, and that 'by processing failures one by one, they fail to produce systemic solutions', as discussed in M. Sparrow, *The Regulatory Craft: Controlling Risks, Solving Problems, and Managing Compliance* (Brookings Institution Press, 2000).
46 S. Hedman, 'Expressive functions of criminal sanctions in environmental law', *George Washington Law Review* (1991) Vol. 59, Issue 4, 889–899, 898.

enforcement tools when faced with the complex web of forces and factors that influence individuals' behaviour in our globalised society. In a context characterised by the emergence and subsequent diffusion of regulatory powers among economic actors, the state's enforcement tools (e.g. the police and other centralised enforcement agencies) fall short in securing adequate protection against the risks created by the sophisticated operations of businesses and corporations.[47] Therefore, an effective strategy to address and prevent environmental crimes requires a move from a top-down to a bottom-up approach to enforcement; this bottom-up approach would need to focus not only on the role of government agencies and their enforcement and prosecutorial powers, but also on firms (non-state actors), social institutions (schools), consumers, and NGOs.

In this perspective, Gant and Grabosky have advocated a strategy which is primarily based on improving the compliance and environmental performance of business actors, while leaving hard enforcement mechanisms as a last resort.[48] This strategy advances a crime prevention model to supplement sanctions and other hard enforcement tools with non-coercive strategies – such as information, self-regulation by individual companies and industrial associations, commercial influences and market forces, and the use of incentives and inducements for environmental compliance and otherwise environmentally beneficial types of conduct – and emphasises the activity of non-state actors, specifically private enterprises and non-governmental organisations. In this framework, criminal law and other types of enforcement mechanisms would still retain an important role either as a means of last resort in cases where preventive strategies failed to deliver the expected results, or as an additional tool to boost compliance through the threat of sanctions.

The above discussion reveals how legal scholars and social scientists alike often appraise the value of legal and 'extra-legal' responses to environmental harms from their respective disciplinary standpoints. On the one hand, as socio-legal approaches to environmental harms penetrate the realm of legal regulation, they are gradually prompting a movement away from primary reliance on criminal sanctions in favour of regulatory mixes and alternative responses. On the other hand, many criminologists, while critically assessing the limits of strictly legalistic and criminal law-based responses, ultimately acknowledge the value of criminal law, if only as a means of last resort to reserve to the most serious environmental violations. By bringing together legal and social science perspectives, this volume probes different disciplinary viewpoints and aims to identify points of contact and opportunities for dialogue and mutual learning.

---

47 See J. Braithwaite, 'The new regulatory state and the transformation of criminology', *British Journal of Criminology* (2000) Vol. 40, Issue 2, 222–238.
48 P. Grabosky and F. Gant, *Improving Environmental Performance, Preventing Environmental Crime*, Australian Institute of Criminology, Research and Public Policy Series, No. 27 (Australian Institute of Criminology, Canberra, 2000). Available at www.aic.gov.au/media_library/publications/rpp/27/rpp027.pdf (accessed 22 January 2017).

4 Scope and aims of this book

As we have seen in the previous sections of this introductory chapter, a range of regulatory and policy strategies exist to tackle environmental harms, and those strategies all have strengths and limitations. In particular we have seen that current approaches to environmental crimes are typically hindered by their singular disciplinary focus (and their reliance upon theories and ideas from *either* law *or* social science). Instead, an interdisciplinary approach drawing upon both legal and social scientific perspectives has significant potential, and the preceding analysis highlighted key points of convergence and complementarity between these approaches. The rest of the book's chapters build upon these themes, with each of the book's three parts focusing on a different aspect of developing a socio-legal agenda to environmental harms.

The chapters in the book's first part, 'Conceptualising a socio-legal approach to environmental harms', offer an overview of the key components of legal and criminological approaches to environmental harms. The two chapters, respectively by Nigel South and by Ruth E. McKie, Paul B. Stretesky, Michael J. Lynch, and Michael A. Long, introduce in different ways the green criminology approach to environmental crimes and explore potential interactions and complementarities between law and green criminology. Specifically, Nigel South's chapter 'Environmental crimes and harms: a green criminology approach and socio-legal challenges' (Chapter 2), shows how the green criminology perspective is uniquely placed to tackle contemporary environmental harms. The chapter also outlines the definition of environmental crimes, its different dimensions, and explores, from a social science perspective, the role that criminal law can play in tackling these offences. In 'Green criminology and the prevention of ecological destruction' (Chapter 3), Ruth E. McKie, Paul B. Stretesky, Michael J. Lynch, and Michael A. Long offer historical and theoretical context by discussing the development of key green criminology ideas and showing how these ideas can illuminate the limitations of traditional legal approaches – particularly for addressing the global dimensions and diversity of environmental crimes. By recognising the impact of multiple societal and economic processes on individual conducts and behaviours, the authors ultimately ask: 'Given the current global economy, can tough enforcement protect the planet?'

Ludwig Kramer's chapter, 'The EU and the protection of the environment through criminal law' (Chapter 4), highlights the role of criminal law in addressing environmental crimes, and provides a detailed analysis and critical evaluation of the EU directive on the protection of the environment through criminal law. Finally, Michael G. Faure's chapter, 'A law and economics approach to environmental crime' (Chapter 5), offers an interesting analysis on the added value of employing a combined law and economics approach to define the most appropriate responses to environmental offences. Taken together, then, the four chapters in the book's first part illuminate key aspects of both criminological and legal perspectives on environmental harms.

The second part of the book, 'Assessing the limitations of current approaches to environmental harms', highlights areas in which greater disciplinary cooperation is needed to obtain a fuller understanding of environmental harms. Deficiencies of current approaches to different kinds of environmental harms in a wide range of contexts around the world are explored, highlighting how such limitations can be overcome by linking criminological and legal insights. Dawn Rothe and Victoria E. Collins' chapter, 'International financial institutions as facilitators of environmental crimes' (Chapter 6), highlights the under-examined role of international financial institutions in promoting these offences. On the other hand, Daniel Jacobs and Marcelo Varella's chapter, 'Learning lessons from deepwater disasters: common ground in oil exploration in Brazil and the United States' (Chapter 7), presents a comparative view of the US and Brazilian legal frameworks against maritime pollution in order to highlight the need of a stronger enforcement approach, and identify aspects in which countries can learn from each other's mistakes and best practices. Finally, in 'Toxic ships, environmental crimes, and the North–South discourse' (Chapter 8) Jona Razzaque explores environmental harms associated with shipbreaking, underscoring the role of global inequalities in these harms, and the failure of existing conventions to provide appropriate redress for environmental harm.

The third part of the book, 'Forging socio-legal solutions to environmental harms: lessons from around the world', uses real-world examples to illustrate the practical applications of a socio-legal approach to environmental crimes. In particular, the chapters in this section underscore the idea that environmental crimes are diverse and occur in different forms in disparate areas of the world. To understand such complexity, a multifaceted approach is needed, which draws upon the knowledge and perspectives developed in both social science and legal disciplines. Focusing on remediating, minimising, and responding to environmental offences, those chapters illustrate how the application of social science approaches and research findings to legal frameworks may help design innovative response strategies. For example, in 'Determining the public interest in environmental enforcement, sanctioning, and prosecution' (Chapter 9), Anne Brosnan offers a practitioner's perspective of the UK Environment Agency, and discusses how socio-legal considerations are taken into account in determining the most appropriate enforcement strategy, and the decision whether to prosecute. In 'The legal and social context of wildlife trafficking' (Chapter 10), Tanya Wyatt looks globally at a specific type of crime – wildlife trafficking – and shows how cultural and political dynamics can influence the negotiation of international law agreements and the ultimate effectiveness of international law responses. In 'Eco-crime and green activism' (Chapter 11), Reece Walters shows how activists in the UK have used alternative strategies to raise awareness of environmental crimes and highlights the important role of environmental activism in responding to such harms. His analysis suggests that social science scholarship on social movements is also relevant to the study of environmental crimes. Finally, in 'The criminalisation of the intentional destruction of cultural heritage' (Chapter 12), Ana Filipa Vrdoljak expands the scope of analysis to include crimes against world heritage and universal cultural values. In this perspective, the author critically examines how international law instruments originally conceived to address the intentional destruction of cultural property are currently deployed to protect the cultural (and natural) heritage of all humanity. Looking at the use of internet and social media by terrorist groups, this chapter also highlights the challenges that international law faces in the digital era where the removal of traditional boundaries have created new avenues for the penetration and spreading of criminal attacks against cultural heritage.

5 The merits and complications of a socio-legal approach

What specifically can a socio-legal approach contribute to the study of environmental crimes and harms? What do we gain by bringing together the insights of social science disciplines and legal perspectives? Criminology, the social science discipline given the most attention in this edited volume, has traditionally focused on crime prevention, and therefore can offer insight into 'the human beings who infringe the criminal code' and 'the environment of these persons'.[49] More specifically, criminological scholarship offers significant potential for illuminating the motivations behind environmental crimes, and the circumstances that facilitate or encourage the commission of these offences – knowledge that is necessary to design the most effective prevention strategies. On the other hand, although legal responses have traditionally focused on reacting to offences perpetrated against the environment, more recent legal developments demonstrate awareness of the limitations of such an *ex post* approach to effectively address the multiple types of environmental crimes and to ultimately prevent these crimes. New strategies have therefore been conceived and the various contributions to this book illuminate the interface between these developments and more traditional approaches, and suggest mechanisms for encouraging greater collaboration between the two disciplines. Finally, it is important to recognise that environmental legal scholarship can also contribute to criminological ideas, as shown by Eck and Eck's assertion in a leading criminological journal that environmental laws that target pollution might serve as a model for policies targeting other kinds of more traditional crimes.[50]

As editors of this book, we contend that the prevention of environmental crimes deserves greater attention from scholars and that both law and criminology can contribute significantly to this enterprise. By bringing together legal and social science knowledge, we can widen the range of strategies available to address the consequences of environmental offences. In particular, we can look

---

49 S. Hurwitz and K.O. Christiansen, *Criminology: The New and Completely Revised Edition of the Standard Scandinavian Study* (George Allen & Unwin, 1983) 4.
50 J.E. Eck and E.B. Eck, 'Crime place and pollution: Expanding crime reduction options through a regulatory approach', *Criminology & Public Policy* (2012) Vol.11, Issue 2, 281.

beyond just criminal justice approaches to consider alternative strategies that focus on *preventing* environmental crimes rather than simply responding to them. Such preventive strategies are particularly important in the environmental field since it is often not possible to restore the environment once damage has occurred.[51]

Widening the range of strategies available to address environmental crimes is also essential given these acts' deep variety. Such variety is evident in the diverse nature of offenders, motivations, contexts, and geographies of these crimes. A wide range of strategies means that authorities can produce targeted responses that strengthen enforcement and lead to an enhanced deterrent and preventive effect. Yet such alternative strategies should be seen as a complement to criminal law, rather than a substitute. Criminal law still has value, despite its limitations identified in this introduction and in multiple chapters of this book. Criminal law is particularly important for serious offences because its expressive and symbolic functions are unique; such functions also explain the recent EU intervention legislation in this field.[52] But criminal law sanctions must be effective and enforced for criminal law to have a preventive role. Ultimately, criminal law is one tool of many in the spectrum of strategies advanced by law and social science scholarship that constitute an effective, socio-legal approach to environmental harms.

Bibliography

Adler, R.H., and Lord, C. (1990–1991). Environmental crimes: Raising the stakes. *George Washington Law Review*, 59, 781–861.
Akers, R.L. (1990). Rational choice, deterrence, and social learning theory in criminology: The path not taken. *The Journal of Criminal Law & Criminology*, 81(3), 654.
Ayres, I., and Braithwaite, J. (1992). *Responsive Regulation: Transcending the Deregulation Debate*. New York, NY: Oxford University Press.
Becker, G. (1968). Crime and punishment: An economic approach. *Journal of Political Economy*, 76(2), 169–217.
Berk, R.A., Campbell, A., Klap, R., and Western, B. (1992). The deterrent effect of arrest in incidents of domestic violence: A Bayesian analysis of four field experiments. *American Sociological Review*, 57(5), 698–708.
Braithwaite, J. (2000). The new regulatory state and the transformation of criminology. *British Journal of Criminology*, 40(2), 222–238.

---

51 As Lazarus has argued, 'It is often quite hard, if not impossible, to put the pieces of an ecological puzzle back together again in the aftermath of serious environmental degradation. Monetary remedies do not address the damage issue': R. Lazarus, 'Mens rea in environmental criminal law: Reading Supreme Court tea leaves.' *Fordham Environmental Law Review* (2011) Vol. 7, Issue 3, 866.
52 Directive 2008/99 of the European Parliament and of the Council of 19 November 2008 on the protection of the environment through criminal law, OJ L 328/28, 6.12.2008, emphasises the importance of 'more dissuasive penalties' to enhance the protection of the environment.

Bricknell, S. (2010). *Environmental Crime in Australia*. Australian Institute of Criminology Report, Research and Public Policy Series, No. 109. Canberra: Australian Institute of Criminology. Available at www.aic.gov.au/media_library/publications/rpp/109/rpp 109.pdf (accessed 22 January 2017).

Brisman, A. (2008). Crime-environment relationships and environmental justice. *Seattle Journal for Social Justice*, 6(2), 727–817.

Cohen, M. (1992). Environmental crime and punishment: Legal/economic theory and empirical evidence on enforcement of federal environmental statutes. *The Journal of Criminal Law and Criminology*, 82(4), 1054–1108.

de Prez, P. (2000). Beyond judicial sanctions: The negative impact of conviction for environmental offences. *Environmental Law Review*, 2(1), 11–22.

Di Mento, J.F. (1993). Criminal enforcement of environmental law. *Annals of the American Academy of Political and Social Sciences*, 525, 134–146.

Directive 2008/99/EC of 19 November 2008 on the protection of the environment through criminal law, OJ L 328, 6. 12. 2008.

Du Rées, H. (2010). Can criminal law protect the environment? *Journal of Scandinavian Studies in Criminology and Crime Prevention*, 11(2), 109–126.

Eck, J.E., and Eck, E.B. (2012). Crime place and pollution: Expanding crime reduction options through a regulatory approach. *Criminology & Public Policy*, 11(2), 281–316.

Eliason, S.L. (2003). Illegal hunting and angling: The neutralization of wildlife law violations. *Society & Animals*, 11(3), 225–243.

Eman, K., Meško, G., and Fields, C.B. (2009). Crimes against the environment: Green criminology and research challenges in Slovenia. *Journal of Criminal Justice and Security (Varstvoslovje)*, 11(4), 574–592.

Environmental Investigation Agency (EIA). (2008). *Environmental Crimes: A Threat to Our Future*. London: Author.

Farrall, S. (2012). Where might we be headed? Some of the possible consequences of climate change for the criminological research agenda. In S. Farrall, T. Ahmed, and D. French (eds), *Criminological and Legal Consequences of Climate Change* (pp. 7–26). Oxford: Hart Publishing.

Faure, M., and Heine, G. (eds.) (2005). *Criminal Enforcement of Environmental Law in the European Union*. The Hague: Kluwer Law International.

Grabosky, P., and Gant, F. (2000). *Improving Environmental Performance, Preventing Environmental Crime*. Australian Institute of Criminology, Research and Public Policy Series, No. 27. Canberra: Australian Institute of Criminology. Available at http://aic.gov.au/media_library/publications/rpp/27/rpp027.pdf (accessed 22 January 2017).

The Hampton Review. (2005). *Reducing Administrative Burdens: Effective Inspection and Enforcement*. HM Treasury. Available at http://webarchive.nationalarchives.gov.uk/20130129110402/http://www.hm-treasury.gov.uk/bud_bud05_hampton.htm (accessed 22 January 2017).

Hart, H.M. (1958). The aims of the criminal law. *Law and Contemporary Problems*, 23(3), 401–441.

Hedman, S. (1991). Expressive functions of criminal sanctions in environmental law. *George Washington Law Review*, 59(4), 889–899.

Hurwitz, S., and Christiansen, K.O. (1983). *Criminology: The New and Completely Revised Edition of the Standard Scandinavian Study*. London: George Allen & Unwin.

Kagan, R., and Scholz, J.T. (1984). The 'criminology of the corporation' and regulatory enforcement strategies. In K. Hawkins and J.M. Thomas (eds), *Enforcing Regulation* (pp. 67–86). Boston, MA: Kluwer-Nijhoff Publishing.

Lazarus, R. (1993). Assimilating environmental protection into legal rules and the problem with environmental crime. *Loyola Los Angeles Law Review*, 27, 867–891.

Lazarus, R. (2011). Mens rea in environmental criminal law. *Fordham Environmental Law Review*, 7, 3, 861–880.

Locke, C. (1991). Environmental crimes: The absence of 'intent' and the complexities of compliance. *Columbia Journal of Environmental Law, 16*, 311–331.

The Macrory Review. (2006). *Regulatory Justice: Making Sanctions Effective*. London: Cabinet Office. Available at http://webarchive.nationalarchives.gov.uk/20090609003228/http://www.berr.gov.uk/files/file44593.pdf (accessed 22 January 2017).

Ogus, A., and Abbott, C. (2002). Sanctions for pollution: Do we have the right regime? *Journal of Environmental Law*, 14(3), 283–298.

Piliavin, I., Thornton, C., Gartner, R., and Matsueda, R.L. (1986). Crime, deterrence, and rational choice. *American Sociological Review*, 51, 101–119.

Schroeder, C.H. (1993–1994). Cool analysis versus moral outrage in the development of federal environmental criminal law. *William & Mary Law Review*, 35, 251–269.

Situ, Y., and Emmonds, D. (2000). *Environmental Crime: The Criminal Justice System's Role in Protecting the Environment*. Thousand Oaks, CA: SAGE Publications.

Sparrow, M. (2000). *The Regulatory Craft: Controlling Risks, Solving Problems, and Managing Compliance*. Washington, DC: Brookings Institution Press.

Stockdale, M. (1993). English and American wildlife law: Lessons from the past. *Proceedings of the Annual Conference of the Southeastern Association of Fish and Wildlife Agencies*, 47, 732–739.

Tamanaha, B.Z. (1997). *Realistic Socio-Legal Theory: Pragmatism and a Social Theory of Law*. Oxford: Oxford University Press.

Tyler, T. (2001). Trust and law-abidingness: A proactive model of social regulation. *Boston University Law Review*, 81, 361–406.

UNEP and Interpol. (2012). *Green Carbon: Black Trade: Illegal Logging, Tax Fraud and Laundering in the World's Tropical Forests*. Arendal, Norway: UNEP/GRID-Arendal.

Watson, M. (2005). The enforcement of environmental law: Civil or criminal penalties. *Environmental Law & Management*, 17, 1, 3–6.

White, R. (2008). The criminalisation of environmental harm. *Criminal Justice Matters*, 74(1), 35–37.

White, R. (2011). *Transnational Environmental Crime: Toward an Eco-Global Criminology*. Abingdon: Routledge.

White, R., and Heckenberg, D. (2014). *Green Criminology: An Introduction to the Study of Environmental Harm*. Abingdon: Routledge.

Woods, M., and Macrory, R. (2003). *Environmental Civil Penalties: A More Proportionate Response to Regulatory Breach*. London: Centre for Law and the Environment, University College London.

Chapter 2

Environmental crimes and harms: a green criminology approach and socio-legal challenges

Nigel South

1 Introduction

This chapter introduces a 'green' criminological perspective regarding environmental crimes and harms, describing its breadth and providing definitions of relevant terms. The chapter then provides examples of environmental crimes and harms, and the definitional, legal or political challenges these often pose for socio-legal responses. Following a discussion of rights, ethics and the idea of an 'earth jurisprudence', it concludes by considering a proposal for an international law against 'ecocide'.

2 A green perspective for criminology

From around 1990, a 'green' perspective developed within criminology and emphasised the importance of engagement with the bio-physical and socio-economic consequences of various sources of threat and damage to the environment, whether pollution, resource degradation, biodiversity loss or climate change (South, 1998, 2014; also see Lynch, 1990; Clifford, 1998; Sollund, 2008; Walters, 2010; White, 2008). Broadly, the field has covered: corporate criminality and its impact on the environment; health and safety in the workplace where breaches have environmentally damaging consequences; involvement of organised crime and official corruption in the illegal disposal of waste; the impact and legacy of law enforcement and military operations on landscapes, water supply, air quality and living organisms populating these areas – human, animal and plant; as well as forms of law enforcement and rule regulation relevant to such acts (for an overview and examples, see South, Brisman and Beirne, 2013).

2.1 Definitions

In one sense at least, a 'green criminology' is easy to define. It is simply the application of criminological (and related socio-legal and sociological) thinking and techniques to environmental issues. Green criminology has developed in various ways but remains an 'open' framework that does not aim to provide a single or unified 'theory' (Brisman, 2014; South, 1998; South et al., 2013; White, 2008, p. 14). Other similar or overlapping approaches – such as 'conservation criminology' (Gibbs et al., 2010), 'eco-crime' (Walters, 2010) and 'eco-global criminology' (White, 2010) – address the same issues and problems but, at present, 'green criminology' is probably the term most widely used. Key concepts used here can be defined as follows:

- *Green criminology* = the study by criminologists of environmental crimes, harms, laws and regulations.
- *Environmental crime* = environmental harms proscribed by law (e.g. acts or omissions relating to the illegal taking of flora and fauna, pollution offences, transportation of banned substances). Environmental crime that crosses the borders of nation-states is often referred to as *transnational environmental crime* and includes the illegal trade in wildlife, the international transfer of toxic waste and the illicit market in ozone-depleting substances.
- *Environmental harm* = refers to a wide range of injuries to, and degradations of, the natural environment (e.g. forests, deserts, oceans, rivers) due to human use, misuse and poor management, including logging, pollution and the killing of non-human species. Unlike environmental *crime*, environmental *harm* includes both acts and omissions that are *legal* and those that are *illegal* (adapted from Brisman and South, in press).

3 The classification of environmental crimes and harms

In this section the distinction between 'crimes', 'civil offences' and 'harms' is discussed. The following section will then present examples of environmental crimes and harms. Clarifying these terms and providing examples is important because they lie at the heart of a longstanding debate among criminologists and socio-legal scholars. In this instance, the question is whether a 'green criminology' should concern itself only with legally defined crimes or also embrace the study of those activities that lie within lawful practice but by some measures of evidence and in the judgement of observers result in harms to other entities (human, non-human, ecological) that might or should merit legal proscription and response. One or other of the following approaches may be adopted: a *legal-procedural approach*, maintaining the traditional focus on violations of enacted environmental law (including civil and regulatory violations); or the more *critical, socio-legal approach*, examining environmental harms that are not statutorily prohibited but regarded by some as equally or more damaging than some actions that are legal offences. Wolf (2011, p. 501) remarks that 'some scholars may opt for a broad and amorphous definition of environmental crime that includes any behaviors that are considered ecologically harmful or unsustainable', while many others would have 'conceptual and methodological issues with including behaviors that are not prohibited by laws'.

Shover and Routhe (2005, p. 324) have argued that 'criminal conviction of environmental "crime" requires prosecutors to demonstrate either that defendants knowingly, intentionally, or recklessly violated the law or were negligent'. As they observe, this 'can be a high standard to meet in most cases' (Cohen, 1992) and I will return to the question of whether it is necessary – or even desirable – to have to demonstrate 'intentionality' later when discussing a possible law of ecocide. However, these authors also suggest we could consider a category of environmental 'illegalities' which 'by contrast, are violations of rules that do not require demonstration of intent to violate', these 'generally' being 'violations of regulatory rules promulgated and enforced by environmental protection agencies' that carry civil penalties. The latter would overlap with the category of 'harms' often employed in critical criminology to describe the impact of, for example, what are seen as the 'crimes' of the powerful that do not actually break laws but morally and ethically can be seen to be anti-social, damaging or even lethal in consequences. In practical terms, the negative impacts on the environment that result from human activity are enormous in their range and variety, and there is a need for flexibility and gradation in legal and enforcement responses, although this is not, of course, an argument for dilution and trivialisation of response and process (de Prez, 2000).

4 Examples of environmental crimes and harms

As noted above, the aim in this section is simply to provide some examples of environmental crimes and harms, using five general headings.

4.1 Polluting the atmosphere (and beyond)

Air pollution and greenhouse gas emissions are primarily caused by fossil fuel combustion, deforestation and industrial activities. All are continuing to increase, contributing to ozone depletion and climate change, while the World Health Organization estimates that the annual toll of premature deaths caused by air pollution is two million worldwide (Walters, 2010, p. 868; WHO, 2008). Air pollution affects all who live and work in cities or areas of high industrial concentration (WHO, 2008) but it also travels vast distances and crosses national boundaries, with huge implications for commercial regulation or legal control, including problems of identification of sources of origin, finding means of prevention and proceeding with any form of prosecution. Particularly relevant to air pollution is White's (2010, p. 371–2) point that the use of criminal sanctions to punish or prevent continuation of environmental offences can be undermined by 'the international character of capital and the trans-border nature of ... harm [which] make[s] prosecution and regulation extremely difficult'.

Pollution of the space above us does not stop at our atmospheric boundary and beyond this we have already started to extend our human habit of leaving waste behind us, with 'approximately 24,500 objects larger than 10 cm. now orbiting the earth, ranging from dead satellites and discarded rocket parts to loose screws, metal scraps and tiny particles of paint and liquid coolant' (The Week, 2011, p. 13; Amos, 2011).

4.2 Felling the forests and taking over the land

Illegal logging is depleting forestry resources around the world and this has worrying implications for global warming, although the activities, actors and motives involved are complex, with logging pursued for need as well as for greed. Such complexities need to be considered, but so too do the genocidal impacts of some major commercial logging operations and their motives and methods. In the Amazon rainforest, the impact of giant industrial logging companies is devastating not only for the forests but also for the survival chances of the few remaining nomadic hunter gatherer tribes such as the Awá. Boundaries between legality and illegality in the transport and marketing of the harvested timber are often blurred, making it difficult to identify or police criminal involvement (Bisschop, 2012a; Boekhout van Solinge and Kuijpers, 2013; Tacconi, 2007). In other contexts, the commercialisation of indigenous knowledge ('bio-piracy'), the imposition of monopoly-controlled farming technologies (e.g. based on sale of non-re-usable 'terminator' seeds) and the suppression of resistance (Rodriguez-Goyes and South, 2016), all highlight the question of whether community-based and participatory initiatives – supporting, for example, environmental mediation schemes – could be enabled to play a more influential role in responding to what are often legal enterprises that lead to social and environmental harms as well as associated illegal activities.

4.3 Spoiling the soil and disposing of waste

Historically, the prosaic fact of deterioration and loss of good-quality soil has led to the fall of civilisations (Mares, 2010). Today the sustainability of fertile soil is threatened, with deterioration merely slowing in Western nations but probably increasing annually in many other countries (Mares, 2010). Simply losing topsoil is a threat to sustainability, especially as populations grow and climate change disrupts growing cycles. Food security is becoming a pressing global issue. In the future, conditions of scarcity, increases in pricing and selective distribution will exacerbate divisions between the global rich and poor but also create criminogenic forces and illegal markets. At present we do not treat the ground we live on very well despite its importance, but degrade it with the over-use of chemical treatments as well as with an incalculable amount of non-decomposable and often toxic waste that is buried on a daily basis.

'Waste', it must be acknowledged, is a catch-all term, reflecting its pervasiveness as the corollary of a hugely productive and consumptive society. Klenovsek and Mesko (2011, p. 80) point out that there is at present no single internationally adopted definition of 'waste' and that it can 'be defined in numerous ways, depending on its environmental impact, its form, its properties, or its legal definitions (Buckingham and Turner, 2008). Defining waste as hazardous or non-hazardous is usually controversial, and definitions of hazardous waste vary widely from country to country, creating loopholes and making it difficult to measure the volume of hazardous waste trade (Burns and Fuchs 2004).'

Of increasing significance is the problem of electronic waste, extracted from devices such as computers, mobile phones and televisions. Processes of competitive innovation and marketplace advertising drive consumers to desire the latest products when devices become undesirable because they are unfashionable, out-of-date or genuinely obsolete (as occurred following the switchover to digital broadcasting in Europe and North America) (Bisschop, 2012b; Nriagu, 1990; Brisman and South, 2014). The toxic nature of such waste is varied but includes lead that would be found in computer components until recently, the PVC in cables that can produce dioxins when burned, and heavy metals such as mercury, cadmium, barium and beryllium.

4.4 Animal life crimes and species extinction

Abuse, mistreatment or death affecting animals may be visible and stark as in cases of destruction of habitats by war, catastrophe, oil spills or deforestation. On the other hand, mistreatment may be less visible and indeed socially accepted when related to farming, medical experiments or clearance of land for building, or where harm results from activities that cause air or water pollution, soil erosion or climate change.

Illegal wildlife trafficking is now a global business rivalling the drugs and arms trades (South and Wyatt, 2011; Wyatt, 2012). The smuggling of live animals or trading of animal parts has been criticised as attracting insufficient law enforcement attention, although Interpol has, in recent years, mounted a number of campaigns and intelligence-sharing operations (McGrath, 2012; McCoy, 2014). Links between the illicit wildlife trade and the illegal drugs trade have also moved the issue up the priority list of US security agencies (Goldenberg, 2012). Increasingly, action is urged in relation to those species identified as 'endangered' and close to extinction (Broswimmer, 2002; Schneider, 2012).

In the past, when criminologists have considered animal abuse, this has generally been in terms of viewing animal life as 'property' or passive objects that can be damaged, violated, stolen or otherwise misappropriated. This lack of attention to the harms and crimes that affect animals is slowly changing (Beirne, 2009) and the notion of 'speciesism' has been adopted to describe the ways in which non-human species are exploited, while there have also been serious calls for the attribution of rights and victim-status to non-human actors or species.

4.5 Polluting the waters of the planet

According to the World Health Organization (2015) prevention of disease related to water quality is a global health challenge with 1 billion people lacking access to improved supplies of clean water, 2 million deaths being attributable to unsafe water, sanitation and hygiene on an annual basis, and cholera still a serious problem in 50 countries and likely to be affecting children in particular. Freshwater ecosystems are in decline everywhere and as Brundtland (2012, p. xi) summarises:

> [T]here is no question that water scarcity is becoming a major issue on our planet. The most important problems are all well-known. These include, *inter alia*: a rapidly growing population with associated changes in lifestyle and consumption patterns; competition between sectors, such as industry, agriculture and energy for precious land and water resources; inadequate access to water supply and sanitation services for what is now becoming known as the 'bottom billion' on this planet; the failure to adequately address the issue of indigenous water rights and include marginalized populations in water decision-making processes; matters related to environmental protection; and, growing tension over transboundary water issues. All of these problems will to some extent be magnified by the growing realization that past and current hydrological patterns will no longer be sufficient or a reliable guide for dealing with future hydro-climatic scenarios.

Human lack of care for the waters of the earth may have instantaneous or slow impact as well as lasting legacies, such as the disposal of radioactive waste or the pollution resulting from the dependence of global economies on oil which has produced a succession of ecological and human tragedies (Johnson, South and Walters, 2016). The record of oil companies in Nigeria has been disastrous for years (South, 2015), but in terms of international media attention it was the Deepwater Horizon oil spill in the Gulf of Mexico that has recently been most notable. In this case, on 20 April 2010, a sea-bed oil well operated by BP exploded, with the immediate effect of killing 11 people and injuring 17 others. The wider impact was that with oil leaking at a high rate of (according to some estimates) around 40,000 barrels per day, pollution affected and destroyed fauna and flora off and along 100 miles of shoreline in Louisiana. Declared the worst ecological disaster in US history, the damage was then compounded by the chemical dispersants used to neutralise the slick: more than 3.5 million litres of chemicals combined with crude oil that in turn posed their own severe threat to public health. In the aftermath of the explosion, President Obama declared that 'If our laws were broken ... we will bring those responsible to justice' (Uhlmann, 2010). Subsequently, reports of warnings that were ignored and departures from standard industry practice led to suggestions that criminal charges could be brought against BP, and possibly other implicated companies (Transocean and Halliburton), on the same basis as those in the Exxon Valdez case (using US legislation, principally the Clean Water Act, the Migratory Bird Treaty Act and the Refuse Act). It is worth paying attention here to the comments made by Uhlmann (2010), who observed of this situation that

> All three of the environmental laws that may have been broken provide for criminal penalties, but only the Clean Water Act includes felony charges. For the government to prove a felony violation of the act it would need to demonstrate that the defendant knew oil would be discharged into United

States waters. A felony violation can be easy to prove when a business dumps waste into a river, but it's harder in the case of an oil spill.

In such a case it is hard to prove knowing *intent*, understandably so as clear intent in such a case is unlikely. Companies have no incentive to intentionally commit massive environmental damage with resulting financial losses and costs. When this does occur, it is all too often a by-product of placing profit first and failing to give similar priority to considering the consequences of actions. In late January 2013, a plea bargain by BP was accepted in a US court with $4 billion in criminal penalties attached to the agreement. No test of intent was therefore needed as the company pleaded guilty to 11 felony matters including the deaths of oil workers, obstruction of Congress and two misdemeanours. The question of 'intent' will be returned to in later discussion of the history of attempts to formulate an international law of 'ecocide'.

For now, the point is that these impacts on the environment pose legal, ethical and practical challenges, clearly related to human – or anthropogenic – activity. The next section therefore explores some ways in which consideration of rights, ethics and jurisprudence has attempted to express the 'voice' of the earth and non-human species as 'victims' of such activity.

5 Rights, ethics and earth jurisprudence

In the previous section, a number of examples of environmental crimes and harms were outlined and it is argued that these – and similar activities and behaviours – present a challenge for the sustainable future of the planet, humanity and other species. A number of scholars have argued that, in response, new forms of rights and justice are required (Benton, 1998; Brisman, 2013). Cullinan (2010, p. 144), for example, notes that some commentators have 'drawn attention to the need for legal systems to take an evolutionary leap forward by recognizing legally enforceable rights for nature and other-than-human-beings'. Cullinan refers to this body of work as 'the evolution of earth jurisprudence' (see also Burden, 2011) and cites, among others, the work of Stone (1972) who questioned whether the widening of protection and rights to the formerly disempowered should be extended to natural objects such as trees, and Berry (1999, p. 161) who argued that 'we need a jurisprudence that would provide for the legal rights of geological and biological as well as human components of the Earth community. A legal system exclusively for humans is not realistic.'

However, attribution of rights to animals and various other forms of non-human life is highly contested (Beirne, 2009; Sollund, 2008). Even the principles of conservation give rise to controversy and difficult debate, as described by Bekoff (2010, p. 24) in discussing the tensions and questions that can arise between animal welfare and conservation in agreeing what might be meant by 'compassionate conservation':

Should we kill for the sake of conservation? Can conservation biologists do good science, saving species and ecosystems while also being compassionate? Can people who value individual lives work with those who are willing to sacrifice lives for the good of a species or an ecosystem? What role should animal sentience play in such decisions?

Matters of ethics and justice related to species diversity also need to prepare for a new future as 'synthetic biology provides the technology to create life that has not and could not naturally have existed'. Organisations led by Friends of the Earth have already called for a 'moratorium on the release and commercial use of synthetic organisms until proper regulation is in place' (Savulescu, 2012, p. 33).

One way of including the voices of missing victims of environmental crimes, 'quasi-crimes' or harms is to adopt a restorative justice approach. This would respond to the current position which, as Cardwell, French and Hall (2011, pp. 8–9) note, was 'famously captured by Christie (1977) who argued that the State effectively "steals" conflicts from their rightful owners, namely the victim and the accused'. This established argument is, they say, 'given fresh impetus by the issue of environmental crimes, where the victims include not only individuals and their physical or emotional health, but the social, cultural and economic life of entire communities'. As Higgins (2010, p. 143) puts it, applied in such contexts, '[r]estorative justice is built on an understanding of our relationship with nature and the duty to remedy the harm caused' – addressing 'the needs of the beleaguered party to restore that which has been harmed rather than simply fixating on the punishment of the perpetrator'. However, this method may only give voice and rights of participation to immediate human victims unless ways are found to include representatives of other species, ecological systems and future generations (see e.g. Rivers 2012).

5.1 Restorative justice and environmental justice

The idea of restorative justice is in one sense quite simple and has a long history. Its main proponent, Braithwaite (2002), has noted that in earlier work he had

> hypothesized from the historical literature five stages in the history of Western regulation:
>
> 1. A pre-state stage where restorative justice and banishment are dominant
> 2. A weak state stage where corporal and capital punishment dominate
> 3. A strong state stage where professional police and penitentiaries dominate
> 4. A Keynesian welfare state stage where new therapeutic professions such as social work colonize what becomes probation-prison-parole
> 5. A contemporarily evolving new regulatory state phase of community and corporate policing (with a revived restorative justice).
>
> (pp. 7–8)

However, he has subsequently regarded this sequential history as too simple a rendering, noting that 'the important point' is that we have witnessed

> a late modern revival of restorative justice that has its deepest roots in a shift from most regulatory activities having individuals and their bodies as their objects to a world where more of the wrongdoing is done by organizations that are regulated in a mostly restorative fashion.
>
> (p. 8)

This kind of approach to the administration of environmental justice, recognising the rights and voice of victims, and requiring mutual engagement, shared learning and mediation between perpetrator and victim, is practical as well as consonant with green ideals. Importantly, it could be placed within a spectrum of responses in recognition that no one single approach is sufficient (Sahramäki, Korsell and Kankaanranta, 2015), and could be a main feature of the menu of options available to environmental courts as they continue to develop. At the end of the last decade, Pring and Pring (2009) reported there were more than 350 environmental courts and tribunals authorised in some 41 countries. This growth in the number of such courts and proposals for the establishment of an International Environmental Court have, as White (2013) argues, 'mirrored' the increasing importance attached to environmental matters in international forums and law. This recognition demonstrates that the late-modern world is not unaware of the risks and threats facing us (Giddens, 1999, p. 3), and it is the case that, at global, national, regional and local levels, there has been a proliferation of treaties, prohibitions, laws and by-laws relating to environmental crime. However, responses need to be underpinned by effective statutory and regulatory systems, the maintenance of inspection and policing to ensure compliance and – where breaches and violations occur – prosecution, restoration and proportionate penalty. Regrettably, in a well-known pattern, new loopholes open up and new commercial (legal or illegal) opportunities incentivise evasion and avoidance of control measures. In the case of the Deepwater Horizon oil spill mentioned earlier, Uhlmann (2010) noted that:

> No one thinks BP, Transocean or Halliburton *intended* to spill oil into the Gulf. But given good evidence, the government could argue that the companies cut corners or deviated so much from standard industry practice that they knew a blowout could happen. Or, the government could argue that, even if the initial gusher involved only negligence (a misdemeanor under the Clean Water Act) each additional day represents a knowing violation. Both approaches are untested, because there have been so few oil spill cases – but the Gulf disaster warrants trying aggressive strategies.
>
> (Emphasis added)

One approach of a more aggressive nature would be to bypass the problem of proving 'knowing intent' and introduce an international criminal law based on strict liability. Without this, as Higgins (2010, 2012) argues, the defence that 'we did not intend this to happen' will be a repeated response, with environmental destruction apologetically described as 'collateral damage'. This more aggressive stance is one element of the proposal for an international law of ecocide.

6 Ecocide

Outlining the foundations of a theory of intergenerational ecological justice, Weston (2012, p. 261) emphasises the proposition that the community of humankind is collectively made up of generations of the present, the past and the future, with the related implication that rights and obligations also hold across this long intergenerational chain: 'In this manner, the "common heritage" of Earth's natural resources, fresh water systems, oceans, atmosphere, and outer space belongs to all generations in an inter-temporal partnership.' According to this view, reforms of law and governance should build on recognition of, and respect for, the interdependence of ecosystems and the principle of intergenerational equity.

How, then, might we seek to guarantee the protection of this common heritage and abate the process of exclusion from inheritance of a liveable planet that we are setting in motion for future generations (Higgins *et al.*, 2013)?

At present the prospects seem bleak. Reflecting on the Earth Summit in Rio de Janeiro, one environmental journalist (Pearce, 2012, pp. 10–11) wrote:

> An environmental crusade that began 20 years ago in this same city with high hopes that governments could join forces to rescue the planet … has come to an end with a toothless declaration that commits nobody to anything … there is little left of hopes that ministerial agreements at UN meetings can curb environmental destruction. 'We can't legislate sustainable development in the current state of international relations', said Achim Steiner, Director of the UN Environment Programme.

Yet 'curbing environmental destruction' and 'legislating for sustainable development' ought to be urgent priorities across the agendas of those concerned with international relations and environmental security (South, 2012). One proposal for a mechanism to encourage this is to take the concept of 'ecocide' and formulate an internationally applicable law as an additional 'crime against peace' under the Rome Statute of the International Criminal Court.

6.1 A brief note on the institutional history of ecocide

The institutional history of ecocide is, in origin, inextricably bound up with the evolution of the history of the concept of genocide (Gauger *et al.*, 2012; Higgins *et al.*, 2013). The term 'genocide' was initially advanced by Lemkin in 1933 as a conceptual means of combining the idea of barbarity and vandalism, drawing together the Greek 'genos' for tribe or race and the Latin 'cide' for destruction

(Lemkin, 1944; Gauger *et al.*, 2012). Importantly, the first formulation of the genocide proposal did not limit destruction to direct killing but included the devastation of cultures, which might embrace destruction of a territory such as a homeland and the denial of access to or erosion of the bases for traditional ways of life, both ecological and cultural. One modern example would be the case of what Samson (2003) has called the 'extinguishment of the Innu'.

With the loss of this breadth in scope, the interpretation and application of 'genocide' came to foreground *intentionality* rather than *consequences* of actions, and this ultimately led to questions about its utility as a device for the protection of those it was supposed to protect (Short, 2010, pp. 6–7). As Gauger *et al.* have shown, it was in the context of consideration of such questions that the suggestion that environmental damage and destruction might be subject to criminalisation first arose. This found one early form in a draft for an International Convention on the Crime of Ecocide by Falk (1973) which covered ecological crimes as well as the idea of cultural ecocide. Although general in scope and implications, Falk's work in the 1970s reflected criticism of the campaign of herbicidal warfare carried out by the USA in Vietnam, in particular the use of Agent Orange. As Zierler (2011, p. 25) reports:

> By the early 1970s, Falk had come to believe that the United States stood guilty of war crimes in Vietnam that amounted to genocide. But why ecocide? For Falk, the strategy of environmental destruction for military purposes represented ... a logic that proceeded on the 'basic rationale of separating the people from their land.' ... By contextualising ecocide as a central component to the wider strategy of the destruction of South Vietnam, Falk [1973: 84] identified 'Agent Orange as an Auschwitz for environmental values ... And just as the Genocide Convention came along to formalize part of what had already been condemned and punished at Nuremberg, so an Ecocide Convention could help carry forward into the future a legal condemnation of environmental warfare in Indochina.'

However, beyond the case of Vietnam, the question of 'intent' remained a problematic issue. Although there may be various reasons why environmental damage might be inflicted intentionally in times of war, during a period of peace, harm is more likely to be a product of lack of care or failure of oversight or a by-product of action pursued for profit but not with the primary intent of causing deliberate damage on a major scale (although there may be cases of wilful negligence leading to significant environmental harm). Between 1984 and 1996, the International Law Commission (ILC) extensively debated the question of whether or not to include ecocide on the emerging list of 'crimes against peace'. After much activity within working groups (some well documented, some less transparent), in 1996 the final Article adopted by the ILC, referred to the *intentional* causing of 'widespread, long-term and severe damage to the natural environment' *within a war*, not peace-time, context (Gauger *et al.*, 2012). Environmental destruction that is unintentionally caused during peace time was not incorporated. This was the final reference to a crime against the environment included in the Rome Statute. It has been suggested that one possible reason why a proposal that at one point seems to have gathered some momentum was then dropped from further consideration lies with concern raised by nuclear states who would be seeking to preserve the right to develop, test and ultimately use nuclear weapons (Tomuschat, 1996; Gauger et al., 2012).

6.2 A proposal for a law of ecocide

The proposal, as developed more recently, argues that nations should act to prevent mass damage, destruction or ecosystem collapse, and that international law should place a duty of care on all nations to provide assistance to any other nations facing ecosystem crises or humanitarian disaster in cases such as overwhelming rising sea levels, tsunamis and floods. This law would be inserted into the Rome Statute by an amendment defining ecocide as 'the extensive damage to, destruction of or loss of ecosystem(s) of a given territory, whether by human agency or by other causes, to such an extent that peaceful enjoyment by the inhabitants of that territory has been severely diminished'. At present under the Statute, the International Criminal Court can concern itself with genocide, crimes against humanity, war crimes and the crime of aggression, where states are unable or unwilling to respond to these. The proposition that ecocide should be added to this list as a fifth 'crime against peace' follows on the basis that it can lead to

> breaches against humanity, nature and future generations; heightened risk of conflict; diminution in the quality of life of all inhabitants of a given territory and of territories further afield; diminution in the health and well being of inhabitants, arising out of or leading to catastrophic disaster, food poverty, water pollution and shortages and unnatural climate change.
> (Higgins, 2012, p. 6)

Fundamentally, Higgins takes a global view of environmental challenges leading to the argument that only an international and transboundary response can be sufficient (Higgins et al., 2013). This would be directed not only at governments and their agencies but also at private sector organisations and, in both cases, those persons holding positions of 'superior responsibility' who should exercise a duty of care to prevent the risk of, or actual, extensive damage to or destruction or loss of ecosystems. Both restorative justice mediation approaches and criminal justice sanctions could be deployed to support and encourage compliance.

This proposal and similar calls for extensions of international law are not without critics, but it is significant and important that debate is occurring. Thus Gilbert (2014, p. 552) recognises that '[t]he reality of global warming has forced the international community to seek various responses, including legal responses' and observes that '[i]t is undoubtedly possible to criminalize "ecocide"'. However, and referring specifically to global warming, he continues by arguing that 'just because it can be made subject to criminal law in no way justifies a comprehensive application of international criminal law to global warming *per se*'. Gilbert is concerned in particular with climate change-induced displacement of humans which he acknowledges is 'automatically to have taken an anthropocentric approach to the problem, from protecting the environment *per se* to protecting human beings dealing with the consequences of climate change'. Gilbert's purpose here is to make the process of criminalisation more compatible with domestic and international criminal law in general. Without taking such an approach, his view is that although in

> some circumstances ... one may be able to prove that those perpetrating acts that give rise to climate change which then forces people to move could be guilty of international crimes set out in the Rome Statute of the International Criminal Court ... the complexity of those crimes, the issues surrounding necessary *mens rea*, causation and remoteness, suggest that successful prosecutions will be rare.

'On the other hand', he adds, '*there is nothing to stop the international community or even states with broad extra-territorial jurisdiction from creating new crimes to protect the environment and those affected by changes thereto*' (emphasis added). Gilbert is not unsympathetic to the idea of a law of ecocide but primarily is sceptical about whether a measure based on international criminal law is an appropriate way of responding to global warming or the specific consequential problem of human displacement. Gilbert points out that law requires clarity and that complexity or ambiguity can diminish the chances of successful prosecution. On this point, while the call for a law of ecocide is attracting support, its formulation may still need some clarification and it is possible that interpretation 'in practice' might not be what was intended 'in theory'. For example, the proposal refers to 'inhabitants' of a territory. Given that there is also explicit reference to 'ecosystems', this term could be interpreted to include non-human species. However, if used within the work of the International Criminal Court, the term 'inhabitants' might conceivably become restricted to 'humanity'. In this way, a law of ecocide might simply be a further reflection of anthropocentrism in law.[1]

7 Conclusion

We may now be approaching what some scientists have referred to as our 'planetary boundaries' – the extent to which we are already over or nearing our planet's ability to cope once nine boundaries are breached by damage (these are: climate

---

1 I am grateful to Ragnhild Sollund, Geoff Gilbert and Avi Brisman for points made here and elsewhere in this chapter.

change, biodiversity loss, biogeochemical cycles, ocean acidification, water consumption, land use, ozone depletion, atmospheric particulate pollution and chemical pollution) (Rockström *et al.*, 2009; The Economist, 2012). Human contributions to these impending breaches are not only those on the major scale of the BP Deepwater Horizon case or the destruction or pollution that may be acts or consequences of war; they also include the daily behaviour of consumers engaged in the slow ecocide of the planet (Agnew, 2013). Yet we do not all wish to recognise this, and even if we do, we may do so uneasily and reluctantly (Norgaard, 2006). According to Giddens (1999, p. 6), late modernity has undermined 'certainty' so it can be argued that we no longer feel sure about the real extent of the risks and limits that we are warned not to exceed. No longer do we 'simply accept' the findings of science, having learned a degree of scepticism and cynicism in a 'context of conflicting, changeable scientific and technological information'. This presents a significant barrier to action but must not be accepted as a licence for disregard or denial. Regrettably, consumer society is highly efficient at producing 'off the shelf' narratives of comfort, and presenting ways in which we can reassure ourselves that it is possible to engage in massive consumption without causing harm. Indeed, a great deal of consumption is sold to us as a way of insulating us from harm (Brisman and South, 2014, pp. 78–88).

Proposals such as those for an international law of ecocide and for an international environmental crime court may not yet be perfectly formed, but at the very least they deserve consideration and debate. In fact, if we are to avoid stepping over the 'planetary boundaries' that seem perilously close, and find ways to manage production and consumption, then these (or similar measures) may need urgent support.

Bibliography

Agnew, R. (2013). The ordinary acts that contribute to ecocide: A criminological analysis. In N. South and A. Brisman (eds), *The Routledge International Handbook of Green Criminology*. London: Routledge.

Amos, J. (2011, 2 September). Space debris: Time to clean up the sky. BBC News, Science and Environment web page. Available at www.bbc.co.uk/news/science-environment-14763668 (accessed 23 January 2017).

Bekoff, M. (2010, 24 August). First do no harm. *New Scientist*, 24–25.

Benton, T. (1998). Rights and justice on a shared planet. *Theoretical Criminology*, 2(2), 149–175.

Beirne, P. (2009). *Confronting Animal Abuse: Law, Criminology, and Human–Animal Relationships*. Lanham, MD: Rowman and Littlefield.

Berry, T. (1999). *The Great Work: Our Way into the Future*. New York, NY: Bell Tower.

Bisschop, L. (2012a). Out of the woods: The illegal trade in tropical timber and a European trade hub. *Global Crime*, 13(3), 191–212.

Bisschop, L. (2012b). Is it all going to waste? Illegal transports of e-waste in a European trade hub. *Crime, Law and Social Change*, 58(3), 221–249.

Boekhout van Solinge, T., and Kuijpers, K. (2013). The Amazon Rainforest: A green criminological perspective. In N. South and A. Brisman (eds.), *The Routledge International Handbook of Green Criminology*. London: Routledge.

Braithwaite, J. (2002). *Restorative Justice and Responsive Regulation.* New York, NY: Oxford University Press.

Brisman, A. (2013). Environmental and human rights: Land, property and crime. In G. Bruinsma and D. Weisburd (eds), *Encyclopaedia of Criminology and Criminal Justice.* New York, NY: Springer.

Brisman, A. (2014). Of theory and meaning in green criminology. *International Journal for Crime, Justice and Social Democracy,* 3(2), 21–34.

Brisman, A., and South, N. (2014). *Green Cultural Criminology: Constructions of Environmental Harm, Consumerism, and Resistance to Ecocide.* London: Routledge

Brisman, A., and South, N. (in press). Methodological approaches and ethical challenges in green criminology. In M. Cowburn, L. Gelsthorpe, and A. Wahidin (eds), *Research Ethics in Criminology and Criminal Justice: Dilemmas, Problems and Issues.* London: Routledge.

Broswimmer, F. (2002). *Ecocide: A Short History of the Mass Extinction of Species.* London: Pluto.

Brundtland, G.H. (2012). Foreword. In H. Bigas (ed.), *The Global Water Crisis: Addressing an Urgent Security Issue: Papers for the InterAction Council, 2011–2012.* Hamilton, Canada: UNU-INWEH.

Buckingham, S., and Turner, M. (2008). *Understanding Environmental Issues.* London: Sage.

Burden, P. (ed.) (2011). *Wild Law: The Philosophy of Earth Jurisprudence.* Adelaide: Wakefield.

Burns, T., and Fuchs, J. (2004). *The International Transport of Hazardous Waste: Some Preliminary Findings from the Basel Convention Data.* Resource document. Available at www.allacademic.com//meta/p_mla_apa_research_citation/1/1/0/8/3/pages110830/p110830-1.php (accessed 3 February 2017).

Cardwell, P., French, D., and Hall, M. (2011). Tackling environmental crime in the European Union: The case of the missing victim? *Environmental Law and Management,* 23(3), 113–121.

Christie, N. (1977). Conflicts as property. *British Journal of Criminology,* 17(1), 1–15.

Clifford, M. (ed.) (1998). *Environmental Crime: Enforcement, Policy and Social Responsibility.* Gaithersburg, MA: Aspen Publishers.

Cohen, M. (1992). Environmental crime and punishment: Legal/economic theory and empirical evidence on enforcement of federal environmental statutes. *Journal of Criminal Law and Criminology,* 82, 1054–1108.

Cullinan, C. (2010). Earth jurisprudence: From colonization to participation. In Worldwatch Institute (eds), *State of the World, 2010: Transforming Cultures.* New York, NY: Worldwatch/W.W. Norton.

de Prez, P. (2000). Excuses, excuses: The ritual trivialisation of environmental prosecutions. *Journal of Environmental Law,* 12, 65–77.

du Rées, H. (2001). Can criminal law protect the environment? *Journal of Scandinavian Studies in Criminology and Crime Prevention,* 2, 109–126.

Economist, The. (2012, 16 June). Boundary conditions: The idea of planet-wide environmental boundaries, beyond which humanity would go at its peril, is gaining ground. *The Economist.* Available at www.economist.com/node/21556897 (accessed 23 January 2017).

Eman, K., Mesko, G., and Fields, C. (2009). Crimes against the environment: Green criminology and research challenges in Slovenia. *Journal of Criminal Justice and Security,* 11(4), 574–592.

Falk, R. (1973). Environmental warfare and ecocide: Facts, appraisals and proposals. *Bulletin of Peace Proposals,* 4, 80–84.

Fussey, P., and South, N. (2012). Heading toward a new criminogenic climate: Climate change, political economy and environmental security. In R. White (ed.), *Climate Change from a Criminological Perspective.* New York, NY: Springer Verlag.

Gauger, A., Rabatel-Fernel, M.P., Kulbicki, L., Short, D., and Higgins, P. (2012). *Ecocide is the Missing 5th Crime against Peace*. London: The Ecocide Project, Human Rights Consortium, School of Advanced Study, University of London. Available at http://sas-space.sas.ac.uk/4830/1/Ecocide_research_report_19_July_13.pdf (accessed 3 February 2017).

Gibbs, C., Gore, M., McGarrell, E., and Rivers III, L. (2010). Introducing conservation criminology: Towards interdisciplinary scholarship on environmental crimes and risks. *British Journal of Criminology*, 50(1), 124–144.

Giddens, A. (1999). Risk and responsibility. *The Modern Law Review*, 62(1), 1–9.

Gilbert, G. (2014). International criminal law is not a panacea: Why proposed climate change 'crimes' are just another passenger on an overcrowded bandwagon. *International Criminal Law Review*, 14, 551–587.

Goldenberg, S. (2012, 8 November). US intelligence teams to track wildlife poachers in Africa and Asia. *The Guardian*.

Groombridge, N. (2013). Matter all over the place: Litter, criminology and criminal justice. In N. South and A. Brisman (eds), *The Routledge International Handbook of Green Criminology*. London: Routledge.

Higgins, P. (2010). *Eradicating Ecocide: Laws and Governance to Prevent the Destruction of Our Planet*. London: Shepheard-Walwyn.

Higgins, P. (2012). *Closing the Door to Dangerous Industrial Activity: A Concept Paper for Governments to Implement Emergency Measures*. London. Available at http://eradicatingecocide.com/wp-content/uploads/2012/06/Concept-Paper.pdf (accessed 22 January 2017).

Higgins, P., Short, D., and South, N. (2013). Protecting the planet: A proposal for a law of ecocide. *Crime, Law and Social Change*, 59(3), 251–266.

Jackson, S. (2006). Un/natural disasters, here and there. Understanding Katrina – Perspectives from the Social Sciences. Social Sciences Research Council, New York. Available at http://understandingkatrina.ssrc.org/Jackson (accessed 3 February 2017).

Johnson, H., South, N., and Walters, R. (2016). The commodification and exploitation of fresh water: Property, human rights and green criminology. *International Journal of Law, Crime and Justice*, 44, 146–162.

Klenovsek, A., and Mesko, G. (2011). International waste trafficking: Preliminary explorations. In G. Mesko, D. Dimitrijevic and C. Fields (eds), *Understanding and Managing Threats to the Environment in South Eastern Europe*. Dordrecht: Springer.

Lemkin, R. (1944). *Axis Rule in Occupied Europe: Laws of Occupation – Analysis of Government – Proposals for Redress*. Washington, DC: Carnegie Endowment for International Peace.

Lynch, M. (1990). The greening of criminology: A perspective on the 1990s. *The Critical Criminologist*, 2(3), 1–4, 11–12.

Lynch, M., Burns, R., and Stretesky, P. (2010). Global warming and state-corporate crime: The politicization of global warming under the Bush administration. *Crime, Law and Social Change*, 54, 213–239.

Lynch, M., and Stretesky, P. (2003). The meaning of green: Contrasting criminological perspectives. *Theoretical Criminology*, 7(2), 217–238.

Mares, D. (2010). Criminalizing ecological harm: Crimes against carrying capacity and the criminalization of eco-sinners. *Critical Criminology*, 18(4), 279–293.

McCoy, T. (2014, 4 December). Wanted: The world's worst eco-fugitives. *The i*, p. 32.

McGrath, M. (2012, 12 July). UK laws 'spurring trade in endangered species'. BBC News, Science and Environment web page. Available at www.bbc.co.uk/news/science-environment-18408186 (accessed 23 January 2017).

Norgaard, K. (2006). 'We don't really want to know': Environmental justice and socially organized denial of global warming in Norway. *Organization and Environment*, 19(3), 347–370.

Nriagu, J. (1990). Global metal pollution: Poisoning the biosphere? *Environment: Science and Policy for Sustainable Development*, 32, 7.

Pearce, F. (2012, 6 March). Earth summit signals move to give nature a price tag. *New Scientist*, 2871, 10–11.

Pring, G., and Pring, C. (2009). *Greening Justice: Creating and Improving Environmental Courts and Tribunals*. The Access Initiative. Available at www.law.du.edu/documents/ect-study/greening-justice-book.pdf (accessed 23 January 2017).

Rivers, L. (2012). Restorative justice in the mock ecocide trial sentencing process. The Hamilton Group. Available at www.thehamiltongroup.org.uk/common/ecocide-sentence.asp (accessed 23 January 2017).

Rockström, J., Steffen, W., Noone, K., Persson, Å., Chapin, F., Lambin, E., Lenton, T., Scheffer, M., and Folke, C. (2009). A safe operating space for humanity. *Nature*, 461(7263), 472–475.

Rodriguez-Goyes, D., and South, N. (2016). Land grabs, bio-piracy and the inversion of justice in Colombia. *British Journal of Criminology*, 56(3), 558–577.

Ruggiero, V., and South, N. (2010). Green criminology and dirty-collar crime. *Critical Criminology*, 18(4), 251–262.

Samson, C. (2003). *A Way of Life That Does Not Exist: Canada and the Extinguishment of the Innu*. London: Verso.

Sahramäki, I., Korsell, L., and Kankaanranta, T. (2015). Prevention of environmental crime through enforcement – Finland and Sweden compared. *Journal of Scandinavian Studies in Criminology and Crime Prevention*, 16(1), 41–59.

Savulescu, J. (2012, 19 April). Master the new loom before life's tapestry unravels at our hands. *Times Higher Education*, 32–33.

Schneider, J. (2012). *Sold into Extinction: The Global Trade in Endangered Species*. Westport, CT: Praeger.

Short, D. (2010). Cultural genocide and indigenous peoples: A sociological approach. *The International Journal of Human Rights*, 14(6–7), 831–846.

Shover, N., and Routhe, N. (2005). Environmental crime. In M. Tonry (ed.), *Crime and Justice*. Chicago, IL: University of Chicago Press.

Sollund, R. (ed.) (2008). *Global Harms: Ecological Crime and Speciesism*. New York, NY: Nova Science.

South, N. (1998). A green field for criminology? A proposal for a perspective. *Theoretical Criminology*, 2(2), 211–234.

South, N. (2012). Climate change, environmental (in)security, conflict and crime. In S. Farrall, D. French, and T. Ahmed (eds), *Climate Change: Legal and Criminological Implications* (pp. 97–111). Oxford: Hart.

South, N. (2014). Green criminology: Reflections, connections, horizons. *International Journal for Crime, Justice and Social Democracy*, 3(2), 6–21.

South, N. (2015). Green criminology, brown crime and problems of despoiling, disposal and de-manufacturing in global resource industries. In T. Wyatt (ed.), *Green Crime: Hazardous Waste and Pollution*. London: Springer.

South, N., Brisman, A., and Beirne, P. (2013). A guide to a green criminology. In N. South and A. Brisman (eds), *The Routledge International Handbook of Green Criminology*. London: Routledge.

South, N., and Wyatt, T. (2011). Comparison of the illicit wildlife and drug trades: An exploratory study. *Deviant Behavior*, 32(6), 338–561.
Stone, C. (1972). Should trees have standing? Towards legal rights for natural objects. *Southern California Law Review*, 45, 450–501.
Tacconi, L. (ed.) (2007). *Illegal Logging: Law Enforcement, Livelihoods and the Timber Trade*. London: Earthscan.
Tomuschat, C. (1996). Crimes against the environment. *Environmental Policy and Law*, 26, 6.
Uhlmann, D (2010, 6 June). Prosecuting crimes against the earth. *New York Times* Op-Ed, p. A27. Available at www.nytimes.com/2010/06/04/opinion/04uhlmann.html?_r=1 (accessed 23 January 2017).
Walters, R. (2010). Eco-crime. In J. Muncie, D. Talbot and R. Walters (eds), *Crime: Local and Global* (pp. 173–208). Collumpton: Willan.
Week, The. (2011, 1 October). Space junk. *The Week*, p. 13.
Weston, B. (2012). The theoretical foundations of intergenerational ecological justice: An overview. *Human Rights Quarterly*, 34, 261.
White, R. (2008). *Crimes against Nature: Environmental Criminology and Ecological Justice*. Cullompton: Willan.
White, R. (2010). Globalisation and environmental harm. In R. White (ed.), *Global Environmental Harm: Criminological Perspectives* (pp. 3–19). Cullompton: Willan.
White, R. (ed.) (2012). *Climate Change from a Criminological Perspective*. New York, NY: Springer Verlag.
White, R. (2013). Environmental crime and problem-solving courts. *Crime, Law and Social Change*, 59(3), 267–278.
Wolf, B. (2011). Green-collar crime: Environmental crime and justice in the sociological perspective. *Sociology Compass*, 5(7), 499–511.
WHO. (2008). *Air quality and health*. Available at www.who.int/mediacentre/factsheets (accessed 3 February 2017).
WHO. (2015). *Facts and figures on water quality and health*. Previously available at www.who.int/water_sanitation_health/facts_figures/en.
Wyatt, T. (2012). *Green Criminology and Wildlife Trafficking: The Illegal Fur and Falcon Trades in Russia Far East*. Saarbrücken, Germany: LAP Lambert Academic Publishing.
Zierler, D. (2011). *The Invention of Ecocide*. Athens, GA: University of Georgia Press.

Chapter 3

Green criminology and the prevention of ecological destruction

Ruth E. McKie, Paul B. Stretesky, Michael J. Lynch and Michael A. Long

Introduction

Early efforts by criminologists to call attention to environmental crime, law and justice have been met with significant resistance. But times have changed and substantial concern over local and global environmental problems has opened up political opportunities for criminologists to study environmental crime. As a result, an area of study known as "green criminology" has emerged (Lynch, 1990; South, 1998). As green criminology develops, it also contributes to the general environmental literature, offering solutions and critiques of environmental regulations and policies. This chapter is concerned with the scholarly literature that green criminologists produce. We ask, "How does green criminology inform the study of environmental crime?" To answer this question, we consider laws and policies and especially the emergence of global environmental enforcement. In particular, we explore how traditional legal approaches to environmental crime are not appropriate solutions to environmental crime. Moreover, we review important multinational environmental agreements (or MEAs), including the benefits and limits of this type of global approach to enforcement. We suggest that while green criminologists recognize potential gains that may result from stronger regulation, they also point out the structural limits that prevent the law from slowing rates of ecological destruction. We emphasize that appropriate responses to environmental violations must consider the political economy and "treadmill of production" (Schnaiberg 1980), proposing that environmental law must recognize that the base of current economic structures of capitalism increase and perpetuate environmental crimes.

Prior to that discussion, however, it is necessary to briefly define green criminology and differentiate between the studies of crime and harm. The differentiation between crime and harm is central to green criminology because crime is politically situated and therefore depends upon time and place.

I Origins of green criminology: from crime to harm

Historically, criminologists have directed their attention towards individuals who have violated the criminal law (Lynch, Stretesky, and Long, 2015). That is, criminologists study behavior that the law defines as crime (Tappan, 1947). These studies of crime have largely concentrated on street crime (or the crimes of murder, rape, robbery, aggravated assault, larceny, motor vehicle theft, and arson), while ignoring corporate and white-collar crime. This condition began to change when Sutherland (1940) questioned why the "robber barons" of the time were not studied by sociologists interested in crime (see also Ross 1907 [1973]). Sutherland's (1947, p. 24) emphasis on white-collar crime led him to suggest that criminology needed to expand its focus:

> [T]he legal definitions should not confine the work of the criminologist, and he [sic] should be completely free to push across the barriers of legal definitions whenever he [sic] sees behavior outside the legal field which resembles the behavior within.

Today, of course, the study of white-collar and corporate crime is much more commonplace (Alalehto, 2015; Hunter, 2015). Many criminology textbooks include a chapter on corporate and white-collar crime and most colleges and universities teach a course on the subject. What has been relatively slow to develop is attention to environmental issues within the discipline of criminology (Stretesky, 2008; Zilney, McGurrin, and Zahran, 2006). This condition has also changed with the emergence of corporate environmental crime research. For instance, in 1988 Block and Bernard produced one of the first studies to examine the way corporate power and organized crime can undermine environmental law in their analysis of illegal toxic waste disposal (see also Lynxwiler, Shover, and Clelland, 1983). Nevertheless, it was not until Michael J. Lynch (1990) revisited previous arguments against the narrow position that crime is an act that violates the law to argue that a new class of "green crime" be considered by scholars. This green criminology developed to account for the tremendous amount of ecological destruction occurring across the globe (Lynch, 1990). The problem, according to Lynch, is that criminologists often concentrate on individual causes of crime and therefore tend to ignore the larger structural conditions that promote environmental harm. As a result of this individual level focus, green crimes and their associated harms are often excluded from criminological discourse (see also Lynch, Stretesky, and Long, 2015). Following Lynch's call for a green criminology, various definitions of environmental and green crime emerged (see Clifford and Edwards, 2012). For example, orthodox criminologists interested in environmental crime emphasize state-based definitions of crime. Consider Situ and Emmons (1999: 4) who suggest that environmental crime is an act that "violates existing environmental laws." Critical green criminologists, however, call for a more comprehensive definition of green crime that encompasses illegal and legal – but harmful – acts that are acceptable according to the law.

The notion that criminology – and especially a green criminology – can focus on more than acts defined as crime within the criminal law has important roots in the development of the criminology of social harm. Following the famous

Sutherland–Tappan debates (Friedrichs, 1996), the notion of harm-based crime began to take shape in the 1970s when Schwendinger and Schwendinger (1970) proposed a human rights definition of crime situated within a working-class perspective. Specifically, they argued:

> Culprits, who were at the highest levels of government, have not been prosecuted for their crimes against humanity. Nor have thousands of criminologists shown professional concern with these crimes. Their reasoning is simple: the perpetrators have not been defined or sanctioned as criminals by the state.
> (Schwendinger and Schwendinger 1977: 8)

More recently, this social harm approach is emphasized in the work of Hillyard and Tombs (2007, p. 15) who stress that criminologists should study

> deleterious activities of local and national states and of corporations upon people's lives, whether in respect of lack of wholesome food, inadequate housing or heating, low income, exposure to various forms of danger, violations of basic human rights, and victimization to various forms of crime ... that affect many people throughout their life cycle.

It is within this context of the development of social harm that the study of green crime has fully emerged (Beirne and South, 2007; Kramer and Michalowski, 2012; Lynch *et al.*, 2013; White and Heckenberg, 2014; Stretesky, Long, and Lynch, 2013; Westerhuis, Walters, and Wyatt, 2013; Zaitch, van Solinge, and Müller, 2014). For instance, criminologists such as Lynch *et al.* (2013) argue that harm-based notions of crime are needed to better understand green crime and its solutions. They suggest that a green crime is "an act that causes or has the potential to cause significant harm to ecological systems for the purpose of increasing or supporting the accumulation" of wealth under capitalism (Stretesky, Long, and Lynch 2013, p. 2; see also Lane, 1998). Thus, a definition of green crime that places the ecology and economy on equal footing and accounts for class exploitation is critical if ecological destruction will be prevented over the long term. Furthermore, this leads to the re-evaluation of who are in fact violating these environmental laws, including the group of actors that Sutherland (1940) engaged with in his advancement of criminological discourse. That is, what environmental crimes do states and/or corporations commit, and how can environmental law come to prevent these crimes?

Today, many criminological texts focus on environmental crime and green criminology to adopt a definition of green crime situated within a social harms approach. That is, the social harms approach is dominant within green criminology. As a result, green criminologists study a variety of environmental harms such as climate change (Agnew, 2012; Brisman, 2012; Farrall, Ahmed and French, 2012; White, 2012), logging (van Solinge, 2014; Wyatt, 2014), green victims (Hall, 2012, 2013; Jarrell and Ozymy, 2012; Williams, 1996), hazardous, toxic, and electronic waste (Bisschop, 2012; Gibbs *et al.*, 2011; Ruggiero and South, 2010; Tompson and Chainey, 2011; Walters, 2007), environmental genocide (Brook, 1998); illegal fishing (Hauck, 2008, 2009; Sander *et al.*, 2014); food (Croall, 2007; Walters, 2006), poaching and wildlife trafficking (Lemieux and Clarke, 2009; Pires and Clarke, 2012; Wellsmith, 2010; Wyatt, 2013), chemical releases (Katz, 2010; Lynch and Barrett, 2015; Walters, 2009, 2010), natural resource conflict (Bavinck, Pellegrini, and Mostert, 2014; South, 2007), and environmental injustice (Brisman, 2008; Lynch and Stretesky, 2003; South and Brisman, 2013; Stretesky, 2008). The position that many green criminologists take is that determining harm and crime will have to come through scientific research since the environment cannot speak to us directly – but only through science – wherein political systems favor the economy over the ecology (Lynch and Stretesky, 2011, 2014). Therefore, green criminologists must incorporate scientific research if they are to offer solutions to current environmental laws that fail to deter environmental crime.

2 Environmental enforcement across the globe

In green criminology, there is a major emphasis on the enforcement of environmental laws. The traditional focus of regulatory enforcement is that it will "detect, deter and punish" environmental offenders through administrative actions, civil proceedings, and criminal prosecutions (Pink, 2013; Ross, 1996; White, 2013). On a global scale, environmental enforcement varies considerably because different countries have different environmental laws relative to their position in the world economy. That is, the cross-national distribution of environmental enforcement appears to be based on economic relationships and conditions. For example, the environmental Kuznets curve (or EKC) suggests that as a country's economy develops, its environmental quality deteriorates (Dinda, 2004: except see Harbaugh, Levinson, and Wilson, 2002; Stern, 2004). At some point, however, the Kuznets curve predicts that the wealth of a country changes environmental behavior so that more wealthy countries can afford to pay attention to the environment and therefore environmental laws are implemented and enforced in a way that improves environmental conditions.

Green criminologists note that multinational corporations and wealthy states may take advantage of countries that are developing – by directing development-related investment to those countries – precisely because they have weak environmental laws and enforcement mechanisms (Lopez and Mitra, 2000). Therefore, the environmental costs avoided by wealthier countries are displaced beyond national boundaries to developing states (Mason, 2005) while maintaining and lengthening capitalist modes of production and consumption that perpetuate ecological destruction.

This is most apparent when examining green crime on an international scale and with reference to environmental justice (Torras and Boyce, 1998). Brack (2002) points out that most environmental crime is global in nature because pollution and waste are not confined by political boundaries (see also White, 2013). Walters

(2007, p. 187) also recognizes that "green criminology internationalizes the domain of criminology discourse by focusing on actions that threaten the ongoing development and sustainability of the planet." Consider the impact of carbon dioxide. While countries such as China, the United States and India release significant amounts of carbon dioxide annually, the impact of climate change is felt in countries and locations throughout the globe. As an example of this impact, consider that in 2002 the Pacific island Tuvalu – under the threat of being engulfed by rising seas brought about by melting ice caps – brought a suit against the United States for refusing to commit to lowering its greenhouse gases which are thought to contribute to the problem (Jacobs, 2005).

In recognition of the widespread implications of environmental and social harm, green criminologists tend to refer to and call for stronger enforcement of national laws and international environmental agreements that are based on notions of social and ecological justice to limit or prohibit actions that harm the biosphere and threaten life on earth (Eman, Meško, and Fields, 2009; Gibbs *et al.*, 2011; White, 2011a; Wyatt, 2012). Moreover, calls for a social harm-based notion of green crime are nearly universal in green criminology. Recently, for instance, Gibbs *et al.* (2011, p. 269) suggest that "E-waste is an excellent example of an environmental risk that involves some issues of compliance, but is not *necessarily criminalized*." These calls to examine harm as green crime are often connected to international enforcement and are redefining the discipline of criminology. For instance, Walters (2012, p. 103) notes that the Interregional Crime and Justice Institute at the United Nations "has established a ... categorization of transnational organized environmental crime based on various international protocols and multilateral agreements." That is, international protocols have come to recognize environmental harms as illegal; thus, the discipline of criminology is not simply concerned with green crimes as defined by environmental criminal law.

International enforcement of green crime often takes place through MEAs. An MEA is a legally binding agreement between multiple countries and focused on an environmental issue (Churchill and Ulfstein, 2000). There are hundreds of MEAs in existence worldwide, although the exact number of environmental agreements is in contention (Mitchell, 2003). Although there are several major MEAs that tend to be studied with some frequency, green criminologists have largely emphasized two: the Convention on International Trade in Endangered Species of Wild Fauna and Flora or CITES (Green, Ward, and McConnachie, 2007; Wellsmith, 2010; White and Heckenberg, 2014) and the Basel Convention (Gibbs *et al.*, 2010; Walters, 2007; White, 2011b). These two MEAs cover a majority of wildlife and hazardous waste crime. We briefly examine both MEAs, pointing out their relationship to green criminology, but note that there are several other major ones that are also relevant to green criminology, including those that focus on "nature conservation, hazardous substances management, atmospheric emissions controls and marine environment protection" (Rose, 2011, p. 3). We list these MEAs in Table 3.1 below, drawing upon the organization of Rose (2011) to demonstrate the variety and complexity of global regulation of green crime.

Table 3.1 Major multi-lateral environmental agreements (n=18)

Nature Conservation
1. Convention on Wetlands of International Importance especially as Waterfowl Habitat
2. Convention for the Protection of World Cultural and Natural Endangered Species
3. Convention on International Trade in Endangered Species of World Fauna and Flora
4. Convention on the Conservation of Migratory Species of Wild Animals
5. Convention of Biological Diversity
6. United Nations Convention to Combat Desertification
7. International Treaty on Plant Genetic Resources for Food and Agriculture

Hazardous Materials
8. Basel Convention on the Control of Transboundary Movements of Hazardous Waste and their Disposal
9. Rotterdam Convention on the Prior Informed Consent Procedure for Certain Hazardous Chemicals and Pesticides in International Trade
10. Cartagena Protocol on Biosafety to the Convention on Biological Diversity
11. Stockholm Convention on Persistent Organic Pollutants

Atmospheric Emissions
12. Vienna Convention for the Protection of the Ozone Layer
13. Montreal Protocol on Substances that Deplete the Ozone Layer
14. United Nations Framework Convention on Climate Change
15. Kyoto Protocol to the United Nations Framework Convention on Climate Change

Marine Environment
16. International Convention for the Regulation of Whaling
17. Convention on the Prevention of Marine Pollution by Dumping of Wastes and Other Matter
18. United Nations Convention on the Law of the Sea

Source: Adapted from Gregory Rose (2011, pp. 4–5). Interlinkages between Multi-Lateral Environmental Agreements: International Compliance Cooperation. In Paddock et al. (eds), *Compliance and Enforcement in Environmental Law* (pp. 3–33). IUCN Academy of Environmental Law Series. Cheltenham, UK: Edward Elgar Publishing.

CITES is an example of an MEA that was adopted in 1963 in response to endangered species. The aim of the conservation agreement is to monitor and prevent the international trade in animals and plants when their survival is threatened (Wijnstekers, 2003). Thus, CITES lists species threatened with extinction, species where trade must be controlled to prevent them from becoming endangered, and species where at least one country has asked for help in controlling trade (Wijnstekers, 2003). Each of the 181 member countries signed to the convention implements CITES through its own environmental laws and enforcement mechanisms (CITES, 2013). For instance, in the United States, CITES is implemented through the Endangered Species Act, the Lacey Act, African Elephant Conservation Act, and Wild Bird Conservation Act. These acts are largely enforced through the U.S. Fish and Wildlife Services and offenders may be prosecuted by the United States Department of Justice. In the United Kingdom, CITES is also implemented by a variety of acts such as the Wildlife and Countryside Act 1981 and the Natural Environment and Rural Communities

Act 2006. These acts are enforced by the UK police and Border Force and supported by the National Wildlife Crime Unit. Green criminologists such as Lemieux and Clarke (2009) have found that the impact of CITES ban in the case of ivory trade has helped to prevent the killing of elephants worldwide. However, they note that countries that reside near state actors that do not implement CITES continue to face higher than average elephant poaching because, they suspect, poachers have access to nearby unregulated markets. By drawing on a situational crime prevention framework, the researchers note that unregulated markets must be closed, including "all those in neighboring countries ... otherwise the poached ivory will continue to be transported to where it can easily be sold" (Lemieux and Clarke, 2009). Thus, treaties like CITES are only effective when the problem is addressed by all countries and not just a few. As a result, it is important to (1) remove access to unregulated ivory markets through modifications to MEAs and (2) create new pro-environmental domestic laws in countries where those laws do not yet exist.

The Basel Convention is another MEA that was adopted in 1989 to combat the transfer of hazardous waste between nations – especially waste from developed to less developed nations. As is the case with CITES, each of the 182 states that have signed the Basel Convention have agreed to reduce the toxicity of the waste they generate and promote sound environmental management where the waste is generated (Basel Convention, 2011). Developed countries have also agreed to aid less developed countries with best waste management practices. Moreover, the implementation of Basel is largely based on the enforcement practices and resources in each country. In particular, within its Articles, the Protocol emphasizes that (1) hazardous waste reduction should be promoted over hazardous waste disposal; (2) there should be restrictions on the "transboundary" movement of hazardous wastes; and (3) that states can create and enforce a regulatory system that governs when waste can be moved between countries. Unfortunately, these goals are hard to realize because of varying definitions of hazardous waste (i.e. waste is often redefined in order to comply with Basel) and because legislation is lacking in many countries. In addition, state enforcement mechanisms concerning hazardous waste are not consistent (Rummel-Bulska, 1998). As a result, enforcement is left to a variety of actors and networks that include governmental and non-governmental organizations. For instance, organizations and networks that attempt to enforce the Basel Protocol include "the World Customs Organization (WCO), the International Criminal Police Organization (Interpol), the Transfrontier Shipments cluster of the European Union Network for the Implementation and Enforcement of Environmental Law (IMPEL-TFS), the International Network for Environmental Compliance and Enforcement (INECE), the Asian Network for Prevention of Illegal Transboundary Movements of Wastes" (Voinov-Kohler, 2011, p. 214). Moreover, other non-profit organizations have emerged worldwide that work toward the ideals of the Basel Protocol. For instance, the Basel Action Network (or BAN) has worked to implement the principles of the Basel Protocol through environmental litigation, anonymous tips concerning the shipment of hazardous waste across borders (see http://ban.org/hilights/highlights08.html); education about Basel principles to the public and corporations, and public whistleblowing campaigns that post leaked documents from companies and governments that violate principles of the Basel Protocol (see http://archive.ban.org/main/whistle.html). While these efforts help to implement the Protocol, they are, nevertheless uncoordinated and arbitrary (Stretesky and Knight, 2013). Moreover, regulators and law enforcement in most Basel countries lack adequate training and do not have appropriate technology to identify waste (Bisschop, 2015). Nevertheless, Gibbs et al. (2010) note that most countries have passed legislation to regulate hazardous waste under Basel even if its implementation is highly uneven across nations. For instance, they suggest that while the European Union has banned the export of E-waste to developing nations, the United States "continues to export many forms of E-waste via an ineffective notification and consent process" (Gibbs et al., 2010, p. 135).

States – often influenced by powerful corporate interests – have thwarted global efforts to better define, identify, and enforce environmental crime (White, 2011b). For instance, not all states ratify MEAs, and those that do may not possess the resources and ability to enforce the agreements they ratify. These types of regulatory failures reduce the effectiveness of deterrent messages (Wheeler, 2001) and allow a safe haven for environmental criminals. In response to calls for more environmental enforcement there has been a simultaneous emphasis on the part of corporations to demand more "flexible" and "cooperative" enforcement. Flexible enforcement allows producers to try out new technologies that have the potential to improve environmental performance in the production process rather than rely on "end of the pipe" technology solutions or "add-on measures" that are often less effective, yet mandated by law (Frondel, Horbach, and Rennings, 2007; Vig and Kraft, 2012). Cooperative enforcement promotes solutions that emphasize shared enforcement. For example, companies have proposed that they be allowed to "self-police" environmental violations and find solutions to their own problems without hiding information and internal environmental audits from the state because they fear punishment (Stretesky, 2006). This new enforcement ideology only serves to decrease traditional enforcement staff as they are not as essential in the regulation process when companies police themselves (Jarrell and Ozymy, 2012). Thus, flexible and cooperative enforcement reduces the role states play in managing corporate environmental law violations. As a result of this trend, some researchers suggest that global enforcement will become largely irrelevant and give way to a new modernized world where states are obstacles to environmental performance and corporations will strive to put the ecology on an equal footing with the economy (Mol and Spaargaren, 1993). That is, states – often influenced by corporate actors – will reach a point whereby environmental improvement is not compromised over economic performance, nor economic performance compromised by environmental regulation.

Unfortunately, evidence that major environmental improvement will be gained without enforcement is unlikely. For instance, Stretesky's (1996) results suggest that self-policing policies in the United States that potentially waive civil and criminal penalties if companies correct and report violations are unlikely to be successful without the threat of traditional enforcement mechanisms. Moreover, Stretesky notes, for example, that most self-policing reports are for record-keeping violations and not illegal behavior. In short, the new emphasis on combating environmental harm through flexible and cooperative enforcement is not likely to reduce ecological disorganization (Gould, Pellow, and Schnaiberg, 2008). As Lynch, Burns, and Stretesky (2014, p. 179) suggest, "environmental laws and regulations are meaningless absent consistent monitoring and enforcement practices."

3 The injustice of environmental enforcement

Environmental justice is one concern that is often raised by green criminologists (United States Environmental Protection Agency, 2015). In the United States, the Environmental Protection Agency (or EPA) proposes that environmental justice is:

> [T]he fair treatment and meaningful involvement of all people regardless of race, color, national origin, or income with respect to the development, implementation, and enforcement of environmental laws, regulations, and policies ... It will be achieved when everyone enjoys the same degree of protection from environmental and health hazards ...

This definition of environmental justice has clear implications for green criminology because the enforcement of environmental laws should be unbiased. Criminal justice scholarship commonly investigates whether policies and processes are just, fair, unbiased, and/or non-discriminatory (Belknap, 2014; Chambliss and Seidman, 1971; Cole, 2000; Miller, 1996). As a result, it is not surprising that green criminologists are interested in criminal justice components such as police, courts, and corrections for evidence of racial, ethnic, economic, and gender inequality. Indeed, many popular criminal justice texts place a great deal of emphasis on discussions of fairness and inequality (Reiman, 1979; Walker, 1994) and several focus on investigating, arresting, and punishing environmental criminals (Clifford and Edwards, 2012; Situ and Emmons, 1999).

In the United States, early environmental justice studies with criminal justice implications focused on court-related responses to environmental crime. These early studies were a response to the Federal Government's commitment to environmental justice through Executive Order 12898 that was signed by Bill Clinton in 1994. Importantly, that order states that each federal "agency shall make achieving environmental justice part of its mission by identifying and addressing, as appropriate, disproportionately high and adverse human health or environmental effects of its programs, policies, and activities." As the political momentum for the Order was building, legal scholars Marianne Lavelle and Marcia Coyle (1992) published the first penalty study that investigated whether courts punish environmental offenders more harshly if they carry out their crimes in white and affluent neighborhoods. Importantly, the scholars examined violations of the U.S. Clean Air Act, Clean Water Act, Safe Drinking Water Act, Comprehensive Environmental Response, Compensation, and Liability Act, and/or the Resource Conservation and Recovery Act. Their analysis suggests that the federal courts are sending potential environmental offenders the message that they will not be as severely punished when they offend in a disadvantaged community. Researchers such as Konisky (2009) have found similar bias with respect to facility inspections. Stretesky and Lynch (2011) also found that coal strip mining operations located in poor communities commit environmental violations more frequently, but are inspected less often than operations in affluent communities. Thus, it appears that corporations feel more empowered to violate the law in minority and poor communities within the United States.

Green criminology scholarship also suggests that the concept of environmental justice could be extended to acts of environmental crime across the globe (Lynch, Nalla, and Miller, 1989). That is, environmental injustices under individual state positions such as domestic policy more likely affecting disadvantaged communities are replicated cross-nationally whereby the same environmental injustices influencing environmental law enforcement then become disproportionately distributed between developed and developing countries. For instance, international agreements may not be equally enforced and some countries are at a disadvantage and may rely on civil society organizations to help them carry out natural resource policing and protection (Adeola, 2000; Prakash and Potoski, 2012). Importantly, even non-profit organizations are unevenly distributed across the global landscape. For instance, Stretesky and Knight (2013) found that international non-governmental organizations are disproportionately organized within high-income countries around the world. This finding is important and reveals how the economic characteristics of a country may influence voluntary monitoring efforts that are critical to environmental enforcement and are often supplemented by civil society and related to major MEAs. In short, global inequality may shape monitoring efforts between and within countries and determine where and how environmental enforcement agencies carry out law enforcement efforts. This area of research remains underdeveloped but has global implications since environmental enforcement organizations may be unequally distributed across countries according to available resources, meaning that poor countries do not have the type of pressure for environmental enforcement that rich countries enjoy (Stretesky and Knight, 2013).

4 Limits of environmental law

As noted, the general approach to environmental enforcement is based on the idea of deterrence (Ehrlich, 1996). General deterrence reasoning suggests that environmental crime can be reduced because punishment lowers the probability that others will engage in environmental crime. That is, the environmental offender is punished to demonstrate what will happen to those who may contemplate environmental crime (Zimring and Hawkins, 1973). Specific deterrence is aimed at the offender and punishment is supposed to prevent future offending. Of course, general and specific deterrence are based on the idea that environmental offenders are rational actors and that their offenses will likely be discovered in a reasonable period of time and then result in a punishment that is proportional to the benefit derived from the crime. Some criminologists – including green criminologists – suggest that corporations can be deterred (Simpson et al., 2013). Moreover, empirical studies that examine the perceptions of managers working in production plants suggest that environmental performance is primarily determined by the government's signals that environmental laws will be enforced (Delmas and Toffel, 2008; Doonan, Lanoie, and Laplante, 2005; May, 2005). These deterrent effects, however, must be examined in the context of environmental sustainability. For instance, given the current global economy, can tough enforcement protect the planet? We doubt it. That is, the system of global capital demands ever-expanding levels of production (Schnaiberg, 1980). Thus, capitalists must increase production to accumulate profit and survive. As a result, when it comes to the environment, capitalism has no limits (Magdoff and Foster, 2011). The increasing rate of ecological withdrawals and additions is evidence of this interaction between the economy and ecology. Moreover, this treadmill of production (Schnaiberg, 1980) is unsustainable in the long run.

As evidence of this problem, scientists have created an "ecological footprint" to measure how much of the earth's resources humans consume (see Wackernagel and Rees, 1997). In the aggregate, the footprint suggests that today we consume more resources (approximately 1.5 times more quickly) than the earth's ecosystems can produce. That means we must use some of the earth's capital to live. It also means that the earth's ecosystems produce less than they did before, and that life on earth is not sustainable. This economic behavior pushes us closer to important planetary boundaries that, if crossed, mean that the earth (and therefore humans living on earth) may not survive (see Rockström et al., 2009).

Punishing offenders will do little to alter the long-term trends in withdrawals and additions that are harming the biosphere since these trends are largely determined by global economics. Thus, the strong enforcement of environmental laws may deter environmental crime within the limits of capitalism, but in the long run this regulatory behavior does little to encourage sustainability. Additional support for this position is given in Figure 3.1 which documents the recent trend in criminal enforcement in the United States by the Department of Justice between the years of 1995 and 2012.

While criminal enforcement declines slightly during this time, the overall level of chemical releases (i.e. "toxic releases") that is tracked by the U.S. government fluctuates considerably. Moreover, carbon dioxide emissions – thought to influence climate change – continue to remain well above the sustainable level and do not decrease significantly over time (Solomon et al. 2009). In short, in the case of the United States it does not appear that there is much improvement in the types of emissions that matter as a result of the criminal enforcement of environmental

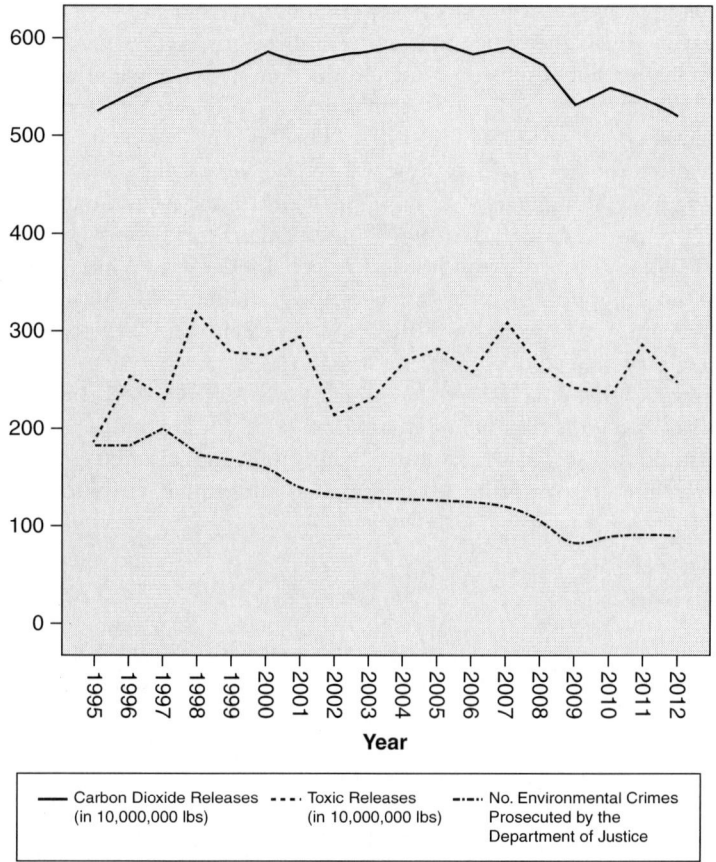

Figure 3.1 United States trends in criminal prosecutions, toxic releases and carbon dioxide emissions, 1995–2012
Source: U.S. Department of Environmental Protection and the U.S. Department of Justice.

laws. Deterrence does not promote better environmental performance on a grand scale. Many criminologists would, of course, be quick to counter that toxic releases and carbon emissions listed in Figure 3.1 are not the specific releases being targeted by criminal enforcement, and that is exactly our point. These are the releases that should be criminalized according to scientific evidence that they are harming the planet as they are pushing us toward planetary boundaries that, if crossed, threaten the earth's biosphere (Rockström *et al.*, 2009). Therefore, a green criminological approach recommends using scientific evidence such as the ecological footprint to advance environmental enforcement. Moreover, it allows environmental enforcement to move beyond traditional methods of deterrence, and rather recommend re-evaluating production and consumption practices that threaten the earth's biosphere.

Criminologists also recognize that corporations are rational – within the systems and context in which they operate – and are therefore likely to avoid "high cost" environmental regulations by locating production in low-income areas and less developed countries in order to avoid financial punishment that comes with environmental compliance (Scholz, 1997). This type of "rational" behavior may end up dictating the flow of environmental hazards across the globe. For instance, Lawrence Summers infamously stated in his World Bank Memo dated December 12, 1991, "Just between you and me, shouldn't the World Bank be encouraging more migration of the dirty industries to the LDCs? ... While production is mobile the consumption of pretty air is a non-tradable." We suggest, then, that deterrence is unlikely to work on those companies that would simply relocate to a different country to avoid regulations and increase profit. Furthermore, deterrence strategies are unlikely to reduce environmental injustices, but rather perpetuate the unequal distribution of environmental harm among poor states. Thus, environmental law must also take into account the rational offender and adopt a suitable response to corporate processes that undermine current enforcement practices.

5 Conclusion

Green criminology emerged in response to orthodox criminology's neglect of environmental harm. As a result, it has drawn heavily upon notions of social harm, environmental justice, and political economy. Although green criminologists recognize the potential gains that may result from refocusing the discipline on crimes of the powerful, there is also a deep recognition that any regulatory solutions are situated within a political economy that encourages environmental disorganization and social inequality – especially related to environmental injustices. That is, deterring environmental crime may be a short-term feel-good strategy that does little to protect the earth in the long run, especially given that the ecological footprint is steadily increasing over time. Current projections of the earth's ecological footprint in 2050 suggest that we will consume nearly three planets' worth of resources annually, exceeding greatly what the earth can handle (see www.footprintnetwork.org/en/index.php/GFN/page/at_a_glance). Unfortunately, this condition is not something that can be easily addressed through the strict detection and punishment of environmental crime. In fact, regulation will do very little to protect the earth's biosphere in the long run. Although green criminologists recognize the potential gains that may result from stronger regulation, their more radical base also emphasizes the structural limits that prevent the law from slowing rates of ecological destruction. That is, because the law is a reflection of the political economy and the "treadmill of production," green crime will be allowed within the confines of the law. This treadmill of production therefore shapes the law and produces a "treadmill of crime" that encourages greater levels of ecological destruction over time (Stretesky, Long, and Lynch, 2013). We propose, then, that it is not the law that must change to protect the environment, but the mode of production that ultimately shapes the law. An understanding of these limits of law lends an important and critical voice to the study of environmental crime, law, and justice that opposes popular modernization arguments which suggest that the economy can someday grow without causing harm to the ecology (i.e. that the ecology and economy will "decouple" (see Jorgenson and Clark, 2012)).

Criminologists therefore should offer definitions to crime that are international in focus and serve to reinforce an alternative economic base that does not reinforce capitalism and the accumulation of capital that is only attainable through substantial increases in production. As a result, we continue to emphasize that "green crime is an act that causes or has the potential to cause harm to the Earth's biosphere for the purpose of accumulation." Therefore, environmental law must be prepared to learn from and adapt to this alternative economic base proposed by criminologists if it wants to successfully manage and prevent further green crimes.

Bibliography

Adeola, F.O. (2000). Cross-national environmental injustice and human rights issues: A review of evidence in the developing world. *American Behavioral Scientist*, 43(4), 686–706.
Agnew, R. (2012). Dire forecast: A theoretical model of the impact of climate change on crime. *Theoretical Criminology*, 16(1), 21–42.
Alalehto, T. (2015). White collar criminals: The state of knowledge. *The Open Criminology Journal*, 8, 28–35.
Basel Convention. (2011). *Controlling Transboundary Movements of Hazardous Wastes*. Geneva, Switzerland: Secretariat of the Basel Convention. Available atwww.basel.int/Portals/4/Basel%20Convention/docs/pub/leaflets/leaflet-control-procedures-en.pdf (accessed 22 January 2017).
Bavinck, M., Pellegrini, L., and Mostert, E. (2014). *Conflicts over Natural Resources in the Global South: Conceptual Approaches*. London: CRC Press.
Beirne, P., and South, N. (eds) (2007). *Issues in Green Criminology: Confronting Harms against Environments, Humanity and Other Animals*. Cullompton: Willan Publishing.
Belknap, J. (2014). *The Invisible Woman*. Stamford, CT: Cengage.
Bisschop, L. (2012). Is it all going to waste? Illegal transports of e-waste in a European trade hub. *Crime, Law and Social Change*, 58(3), 221–249.
Bisschop, L. (2015). *Governance of the Illegal Trade in E-Waste and Tropical Timber: Case Studies on Transnational Environmental Crime*. Farnham: Ashgate.
Block, A., and Bernard, T. (1988). Crime in the waste oil industry. *Deviant Behavior*, 9(2), 113–129.
Brack, D. (2002). Combatting international environmental crime. *Global Environmental Change*, 12(2), 143–147.
Brisman, A. (2008). Crime–environment relationships and environmental justice. *Seattle Journal of Social Justice*, 6, 727–907.
Brisman, A. (2012). The cultural silence of climate change contrarianism. In R. White (ed.), *Climate Change from a Criminological Perspective* (pp. 41–70). New York, NY: Springer.
Brook, D. (1998). Environmental genocide. *American Journal of Economics and Sociology*, 57(1), 105–113.

Chambliss, W., and Seidman, R. (1971). *Law, Order and Power*. Reading, MA: Addison–Wesley.
Churchill, R., and Ulfstein, G. (2000). Autonomous institutional arrangements in multilateral environmental agreements: A little-noticed phenomenon in international law. *American Journal of International Law*, 94(4), 623–659.
CITES. (2013). How CITES works. Available at www.cites.org/eng/disc/how.php (accessed 22 January 2017).
Clifford, M., and Edwards, T. (2012). *Environmental Crime*. Burlington, MA: Jones and Bartlett.
Cole, D. (2000). *No Equal Justice*. New York, NY: The New Press.
Croall, H. (2007). Food Crime. In P. Beirne and N. South (eds), *Issues in Green Criminology: Confronting Harms against Environments, Humanity and Other Animals* (pp. 206–229). Cullompton: Willan Publishing.
Delmas, M., and Toffel, M. (2008). Organizational responses to environmental demands: Opening the black box. *Strategic Management Journal*, 29(10), 1027–1055.
Dinda, S. (2004). Environmental Kuznets curve hypothesis: A survey. *Ecological Economics*, 49(4), 431–455.
Doonan, J., Lanoie, P., and Laplante, B. (2005). Determinants of environmental performance in the Canadian pulp and paper industry: An assessment from inside the industry. *Ecological Economics*, 55(1), 73–84.
Ehrlich, I. (1996). Crime, punishment, and the market for offenses. *The Journal of Economic Perspectives*, 10(1), 43–67.
Eman, K., Meško, G., and Fields, C.B. (2009). Crimes against the environment: Green criminology and research challenges in Slovenia. *Journal of Criminal Justice and Security*, 11(4), 574–592.
Farrall, S., Ahmed, T., and French, D. (2012). *Criminological and Legal Consequences of Climate Change*. Oxford: Hart Publishing.
Friedrichs, D. (1996). *Trusted Criminals*. Belmont, CA: Wadsworth.
Frondel, M., Horbach, J., and Rennings, K. (2007). End-of-pipe or cleaner production? An empirical comparison of environmental innovation decisions across OECD countries. *Business Strategy and the Environment*, 16, 571–584.
Gibbs, C., Gore, M., McGarrell, E., and Rivers, L. (2010). Introducing conservation criminology towards interdisciplinary scholarship on environmental crimes and risks. *British Journal of Criminology*, 50(1), 124–144.
Gibbs, C., McGarrell, E., Axelrod, M., and Rivers, L. (2011). Conservation criminology and the global trade in electronic waste: Applying a multi–disciplinary research framework. *International Journal of Comparative and Applied Criminal Justice*, 35(4), 269–291.
Green, P., Ward, T., and McConnachie, K. (2007). Logging and legality: Environmental crime, civil society, and the state. *Social Justice*, 34(2), 94–110.
Gould, K., Pellow, D., and Schnaiberg, A. (2008). *The Treadmill of Production: Injustice and Unsustainability in the Global Economy*. Boulder, CO: Paradigm.
Hall, M. (2012). Environmental victims: Challenges for criminology and victimology in the 21st century. *Journal of Criminal Justice and Security*, 13(4), 371–391.
Hall, M. (2013). *Victims of Environmental Harm: Rights, Recognition and Redress under National and International Law*. Abingdon: Routledge.
Harbaugh, W., Levinson, A., and Wilson, D.M. (2002). Reexamining the empirical evidence for an environmental Kuznets curve. *Review of Economics and Statistics*, 84(3), 541–551.

Hauck, M. (2008). Rethinking small-scale fisheries compliance. *Marine Policy*, 32(4), 635–642.

Hauck, M. (2009). Crime, environment and power: revisiting the abalone fishery. *South African Journal of Criminal Justice*, 22(2), 229–245.

Hillyard, P., and Tombs, S. (2007). From crime to social harm? *Crime, Law and Social Change*, 48(1), 9–25.

Hunter, B. (2015). *White-Collar Offenders and Desistance from Crime: Future Selves and the Constancy of Change*. Abingdon: Routledge.

Jacobs, R.E. (2005). Treading deep waters: Substantive law issues in Tuvalu's threat to sue the United States in the International Court of Justice. *Pacific Rim Law & Policy Journal*, 14, 103–128.

Jarrell, M.L., and Ozymy, J. (2012). Real crime, real victims: Environmental crime victims and the Crime Victims' Rights Act (CVRA). *Crime, Law and Social Change*, 58(4), 373–389.

Jarrell, M.L., and Ozymy, J. (2014). Few and far between: Understanding the role of the victim in federal environmental crime prosecutions in the United States. *Crime, Law and Social Change*, 61(5), 563–584.

Jorgenson, A.K., and Clark, B. (2012). Are the economy and the environment decoupling? A comparative international study, 1960–2005. *American Journal of Sociology*, 118(1), 1–44.

Katz, R. (2010). The corporate crimes of Dow Chemical and the failure to regulate environmental pollution. *Critical Criminology*, 18(4), 295–306.

Konisky, D. (2009). Inequities in enforcement? *Journal of Policy Analysis and Management*, 28(1), 102–121.

Kramer, R., and Michalowski, R. (2012). Is global warming a state–corporate crime? In R. White (ed.), *Climate Change from a Criminological Perspective* (pp. 71–88). New York, NY: Springer.

Lane, P. (1998). Ecofeminism meets criminology. *Theoretical Criminology*, 2(2), 235–248.

Lavelle, M., and Coyle, M. (1992). Unequal protection. *National Law Journal*, 15(3), S1–S12.

Lemieux, A.M., and Clarke, R.V. (2009). The international ban on ivory sales and its effects on elephant poaching in Africa. *British Journal of Criminology*, 49(4), 451–471.

Lopez, R., and Mitra, S. (2000). Corruption, pollution, and the Kuznets environment curve. *Journal of Environmental Economics and Management*, 40(2), 137–150.

Lynch, M., and Barrett, K. (2015). Death matters: Victimization by particle matter from coal fired power plants in the US, a green criminological view. *Critical Criminology*, 23(3), 219–234.

Lynch, M., and Stretesky, P. (2014). *Exploring Green Criminology: Toward a Green Criminological Revolution*. Farnham: Ashgate.

Lynch, M., Nalla, M., and Miller, K. (1989). Cross-cultural perceptions of deviance. *Journal of Research in Crime and Delinquency*, 26(1), 7–35.

Lynch, M.J. (1990). The greening of criminology: A perspective for the 1990s. *The Critical Criminologist*, 2(3), 3–4, 11–12.

Lynch, M.J., and Stretesky, P.B. (2003). The meaning of green contrasting criminological perspectives. *Theoretical Criminology*, 7(2), 217–238.

Lynch, M.J., and Stretesky, P.B. (2011). Similarities between green criminology and green science: Toward a typology of green criminology. *International Journal of Comparative and Applied Criminal Justice*, 35(4), 293–306.

Lynch, M.J., Burns, R.G., and Stretesky, P. (2014). *Environmental Law, Crime, and Justice* (2nd edn). El Paso, TX: LFB Scholarly.

Lynch, M.J., Long, M.A., Barrett, K.L., and Stretesky, P.B. (2013). Is it a crime to produce ecological disorganization? Why green criminology and political economy matter in the analysis of global ecological harms. *British Journal of Criminology*, 53(6), 997–1016.

Lynch, M.J., Stretesky, P.B., and Long, M.A. (2015). *Defining Crime: A Critique of the Concept and its Implication*. Basingstoke: Palgrave Macmillan.

Lynxwiler, J., Shover, N., and Clelland, D. (1983). The organization and impact of inspector discretion in a regulatory bureaucracy. *Social Problems*, 30(4), 425–436.

Magdoff, F., and Foster, J.B. (2011). *What Every Environmentalist Needs to Know about Capitalism*. New York, NY: NYU Press.

Mason, M. (2005). *The New Accountability: Environmental Responsibility across Borders*. London: EarthScan.

May, P.J. (2005). Regulation and compliance motivations: Examining different approaches. *Public Administration Review*, 65(1), 31–44.

Miller, J. (1996). *Search and Destroy*. Cambridge: Cambridge University Press.

Mitchell, R. (2003). International environmental agreements: A survey of their features, formation, and effects. *Annual Review of Environment and Resources*, 28(1), 429–461.

Mol, A., and Spaargaren, G. (1993). Environment, modernity and the risk society: The apocalyptic horizon of environmental reform. *International Sociology*, 8, 431–459.

Pink, G. (2013). *Law Enforcement Responses to Transnational Environmental Crime: Choices, Challenges, and Culture*. Transnational Environmental Crime Project Working Paper 4. Department of International Relations, School of International, Political and Strategic Studies. Canberra: Australian National University.

Pires, S., and Clarke, R.V. (2012). Are parrots CRAVED? An analysis of parrot poaching in Mexico. *Journal of Research in Crime and Delinquency*, 49(1), 122–146.

Prakash, A., and Potoski, M. (2012). Voluntary environmental programs: A comparative perspective. *Journal of Policy Analysis and Management*, 31(1), 123–138.

Reiman, J. (1979). *The Rich Get Richer and the Poor Get Prison*. New York, NY: John Wiley.

Rockström, J., Steffen, W., Noone, K., Persson, Å., Chapin, F.S., Lambin, E.F., and Lenton, T.M. (2009). A safe operating space for humanity. *Nature*, 461(7263), 472–475.

Rose, G. (2011). Interlinkages between multi-lateral environmental agreements: International compliance cooperation. In L. Paddock, D. Qun, L. Kotze, D. Markell, K. Markowitz and D. Zaelke (eds), *Compliance and Enforcement in Environmental Law* (pp. 3–31). Cheltenham: Edward Elgar.

Ross, D. (1996). A review of EPA criminal, civil and administrative enforcement data: Are the efforts measurable deterrents to environmental criminals? In S.M. Edwards and T.D. Edwards (eds), *Environmental Crime and Criminality: Theoretical and Practical Issues* (pp. 55–76). New York, NY: Garland Publishing.

Ross, E.A. (1973) [1907]. *Sin and Society: An Analysis of Latter-Day Iniquity*. New York, NY: Harper and Row.

Ruggiero, V., and South, N. (2010). Green criminology and dirty collar crime. *Critical Criminology*, 18(4), 251–262.

Rummel-Bulska, I. (1998). Compliance with and enforcement of the Basel Convention on the control of transboundary movements of hazardous wastes and their disposal. In *Proceedings of the Fifth International Conference on Environmental Compliance and Enforcement* (pp. 419–432). Washington, DC: INECE. Available at www.inece.org/5thvol1/5thTOC.htm (accessed 22 January 2017).

Sander, K., Lee, J., Hickey, V., Mosoti, V.B., Virdin, J., and Magrath, W.B. (2014). Conceptualizing maritime environmental and natural resources law enforcement–The case of illegal fishing. *Environmental Development*, *11*, 112–122.

Schnaiberg, A. (1980). *From Surplus to Scarcity*. New York, NY: Oxford University Press.

Scholz, J.T. (1997). Enforcement policy and corporate misconduct: The changing perspective of deterrence theory. *Law and Contemporary Problems*, 60(3), 253–268.

Schwendinger, H., and Schwendinger, J. (1970). Defenders of order or guardians of human rights. *Issues in Criminology*, 5(2), 123–157.

Schwendinger, H., and Schwendinger, J. (1977). Social class and the definition of crime. *Crime and Social Justice*, 7, 4–13.

Simpson, S.S., Gibbs, C., Rorie, M., and Slocum, L.A. (2013). Empirical assessment of corporate environmental crime–control strategies. *Journal of Criminal Law and Criminology*, 103(1), 231–278.

Situ, Y., and Emmons, D. (1999). *Environmental Crime: The Criminal Justice System's Role in Protecting the Environment*. Thousand Oaks, CA: Sage Publications.

Solomon, S., Plattner, G.K., Knutti, R., and Friedlingstein, P. (2009). Irreversible climate change due to carbon dioxide emissions. *Proceedings of the National Academy of Sciences*, 106(6), 1704–1709.

South, N. (1998). A green field for criminology? A proposal for a perspective. *Theoretical Criminology*, 2(2), 211–233.

South, N. (2007). The "corporate colonisation of nature": Bio-prospecting and bio-piracy and the development of green criminology. In P. Beirne and N. South (eds), *Issues in Green Criminology: Confronting Harms against Environments, Humanity and Other Animals* (pp. 230–247). Cullompton: Willan Publishing.

South, N., and Brisman, A. (2013). Critical green criminology, environmental rights and crimes of exploitation. In S. Winlow and R. Atkinson (eds), *New Directions in Crime and Deviancy* (pp. 99–110). Abingdon: Routledge.

Stern, D.I. (2004). The rise and fall of the environmental Kuznets curve. *World Development*, 32(8), 1419–1439.

Stretesky, P. (1996) Environmental equity? A Response to Clark, Lab and Stoddard's review of the literature. *Social Pathology*, 2: 293–298.

Stretesky, P.B. (2006). Corporate self-policing and the environment. *Criminology*, 44(3), 671–708.

Stretesky, P.B. (2008). The neglect of race and class in environmental crime research. In M.J. Lynch and R. Paternoster (eds), *Racial Divide: Racial and Ethnic Bias in the Criminal Justice System* (pp. 241–260). Monsey, NY: Criminal Justice Press.

Stretesky, P.B., and Knight, O. (2013). The uneven geography of environmental enforcement INGOs. In D. Westerhuis, R. Walters, and T. Wyatt (eds), *Emerging Issues in Green Criminology: Exploring Power, Justice and Harm* (pp. 173–196). Basingstoke: Palgrave Macmillan.

Stretesky, P., and Lynch, M. (2011). Coal strip mining, mountaintop removal, and the distribution of environmental violations across the United States, 2002–2008. *Landscape Research*, 36(2), 209–230.

Stretesky, P.B., Long, M.A., and Lynch, M.J. (2013). *The Treadmill of Crime: Political Economy and Green Criminology*. Abingdon: Routledge.

Sutherland, E.H. (1940). White-collar criminality. *American Sociological Review*, 5(1), 1–12.

Sutherland, E.H. (1947). *Principles of Criminology* (4th edn). New York, NY: J.P. Lippincott.

Tappan, P.W. (1947). Who is the criminal? *American Sociological Review*, 12(1), 96–102.

Tompson, L., and Chainey, S. (2011). Profiling illegal waste activity: Using crime scripts as a data collection and analytical strategy. *European Journal on Criminal Policy and Research*, 17(3), 179–201.

Torras, M., and Boyce, J.K. (1998). Income, inequality, and pollution: A reassessment of the environmental Kuznets curve. *Ecological Economics*, 25(2), 147–160.

United States Environmental Protection Agency. (2015). Environmental Injustice. Available at www.epa.gov/environmentaljustice (accessed 22 January 2017).

van Solinge, T.B. (2014). Researching illegal logging and deforestation. *International Journal for Crime, Justice and Social Democracy*, 3(2), 36–49.

Vig, N.J., and Kraft, M.E. (2012). *Environmental Policy: New Directions for the Twenty-First Century*. Thousand Oaks, CA: Sage.

Voinov-Kohler, J. (2011). Compliance with and enforcement of the Basel Convention: Latest developments and things to come during the tenth meeting of the Conference of the Parties. In *The Proceedings of INECE's 9th International Conference on Environmental Compliance and Enforcement* (pp. 214–220). Washington, DC: INECE Secretariat. Previously available at http://inece.org/conference/9/proceedings/28_Kohler.pdf.

Wackernagel, M., and Rees, W.E. (1997). Perceptual and structural barriers to investing in natural capital: Economics from an ecological footprint perspective. *Ecological Economics*, 20(1), 3–24.

Walker, S. (1994). *Sense and Nonsense about Crime and Drugs*. Belmont, CA: Wadsworth.

Walters, R. (2006). Crime, bio-agriculture and the exploitation of hunger. *British Journal of Criminology*, 46(1), 26–45.

Walters, R. (2007). Crime, regulation and radioactive waste in the United Kingdom. In P. Beirne and N. South (eds), *Issues in Green Criminology: Confronting Harms against Environments, Humanity and Other Animals* (pp. 186–205). Cullompton: Willan Publishing.

Walters, R. (2009). *Crime is in the Air: Air Pollution Control and Regulation in the UK*. London: Centre for Crime and Justice Studies, King's College London. Available at http://sheffieldeastend.org.uk/Crimeisintheair.pdf (accessed 22 January 2017).

Walters, R. (2010). Toxic atmospheres air pollution, trade and the politics of regulation. *Critical Criminology*, 18(4), 307–323.

Walters, R. (2012). Dirty collar crime and the environment. In *Proceedings of Crime, Justice and Social Democracy: An International Conference*, Volume 2 (pp. 103–112). Brisbane: Queensland University of Technology.

Walters, R., and Martin, P. (2014). Crime and the commodification of carbon. In D. Westerhuis, R. Walters, and T. Wyatt (eds), *Emerging Issues in Green Criminology: Exploring Power, Justice and Harm* (pp. 93–104). Basingstoke: Palgrave Macmillan.

Westerhuis, D., Walters, R., and Wyatt, T. (eds) (2013). *Emerging Issues in Green Criminology: Exploring Power, Justice and Harm*. Basingstoke: Palgrave Macmillan.

Wellsmith, M. (2010). The applicability of crime prevention to problems of environmental harm: A consideration of illicit trade in endangered species. In R. White (ed.), *Global Environmental Harm: Criminological Perspectives* (pp. 132–149). Cullompton: Willan Publishing.

Wheeler, D. (2001). Racing to the bottom? Foreign investment and air pollution in developing countries. *The Journal of Environment and Development*, 10(3), 225–245.

White, R. (2011a). Environmental law enforcement: The importance of global networks and collaborative practices. *Australasian Policing*, 3(1), 12–16.

White, R. (2011b). *Transnational Environmental Crime: Toward an Eco-global Criminology*. Abingdon: Routledge.

White, R. (2012). The criminology of climate change. In R. White (ed.), *Climate Change from a Criminological Perspective* (pp. 1–11). New York, NY: Springer.
White, R. (2013). *Crimes against Nature: Environmental Criminology and Ecological Justice*. Abingdon: Routledge.
White, R., and Heckenberg, D. (2014). *Green Criminology: An Introduction to the Study of Environmental Harm*. Abingdon: Routledge.
Wijnstekers, W. (2003). *The Evolution of CITES: Pre-COP 11 Abridged Electronic Edition*. March 2000. Geneva: CITES Secretariat.
Williams, C. (1996). An environmental victimology. *Social Justice*, 23(4), 16–40.
Wyatt, T. (2012). *Green Criminology and Wildlife Trafficking: The Illegal Fur and Falcon Trades in Russia Far East*. England: Lambert Academic Publishing.
Wyatt, T. (2013). *Wildlife Trafficking: A Deconstruction of the Crime, the Victims, and the Offenders*. Basingstoke: Palgrave Macmillan.
Wyatt, T. (2014). The Russian Far East's illegal timber trade: An organized crime? *Crime, Law and Social Change*, 61(1), 15–35.
Zaitch, D., van Solinge, T.B., and Müller, G. (2014). Harms, crimes and natural resource exploitation: A green criminological and human rights perspective on land-use change. In M. Bavinck, L. Pellegrini, and E. Mostert (eds), *Conflicts over Natural Resources in the Global South: Conceptual Approaches* (pp. 91–104). Boca Raton, FL: CRC Press.
Zilney, L., McGurrin, D., and Zahran, S. (2006). Environmental justice and the role of criminology. *Criminal Justice Review*, 31(1), 47–62.
Zimring, F.E., and Hawkins, G.J. (1973). *Deterrence: The Legal Threat in Crime Control*. Chicago, IL: University of Chicago Press.

Chapter 4

The EU and the protection of the environment through criminal law

Ludwig Kramer

I The making of Directive 2008/99

In 2008, the European Union (EU) adopted, after seven years of discussion, a directive on the protection of the environment through criminal law.[1] This decision put an end to discussions in Europe which had been going on for almost 15 years. Indeed, in the early 1990s, the Council of Europe started the discussions on the elaboration of a Convention on the protection of the environment through criminal law. This Convention was opened to signature in 1998. By early 2017, it had been signed by 13 countries and only ratified by Estonia. Thus, it has not entered into force, and as the number of signatures has not changed over the last eight years, it may well be assumed that this Convention will never enter into force. The reason for this appears to have been the introduction of criminal liability for legal persons which seems to be unacceptable to some countries.

In order to overcome the blocking of the Convention, Denmark suggested, in 2000,[2] adopting an instrument under the Treaty on European Union. By that time, such instruments were capable of being adopted by a sort of intergovernmental decision under the Treaty on European Union (TEU).[3] Member States largely agreed to that proposal. However, before its formal adoption, the Commission presented a proposal for an EU directive on the protection of the environment through criminal law which it based on the present Article 192 of the

---

1 Directive 2008/99 on the protection of the environment through criminal law, OJ 2008, L 329 p. 28.
2 Initiative of the Kingdom of Denmark with a view to adopting a Council framework Decision on combating serious environmental crime, OJ 2000, C 39 p. 4.
3 See Article 31(1.e) of the Treaty on European Union (version before 2009): 'Common action on judicial cooperation in criminal matters shall include ... progressively adopting measures establishing minimum rules relating to the constituent elements of criminal acts and to penalties in the fields of organised crime, terrorism and illicit and illicit drug trafficking.' Article 34(2): '... acting unanimously on the initiative of any Member State or the Commission, the Council may ... (b) adopt framework decisions for the purpose of approximation of the laws and regulations of the Member States.'

Treaty on the Functioning of the European Union (TFEU).[4] Long discussions followed regarding whether the EU was indeed competent to deal with criminal matters or whether this was of the competence of the Member States, who would deal with it through intergovernmental cooperation under the TEU. Finally, the Council opted for the application of the TEU and adopted a Framework Decision.[5]

The Commission appealed to the Court of Justice, arguing that the provisions of the TEU only applied when the former EC Treaty gave no competence to the European institutions.[6] As, however, measures to protect the environment through criminal law could be based on the present Article 192 TFEU, there was, according to the Commission, no room for applying the provisions of the TEU. The Court of Justice held that it appeared from the objective and the content of the Framework Decision that its principal objective was the protection of the environment. In this area, the EU was competent; this included competence to fix criminal sanctions for the infringement of provisions that were intended to protect the environment.[7]

The Commission then proposed a new directive on the protection of the environment through criminal law.[8] Before a decision on that proposal was taken, however, a second judgment of the Court of Justice intervened.[9] The Court confirmed its earlier judgment, according to which the EU was competent to adopt provisions on criminal sanctions for breaches of EU law:

> [W]hen the application of effective, proportionate and dissuasive criminal penalties by the competent national authorities is an essential measure for combating serious environmental offences, the Community legislature may require the Member States to introduce such penalties in order to ensure that the rules which it lays down in that field are fully effective.

However, the Court then continued: 'By contrast, and contrary to the submission of the Commission, the determination of the type and level of the criminal

---

4 European Commission, Proposal for a European Parliament and Council Directive on the protection of the environment through criminal law, COM (2001) 139 – OJ 2001, C 180E, p. 238; amended COM (2002) 544 Final – OJ 2003, C 20E, p. 284.
5 Council Framework Decision 2003/80/JHA of 27 January 2003 on the protection of the environment through criminal law, OJ 2003, L 29 p. 55.
6 See Article 47 TEU (version prior to 2009): '... nothing in this Treaty shall affect the Treaties establishing the European Communities or the subsequent Treaties modifying or supplementing them.'
7 Case C-176/03 *Commission v Council* [2005] ECR I-7879. Eleven of the then 15 EU Member States – Austria, Belgium, Italy and Luxemburg did not intervene – had intervened on the side of the Council; the European Parliament had intervened on the side of the Commission.
8 European Commission, Proposal for a Directive of the European Parliament and of the Council on the protection of the environment through criminal law, COM (2007) 51 final.
9 Case C-440/05 *Commission v Council* [2007] ECR I-9097.

penalties to be applied does not fall within the Community's sphere of competence.' For this last statement, the Court did not give a single word of justification. And one might well wonder how the Commission could ensure that the criminal penalties are indeed effective and dissuasive if it is not competent to deal with such questions. It rather appears that the Court wanted to put an end to the political conflict on EU competence in criminal matters, an area that Member States considered to be an essential part of their national sovereignty.

This may be so. The European Parliament suggested that the Commission proposal on the protection of the environment through criminal law be adapted to the judgment of the Court.[10] And the Council made this adaptation itself, finally adopting Directive 2008/99 on the basis of the present Article 192 TFEU.

The Lisbon Treaties did not bring any significant change to the situation as far as the environment is concerned. Articles 82ss TFEU provide for judicial cooperation in criminal matters. Article 83 TFEU allows the European Parliament and the Council to adopt directives that establish

> minimum rules concerning the definition of criminal offences and sanctions in the areas of particularly serious crime with a cross-border dimension. These areas of crime are the following: terrorism, trafficking in human beings and sexual exploitation of women and children, illicit drug trafficking, illicit arms trafficking, money laundering, corruption, counterfeiting of means of payment, computer crime and organised crime.

The Council was given power to unanimously identify other areas of crime.

Article 83(2) TFEU provides:

> If the approximation of criminal laws and regulations of the Member States proves essential to ensure the effective implementation of a Union policy in an area which has been subject to harmonisation measures, directives may establish minimum rules with regard to the definition of criminal offences and sanctions in the area concerned.

Although it is not beyond doubt whether environmental legislation, adopted under Article 192 TFEU, constitutes 'harmonisation measures', it is assumed here that the EU would now be competent to adopt measures, including sanctions, in the area of environmental criminal law, although it has not made use of this possibility so far.

2 Criminal offences under Directive 2008/99

According to Directive 2008/99, nine acts shall be classified as environmental crime, when they are illegal and committed intentionally or with serious negligence. 'Illegal' is an act which breaches:

10 European Parliament, Legislative Resolution A6-154/2008 of 15 April 2008.

- either EU legislation which is mentioned in Annex A to the Directive;
- or Euratom legislation which is enumerated in Annex B to the Directive;
- or a provision of national law which implements EU legislation of either Annex A or B.

Annex A lists 61 EU directives and eight regulations, including some legislation of the transport, internal market and agricultural sector. Annex B lists three directives on nuclear energy.

Article 3(a) concerns the emission into the environment of a quantity of materials or of ionizing radiation which causes or is likely to cause serious damage to persons or to the environment.[11] 'Materials' do not include waste materials, as follows from Article 3(b). As Directive 2008/56 on the protection of marine waters is not mentioned in the annexes to Directive 2008/99, the discharge of substances into marine waters is not an offence. The notion 'substantial damage' is sufficiently vague to leave public authorities a broad margin of discretion in terms of whether or not they should tackle a specific discharge or emission. Article 3(b) deals with the management and the elimination of waste[12] and obliges all Member States to consider the management of a non-authorised landfill or the non-authorised discharge into the environment of waste a crime – which had, until then, frequently not been the case. This requirement is nuanced, however, by the supplementary requirement that there must be serious damage to persons or to the environment. Therefore, the fact alone that a non-authorised landfill is operated is not sufficient to qualify the act as a criminal offence.

This provision is completed by Article 3(c) which classifies as environmental crime the non-authorised shipment of a non-negligible quantity of waste.[13]

Article 3(d) deals with the operation of a plant in which a dangerous activity is carried out or in which dangerous materials are stored or used.[14] The Directive

---

11 Directive 2008/99, Article 3(a): '[constitutes a criminal offence:] the discharge, emission or introduction of a quantity of materials or ionising radiation into air, soil or water, which causes or is likely to cause death or serious injury to any person or substantial damage to the quality of air, the quality of soil or the quality of water, or to animals or plants.'
12 Directive 2008/99, Article 3(b): '[constitutes a criminal offence:] the collection, transport, recovery or disposal of waste, including the supervision of such operations and the after-care of disposal sites, and including action taken as a dealer or a broker (waste management), which causes or is likely to cause death or serious injury to any person or substantial damage to the quality of air, the quality of soil or the quality of water, or to animals or plants.'
13 Directive 2008/99, Article 3(c): '[constitutes a criminal offence:] the shipment of waste, where this activity falls within the scope of Article 2(35) of Regulation (EC) No1013/2006 of the European Parliament and of the Council of 14 June 2006 on shipments of waste and is undertaken in a non-negligible quantity, whether executed in a single shipment or in several shipments which appear to be linked.'
14 Directive 2008/99, Article 3(d): '[constitutes a criminal offence:] the operation of a plant in which a dangerous activity is carried out or in which dangerous substances or preparations are stored or used and which, outside the plant, causes or is likely to

does not define a 'dangerous substance'. It is likely that arms or drugs will not be included in this notion.

Article 3(e) deals with nuclear materials or hazardous radioactive substances and introduces a comprehensive ban on dealing with them.[15] Again, however, the handling of these materials must be likely to cause damage to humans or to the environment.

The next three provisions deal with crime against biodiversity issues. Article 3(f) incriminates the impairment of species of fauna and flora;[16] Article 3(g) concerns the trade in protected species[17] and Article 3(h) the significant deterioration of a protected habitat.[18]

The last offence concerns ozone-depleting substances. Article 3(i) considers 'the production, importation, exportation, placing on the market or use of ozone-depleting substances' to be a criminal offence.

The first surprising aspect of the Directive's approach is the lack of updating. It appears that since 2006 – thus even before the formal adoption of the Directive – the lists of annexes A and B have never been updated, despite the fact that Recital 15 of Directive 2008/99 stated: 'Whenever subsequent legislation on environmental matters is adopted, it should specify where appropriate, that this Directive will apply. Where necessary, Article 3 should be amended.' There is an impressively long list of EU regulations and directives which are not included in annexes A or B.[19]

cause death or serious injury to any person or substantial damage to the quality of air, the quality of soil or the quality of water, or to animals or plants.'
15 Directive 2008/99, Article 3(e): '[constitutes a criminal offence:] the production, possession, handling, use, holding, storage, transport, import, export or disposal of nuclear materials or other hazardous radioactive substances which causes or is likely to cause death or serious injury to any person or substantial damage to the quality of air, the quality of soil or the quality of water, or to animals or plants.'
16 Directive 2008/99, Article 3(f): "[constitutes a criminal offence:] the killing, destruction, possession or taking of specimens of protected wild fauna or flora species, except for cases where the conduct concerns a negligible quantity of such specimens and has a negligible impact on the conservation status of the species.'
17 Directive 2008/99, Article 3(f): '[constitutes a criminal offence:] trading in specimens of protected wild fauna and flora species or parts or derivatives thereof, except for cases where the conduct concerns a negligible quantity of such specimens and has a negligible impact on the conservation status of the species.'
18 Directive 2008/99, Article 3(h): '[constitutes criminal offence:] any conduct which causes the significant deterioration of a habitat within a protected area.'
19 Only the most relevant regulations and directives can be mentioned here: Regulation 1907/2006 on chemical (REACH), OJ 2006, L 396 p. 1; Directive 2007/60 on flood risks, OJ 2007, L 288 p. 7; Regulation 1005/2008 to prevent, deter and eliminate illegal, unreported or unregulated fishing, OJ 2008, L 286 p. 1; Regulation 1102/2008 banning the export of mercury, OJ 2008, L 304 p. 74; Regulation 1272/2008 on the classification, packaging and labelling of chemicals, OJ 2008, L 250 p. 1; Directive 2008/50 on air pollution, OJ 2008, L 152 p. 1; Directive 2008/56 on the protection of marine waters, OJ 2008, L 164 p. 19; Directive 2008/105 on pollutants in fresh water, OJ 2008, L 348 p. 84; Regulation 443/2009 on CO_2 emissions from

Another set of regulations and directives which are listed in the annexes were replaced by new versions of legislation.[20] At least for those texts which brought substantive amendments to the legislation, the principle of *nullum crimen sine lege* applies and makes it more than doubtful whether the different acts may be considered a criminal offence under Directive 2008/99. The omission to update can only be understood in the sense that the EU institutions and, in particular, the Commission lost the interest in monitoring Directive 2008/99.

3 The liable persons

The Directive concerns natural and legal persons. However, it is well known that German law in particular does not consider that a legal person may be criminally liable. Germany has maintained and is maintaining this position in all international and EU negotiations. With regard to Directive 2008/99, the problem was solved by the inclusion of Article 6 which provides that 'legal persons can be held liable for offences, where such offences have been committed for their benefit by any person who has a leading position within the legal person'. This text thus provides for a liability of a legal person under certain circumstances, but not for a *criminal* liability. Member States may therefore provide for criminal liability of legal persons in their national legislation, but they are not obliged to do so.[21]

It should be underlined that neither the Council of Europe draft Convention on criminal environmental liability nor the Commission proposal for a directive of 2001 – both texts mentioned above – had suggested the introduction of full

---

passenger cars, OJ 2009, L 140 p. 1; Regulation 595/2009 on emissions from heavy duty vehicles, OJ 2009, L 188 p. 1; Regulation 1007/2009 on trade in seal products, OJ 2009 L 286 p. 36; Regulation 1107/2009 on pesticides, OJ 2009, L 309 p. 1; Directive 2009/28 on renewable energy, OJ 2009, L 140 p. 16; Directive 2009/31 on carbon capture and storage, OJ 2009, L 140 p. 114; Directive 2009/71 on nuclear installations, OJ 2009, L 172 p. 18; Directive 2009/125 on the eco-design of products, OJ 2009, L 285 p. 10; Directive 2009/128 on the use of pesticides, OJ 2009, L 309 p. 71; Regulation 895/2010 on timber and timber products, OJ 2010, L 295 p. 23; Directive 2010/31 on the energy performance of buildings, OJ 2010, L 153 p. 13; Directive 2010/63 on the protection of animals used for scientific purposes, OJ 2010, L 276 p. 33; Directive 2011/70 on radioactive waste, OJ 2011, L 199 p. 48; Directive 2013/30 on offshore gas and oil activities, OJ 2013, L 178 p. 66.

20 For example: Directive 2008/98 on waste, OJ 2008, L 312 p 3; Regulation 1005/2009 on ozone-depleting substances (replacing Reg. 1037/2000), OJ 2009, L 286 p. 1; Regulation 1107/2009 on pesticides (replacing Directive 91/414), OJ 2009, L 309 p. 1; Directive 2009/42 on contained use of GMOs (replacing Directive 90/219) OJ 2009, L 175 p. 75; Directive 2009/147 on birds (replacing Directive 79/409), OJ 2010, L 20 p. 7; Directive 2010/75 on industrial emissions (replacing Directives 2008/1, 2000/76 and others), OJ 2010, L 334 p. 17.

21 See also Commission, Explanatory Memorandum to its proposal for a directive, COM (2007) 51, p. 8: 'It is not specified whether the liability of legal persons should be a criminal one. Thus, Member States that do not recognise the criminal liability of legal persons in their national law are not obliged to change their national systems.'

criminal environmental liability of legal persons all over Europe or the EU; apparently, the objections from Germany to such an approach appeared too great.

In EU competition matters, where illegal concerted practices between legal persons (companies) – mergers, abuse of a dominant position, etc. – are frequent in a market economy, the EU legislature chose a simple way to overcome the problem of criminal liability of legal persons. The investigation procedure is rather similar to that of a criminal offence: the incriminated actions must have been committed intentionally or negligently, and the burden of proof lies with the public authorities. However, Article 23(5) of the relevant Regulation simply states that the fines which are pronounced against a company 'shall not be of a criminal nature'.[22] This approach has several advantages. First, it allows the European Commission to pronounce the administrative fines, whereas in the EU and the EU Member States' national legal orders, criminal sanctions have to be pronounced by the courts. Second, the fines which the Commission may fix can include up to 10 per cent of the annual turnover of the incriminated company, sums which a court within the EU has never pronounced in a criminal case. Third, the instruction is easier, can be made more quickly and may be addressed against several companies at a time.

Directive 2003/87 on greenhouse gas emission allowance trading[23] provides in Article 16 that an operator shall be liable to pay a sum of €100 euro per tonne of CO_2 equivalent emitted by him and for which he is not able to surrender the necessary allowances. Intention or negligence is not required. This administrative sanction may quickly add up to be very considerable – and thus, from the point of view of the environment, very effective – amounts.[24]

These examples show that EU environmental legislation, including Directive 2008/99, could introduce administrative sanctions against legal persons, which would be effective and dissuasive. In its first proposal for Directive 2008/99, the Commission had made a modest proposal in this sense.[25] In its proposal of 2007, the Commission had proposed (administrative or criminal) fines up to €1.5 million for legal persons, as well as other administrative obligations such as the reinstatement of the environment, exclusions from entitlement to public benefits or the temporary or permanent disqualification from the practice of industrial or commercial activities.[26] However, all these proposals were bluntly rejected by the European Parliament and the Council.

---

22 Regulation 1/2003 on the implementation of the rules on competition laid down in Articles 81 and 82 of the Treaty, OJ 2003, L 1 p. 1, Article 23(5).
23 Directive 2003/87, OJ 2003, L 275 p. 32. That Directive is not listed in the annexes to Directive 2008/99.
24 See, for example, Case C-203/12 *Billerud Karlsborg and Billerud Skärblacka v Naturvårdsverket* (judgment of 17 October 2013) where two Swedish companies had to pay more than €2.1 million.
25 European Commission (n. 4, above), Article 4(b).
26 European Commission, Proposal for a directive, (n. 8, above), Article 7.

4 The incriminated acts

What is striking about the list of acts in Article 3 that constitute a criminal offence is that the acts in Article 3(a), (b), (d), (e) and (f) are qualified by supplementary requirements. Thus, it is not enough to discharge a quantity of materials into water, in breach of existing EU water protection legislation, intentionally or with negligence. The material must furthermore cause or be likely to cause death or serious injury to persons or substantial damage to the environment. It is not enough to dispose of waste in breach of existing EU provisions on the treatment or disposal of waste. The disposed waste must also cause or be likely to cause damage to persons or to the environment. The same approach was chosen for the illegal operation of a plant, the illegal handling of radioactive material, the illegal destruction of fauna or flora species or the illegal trade with such species. Only the illegal trade in waste (Article 3(c)), causing the significant deterioration of a natural habitat within a protected site (Article 3(h)) and the handling of ozone-depleting substances (Article 3(i)) are not qualified by such a supplementary requirement.

Such a supplementary requirement rests on a deliberate choice. This may be illustrated by a simple example. It is possible to classify as a criminal offence when a person drives a car and has drunk alcohol; the legislation may provide for zero tolerance or consider the driving a criminal offence when a specific threshold of alcohol has been exceeded. But it is also possible only to classify as a criminal offence the driving of a car when damage is caused to persons or property, or when there are clear signs that the driver is no longer able to drive a car without risk to persons or property. How the legislature decides is a question of societal choice, which might be influenced by the frequency and gravity of accidents, the level of public concern, the density of the population, etc.

The environmental criminal offences that are enumerated in Article 3 should, in this author's opinion, practically all be classified as criminal offences even without the supplementary qualification of damage or risk of damage to persons or the environment. It is sufficient that there is a breach of existing legislation and that the act was committed intentionally or with serious negligence. For example, the discharge of sewage sludge into waters in the EU has been prohibited since the end of 1998;[27] the unauthorised discharge of waste has been prohibited since 1977.[28] However, it is well known that sewage sludge continues to be discharged into waters and that waste even today continues to be discharged in unauthorised landfills or in the wild.[29] If one takes the protection of the environment seriously,

---

27 Directive 91/271 on urban waste-water treatment, OJ 1991, L 135, p. 40, Article 14(3).
28 Directive 75/442 on waste, OJ 1975, L 194 p. 23, Article 4.
29 In a press release of 20 February 2014, the European Commission announced that it was taking legal action – sending a reasoned opinion – under Article 258 TFEU against Romania, because 19 landfills and two tailing ponds were operating in that country in breach of EU law, 'representing a serious risk for human health and the environment' (Commission, Memo/14/116 of 20 February 2014, point 19). The

there is no reason whatsoever to consider such activities as a criminal offence only when – beyond the operation of an unauthorised landfill or the illegal discharge of sewage sludge – supplementary risks are created for humans or the environment; rather, the operation itself already constitutes a risk for the environment. Issues of small quantities or other borderline cases may easily be solved by flexible handling of the fines.

Also, trade in endangered species of fauna and flora is, as a rule, prohibited under EU law.[30] Why, then, should a trader of such endangered species only commit a criminal offence when the trading has a non-negligible impact on the conservation status of the species (Article 3(g))? A person who trades in military weapons, the trade of which is prohibited, does not commit a criminal offence only in the case that there is a substantial risk to humans. Illegal trade in waste is a criminal offence *per se* (Article 3(c)); it is difficult to see the logic behind the different treatment of illegal trade in species.

The EU legislation decided, in the majority of the cases enumerated in Article 3, in favour of a more restrictive approach, requiring a concrete risk; only in Article 3(c), (h) and (i) did it let the abstract risk suffice. It appears to this author that the EU did not take environmental concerns completely seriously.

The objection to this reasoning – that national law could adopt more stringent provisions than EU law – is not convincing. In the meantime, it has become obvious that Member States do not like to extend the protection of the environment beyond the level that they had agreed at EU level, mainly for fear of a competitive economic disadvantage.[31] Rather, national environmental law has a tendency to align with EU law.

5 Administrative and criminal law

Recourse to criminal law is further made difficult by the application of administrative law. In most EU Member States, it is possible for the administration to pronounce an administrative sanction against a person who impairs the environment. When this is done, the criminal law recedes and becomes inapplicable. Most legal orders in Member States contain some written or unwritten rules on this relationship between administrative and criminal law – for example, by qualifying a certain act as 'criminal' when a specific threshold is exceeded or a specific

---

reasoned opinion itself is not made public, due to the secretive policy of the Commission in this regard. It is therefore not known whether the Commission considers the operating of the landfills as being a risk *per se*, or whether it has other reasons to believe that there is a risk. And no information is given as to why the Romanian authorities do not take criminal legal action against the operators of the landfills.

30 Regulation 338/97 on the protection of species of wild fauna and flora by regulating trade therein, OJ 1997, L 61 p. 1.
31 See in particular J.J. Jans, L. Squintani, A. Aragao, R. Macrory and B.W. Wegener (2010). 'Gold plating' of European environmental measures? (2010) *Journal of European Environmental & Planning Law* 6 (4) 417–435.

result has occurred. Directive 2008/99 did not touch at all on this relationship. For administrative authorities, police officers and public prosecutors, this situation shifts the balance of action very considerably to the side of the administration. Administrative authorities are not bound by the formalised procedures of criminal law, but may use one of the many sanctions that are at their disposal to address the wrongdoer; they can pronounce the sanction themselves, without having to wait for a court to issue a judgment. Criminal prosecution will normally have to wait for the outcome of the administrative activity. This might be different in very serious cases, but is certainly the norm in day-to-day breaches of the law.

An example might again illustrate this point.[32] In 2005, an applicant obtained, by the regional Spanish government of Extremadura, permission to construct, within habitats that were protected under EU law, on a surface of 134 hectares, some 250 bungalows, 310 houses, two hotels, a golf course, a marina and various other sport and leisure installations. The permission was attacked in court and the Regional Court of Extremadura quashed the permission as illegal. On appeal, the Supreme Court of Spain confirmed the decision.

Taking criminal action against the constructor in the Extremadura case appears, at the present state of the law, almost impossible, as he had a permit from the competent authorities and one cannot seriously argue that he knew or should have known (grave negligence) that this permit was in breach of EU and Spanish law. Taking criminal action against the officials who issued the permit, nine years after it was issued, is not the easiest case,[33] and the Spanish criminal authorities waited until the final outcome of the case, without taking criminal action in the interim; this can hardly be reproached. However, the damage to the environment exists. It appears that criminal law is hardly able to solve such cases.

When an administration sides with a wrongdoer – in particular by granting a permit – criminal law becomes almost inapplicable. Most legal orders within the EU do not provide for criminal liability of officials who act in breach of their legal obligations. Such cases are relatively frequent in environmental law: where an official does not monitor – measure, inspect, etc. – the emissions of an industrial plant, the discharges into water, or the respect of provisions on waste, where the safety provisions of an industrial plant, the labelling requirements of a product or the disposal of radioactive waste are not controlled – the official acts by omission and there is no reason not to treat him according to criminal law. It should be repeated, however, that most legal orders – including EU law – do not have provisions for the criminal liability of officials in environmental matters.

There is one other aspect of criminal environmental law which might be usefully discussed in the context of the Extremadura case, mentioned above. When a

---

32 Tribunal Supremo of Spain, case 2940/2011, Diputación de Cáceres a.o., judgment of 21 January 2014.
33 The permit was part of a Governmental Decree. Thus, legal action would have to be taken against the regional prime minister and some of his advisors. Spanish law provides for criminal liability of officials, however.

manufacturer of a pesticide obtains a permit to put his product into circulation, this permit is given without relieving the manufacturer of his civil and criminal liability in the event that the product causes damage.[34] The underlying reason for this legal provision is that the manufacturer is not obliged to put his product on the market. When he does so, he assumes full responsibility for it. In the same way, the constructor in the Extremadura case should remain criminally liable for the significant deterioration of the two habitats in question. He also was not obliged, by virtue of the permit, to complete the project. In constructing, he assumes full civil and criminal responsibility for his actions. As far as can be seen, however, such an approach for developers or constructors has not yet been adopted by courts within the EU.

6 The Directive's approach in daily practice

The 28 Member States transposed the Directive into national law, with the exception of France which was of the opinion that its national legislation already complied with the Directive's requirements. Overall, Member States sent to the Commission 883 pieces of national law as transposition measures.[35] No assessment or other evaluation of this transposing legislation by the Commission is known; it is thus not clear whether the national legislation really is proportionate, effective and dissuasive.

In the following, some examples are given to demonstrate how difficult the application of Directive 2008/99 is in practice.

6.1 Air pollution in agglomerations

Air pollution is a serious problem within the EU, in particular in urban agglomerations. The Commission estimates that there are about 420,000 premature deaths per year within the EU due to air pollution.[36] A United Kingdom estimate gives the figure of some 29,000 annual premature deaths in the United Kingdom, with some 4,300 deaths in the London agglomeration alone.[37]

---

34 See, for example, Regulation 1107/2009 concerning the placing of plant protection products on the market, OJ 2009, L 309 p. 1, Article 73: 'The granting of authorisation and any other measures in conformity with this Regulation shall be without prejudice to general civil and criminal liability in the Member States of the producer and, where applicable, of the person responsible for placing the plant protection product on the market or using it.'
35 There is a great diversity among Member States: while the UK notified the Commission with 290 pieces of national law, Ireland with 144 pieces, Belgium with 115 pieces, and Finland with 93 pieces, Bulgaria, Germany, Estonia, Greece, Spain, Italy, Netherlands, Austria, Poland and Portugal notified only one piece of legislation.
36 European Commission, A Clean Air Programme for Europe, COM (2013) 718, p. 2.
37 Committee on the Medical Effects of Air Pollutants (COMEAP). *The Mortality Effects of long-term Exposure to Particulate Air Pollution in the United Kingdom*. Didcot, 2010.

The main legal instrument at EU level is Directive 2008/50 on ambient air quality.[38] The Directive fixed for a number of pollutants concentration levels in the air that were not to be exceeded. The general deadline for compliance was 2010; however, Member States could prolong this period by five years, when they elaborated a clean-up plan.[39]

Under Directive 2008/99, the unlawful emission into the air of materials that cause damage to humans or the environment constitutes a criminal offence. However, Directive 2008/50 – not even listed in the Annex A to Directive 2008/99 – does not limit or prohibit the emission of materials into the air; it only limits the concentration of materials (pollutants) in the air. Thus, whatever the deadline for compliance under Directive 2008/50 is, there is no criminal offence under it. To this has to be added the fact that the concentration of materials (pollutants) in the air that cause the premature death of persons is due to the emission of pollutants from many individual sources – cars, trucks, heating systems, industrial activity, etc. No individual person can normally be accused of emitting, intentionally or with grave negligence, materials into the air which cause damage to persons or the environment: EU law does not prohibit such emissions into the air or discharges into the water. Annex A to Directive 2008/99 enumerates some directives which limit such discharges into waters.[40] However, in the meantime, successful lobbying, in particular by the United Kingdom and by industry, forced the EU to change its water policy and these directives were repealed.

The result is that the premature death of persons appears to be a sort of *force majeure*, where criminal law cannot intervene. As there is no EU provision that prohibits the emission of pollutants into the air, it is also not possible to take action against officials who did not bring air quality into the limits of Directive 2008/50. Thus, the serious air pollution in London, the UK and the EU as a whole is not relevant under Directive 2008/99.

Annex A to Directive 2008/99 lists two Directives on air pollution from cars.[41] Apart from the fact that the more recent directives on CO_2 emissions from cars

---

38 Directive 2008/50 (n. 20, above).
39 In case C-404/13, *The Queen, on the Application of ClientEarth, v The Secretary of State for the Environment, Food and Rural Affairs*, ECLI:EU:C:2014:2382, the Court of Justice implicitly decided that the 2015 deadline could be further prolonged by national authorities, as the directive requested compliance 'as soon as possible' only.
40 See, for example, the following directives which are listed in annex A to Directive 2008/99: Directive 82/176, OJ 1982, L 81 p. 29 (mercury discharges from chloralkali industry), Directive 83/513, OJ 1983, L 291 p. 1 (cadmium discharges), Directive 84/156, OJ 1984, L 74 p. 49 (mercury discharges from other industries), Directive 84/491, OJ 1984, L 274 p. 11 (discharges of hexachlorocyclohexane), etc. All these directives have been repealed in the meantime.
41 Directive 70/220 on the approximation of the laws of the Member States on measures to be taken against air pollution by emissions from motor vehicles, OJ 1970, L 76 p. 1; Directive 72/306 on the approximation of the laws of the Member States relating to the measures to be taken against the emission of pollutants from diesel engines for use in vehicles, OJ 1972, L 190 p. 1.

and trucks, mentioned above,[42] are not listed in Annex A, these two directives only concern air pollution emissions from new cars. There is no provision in EU law that obliges existing cars to be retrofitted with filters or other systems to adapt their emissions to those of new cars. This means in practice that, with a lifetime of a normal car of 12–15 years, the full effect of air pollution reduction measures in the vehicles field will be delayed by 10–15 years.

Also, the inclusion of Directives 70/220 and 72/306 in the annex to Directive 2008/99 is some sort of 'greenspeak' legislation. Indeed, cars are permitted according to a complex system of checking and verifications. It is not really imaginable that such a permit would be granted to a new car when it exceeds the limits of air emissions; a new car put on the market is thus never 'unlawful'. Furthermore, one cannot imagine that the emissions of a specific new car cause or are likely to cause death or serious injury to a person or substantial damage to the environment – unless someone wants to commit suicide in his garage. The inclusion of the two Directives shows once more that the EU legislature was not very careful in drafting the Directive.

6.2 Waste water treatment

In case C-301/10,[43] the EU Court of Justice found that the waste water treatment system for London was 'sufficient in dry weather, but not sufficient in the slightest in the course of rainfalls'. This has the consequence that, in rainy weather, considerable quantities of untreated waste water go into the river Thames, which is not in compliance with Directive 91/271 on urban waste water treatment.[44]

Directive 91/271 is listed in Annex A to Directive 2008/99. The discharge of the waste water is unlawful. It may be assumed that the untreated waste water contains considerable quantities of 'materials'. Moreover, one may argue that the persons within the UK authorities who were responsible for undertaking the necessary construction work in order to bring the waste water treatment system into compliance with the requirements of Directive 91/271 omitted to do so and that this omission constitutes an intentional act.[45] However, any prosecutor in such a case would have to prove that the discharge caused or was likely to cause 'death or serious injury to any person or substantial damage to the quality of air, the quality of soil or the quality of water, or to animals or plants' (Article 3(a)).

---

42 See Regulations 442/2009 and 595/2009 (n. 20, above).
43 Case C-301/10, *Commission v United Kingdom* (judgment of 18 October 2010).
44 Directive 91/271, OJ 1991, L 135 p.40 (n. 28, above).
45 See Case C-301/10 (n.44, above), paragraph 92: 'It was therefore incumbent upon the United Kingdom to initiate in good time the procedures necessary for implementing Directive 91/271 in the national legal order, so that those procedures [projects designed to ensure compliance which are costly and achievable over a number of years, see paragraph 91] were completed within the time-limit ... of that directive, namely 31 December 2000.'

And the efforts in cost and in time to prove such effects are so considerable that, in practice, prosecutors do not undertake them – all the more so as the environment cannot protest.

London's discharge of waste water in breach of Directive 91/271 is thus normally not relevant under Directive 2008/99.

6.3 Radioactive waste

Some years ago, the French authorities discovered that radioactive hospital waste and other radioactive waste had been illegally dumped at ordinary municipal landfills. The application of Directive 2008/99 was not possible, as there was no proof that this unlawful dumping had caused or was likely to cause death or serious injury to persons or substantial damage to the quality of the environment (Article 3(e)). And the Directive of 2011 on radioactive waste[46] – as well as the Directive on the safety of nuclear installations[47] – is not listed in Annex B to Directive 2008/99.

At the end of 2013, media in the EU reported that Italian authorities feared that toxic nuclear and industrial waste, dumped illegally by the Neapolitan mafia, was responsible for a surge in cancers in southern Italy; the Italian Senate investigated a link between buried pollutants and a rise of almost 50 per cent in tumours which was found in the inhabitants of several towns around Naples.

The application of Directive 2008/99 to this case is not possible, first, because most of the unlawful activities occurred prior to 2010 – the date of entry into effect of Directive 2008/99 – and, second, because it is not possible to identify an individual person who did the dumping; the term 'mafia' is too vague.

6.4 Deterioration of habitats

In case C-258/11,[48] the Court of Justice found that the permanent loss of an area of 1.47 hectares of a habitat of 270 hectares which is part of the EU Natura 2000 network constituted a significant deterioration of a habitat;[49] the Extremadura regional government in the Extremadura case, mentioned above, cannot really have considered that a construction on 134 hectares was insignificant.

It is obvious that day by day parts of EU-protected natural habitats are used for the construction of energy or transport projects, urban development, agricultural activities or infrastructure purposes, without any consideration ever being

---

46 Directive 2011/70/Euratom of 19 July 2011 establishing a Community framework for the responsible and safe management of spent fuel and radioactive waste, OJ 2011, L 199 p. 88.
47 Directive 2009/71/Euratom of 25 June 2009 establishing a Community framework for the nuclear safety of nuclear installations, OJ 2009, L 172 p. 18.
48 Case C-258/11 *Sweetman and Others* (judgment of 11 April 2013).
49 The case was assessed under Directive 92/43, OJ 1992, L 206 p. 7 (Habitat protection Directive).

made regarding whether such projects lead to criminal liability under Directive 2008/99. In many, if not in most cases, the administrative permit that is granted for such projects will lead to the project not being 'unlawful'. And, as mentioned, the criminal liability of officials who grant such permits is practically never examined.

6.5 Nitrates in waters

The Commission stated in 2010 that at least 30–40 per cent of rivers and lakes within the EU showed symptoms of eutrophication.[50] A large part of nitrate inputs into waters which cause eutrophication comes from agricultural sources. Directive 91/676 on the protection of waters from nitrates of agricultural sources[51] limits the amount of livestock manure applied to the land to 170 kg nitrogen per hectare. This means in substance that the number of cattle per hectare has to be limited, when the levels of the Directive are exceeded or at risk of being exceeded. However, Directive 91/676 allows derogation from the amounts indicated, subject to Commission approval.

Instead of progressively enforcing the Directive, the Commission granted derogations, arguing that the objectives of the Directive were not put at risk. These derogations have been granted since 2002 and extend, at present, until 2016.[52] In this way, the provisions of the Directive are simply not applied. At the same time, Directive 2008/99, Article 3(a), which makes it a criminal offence to unlawfully discharge materials into waters that are likely to cause significant damage to water, is bypassed by the very national and EU authorities that should enforce the provisions of the Directive.

A special case is France. The problem of nitrates in water, in particular in Bretagne and Normandy, is well known. The French authorities have delayed the

---

50 Report from the Commission to the Council and the European Parliament on implementation of Council Directive 91/676/EEC concerning the protection of waters against pollution caused by nitrates from agricultural sources based on Member States reports for the period 2004–2007 SEC(2010) 118, Commission, COM (2010) 47.
51 Directive 91/676, OJ 1991, L 375 p. 1.
52 Commission Decision 2002/915, OJ 2002, L 319 p. 24 (Denmark), Decision 2005/294, OJ 2005, L 94 p. 34 (Denmark); Decision 2005/880, OJ 2005, L 324 p. 89 (Netherlands); Decision 2007/697, OJ 2007, L 284 p. 27 (Ireland); Decision 2007/863, OJ 2007, L 337 p. 122 (UK – Northern Ireland); Decision 2008/64, OJ 2008, L 16 p. 28 (Belgium – Flanders); Decision 2008/69, OJ 2008, L 32 p. 21 (Belgium – Wallonia); Decision 2008/664, OJ 2008, L 217 p. 16 (Denmark); Decision 2009/431, OJ 2009, L 141 p. 48 (UK – England, Scotland, Wales); Decision 2010/65, OJ 2010, L 35 p. 18 (Netherlands); Decision 2011/127, OJ 2011, L 51 p. 19 (Ireland); Decision 2011/128, OJ 2011, L 51 p. 21 (UK – Northern Ireland); Decision 2011/489, OJ 2011, L 200 p. 23 (Belgium – Flanders); Decision 2011/777, OJ 2011, L 287 p. 36 (Italy – Emilia Romagna, Lombardia, Piemonte, Veneto); Decision 2012 659, OJ 2012, L 295 p. 20 (Denmark); Decision 2013/781, OJ 2013, L 346 p. 65 (UK – England, Scotland, Wales).

designation of those zones, which came under Directive 91/676 and which should have been designated by 1993(!). For this reason, France was twice condemned by the Court of Justice.[53] Nevertheless, as the relevant zones had not been designated, there was no need to apply the restrictions provided for in Directive 91/676. The result is that the Directive continues not to be applied in full in France, 20 years after its entry into effect. And the Commission has not taken steps to have an administrative fine imposed on France under Article 260 TFEU – probably because the issue is politically too delicate.

As there is no legal provision in France that limits the quantity of nitrates in waters in conformity with Directive 91/676, there is also no unlawful activity by French farmers that is punishable under Directive 2008/99.

6.6 Inundations

Extended precipitations may lead to inundations within the EU. Following severe inundations in Central Europe in the years 2002 and 2004, the EU adopted a Directive on the assessment and management of flood risks.[54] The Directive provides that by the end of 2011, Member States had to make preliminary risk assessments in order to identify the areas at risk of floods. By the end of 2013, Member States had to develop flood risk maps indicating areas with a low probability of floods, areas with a medium probability (likely return of floods within 100 years) and areas with a high probability. By 2015, Member States had then to establish a flood risk management plan containing measures to prevent floods occurring as well as to minimise their negative consequences.

The indicated dates are minimum dates: nothing prevented the Member States from adopting legislation and taking measures earlier.

Leaving aside instances of specific, concrete inundations, it should be pointed out that early, careful and serious implementation and application of the provisions of the Directive, including considerations of climate change and its impact, are likely to very considerably reduce the risk of floods and of their negative consequences.

Directive 2007/60 is not listed in the Annex A to Directive 2008/99, although it existed at the time of adopting the latter Directive. A criminal offence could, at best, be seen in the omission of the responsible authorities to make the provisions of the Directive operational and adopt the necessary flood prevention and mitigation measures as quickly as possible. However, hardly any public prosecutor would take such a case up.

These comments are mainly destined to draw attention once more to the fact that environmental and human disasters are often not acts of *force majeure*, but may be prevented by policies and actions that take the protection of the environment seriously.

---

53 Case C-258/00 *Commission v France* [2002] ECR.I-5959; Case C-193/12 *Commission v France* (judgment of 13 June 2013).
54 Directive 2007/60, OJ 2007, L 288 p. 27.

6.7 Ecocide

A citizen initiative – started under Article 11(4) TEU – suggests making 'ecocide' a crime, first at EU and later at global level. 'Ecocide' is, parallel to 'genocide', defined as

> the extensive damage to, destruction of or loss of ecosystem(s) of a given territory, whether by human agency or by other causes, to such an extent that (1) peaceful enjoyment by the inhabitants has been severely diminished or (2) peaceful enjoyment by the inhabitants of another territory has been severely diminished.

As examples, deforestation, oil spills, unconventional extraction of fossil fuels through tar sands or the loss of biodiversity are quoted:

> Ecocide is a crime for which no intent is necessary. Even if ecocide is not intended but rather the side-effect of another (probably profit-generating) activity, companies and CEOs must still be liable for the damage they cause.[55]

At present, the proposals appear to be difficult to fit into any legal concept. The definition of ecocide might be good for biological purposes, but it does not fit into a criminal law system. A strict criminal liability contradicts all principles of criminal law in Europe. Financing activities which lead to ecocide shall also be punishable, but no explanation is given as to how this is to be worked out. No explanation is given either about the suggestion by the initiative to hold heads of State, directors of banks and heads of legal persons accountable.

As the questions of substantive law are entirely unsettled, it appears of little interest to discuss the establishment of a European criminal court of environment and health and of an international criminal court with the same responsibilities.

7 Some concluding comments

If one looks at Directive 2008/99 and its application in day-to-day practice, the following observations may be made:

1 Directive 2008/99 has broad, sometimes vague definitions of what constitutes an environmental criminal offence. This makes the Directive frequently inapplicable.
2 The Directive does not foresee any criminal liability of legal persons, which is a relic of early industrialisation, preserved more for ideological than serious reasons.

---

55 www.endecocide.eu; Charter of Brussels for the creation of a European and an International Criminal Court of the Environment and Health (November 2013–January 2014).

3   Cases where Directive 2008/99 or its national implementing counterpart legislation is applied appear to be relatively rare. Only the illegal trade in waste materials seems to be prosecuted with some zeal in the majority of Member States.
4   EU institutions neither update the annexes to the Directive nor monitor the Directive. They appear to have lost interest in its monitoring.
5   It is obvious that administrative sanctions in the environmental area are more flexible than criminal sanctions. Nothing would prevent the EU authorities – if they had the political will – from laying down provisions for administrative sanctions and keeping criminal sanctions for really serious cases. This seems to be the practice in the majority of EU Member States anyway.
6   Directive 2008/99 has not made a significant impact in the attempts to protect the environment. It can more easily be compared to a flagship than to a battle-horse. Its overall importance is very limited, and so is its added value to national criminal legislation.
7   Where a Member State wishes to protect the environment through criminal law, it can do so and does not really need the Directive. Where a Member State does not have this political will, it may abide, word by word, with the Directive and then claim that it fully complies with its EU requirements with regard to the protection of the environment through criminal law – and yet ensure no or very little supplementary protection.

This chapter has concentrated on the content of Directive 2008/99 as an instrument to protect the environment through criminal law. It has neither looked into the question of ship-source water pollution, on which separate directives exist,[56] nor looked into the activities of the national, regional and local police in taking up environmental criminal activities; nor has it looked into the efforts of public prosecutors and courts to address these issues, or at the level and effect of national sanctions and of numerous other practical issues surrounding environmental crime.

In general, it appears that the EU undertook one isolated step to legislate on criminal offences in environmental matters. This initiative led to the adoption of Directive 2008/99. Since then, practically no initiative had been taken by the EU institutions as at the end of 2015: no reporting; no legal action against Member States that had not transposed correctly Directive 2008/99 into their national legal order;[57] no attempt to find out whether the Directive is working, where deficiencies are, what the obstacles were for its application in daily practice in the

---

56   Directive 2005/35, on ship-source pollution and on the introduction of penalties, particularly criminal penalties, for infringements, OJ 2005, L 255 p. 11; Directive 2009/123 amending Directive 2005/35 on ship source pollution and the introduction of penalties for infringements, OJ 2009, L 280 p. 52.
57   Actions which the Commission undertakes under Article 258 TFEU are kept confidential until the Commission appeals to the Court of Justice. The statement above thus only refers to court proceedings.

Member States; no comparison of the sanctions actually applied within the Member States; no consideration of establishing administrative sanctions, etc. In view of all this, the conclusion is that the added value of Directive 2008/99 to the fight against environmental impairment and environmental crime is limited.

Bibliography

Charter of Brussels for the creation of a European and an International Criminal Court of the Environment and Health, available from www.endecocide.org/downloads (accessed 22 January 2017).

Committee on the Medical Effects of Air Pollutants (COMEAP). (2010). *The Mortality Effects of Long-Term Exposure to Particulate Air Pollution in the United Kingdom*. Didcot: COMEAP Secretariat.

Council Directive 70/220/EEC of 20 March 1970 on the approximation of the laws of the Member States on measures to be taken against air pollution by emissions from motor vehicles, Official Journal 1970, L 76, p. 1.

Council Directive 72/306/EEC of 2 August 1972 on the approximation of legislation of the Member States on measures to be taken against emissions of pollutants from diesel engines for use in vehicles, Official Journal 1972, L 190, p. 1.

Council Directive 75/442/EEC of 15 July 1975 on waste, Official Journal 1975, L 194, p. 23.

Council Directive 91/271/EEC of 21 May 1991 concerning urban waste water treatment, Official Journal 1991, L 135, p. 40.

Council Regulation (EC) No. 338/97 of 9 December 1996 on the protection of species of wild fauna and flora by regulating trade therein, Official Journal 1997, L 61 p. 1.

Council Regulation (EC) No 1/2003 of 16 December 2002 on the implementation of the rules on competition laid down in Articles 81 and 82 of the Treaty, Official Journal 2003, L 1, p. 1.

Council Framework Decision 2003/80/JHA of 27 January 2003 on the protection of the environment through criminal law, Official Journal 2003, L 29, p. 55.

Directive 2007/607EC of the European Parliament and of the Council of 23 October 2007 on the assessment and management of flood risks, Official Journal 2007, L 288, p. 27.

Directive 2003/87 of the European Parliament and of the Council of 13 October 2003 establishing a scheme for greenhouse gas emission allowance trading within the Community and amending Council Directive 96/61/EC, Official Journal 2003, L 275, p. 32.

Directive 2005/35, of the European Parliament and of the Council of 7 September 2005 on ship-source pollution and on the introduction of penalties, particularly criminal penalties, for infringements, Official Journal 2005, L 255, p. 11.

Directive 2008/99 of the European Parliament and of the Council of 19 November 2008 on the protection of the environment through criminal law, Official Journal 2008, L 329, p. 28.

Directive 2009/123 of the European Parliament and of the Council of 21 October 2009 amending Directive 2005/35 on ship-source pollution and the introduction of penalties for infringements, Official Journal 2009, L 280, p. 52.

Directive 2009/71/Euratom of 25 June 2009 establishing a Community framework for the nuclear safety of nuclear installations, Official Journal 2009, L 172, p. 18.

Directive 2011/70/Euratom of 19 July 2011 establishing a Community framework for the responsible and safe management of spent fuel and radioactive waste, Official Journal 2011, L 199, p. 88.

European Commission, Proposal for a European Parliament and Council Directive on the protection of the environment through criminal law, COM (2001) 139; amended COM (2002) 544, final.
European Commission, Explanatory Memorandum to its Proposal for a Directive on the protection of the environment through criminal law, COM (2007) 51, p. 8.
European Commission, Proposal for a Directive of the European Parliament and of the Council on the protection of the environment through criminal law, COM (2007) 51, final.
European Commission, A Clean Air Programme for Europe, COM (2013) 918, final.
European Commission, Memo/14/116 of 20 February 2014 on Infringement Packages.
European Parliament, Legislative Resolution A6-154/2008 of 15 April 2008.
European Topic Centre on Air and Climate Change. (2009, June). *Assessment of the Health Impacts of Exposure to PM 2.5 at a European Level*. ETC/ACC Technical Paper 2009/1.
Jans, J., Squintani, L., Aragao, A., Macrory, R. and Wegener, B.W. (2010). 'Gold plating' of European environmental measures? *Journal of European Environmental & Planning Law*, 6(4), 417–435.
Regulation 1107/2009 of the European Parliament and of the Council of 21 October 2009 concerning the placing of plant protection products on the market, and repealing Council Directives 79/117/EEC and 91/414/EEC, Official Journal 2009, L 309, p. 1.

Court cases and related files

Court of Justice, Case C-258/00, *Commission v France* [2002] ECR I-5959.
Court of Justice, Case C-176/03 *Commission v Council* [2005] ECR I-7879.
Court of Justice, Case C-440/05 *Commission v Council* [2007] ECR I-9097.
Court of Justice, Case C-301/10, *Commission v United Kingdom*, judgment of 18 October 2010.
Court of Justice, Case C-203/12, *Billerud Karlsborg and Billerud Skärblacka v Naturvårdsverket*, judgment of 17 October 2013.
Court of Justice, Case C-258/11, *Sweetman and Others v An Bord Pleanála*, judgment of 11 April 2013.
Court of Justice, Case C-193/12 *Commission v France*, judgment of 13 June 2013.
Court of Justice, Case C-404/13, *The Queen, on the application of ClientEarth v The Secretary of State for the Environment, Food and Rural Affairs*, judgment of 19 November 2014.
Tribunal Supremo of Spain, Case 2940/2011, Diputación de Cáceres a.o., judgment of 21 January 2014.

Chapter 5

A law and economics approach to environmental crime

Michael G. Faure

1 Introduction

A question that has often been asked is what is the added value of the criminal law as far as remedying environmental pollution is concerned. Is there any such added value at all? In this chapter we will attempt to address that question by using the economic analysis of law. The economic analysis of law can be considered as a useful instrument, given not only solid theoretical foundations but also an increasing interest in the empirics of environmental crime. Moreover, in the economic analysis the added value of the criminal law has been stressed, especially when compared with other instruments such as private and administrative law.

Traditional lawyers may have difficulties accepting an economic perspective to law and especially to criminal law. That may, however, be less the case if it concerns environmental criminal law or other types of so-called white collar crime. The traditional opposition to the economic analysis of law is related to the fact that traditional law and economics was based on the so-called rational choice theory. This assumes that the behaviour of rational human beings is based on a cost–benefit analysis which is affected by an exposure to legal rules. This approach may be more difficult to accept with traditional criminality than with economic crime, often committed by corporations where cost–benefit analysis is a part of daily life. Hence, in this chapter, I will largely base myself on the classic economic approach to criminal law in the way that this has *inter alia* been developed in seminal works of the Nobel Prize-winning Chicago economists Gary Becker and George Stigler.[1] The reader should, however, be aware of the fact that the rational choice approach is definitely no longer the only approach followed in the economic analysis of law. There is now increasing attention given to another approach, largely inspired by cognitive psychology, referred to as behavioural law and economics. To some extent, these behavioural insights are also applied to criminal law, although those developments are still in an early stage.[2]

---

1 Becker (1962), Becker (1968) and Stigler (1970).
2 See *inter alia* McAdams and Ulen (2009).

One important difference between environmental criminal law and a rather traditional criminal law is the so-called administrative dependence of environmental criminal law. In fact, not every pollution constitutes a criminal offence. In many legal systems, pollution is only criminalized when at the same time it violates regulatory norms, or at least an administrative obligation (such as a condition of a permit). This has important consequences, also for the way in which the conditions for criminal liability have been formulated in the law. Moreover, the existing strong link between administrative law and criminal law in this domain also has consequences at the practical level for the enforcement of environmental criminal law.

In this chapter, I will use the traditional economic approach to crime to analyse environmental criminal law. As just mentioned, one advantage of this economic approach is that a lot of attention has been given to the question why it would be necessary to use the criminal law in order to protect the environment. After this introduction, I will therefore first present the economic arguments for regulation. The simple reason is that without (public) regulation, the question of the necessity of criminalization does not even arise. The criteria for regulation therefore also provide insights on why public enforcement of environmental law may be indicated (2). This leads automatically to the question why this public enforcement should, under specific circumstances, take the form of criminal rather than administrative law (3). Next, I will pay attention to the structure of environmental criminal law (4) to turn to policy questions related to the enforcement of environmental criminal law (5–7). This enforcement question is interesting since it will also allow a brief discussion of some of the results of the empirical literature with respect to environmental criminal law. This will finally lead to some more general questions related to the effectiveness of environmental criminal law (8), and the role of reputational sanctions (9). A few concluding remarks will end the chapter (10).

2 Arguments for regulation and arguments in favour of public enforcement

2.1 Weaknesses of private law

A first question that can arise is why the criminal law should be used at all to deal with problems of environmental pollution.[3] In order to answer that question, first the question has to be answered when public enforcement or environmental law is needed. A first argument that is often heard is that this has to do with weaknesses in private law and private enforcement and more particularly in the fact that liability rules would not provide a sufficiently deterrent effect.[4] There are many reasons for this. Often, environmental pollution causes damage to non-identifiable

---

3 See further Faure (2009), 320–345.
4 For a summary of the limits of tort law, see *inter alia* Wilde (2013) and Liu (2013).

victims. It is rather the entire community that suffers harm. In other cases, victims can simply not use liability rules given problems of causation. Also, there may be a long time-lapse (so-called latency) between the moment of the wrongdoing and the moment that the damage occurs. As a result of this long time-frame, problems of proof and causation are only exacerbated. For those and many other reasons, it is often difficult, if not impossible, to apply private enforcement to environmental pollution.[5]

A second problem closely linked to the issues just mentioned is that the application of private law is often not possible since there may not always be a solvent injurer who is able to compensate the damage suffered by the victim. In reality, enterprises can in some cases create an environmental harm of which the amount is substantially higher than their personal wealth.[6] Hence, if the cost of the damage is higher than the personal wealth of the polluter, a problem of lacking incentives and underdeterrence may arise.[7]

2.2 Low probability of detection

A third reason advanced in economic literature (in addition to a low deterrent effect of a liability suit and the judgment proof problem just mentioned) to justify public enforcement is the fact that the probability of detection with environmental pollution may often be lower than 100%.[8]

The problem with private law is that a polluter is only forced to pay damages equal to the harm suffered by the victim. In many classic tort cases, that may not pose a problem. If, for example, a cyclist hits a pedestrian and is forced to compensate the damage to the pedestrian as a result of the accident, civil liability can provide optimal incentives to the cyclist to take efficient care measures aiming at the prevention of the accident.[9] However, from the moment that there is a probability that the injurer can escape the law suit and that hence the probability that he will have to compensate for the damage is lower than 100%, an underdeterrence problem arises.

A simple example can illustrate this: suppose that a tourist wants to import a nice turtle from Lomé (capital of Togo) to Belgium where the turtle would be a protected animal under the CITES Convention and that the tourist does not

---

5 For a summary of the problems with private enforcement of environmental law, see also Brans (2001) and Bergkamp (2001).
6 Just think of the example of the Deepwater Horizon incident which allegedly caused damage of which the estimates vary between $20 billion and $40 billion. If the incident had not been caused by one of the largest oil and gas operators in the world (BP), an insolvency problem would almost inevitably have risen.
7 See Shavell (1986).
8 See on that point more particularly Posner (1985).
9 Assuming that in this case no insolvency problems arise or that any that did arise would be solved through a compulsory insurance. For the example of a cyclist, that may obviously not be the case, but if the injurer were a car driver, it would. For the basic theory, see Shavell (1980).

possess the necessary certificates for the transport. Assume that this turtle would have a value to the tourist of €1,000 and that the fine that would be imposed if the illegal import were discovered would be €10,000. Since the tourist can hide the turtle in his luggage, he can reduce the probability of detection to 10%. Moreover, the tourist having an excellent lawyer, he can also reduce the probability of being convicted to pay the fine to 50%. A simple calculation teaches that the expected costs for the tourist would be 10% x 50% x €10,000 = €500, whereas the advantage to him would be €1,000. A rational criminal would hence decide to commit the crime since the expected benefits are higher than the expected costs.[10]

This simple example shows that problems arise when the probability of detection is lower than 100%. In that case, the sanction should be higher in order to outweigh the low probability of detection. This can in general not be achieved with tort law since tort law in principle only forces the injurer to compensate the victim the amount of the damage suffered and not more. This shows yet another shortcoming of private law in a case where the probability of detection is less than 100%. For optimal deterrence, a higher sanction has to be imposed (of, in our example, €20,000) to outweigh the low probability of detection. This cannot be provided through private law, which explains the need for regulation and public enforcement in order to compensate for the low detection rate.[11]

These arguments hence correspond with the classic criteria for regulation (and hence for public enforcement) as they are *inter alia* powerfully presented in the work of Steven Shavell.[12] A first conclusion that can be reached therefore is that there are apparently strong arguments in favour of regulation of environmental harm, given the indicated weaknesses of private law and private enforcement. That, however, does not answer the question why environmental harm should necessarily be criminalized.

3 Administrative or criminal law?

So far, we presented the traditional economic arguments to explain why environmental pollution cannot merely be remedied via the private law and why public enforcement is indicated. The main reason is the low probability of detecting environmental crime. However, this does not necessarily explain why one should have to use the criminal law. Indeed, the low probability of detection could well be compensated by imposing a high fine on the polluter. Fines have always been considered the preferred sanction in economic theory for the simple reason that the costs of imposition are low and fines in fact only generate money for the public budget.[13] Monetary sanctions can in principle have both a criminal

---

10 See also Faure and Svatikova (2012), 5.
11 See Skogh and Stuart (1982) and Skogh (1973).
12 See *inter alia* Shavell (1984).
13 Shavell (1985) and Posner (1980).

and an administrative nature. All things being equal, the administrative procedure has the major advantage that it is usually less costly than the criminal procedure. Administrative fines can, within what is sometimes referred to as 'administrative penal law',[14] be imposed by administrative authorities after a relatively simple procedure and usually require a relatively low threshold of proof. Compared with the criminal law, the costs of the administrative procedure are lower.[15] All things being equal, it can therefore be argued that if optimal deterrence can be achieved through fines, it seems desirable to use the less costly administrative law instead of the relatively more costly criminal procedure. This has led many scholars to argue that the imposition of relatively modest fines through the criminal procedure is inefficient since a similar result could be achieved at lower costs through administrative law. More particularly, Ogus and Abbot have therefore argued that in the UK more use should be made of administrative fines (and other administrative sanctions for that matter) to enforce violations of environmental regulations.[16] A clear normative conclusion from this literature is therefore that in many more instances than is the case today, administrative law could be used to deter environmental pollution, especially when the penalties consist of relatively low fines or other (not too infringing) administrative sanctions.

There are, however, two important reasons why optimal deterrence cannot under all circumstances be achieved merely with administrative fines.

3.1 Need for non-monetary sanctions

The first reason is that since the probability of detection of environmental pollution can in practice often be very low, the optimal sanction to deter pollution may become very high. The likelihood that this optimal fine might outweigh the individual wealth of an offender is relatively high. Environmental polluters are often organized as corporate entities that benefit from limited liability.[17] Hence, there is always a risk that environmental harm may cause costs that are higher than the assets of the firm or, in the criminal law context, that the optimal fine (to outweigh a low detection rate) will be much higher than the assets of the firm. Indeed, the optimal monetary sanction required for deterrence so frequently exceeds the offenders' assets that non-monetary sanctions, such as imprisonment, are necessary. The major advantage of the fine (lower administrative costs) therefore only leads to favouring this type of sanction when the risk of insolvency can be controlled. It should also be recalled that the probability of an administrative fine being imposed will be much higher (given a lower procedural

---

14 This expression 'administrative penal law' may be confusing to some who consider 'penal' synonymous with 'criminal'. In the literature, this notion is used to refer to a system whereby administrative authorities impose penalties.
15 See *inter alia* Faure and Svatikova (2012) and Faure, Ogus and Philipsen (2009).
16 Ogus and Abbot (2002a) and Ogus and Abbot (2002b).
17 Hansmann and Kraakman (1991), 1879, and Cortenraad (1999).

threshold) than that of a criminal fine. As a result, the administrative fine should not necessarily be nearly so large as the criminal fine. This can again reduce the insolvency problem.

3.2 Error costs

There is a second reason why, from an economic perspective, very high sanctions (such as imprisonment) cannot be imposed through an administrative regency. There is a clear economic reason why society does not want to impose very stringent sanctions, such as imprisonment (but also high fines), through an administrative proceeding. The reason is that the costs of the administrative proceedings may be lower than the costs of the criminal proceedings, but the accuracy of the latter (where the investigations are often undertaken by professional lawyers) may be a lot higher.

This aspect is also important because a task of criminal law is not only to apply optimal sanctions to the guilty but also to avoid punishing the innocent. This is referred to as the goal of reduction of error costs.[18] The error costs are obviously a lot higher when very serious sanctions, such as imprisonment, may be imposed, rather than monetary sanctions only. It is therefore understandable that less costly administrative proceedings are chosen in all cases where the consequences (and thus the error cost) will not be too high in the event of a wrongful conviction. Arguably, it is also a goal of the administrative procedure to avoid punishing the innocent as well (and thus reducing error costs), although the administrative procedure operates at a lower standard. That explains why administrative law (and the corresponding administrative procedure) will be reserved for cases where relatively low penalties can suffice to provide deterrence.

The policy lesson from this economic literature is therefore rather straightforward: in cases where optimal deterrence of environmental polluters can be achieved through relatively modest sanctions (such as not excessively high administrative fines or other administrative sanctions), the use of the less costly administrative penal law may be warranted. However, in cases where the probability of detection is relatively low, social harm and the potential gain to the polluter is high and thus a more severe sanction is needed, it may be warranted to use the more costly criminal procedure in order to reduce error costs. This is certainly the case when the optimal fine would reach the insolvency limit and non-monetary sanctions are thus needed for deterrence, but equally where for the same reason very high administrative fines would have to be imposed. In reality, in many legal systems there are now possibilities to use either the criminal law or administrative penal law for particular environmental offences or in some cases even a combination of those.[19]

18 Miceli (1990).
19 For a discussion on the optimal use of criminal sanction in addition to administrative penalties, see Garoupa and Gomez-Pomar (2004).

4 Optimal environmental criminal law

4.1 Goal of environmental criminal law

4.1.1 Raising polluters' expected costs

The basic idea of the economic analysis of criminal law, as it has been developed by Gary Becker and others, is that the potential polluter will make a cost–benefit calculation concerning the potential violation and will base this decision to commit the crime or not on the result of this cost–benefit analysis.[20] Hence, the idea is that the crime will not be committed when the potential costs are higher than the benefits. From this simple economic perspective, the goal of (environmental) criminal law can be relatively easily identified as increasing the expected costs of the potential polluter.[21]

These expected costs consist on the one hand of the sanction that can be imposed but on the other hand also on the probability of detection that will have to be multiplied with the probability of conviction. An example may illustrate this.

Suppose that the advantages of an environmental crime (e.g. costs that do not have to be invested in pollution prevention technology) are €10,000 and the sanction that could be imposed in case of a conviction is €100,000. If the probability of detection is 10% and the probability of a conviction is 50%, the expected costs for the potential polluter are hence 10% x 50% x €100,000 = €5,000. According to this simple example, the potential polluter will commit the crime since his private benefits are higher than the expected costs. The goal of criminal policy would in that case consist of increasing the expected costs for the potential polluter. The idea is hence that potential polluters will change that behaviour on the basis of information concerning costs and benefits. Criminal policy can rarely influence the advantages to the potential polluter. Influencing the costs is possible, but an important aspect of that consists also of communicating those costs to potential polluters.[22] The potential polluter will change his behaviour on the basis of his (subjective) perception, consisting of the result of the probability multiplied with the sanction.

Concerning the costs, society has a basic choice between either increasing the probability of detection or increasing the sanction. However, the choice between those options has important economic consequences.

4.1.2 Increasing the probability of detection or the sanction?

Suppose that the potential polluter could have a benefit from the crime we just described of €2,000. The probability of detection and conviction is 1% and the sanction is €100,000. Hence, the expected costs for the potential polluter are 1% x €100,000 = €1,000, whereas the benefits are €2,000. Criminal policy should

---

20 This builds further on Faure (2009).
21 For an excellent summary of the economic analysis of crime, see Bowles (1982).
22 That is why it will be agreed below (see section 6) that an information strategy should be a part of an optimal enforcement policy.

hence, if one wants to obtain efficient deterrence, increase the expected costs. This can be done by increasing either the probability of detection or the sanction. If either the probability of detection or the magnitude of the sanction is doubled, expected costs would be €2,000, which is equal to the sanction and hence efficient deterrence would be achieved.

However, Stigler, but also others, has indicated that the choice between those options is not neutral. At first blush, one could hold that increasing the sanction is easier than increasing the probability of detection. The simple reason is that increasing the sanction (specifically when it consists of a fine) is much cheaper than increasing the probability of detection.[23] This would lead to the advice that it is easier to increase the sanction than the probability of detection simply because it would cost less. This has, however, been criticized, also because empirical research has indicated that the probability of detection has a more important deterrent effect than increasing the sanction.[24] Moreover, it is not always possible to increase the sanction in an unlimited way given the insolvency problem. Also, having a very low probability of detection and a high sanction would lead to the situation that only a few polluters would be confronted with a (very high) sanction and others would not be sanctioned at all. This could also be considered unfair.[25]

However, it remains important that from an economic perspective also the costs of enforcement are a deciding factor in the choice between different enforcement instruments and sanctions. Given the fact that enforcement costs are high as well, a 100% compliance is, according to some, neither possible nor desirable.[26] It is important to remember that a reduction of the probability of detection will have to be compensated with a higher sanction if the expected costs for the potential polluter should remain equal.[27]

4.2 Optimal sanctions

We have already indicated that from an economic perspective the probability of detection should be balanced against the amount of the sanction in order to reach an optimal sanctioning system.[28] To which conclusion does the previous analysis lead concerning the optimal sanctions to be applied to environmental crime?

1   When optimal deterrence can be achieved equally through fines and prison sanctions, fines are preferred since they are less costly to impose than prison sanctions.[29]

23 See in particular Polinsky and Shavell (1991), 618 and following.
24 See e.g. Ehrlich (1973).
25 See Polinsky and Shavell (2000).
26 See Ogus and Abbot (2002b).
27 See Polinsky and Shavell (1979).
28 See also Easterbrook (1983), 293.
29 See among many others Polinsky and Shavell (1991), Polinsky and Shavell (1979) and for a summary Bowles (1982).

2   When the expected costs for the potential polluter have to be increased, increasing the sanction (if this is possible without increasing costs) has an advantage compared with increasing the probability of detection. Increasing the sanction can in principle be done at lower cost.
3   However, it is equally important to take into account the costs of the sanction. Many economists have for that reason shown themselves to be opponents of prison sanctions, simply because the costs of the implementation of those sanctions are much higher than the costs of imposing fines. That is why the fine has been advanced as the ideal sanction in case of corporate crimes such as environmental crime.[30] This was, however, criticized by Coffee[31] as well as by Shavell[32] who argued that fines can only work as an effective deterrent if there is no insolvency problem.
4   The problem is indeed that, in case of insolvency, fines will not have a deterrent effect. Since the probability of detection in case of environmental crime is often relatively low, the optimal sanction to reach effective deterrence should be relatively high to compensate this low probability of detection. The problem for the judge is that the probability of detection is a given which can *ex post* no longer be influenced. Hence, given the (low) probability of detection, the judge will have to fix the optimal sanction. In some cases, the fine may then be higher than the individual wealth of the potential polluter. In that case, non-monetary sanctions become necessary. Hence, the advantage of the fine (low-cost sanction) can only be used as long as there is no insolvency problem.[33]
5   However, the application of non-monetary sanctions remains very costly. It is for that reason that economists have often held that it may be more effective to increase the probability of detection in order to avoid a costly non-monetary sanction.[34] The combination of a low probability of detection and a high fine is therefore only efficient as long as one does not reach the solvency limits of the polluter. This shows that monetary sanctions can be applied as long as possible, taking into account the individual wealth of the polluter. Once the solvency limits are reached, it may become less costly to increase the probability of detection in order to avoid the necessity to apply non-monetary sanctions which may be more costly.[35]

Of course, in practice this may constitute a large problem for the judge since information on all the elements that influence the optimal sanctioning policy may not always be easy to obtain. At a policy level, an important lesson is that it may

30 Posner (1980).
31 Coffee (1980).
32 Shavell (1985).
33 See Segerson and Tietenberg (1992).
34 See Ehrlich (1973).
35 On this trade-off between the probability of detection and the magnitude of the sanctions, see also Polinsky and Shavell (1979) and Posner (1980).

in some cases be important to invest additionally in increasing the probability of detection of environmental crime, especially when there is an insolvency risk in order, to avoid having to impose (more costly) non-monetary sanctions.

4.3 Optimal structure of environmental criminal law

There is a great difference in the way criminal law is used to protect classical interests such as life, health or property and the way in which the environment is protected through the criminal law. Traditional interests enjoy a far-reaching protection and every infringement is penalized as manslaughter, assault or theft. The environment does not enjoy the same far-reaching protection as these traditional interests. The economic reason behind this is that many 'polluters' equally exercise socially beneficial activities. An environmental criminal law which would simply prohibit all pollution would therefore be socially wasteful. This explains the interweaving of criminal law with administrative law, which was already mentioned in the introduction. Most environmental statutes provide powers to administrative agencies to decide upon the permitted degree of pollution. Thereby, it is these administrative authorities that determine the scope of environmental crime provisions.

Additionally, no general rule of criminal law prohibits polluting. Polluting only constitutes a crime when it violates an administrative norm, and even if a general prohibition existed, compliance with a permit is usually a sufficient justification. Because most environmental crimes consist of a violation of these administrative norms, the administrative agency that sets the (emission) standards determines what kind of behaviour is criminal.

This type of structure may be economically sound because the administrative authorities have an informational advantage over a judge in an individual criminal case. The alternative would be to consider all pollution a crime, leaving the judge to decide which acts warrant punishment. In most cases, a regulatory agency has either a superior knowledge of, or far better access to, the relevant ecological and technological information than a judge does. Requiring a judge to acquire expert knowledge of chemical and toxic substances, and to keep up to date with recent developments in the field of environmental science would be very inefficient, if not impossible. Moreover, administrative agencies acquire information that benefits a large number of people and therefore diminishes the costs of research for society.[36]

Thus, the current structure of criminal environmental law of relying primarily on administrative agencies to determine environmental crimes appears economically sound. Administrative law, however, cannot be the sole source of environmental criminal law since some serious cases of environmental pollution should be directly punishable, even if no violation of administrative provisions is at hand.

---

36 See further on the optimal structure of environmental criminal law, Mandiberg and Faure (2009).

This obviously raises a lot of questions as to how to formulate environmental criminal law from a legal perspective. It would of course go beyond the scope of this chapter to discuss this in detail.[37] It should, however, be stressed that most environmental criminal law is merely an addition to a prior system of administrative decisions concerning the amount and quality of emissions into the environment. Traditionally, criminal law applied as soon as prior administrative decisions (such as permit conditions) were violated, irrespective of whether this caused harm to the environment. Increasingly, one now notices that these mere administrative violations (e.g. of permit conditions) are sanctioned with fines under administrative penal law. This corresponds with the economic reasoning explained above. Most of the offences are also strict liability offences, which require no specific intent or *mens rea*. This corresponds with a general trend to apply strict liability to regulatory offences. However, some legal systems make a distinction between these mere administrative violations on the one hand and situations where there is also an unlawful emission or even situations where there are serious consequences (such as endangerment of human health) resulting from environmental pollution. In those more serious cases, often criminal law applies and specific conditions apply with respect to mens rea. In a recent study, however, Babbitt, Cory and Kruchek hold that although the requisite criminal intent in the case of environmental violations may have been modified (in the sense that it may to some extent have diminished), substantial defences and procedural safeguards still exist. They hence conclude that the danger of wrongful conviction is no greater in the area of environmental crime than in many other areas of criminal law.[38]

5 Enforcement strategy

5.1 The cooperative strategy

In enforcement literature, not necessarily restricted to economic theory, a lot of attention has been paid to the type of strategy that has to be followed to induce compliance of polluters.[39] The literature makes a distinction between two enforcement styles: the economic approach is qualified as the deterrence style, based on the idea that authorities should go hard on polluters and should prosecute in all cases, preferably resulting in severe sanctions. A deterrence model therefore does not rely on agency discretion. A cooperation enforcement style relies more heavily on negotiations between the polluter and the agency whereby the agency, through persuasion and by providing information, tries to bring the polluter to compliance. Within this cooperation model, punishment is not the appropriate instrument, but rather a method of last resort if other instruments (persuasion and information) have failed.[40]

---

37 See Faure and Visser (1995).
38 Babbitt, Cory and Kruchek (2004), 61.
39 See further Faure (2012), 327–330.
40 Van Rooy (2006).

At first blush, the cooperation model does not fit into the economic approach to enforcement. The classic Becker model assumes that the application of strict and deterrent sanctions, in combination with enforcement efforts to increase the detection rate, will provide incentives to the polluter towards compliance. If a cooperation model merely results in the risk that the polluter would, after being detected, still have to invest in abatement technology which he already had to do on the basis of a permit, deterrence will fail. Some economists therefore hold that the cooperation model (which was followed in the Netherlands in the 1990s) stimulates violations of environmental regulation since companies who comply after a first warning do not encounter any negative consequences of their violation.[41] Another problem with the cooperation model is that when a cooperative strategy has failed and the administrative agency has to change its position to a deterrence style, the cooperation and strong links between the polluter and the agency may have made it difficult or even impossible to change to a deterrence approach when necessary. The cooperation strategy has the inherent risk that powerful and knowledgeable companies will *de facto* be able to control and 'capture' the agency. See, for example, a study of environmental law enforcement in Denmark, which showed that cooperative enforcement was undermined by capturing.[42] There is hence always the danger that this cooperation model will lead to situations of collusion and corruption[43] as a result of which compliance will fail.

Another disadvantage of the cooperative strategy is that it can *de facto* be very difficult for enforcement agents to change the strategy: once enforcement agents have, during many years, cooperated with polluters, it becomes practically impossible to change the strategy and act very severely and impose sanctions against 'friends'. That is of course precisely the capturing problem we just referred to. Capturing *de facto* leads to a situation where the relationship between the controllers and the controlled has become so narrow that an effective enforcement has become impossible. De Ridder has expressed this as follows: 'The controller becomes consultant, partner, person of confidence; everything, except controller.'[44]

5.2 Deterrence strategy

However, notwithstanding these limits of the cooperation model, many have also pointed at limits of the deterrence approach. It has been argued that a strict deterrence approach, which does not take into account the fact that as a result of practical difficulties compliance is impossible, may lead to a refusal to comply because the deterrence approach is felt to be unreasonable.[45] Moreover,

---

41 Nentjes and Hommes (1990).
42 May and Winter (1999).
43 Garoupa and Klerman (2004).
44 De Ridder (2004).
45 Hawkins (1984).

enforcement agents may be unwilling to act as 'policeman' in an adversarial relationship with the polluter.[46] The cooperative strategy even receives some support from economists. It would indeed be too simple to reject the cooperation style entirely because of the danger of capturing. An advantage of the cooperation model is that through persuasion, education and information companies can be led towards compliance.[47] One reason to follow the cooperation model can be related to the high costs for the enforcing agency to bring a case to court.[48] Those high costs may also explain why in some cases there is a seemingly high tolerance of the enforcing agency to non-compliance; this can be a strategic response by the agency to a difficult enforcement environment.[49] This may hence provide a rationalization of 'regulatory dealing' between the agency and the polluter. Especially in cases where administrative authorities are well informed and small and medium-size enterprises are not, a cooperative strategy could lead to the situation whereby the controlling agency in fact assists the enterprise towards compliance with environmental regulation.[50] This is also confirmed in a recent experimental study which found that there are substantial learning effects in the sense that compliance with the desired pollution reduction is substantially higher in a second period when the firm was informed about the contents of their obligations.[51]

5.3. Summary

Summarizing, there may not be such a strict distinction between the deterrence and cooperation style. Proponents of the cooperative approach realize that coercion is necessary also in a cooperation model. Braithwaite therefore proposes a successful enforcement strategy to start with informal and less intrusive enforcement options (persuasion and warnings) to move to more punitive options (fines or criminal prosecution) when the cooperation has failed.[52]

In a powerful study, Lofton attributes the differences in enforcement styles between the US (which has a strongly deterrence based enforcement style) and the UK (which followed a cooperative strategy) to differences in cultural values and attitudes on social regulation.[53] Given high opposition of American business to environmental regulation, Lofton argues that only coercion or the threat of coercion worked to ensure compliance with environmental regulation in the US. Introducing a cooperative approach (which has worked in the UK) in the US context would, according to Lofton, have disastrous consequences for the

46 Aalders and Wilthagen (1997), Aalders (2003).
47 Fenn and Veljanovski (1988).
48 Ogus and Abbot (2002b), 293.
49 Heyes and Rickman (1999).
50 See also Johnston (2001).
51 Alpízar, Requate and Schram (2004).
52 Braithwaite (2002).
53 Lofton (2001).

environmental quality in the US. He therefore argues that varying enforcement styles are largely based upon cultural differences. Hence, one can understand that, given the different cultural attitude of industry to environmental regulation in the US, the shift from traditional command and control to a more flexible system of industry's self-regulation is qualified as a 'dangerous journey' by some American commentators.[54]

In addition to this literature on enforcement styles, there is also some (partially empirical) related literature on the effectiveness of specific enforcement approaches. First, it can be recalled that an overview of the empirical literature shows that studies generally find a deterrent effect from increased inspections and government enforcement actions, but less so from increasing penalties.[55] However, a problem is of course that (as was already pointed out by Stigler) costs for increased monitoring can be high. Also, various empirical studies show that even in the absence of frequent prosecutions, inspections deter future violations.[56]

6 Information strategy

We already indicated that the economic model supposes that potential polluters adapt their behaviour on the basis of an analysis of costs and benefits of environmental crime. Within this model, it is of course crucial that the potential polluter obtains correct information on benefits (which he will usually have) but also on expected costs. Hence, it is important not only to produce information concerning the sanctions and the probability of detection, but also concerning the contents of the obligations following from environmental regulations. This again points at the advantage of a cooperative strategy, especially in cases where administrative authorities are well informed, but polluters are not. The cooperative strategy has the advantage that the controllers can assist industry by explaining the content of the obligations. This seems also to correspond with criminological research in the Netherlands which has confirmed that many violations of environmental regulation do not take place wilfully, but rather as a result of a lack of information or knowledge. In these cases, more particularly when it concerns first offenders, a cooperative enforcement style would probably be effective.[57]

If, indeed, many violations take place as a result of lack of information, a deterrence strategy may not be useful and may even be counterproductive. The deterrence strategy seems therefore to be useful only in a perspective where environmental crime is actually the result of a rational cost–benefit analysis. That is obviously not the case if violations take place negligently because of lacking information.

This was also confirmed in a recent study by Prinsen and Vossen who examined violations concerning the Surface Water Protection Act in the Netherlands, where

54 Steinzor (1998).
55 Cohen (2000), Cohen (2001a), 209.
56 For an empirical study of the petroleum sector in Canada, see Eckert (2004).
57 Huisman (2001) and Huisman and Van de Bunt (1997).

32% of enterprises were not aware of the existing regulations and 38% followed the rules spontaneously. Only 21% held that they followed the rules because they were deterred by the prospect of a sanction.[58] This shows that an information strategy, aiming at informing industry about the contents of their publications, could potentially contribute to an important extent to compliance with environmental regulations.

7 Flexibility or obligations?

One could, at first blush, deduce from the economic approach that economists would be in favour of a strict obligation to enforce compliance with environmental regulations at all costs and this, in combination with an obligation for the judge to apply the sanctions provided for in legislation. Reality is, as often, more balanced.

7.1 Enforcement obligation?

The idea behind an enforcement obligation would be that this would reduce the risk of collusion and that the effectiveness of enforcement would be stimulated by removing discretionary behaviour from controlling administrative authorities. Such an obligation would entail a duty of controlling agents to, for example, draft a notice of violation for every violation that would be discovered. It would remove any discretionary powers that are inherent in a cooperative strategy.

Such a strict obligation does not at all correspond with the economic logic. The simple reason is that the costs of such an absolute obligation to enforce would be too high. Stigler already indicated that the social goal of criminal policy is not a maximum enforcement, but an optimum enforcement.[59] Also, Ogus and Abbot clearly concluded as far as environmental law enforcement is concerned: 'Perfect compliance is neither possible nor desirable.'[60] Moreover, we can point at the empirical evidence that we just discussed which showed that environmental crimes are often committed out of ignorance. If that is indeed the case, it is not in society's interest to force controllers to enforce every violation at all cost. Especially when it concerns a first violation where no environmental harm occurs (i.e. no emission), providing information and warning industry can be a more cost-effective enforcement policy.

7.2 Sentencing guidelines?

The result of economic theory is that optimal sanctions in the case of environmental crimes depend upon a variety of elements, such as the probability of

---

58 Prinsen and Vossen (2003).
59 Stigler (1970).
60 Ogus and Abbot (2002b).

detection, the harm caused, available assets of the polluter, the corresponding insolvency risk and the costs of the sanctions to be imposed. Optimal sentencing policy would consist of applying fines as long as possible (in the light of the insolvency risk) and to combine them in a differentiated manner with non-monetary sanctions where necessary.[61] In the reality of sentencing practice, this can be different. This is more particularly the case in the US where strict sentencing guidelines apply, with which the judge in principle should comply. Differently to the economic model, the sentencing guidelines also provide quite often for incarceration as the main penalty in case of violation of environmental regulations. Frank Easterbrook has strongly opposed this idea of strict sentencing guidelines, arguing that 'there is no correct price for crime in the same way that there is no correct price for apples'. He holds that the price of (environmental) crime depends upon a variety of elements, indicated above, which enable the judge to determine the optimal penalty in a differentiated way.[62] Easterbrook therefore supports discretionary sanctioning powers of the judge, arguing that this will allow the judge to differentiate the sanctions in a more precise manner, taking into account relevant economic criteria.

The economic lessons as formulated by Easterbrook seem to be followed in Europe where, if sentencing guidelines exist at all, they seem to provide sufficient flexibility to the judge to differentiate sanctions according to the economic criteria. The Department for the Environment, Food and Rural Affairs (DEFRA) in the UK published a Review of Enforcement in Environmental Regulation which provides for sentencing guidelines, but at the same time it holds that this should not impose a rigid tariff but should merely provide a more systematic framework for more effective and consistent sentencing decisions.[63] Also, recent empirical evidence seems to support Easterbrook's criticism on the sentencing guidelines in the US. Barrett concluded in a study on the application of the sentencing guidelines for environmental crime that 'the sentences imposed in the majority of cases reflected the reluctance of judges to impose significant incarceration for violations of environmental laws'.[64] Also others have recently held that the sentencing guidelines lead to negative outcomes as far as enforcement and deterrence is concerned. Recent research by Babbitt, Cory and Kruchek showed that the practice of lenient sentencing of environmental criminals, as a refusal to apply the guidelines, was well documented. Since the judiciary feels that the guidelines 'overcriminalize' environmental violations, they may systematically sentence (also significant) violations too leniently, which may undermine the deterrent value of environmental enforcement and may trivialize environmental law itself.[65]

---

61 See Cooter and Ulen (2004), 477.
62 Easterbrook (1983), 295 and 325.
63 Parpworth (2007), 21.
64 Barrett (1992), 1421.
65 Babbitt, Cory and Kruchek (2004), 63.

8 Effectiveness of environmental criminal law: Harrington's paradox

8.1 Low expected sanctions

The sparse empirical evidence that is available with respect to the probability of detection and the probability of being prosecuted and convicted shows, at least as far as Europe is concerned, that these are relatively modest, to say the least. Belgian criminological research showed that around 74% of all reports of violation of environmental laws are not prosecuted.[66] Moreover, there is of course a significant proportion of violations that are not detected at all, which leads to a substantial dark number. Similar Belgian research also shows that when eventually a violation is detected, prosecuted and a sanction is imposed, the average fines are relatively low. Research concerning the imposed fines by criminal courts in the region of Ghent (Belgium) showed an average fine of 200,000 Belgian Francs (€5,000).[67] Recent empirical research concerning the Flemish region also shows that the probability of being detected and convicted is lower than 1%.[68] Empirical research also showed that the average fine imposed by the criminal courts for environmental crime in the Flemish region was approximately €1,000.[69] For other countries one can see a similar picture.[70] Also for the Netherlands, Prinsen and Vossen concluded that in fact compliance with the law (in the case concerning the protection of surface waters) costs much more than the expected costs of violation.[71] Similar research performed by German criminologists in the 1990s shows a similar picture: many environmental crimes are, if detected and reported at all, not prosecuted and the penalties consist generally of relatively low fines.[72] Similar data are provided by Ogus and Abbot concerning the situation in the UK: prosecutions follow for less than a quarter of the worst environmental incidents and the amounts of the fines imposed are low relative to the profitability of the contravening activity.[73]

If one takes into account the fact that the economic gain resulting from a violation of environmental statutes can be substantial, it is not difficult to argue that current practice constitutes a serious problem of underdeterrence. In order to outweigh the potential gain to be made (e.g. by deciding not to invest in a water treatment plant), detection and prosecution rates as well as effective sanctions should be substantially higher. Many have therefore held that by delaying an investment in environmental prevention equipment, enterprises can save substantially on

66 Ponsaers and De Keulenaer (2003).
67 Billiet and Rousseau (2003), 131.
68 See Faure and Svatikova (2012).
69 See Billiet and Rousseau (2003).
70 For an overview of the situation in the Flemish region, United Kingdom, the Netherlands and Germany, see Faure and Svatikova (2012).
71 Prinsen and Vossen (2003).
72 See, for example, also Meinberg (1988).
73 Ogus and Abbot (2002a), 497–498.

interests without additional risks.[74] Also, Cohen concluded from a review of empirical literature that there is little evidence of any preventive effect of increasing monetary sanctions and none on the role of criminal (non-monetary) sanctions.[75] These results could lead to the conclusion that environmental criminal law is apparently not able to provide any deterrence. One could even ask the question why many corporations comply relatively well with environmental law, given the fact that benefits of violation are usually higher than the expected costs. A simple application of the Becker model teaches that there should in principle be much more environmental criminality than can be observed today.

This has been referred to in the literature as the Harrington paradox, following a few papers of Winston Harrington who identified this issue.[76] The paradox is the following: the number of inspections (and hence detection) is low; even if violation is detected, sanctions are hardly imposed and yet the level of compliance by firms seems to be relatively high. Apparently, firms may have an incentive to comply with environmental regulations even if their costs of compliance exceed the expected penalty in case of violation. Some further literature which refines and tries to explain the Harrington paradox shows why firms may have these incentives. Heyes and Rickman[77] show that enforcement agencies may use tolerance in some cases and for some types of violations in order to increase compliance in other contexts and for other violations. According to them, this type of regulatory dealing will improve both the rate of compliance and the individual performance of firms. Also others[78] have held that the discovered pattern is less paradoxical than it seems. On the basis of enforcement data from Norway concerning compliance with environmental regulation, they show that enforcement of minor violations is indeed lax, but that serious violations on the other hand are subject to credible threats of hard punishment and that as a result such violations are more uncommon. They therefore hold that these findings are consistent with standard theory.

In sum, these more recent studies show that even though in general the probability of detection for environmental offences may be low and on average the imposed penalties may be low, that should not necessarily mean that firms would be better off with violation than with compliance. In order to analyse this behaviour of firms, it is necessary to address not only actual sentencing policy but also enforcement strategy (which will be addressed below in 8). This corresponds with a review of empirical literature by Cohen who showed that even though there is little evidence on the effect of increasing monetary sanctions, there is generally a deterrent effect from increased inspections and government enforcement actions.[79] There are, moreover, other reasons why firms comply notwithstanding the Harrington paradox.

74 Nentjes and Hommes (1990).
75 Cohen (2000) and Cohen (2001a), 209.
76 Harrington (1988), Harford and Harrington (1991).
77 Heyes and Rickman (1999).
78 For example, Nyborg and Telle (2006).
79 Cohen (2000) and Cohen (2001a), 209.

8.2 Why comply with the law?[80]

8.2.1 Risk aversion

First, the traditional Becker model assumes risk neutrality of the potential polluter. Violating polluters may well be risk averse. Even though the actual probability of detection, prosecution and conviction in case of environmental crime may well be low, in theory the expected penalty can still be high. For most violations of environmental regulations, prison sanctions can still be imposed, even though these are (at least in Europe) rare in practice. Risk aversion of the potential perpetrator can thus provide additional deterrence.[81] Even though the probability of detection is low, on paper many violations of environmental regulation can still give rise to imprisonment, although the probability that prison sanctions would be imposed is, at least in Europe, relatively low.[82] It is therefore possible that a calculating member of a corporate board of directors who is risk averse will still be deterred by the (even low) probability of being confronted with a prison sanction.

8.2.2 Information problems

Second, the economic model of crime is based on available information by the potential perpetrator of the probability of detection and the expected sanction. Even though criminological research shows that both are relatively low, the relevant question is of course whether these are also perceived as such by (risk-averse) potential polluters.[83] Also the Harrington model discussed above, assumes that the monitoring agency has information on the firm's compliance cost. In reality, this assumption may not hold and moreover there can be lacking information and also errors, both on the side of the agency and on the side of the potential polluter.

8.2.3 Subjective perceptions of expected sanctions

There may be another reason why many firms comply notwithstanding low expected sanctions under the criminal law. This is related to the fact that companies base their *ex ante* decision of compliance on their subjective perception of the probability of being detected and prosecuted and the sanctions that can be imposed.[84] They may therefore not be aware of the low expected sanction in reality. The Belgian economist Rousseau found strong empirical backing for this

---

80 This builds further on Faure (2012), 320–327.
81 For a mathematical example, see Bowles (1982), 59.
82 An overview of the application of environmental criminal law in the Netherlands shows not only that many polluters are acquitted, but also that the most often imposed sanction is the fine. See Faure, De Roos and Visser (2001).
83 See also Ogus and Abbot (2002b), 292.
84 See Rousseau (2007) at 17, 19 (noting that firms that are aware of the monetary restrictions are generally more likely to violate, implying that fears of sanctions may actually be more powerful than the sanction itself).

phenomenon: when firms had to pay a monetary sanction during the previous two years, they were on average more in violation in a second period than firms that did not have to pay a fine in the first period.[85] The interpretation is clear: those who did not have to pay a fine before overestimated the expected fine and complied.[86] Firms that were recently fined had a more accurate impression of true expected sanctions and, being aware that they were low, were no longer deterred.[87] This has an important policy implication: fining a polluter with too low a fine can have a perverse learning effect: firms will then be informed about the low expected sanction, whereas those who were not confronted with these low sanctions may still wrongly believe that expected sanctions are higher than they actually are and thus be more persuaded towards compliance.[88] The policy implication seems to be that if the agency or court decides to fine a polluter, it is better not to impose any fine at all than one too low, since otherwise one would destroy wrong, subjective perceptions of potential perpetrators that fines are higher than they actually are.

8.2.4 Other sanctions mechanisms

One reason for compliance is that one could argue that of course not all cases are prosecuted before a criminal court, but that does not necessarily mean that nothing happens. There can in many cases also be good reasons to dismiss a case, simply because the conditions for criminal liability are not fulfilled – for example, because waste was illegally deposited but no perpetrator could be identified. Also, in cases where conditions for criminal liability are fulfilled, mechanisms other than criminal prosecution may exist which could expose the potential polluter to expected costs.[89] Prosecutors can, in some legal systems, also propose a financial payment to the perpetrator and hence deal with the case themselves, in order to avoid the high administrative costs of the criminal prosecution.[90] This may therefore add something, but probably not a lot, to the expected sanction.

More powerful is probably the possibility for some environmental agencies to impose administrative fines. This exists, for example, in legal systems such as Austria and the Netherlands that have, in addition to the criminal law, the possibility of administrative fines.[91] German research shows that the likelihood that

85 Ibid.
86 Ibid.
87 Ibid.
88 Ibid.
89 For example, after the *Exxon Valdez* ran aground in 1989, a five-month trial followed, and subsequent appeals prolonged the ordeal for nearly two decades before the Supreme Court finally rendered the ultimate decision. Totenberg (2008), www.npr.org/templates/story/story.php?storyId=48308288. See generally Braithwaite (1989) (discussing the deterrent effect of shame). Cohen (2001a) (citing Karpoff, Lott and Rankine (1998)).
90 OECD (2009) (using the Netherlands as an example).
91 See Faure and Heine (2005).

these administrative fines (referred to as *Geldbußen*) are imposed for administrative violations (referred to as *Ordnungswidrigkeiten*) is substantially higher than the likelihood of a prosecution in the criminal court.[92] Therefore, a simple conclusion is that in systems that allow administrative fines in addition to criminal prosecution one can add substantially to expected costs and thus to deterrence. The simple reason is that in those systems a dismissal in the criminal procedure does not necessarily mean that nothing happens, as an administrative fine could still be imposed, thus adding to deterrence.[93]

8.2.5 Other costs

In the case of a prosecution before the criminal court, the polluter can be confronted with other costs that are added to the formal penalty which is imposed. One can simply mention the fact that, for example, members of a board of directors may in some legal systems have to appear as defendants before a criminal court over a period of several weeks. This could be a very unpleasant experience, even if the sanction that is ultimately imposed (e.g. a fine) is relatively low. The time spent and the loss of reputation involved in having pictures of those directors on trial appearing in the press may also constitute an additional cost to the perpetrator. Moreover, a conviction for an environmental crime may lead to other costs to the firm. It may, for example, be more difficult to obtain a new permit since the convicted polluter may have lost goodwill with the administrative agency. Empirical research by Decker showed that this is a realistic fear: companies that complied in the past with environmental regulation will more easily receive a new permit.[94] A conviction may even lead to an increase in insurance premiums, which equally may lead to additional deterrence.

9 Reputational sanctions

A criminal prosecution and conviction may (depending upon the nature of the firm, of course) lead to a significant loss of reputation. The reputational loss of being convicted as a polluter can lead to significant costs for a firm and thus constitute additional deterrence.[95] This corresponds to the well-known idea that a criminal conviction would have the benefit of 'naming and shaming'.[96] The value of this 'shaming' approach to crime is debated. Posner does not believe that

---

92 See Meinberg (1988); Lutterer and Hoch (1997).
93 See Firestone (2003), at 147–158 (discussing enforcement options available to the United States Environmental Protection Agency (EPA) and the enforcement choices applied to different parties). Also, in the United States, the EPA has the choice to enforce environmental law administratively or criminally. Ibid. Empirical evidence shows that a substantial portion of cases are prosecuted administratively.
94 Decker (2003).
95 Ogus and Abbot (2002b), 292.
96 See generally on these notions Braithwaite (1989).

shaming would deter corporate crime since 'a corporation can act only through individuals, and there is a constant turnover of these individuals'.[97] However, in a later publication with Rasmusen, Posner seemed to recognize the value of shaming to enforce specific norms.[98] Others are more optimistic and stress that a major advantage of 'shaming' is that it can reach additional deterrence at relatively low costs.[99] The empirical evidence of the deterrent value of reputational loss resulting from shaming is debated.[100]

The issue received some attention with respect to environmental crime: some hold that the mere fact of a criminal conviction can lead to a decrease of stock prices resulting in damage to the company that is substantially higher than the fine imposed.[101] Cohen, however, comes to a different conclusion: he quotes various empirical studies that demonstrated that indeed the stock value of publicly traded firms is reduced upon the announcement of a bad environmental outcome, such as an oil spill or criminal prosecution. However, quoting another study by Karpoff, Lott and Rankine,[102] Cohen holds that the stock price effects are approximately equal to government-imposed penalties, clean-up costs and private settlements, so that there is no additional reputational loss.[103] Moreover, the mere fact of being labelled a 'criminal' violation did not cause any additional reputation loss.

Of course, the latter two effects only play a role in the case of a criminal conviction, not when merely an administrative fine is imposed. The additional costs of going to trial may thus be an argument in favour of criminalizing environmental offences; it is doubtful whether this criminalization can also be based on the premise that a criminal conviction would lead to an additional reputation loss. There seems to be no empirical evidence to support this statement.

10 Concluding remarks

In this chapter I presented the economic reasons for protecting the environment through the criminal law and I moreover discussed the way in which the criminal law provides protection to the environment. The methodology used was the economic analysis of law. For some traditional lawyers, applying economic notions to criminal law may not be that obvious. It appears, however, that many of the economic ideas are in fact in line with ideas also represented in criminal law. For example, the economic notion that the criminal law and criminal procedure are very costly and therefore only have to be applied in exceptional circumstances corresponds well with the notion in environmental criminal law that the criminal

97 Posner (1985), 1228.
98 Posner and Rasmusen (1999).
99 Morris and Tonry (1990), Buell (2006).
100 Harvard Law Review (2003).
101 Karpoff and Lott (1993).
102 Karpoff, Lott and Rankine (1998).
103 Cohen (2001a), 213–214.

sanction should be considered an *ultimum remedium*. The economic approach to environmental criminal law therefore invites reflection on the goals of the criminal law and the added value of criminal law in protecting the environment.

It is also interesting to notice that increasingly the economic approach to environmental criminal law is supported by empirical evidence. This empirical evidence shows that, almost without exception, the probability of detection and the expected sanctions for environmental crime are relatively low. It is therefore clear, as has also been powerfully demonstrated by Harrington, that potential polluters will not only comply with environmental regulations because of the deterrent effect of the criminal law. There are undoubtedly other elements (such as the fear of reputational losses) that can be more decisive factors.

Empirical evidence also shows that, as far as enforcement policy is concerned, one cannot choose either a cooperative or a deterrence perspective in an absolute way. Different types of environmental crime probably need different types of reactions. For those perpetrators who violate because of a lack of information, information strategies based on a cooperation model, gently guiding the perpetrator towards compliance, may be appropriate. For the calculating polluter, rationally saving, for example, on investments in pollution prevention technologies, a dissuasive approach based on deterrent sanctions may be indicated. Precisely because every situation is different, awarding discretionary powers to agents to be able to choose the appropriate reaction depending upon the circumstances is important. For the same reason, it is important to award those discretionary powers also to the judges as far as sanctioning policy is concerned. Enforcement obligations or mandatory sanctioning guidelines cannot be reconciled with the discretionary powers that should be awarded to enforcement agencies and to the judiciary on the basis of the economic approach.

Politicians (but also public opinion) may in some cases have fixed (and sometimes wrong) ideas on the fact that compliance with environmental regulations could only be reached through severe sanctions imposed via criminal law. This is also the perspective followed in the European Union where Directive 2008/99 explicitly refers to the fact that only the criminal law could be able to provide an effective remedy to environmental pollution.[104] The economic approach showed that to a large extent violation of environmental regulation can also be deterred via administrative fines. Given the low probability of detection and relatively low expected sanctions that will be imposed via the criminal system, it is important that, in addition to the criminal law, administrative sanctions (and more particularly administrative fines) are available, which also reduces the necessity to use the costly criminal law system.

Of course, many other issues may affect the effectiveness of environmental criminal law as well, which could not be discussed in this chapter. For example, the criminal liability of legal entities and the way in which corporate crime can be

---

104 See the motivation in the considerations preceding Directive 2008/99 of 19 November 2008, *Official Journal* L328/28 of 6 December 2008.

prosecuted could not be addressed. Moreover, I could only touch upon the empirical findings concerning the effectiveness of environmental criminal law. One reason for this is that the data in this domain are really scarce. Even in Europe, there is no harmonized system of data collection, and decisions (e.g. concerning the necessity of enforcement via criminal law) are often taken based on assumptions, but not on data. If one really wants to increase the effectiveness of environmental criminal law, it is necessary that reliable data are available on the number of violations, the consequences attached to those (transaction, administrative penalty, criminal sanction, other) and the sanction finally imposed. Also at the EU level, these types of data are lacking. In order to increase the effectiveness of environmental criminal law, it is advisable to move to an 'evidence-based' environmental criminal law. For that it is absolutely necessary to create a harmonized system of data collection on inspections, violations, measures taken and sanctions.

Bibliography

Aalders, M., and Wilthagen, T. (1997). Moving beyond command and control: Reflexivity in the regulation of occupational safety and health and the environment. *Law & Policy*, 19, 415–444.

Aalders, M. (2003). Self-regulation and compliance with environmental law from a global perspective. In N. Niessen and A. Bedner (eds), *Towards Integrated Environmental Law in Indonesia* (pp. 21–36). Leiden: CNWS.

Alpízar, F., Requate, T., and Schram, A. (2004). Collective versus random fining: An experimental study on controlling ambient pollution. *Environmental and Resource Economics*, 29(2), 231–252.

Babbitt, C.J., Cory, D.C., and Kruchek, B.L. (2004). Discretion and criminalization of environmental law. *Duke Environmental Law and Policy Forum*, 15, 1–64.

Barrett, J.J. (1992). Sentencing environmental crimes under the United States Sentencing Guidelines: A sentencing lottery. *Environmental Law*, 22, 1421–1449.

Becker, G.S. (1962). Irrational behaviour and economic theory. *Journal of Political Economy*, 70(1), 1–13.

Becker, G.S. (1968). Crime and punishment: An economic approach. *Journal of Political Economy*, 76(2), 169–217.

Bergkamp, L. (2001). *Liability and Environment: Private and Public Law Aspects of Civil Liability for Environmental Harm in an International Context* (pp. 211–218). The Hague: Kluwer Law International.

Billiet, C.M., and Rousseau, S. (2003). De hoogte van strafrechtelijke boetes. Een rechtseconomische analyse van milieurechtspraak (1990–2000) van het Hof van Beroep te Gent. *Tijdschrift voor Milieurecht*, 120–134.

Brans, E.H.P. (2001). *Liability for Damage to Public Natural Resources: Standing, Damage and Damage Assessment* (pp. 35–64). The Hague: Kluwer Law International.

Bowles, R. (1982). *Law and the Economy*. Oxford: Martin Robertson.

Braithwaite, J. (1989). *Crime, Shame and Reintegration*. Cambridge: Cambridge University Press.

Braithwaite, J. (2002). Rewards and regulation. *Journal of Law and Society*, 29(1), 12–26.

Buell, S.W. (2006). The blaming function of entity criminal liability. *Indiana Law Journal*, 81, 473–537.

Coffee, J.S. (1980). Corporate crime and punishment: A non-Chicago view of the economics of criminal sanctions. *American Criminal Law Review*, 17(4), 419–476.

Cohen, M.A. (2000). Measuring the costs and benefits of crime and justice. *Measurement and Analysis of Crime and Justice*, 4, 263–316.

Cohen, M.A. (2001a). Criminal law as an instrument of environmental policy: Theory and empirics. In A. Heyes (ed.), *Law and Economics of the Environment* (pp. 198–216). Cheltenham: Edward Elgar.

Cohen, M.A. (2001b). The crime victim's perspective in cost-benefit analysis: The importance of monetizing tangible and intangible crime costs. In D.P. Farrington, B.C. Welsh, and L.W. Sherman (eds), *Costs and Benefits of Preventing Crime* (pp. 23–50). Boulder, CO: Westview Press.

Cooter, R.D., and Ulen, T. (2004). *Law and Economics* (4th edn). Indianapolis, IN: Addison Wesley.

Cortenraad, W.H.F.M. (1999). *The Corporate Paradox, Economic Realities of the Corporate Form of Organization*. Boston, MA: Kluwer Academic.

De Ridder, J. (2004). Een goede raad voor toezicht, Groningen, inauguration address Boom Juridische Uitgevers, The Hague.

Decker, C.S. (2003). Corporate environmentalism and environmental statutory permitting. *The Journal of Law & Economics*, 46(1), 103–129.

Easterbrook, F. (1983). Criminal procedure as a market system. *Journal of Legal Studies*, 12, 289–332.

Eckert, H. (2004). Inspections, warnings, and compliance: The case of petroleum storage regulation. *Journal of Environmental Economics and Management*, 47, 232–259.

Ehrlich, I. (1973). Participation in illegitimate activities: A theoretical and empirical investigation. *Journal of Political Economy*, 81, 521–552.

Faure, M.G. (2009). Environmental crimes. In N. Garoupa, (ed.), *Criminal Law and Economics* (pp. 320–345). Cheltenham: Edward Elgar.

Faure, M.G. (2012). Effectiveness of environmental law: What does the evidence tell us? *William & Mary Environmental Law and Policy Review*, 36(2), 293–336.

Faure, M.G., and Heine, G. (2005). *Criminal Enforcement of Environmental Law in the European Union*. The Hague: Kluwer Law International.

Faure, M., and Svatikova, K. (2012). Criminal or administrative law to protect the environment? Evidence from Western Europe. *Journal of Environmental Law*, 24(2), 253–286.

Faure, M., and Visser, M.J.C. (1995). How to punish environmental pollution? Some reflections on various models of criminalization of environmental harm. *European Journal of Crime, Criminal Law and Criminal Justice*, 3(4), 316–368.

Faure, M., De Roos, T., and Visser, M. (2001). *Herziening van het Commune Milieustrafrecht*. Deventer: Gouda Quint, 53–59 and 165–168.

Faure, M., Ogus, A., and Philipsen, N. (2009). Curbing consumer financial losses: The economics of regulatory enforcement. *Law & Policy*, 31(2), 161–191.

Fenn, P., and Veljanovski, C. (1988). A positive economic theory of regulatory enforcement. *Economic Journal*, 98(393), 1055–1070.

Firestone, J. (2003). Enforcement of pollution laws and regulations: An analysis of forum choice. *Harvard Environmental Law Review*, 27, 105–176.

Garoupa, N., and Gomez-Pomar, F. (2004). Punish once or punish twice: A theory of the use of criminal sanctions in addition to regulatory penalties. *American Law and Economics Review*, 6(2), 410–433.

Garoupa, N., and Klerman, D. (2004). Corruption and the optimal use of non-monetary sanctions. *International Review of Law and Economics*, 24, 219–225.

Hansmann, H., and Kraakman, R.H. (1991). Toward unlimited shareholder liability for corporate torts. *Yale Law Journal*, 100(7), 1879.

Harford, J.D., and Harrington, W. (1991). A reconsideration of enforcement leverage when penalties are restricted. *Journal of Public Economics*, 45, 391–395.

Harrington, W. (1988). Enforcement leverage when penalties are restricted. *Journal of Public Economics*, 37, 29–53.

Harrington, W., and Heyes, A. (2001). The theory of penalties: 'leverage' and 'dealing'. In A. Heyes (ed.), *The Law and Economics of the Environment* (pp. 185–197). Cheltenham: Edward Elgar.

Hawkins, K. (1984). *Environment and Enforcement, Regulation and the Social Definition of Pollution*. Oxford: Clarendon Press.

Heyes, A., and Rickman, N. (1999). Regulatory dealing – Revisiting the Harrington Paradox. *Journal of Public Economics*, 72(3), 361–378.

Huisman, W. (2001). *Tussen winst en moraal: Achtergronden van regelnaleving en regelovertreding door ondernemingen*. The Hague: Boom Juridisch.

Huisman, W., and Van de Bunt, A.G. (1997). Sancties, Organisatiecriminaliteit en Milieudelicten. *Ars Aequi*, 684–697.

Johnston, J.S. (2001). The law and economics of environmental contracts. In E.W. Orts and K. Deketelaere (eds), *Environmental Contracts: Comparative Approaches to Regulatory Innovation in the United States and Europe*. The Hague: Kluwer.

Karpoff, J. and Lott, J. (1993). The reputational penalty firms bear from committing criminal fraud. *Journal of Law and Economics*, 36, 757–802.

Karpoff, J., Lott, J., and Rankine, G. (1998). *Environmental Violations, Legal Penalties, and Reputation Costs*. John M. Olin Law and Economics Working paper, no. 71, second series, University of Chicago Law School.

Liu, J. (2013). *Compensating Ecological Damage: Comparative and Economic Observations*. Antwerp: Intersentia, 45–93.

Lofton, J.A. (2001). Environmental enforcement: The impact of cultural values and attitudes on social regulation. *Environmental Liability*, 4, 167–181.

Lutterer, W., and Hoch, H.J. (1997). *Rechtliche Steuerung Im Umweltbereich. Funktionsstrukturen Des Umweltstrafrechts Und Des Umweltordungswidrigkeitenrechts. Empirische Untersuchungen Zur Implementation Strafbewehrter Vorschriften Im Bereich Des Umweltschutzes*. Freiburg i.Br. Max Planck Institute for Foreign & International Criminal Law.

Mandiberg, S.F., and Faure, M.G. (2009). A graduated punishment approach to environmental crimes: Beyond vindication of administrative authority in the United States and Europe. *Columbia Journal of Environmental Law*, 34, 447–511.

McAdams, R.H., and Ulen, T.S. (2009). Behavioral criminal law and economics. In N. Garoupa (ed.), *Criminal Law and Economics, Encyclopedia of Law and Economics*, vol. XI (pp. 403–436). Cheltenham: Edward Elgar.

May, P.J., and Winter, S. (1999). Regulatory enforcement and compliance: Examining Danish agro-environmental policy. *Journal of Policy Analysis and Management*, 18(4), 625–651.

Meinberg, V. (1988). Empirische Erkenntnisse zum Vollzug des Umweltstrafrechts. *Zeitschrift für die Gesamte Strafrechtswissenschaften*, 112–157.

Miceli, T. (1990). Optimal prosecution of defendants whose guilt is uncertain. *Journal of Law, Economics and Organisation*, 6(1), 189–201.

Morris, N., and Tonry, N. (1990). *Between Prison and Probation: Intermediate Punishment in a Rational Sentencing System*. New York, NY: Oxford University Press.
Nentjes, A., and Hommes, J. (1990). Handhaving van het Milieurecht. *Tijdschrift voor Milieuaansprakelijkheid*, 1–7.
Nyborg, K., and Telle, K. (2006). Firms' compliance to environmental regulation: Is there really a paradox? *Environmental & Resource Economics*, 35(1), 1–18.
OECD. (2009). *Ensuring Environmental Compliance: Trends and Good Practice*. Paris: OECD Publications.
Ogus, A., and Abbot, C. (2002a). Pollution and penalties. In T. Swanson (ed.), *An Introduction to the Law and Economics of Environmental Policy: Issues in Institutional Design* (pp. 493–516). Oxford: Elsevier.
Ogus, A., and Abbot, C. (2002b). Sanctions for pollution: Do we have the right regime? *Journal of Environmental Law*, 14, 283–300.
Parpworth, N. (2007). Enforcement in environmental regulation: The Defra Review. *Environmental Liability*, 15(1),15–26.
Polinsky, A.M., and Shavell, S. (1979). The optimal trade off between the probability and the magnitude of fines. *American Economic Review*, 9(5), 880–891.
Polinsky, A.M., and Shavell, S. (1991). A note on optimal fines when wealth varies among individuals. *American Economic Review*, 81, 618–621.
Polinsky, A.M., and Shavell, S. (2000). The fairness of sanctions: Some implications for optimal environmental policy. *American Law and Economics Review*, 2, 223–237.
Ponsaers, P., and de Keulenaer, S. (2003). Met strafrecht tegen milieudelicten? Rol en functie van bijzondere inspectiediensten in de strijd tegen milieucriminaliteit, *Panopticon*, 250–265.
Posner, R. (1980). Optimal sentences for white-collar criminals. *American Criminal Law Review*, 17(4), 400–418.
Posner, R. (1985). An economic theory of the criminal law. *Columbia Law Review*, 85, 1193–1231.
Posner, R.A., and Rasmusen, E.B. (1999). Creating and enforcing norms, with special reference to sanctions. *International Review of Law and Economics*, 19, 369–382.
Prinsen, H.M., and Vossen, R.M.M. (2003). Naleving en Handhaving van Regelgeving. Loont het de Moeite? *Justitiële Verkenningen*, 29(9), 54–69.
Van Rooy, B. (2006). *Regulating Land and Pollution in China, Law Making, Compliance, and Enforcement; Theory and Cases*. Dissertation, Leiden: Leiden University Press.
Rousseau, S. (2007). *The Impact of Sanctions and Inspections on Firms' Environmental Compliance Decisions*, 10 (Katholieke Universiteit Leuven, Center for Economic Studies, Working Paper No. 2007-04).
Schwarcz, D. (2003). Shame, stigma and crime: Evaluating the efficacy of shaming sanctions in criminal law. *Harvard Law Review*, 116, 2186–2207.
Segerson, K., and Tietenberg, T. (1992). Defining efficient sanctions. In T.H. Tietenberg (ed.), *Innovation in Environmental Policy* (pp. 63–65). Cheltenham: Edward Elgar.
Shavell, S. (1980). Strict liability versus negligence. *Journal of Legal Studies*, 9(1), 1–25.
Shavell, S. (1984). Liability for harm versus regulation of safety. *Journal of Legal Studies*, 13(2), 357–374.
Shavell, S. (1985). Criminal law and the optimal use of non-monetary sanctions as a deterrent. *Columbia Law Review*, 85, 1232–1262.
Shavell, S. (1986). The judgment proof problem. *International Review of Law and Economics*, 6, 45–58.

Skogh, G. (1973). A note on Gary Becker's 'Crime and Punishment: An Economic Approach'. *Swedish Journal of Economics*, 75(3), 305–311.

Skogh, G., and Stuart, C. (1982). An economic analysis of crime rates, punishment and the social consequences of crime. *Public Choice*, 38(2), 171–179.

Steinzor, R.I. (1998). Reinventing environmental regulation: The dangerous journey from command to self-control. *Harvard Environmental Law Review*, 22, 103–202.

Stigler, G. (1970). The optimum enforcement of laws. *Journal of Political Economy*, 78(3), 526–536.

Totenberg, N. (2008, 27 Feburary). Supreme court weighs Exxon Valdez damages. *NPR*. Retrieved from: www.npr.org/templates/story/story.php?storyId=48308288.

Wilde, M. (2013). *Civil Liability for Environmental Damage: A Comparative Analysis of Law and Policy in Europe and the United States* (2nd edn). Alphen-aan-de-Rijn: Kluwer Law International.

Part II

Assessing the limitations of current approaches to environmental harms

Chapter 6

International financial institutions as facilitators of environmental crimes

Dawn L. Rothe and Victoria E. Collins

1 Crimes of globalization, environment degradation, and beyond

When the term "environmental crimes" is invoked, we often think in terms of toxic dumping, illegal logging, deforestation, or a host of other devastating harms to the natural ecological system. More often than not, the imagined culprits are rogue actors, organized syndicated criminals, corporations, or even state governments. In this chapter, we suggest that international financial institutions (IFIs) (i.e. the World Bank Group and the International Monetary Fund in particular) have been and continue to be a main impetus for and facilitator of environmental crimes. One of the main areas where IFIs play an active role in the degradation of the environment is the mining sector. Our focus in this chapter is on the environmental crimes associated with open-pit mining that are promoted, supported, and funded in some capacity by IFIs. We advocate that the facilitation of the environmental harms of open-pit mining by the international financial institutions can be situated within the literature of crimes of globalization.

The concept of crimes of globalization was first introduced in an article by David and Jessica Friedrichs (2002) where they discussed the impact of the World Bank Group's project, Pak Mun Dam, on the indigenous population and local ecosystem. They suggest that crimes of globalization have characteristics of "state crime, political crime, white-collar crime, state-corporate crime, and finance crime," but do not fit neatly into any of these categories. Specifically, these crimes "involve cooperative endeavors between international financial institutions, transnational corporations, and state or political entities that engage in demonstrably harmful activities in violation of international law or international human rights convention" (Friedrichs and Friedrichs, 2002, p. 18).

In the Pak Mun Dam case, the World Bank helped finance the building of the dam in eastern Thailand in the early 1990s. The process of planning, constructing, and operating this dam was undertaken without obtaining input from the fishermen and villagers who lived along the river. The construction of the dam had a detrimental effect on the environment, flooding the adjacent forests. Many edible plants upon which locals were dependent for their sustenance and for income were lost. Villagers who used the river waters for drinking, bathing, and laundry developed skin rashes. Most importantly, a severe decline in the fish population occurred. As a consequence, the way of life of indigenous fishermen dependent upon abundant fish for food and income was annihilated.

In the wake of the original article focusing upon the World Bank and the case of the Pak Mun Dam, a number of criminologists have applied the concept of crimes of globalization to other circumstances (Friedrichs and Rothe, 2012; Rothe and Friedrichs, 2013). For example, Rothe, Muzzatti, and Mullins (2006) conducted research that explored the interrelationship between the International Monetary Fund and the World Bank, and legacies of colonialism along with foreign policies that set the stage for large-scale atrocities and crimes of states. Exploring the circumstances leading to the sinking of the ferry *Le Joola*, the authors demonstrated that the state of Senegal itself had core liability for this maritime tragedy, with its dramatic loss of lives. The government readily admitted its errors and several ministers either stepped down or were removed from their positions. However, despite unequivocal governmental responsibility, Rothe, Muzzatti, and Mullins advance the case that the sinking could not be characterized simply as a case of state crime. Rather, a thorough investigation and analysis of the reasons and forces behind the *Le Joola* sinking suggested that international financial institutions bore some clear culpability for the disaster. In response to Structural Adjustment Programs (SAPs) imposed by the International Monetary Fund, the Senegalese government was forced to cut spending in many areas. These spending cuts extended to ferry programs central to transportation in Senegal, especially in relation to its geographic location. This had a direct impact on the upkeep and return of the *Le Joola* to open waters. The ferry capsized with only one of its two engines functioning, resulting in the deaths of 1,863 passengers. This was the second largest maritime disaster in history. Most crucially, the authors of this study demonstrated why scholars need to examine the criminogenic effects of policies and practices of international financial institutions in developing countries such as Senegal. These policies and practices privilege capitalistic profit over human lives and a better quality of life for people in developing countries. Accordingly, this is crime against vulnerable human beings (Friedrichs and Rothe, 2012; Rothe and Friedrichs, 2013).

An article by Rothe, Mullins, and Sandstrom (2009) took a parallel approach, exploring the role of international financial institution policies in the conditions leading to the Rwandan genocide in 1994. While the World Bank and the International Monetary Fund did not seek to instigate economic collapse or to promote genocide, their policies and their systematic inattention in Rwanda set the stage for political and economic disaster as well as the genocide itself. The authors suggested that these international financial institutions knowingly violated their own standards, as well as international human rights principles. Through the imposition of harsh conditions tied to their financial aid, they facilitated criminal activities on a massive scale.

In an article published in 2008, Ezeonu and Koku also adopted the concept of crimes of globalization. They demonstrated the key contributing role played by the neo-liberal policies of international financial institutions in sub-Saharan Africa, in expanding the vulnerability of people in this region to HIV infection. They called for more systematic criminological attention to the victimization of people in developing countries as a consequence of the promotion of neo-liberal policies and practices in an increasingly globalized world (see also Ezeonu, 2008).

In a similar vein, Rothe (2010a, 2010b, 2010c) has provided an analysis of the complicity of international financial institutions in heightened levels of corruption and the suppression or violation of human rights in developing countries. Analyzing such complicity seems especially important given that these institutions claim to be engaged in combating corruption in developing countries, including those linked to transnational and multinational corporations. The anti-corruption initiatives include threatening to withhold much-needed economic aid and loans in the absence of action taken against corrupt activities in these countries. Rothe has illustrated the specific role of the international financial institutions in the illegal expropriation of the rich natural resources of the Democratic Republic of Congo by the neighboring countries of Uganda and Rwanda. Beyond theft on a grand scale, Rwandan and Ugandan state forces and militias also engaged in especially atrocious human rights violations conducted against civilian populations, including forced labor, systematic rape, and widespread killing. Through their funding of African states engaged in crimes against both their own citizens and those of neighboring countries, the international financial institutions bear some responsibility for these crimes (Friedrichs and Rothe, 2012; Rothe and Friedrichs, 2013).

Parallel circumstances have arisen in other parts of the world (Friedrichs and Rothe, 2012; Rothe and Friedrichs, 2013). Stanley (2009) has analyzed the role of the international financial institutions in Indonesia. They directed some $30 billion to the Suharto regime, despite its known record of massive corruption, false accounting, and a militaristic appropriation of aid funds. As the World Bank's focus was on supporting Indonesia, the state was able to use funds supposedly intended to reduce poverty in its brutal campaign against civilians in the state of Timor-Leste. This campaign had as its purpose terrorizing people to deter them from voting for independence from Indonesia. One could identify many other cases in Asia and other parts of the world where the international financial institutions have been complicit in supporting corrupt, authoritarian regimes and facilitating their massive violations of human rights.

The concept of crimes of globalization has also been adopted in relation to forms of crime that occur in the context of globalization but do not specifically involve the international financial institutions (Friedrichs and Rothe, 2012; Rothe and Friedrichs, 2013). Wright and Muzzatti (2007) have addressed the global restructuring of agriculture and food systems – agri-food globalization – with some specific attention to the victimization of huge numbers of animals: for example, 58,000 sheep stranded at sea for almost three months in 2003, in violation of animal welfare law. Altogether, policies and practices relating to the global restructuring of agriculture and food systems were driving up food prices, pushing tens of millions of people towards hunger and starvation, and developed country farm subsidies were driving large numbers of farmers in developing countries into desperate circumstances – to the advantage of corporate and high-finance interests in the wealthy countries of the world.

More recently, Rothe and Friedrichs (2014) put forth a volume dedicated to crimes of globalization that provides an extensive and broad overview of the harms and violence perpetrated by international financial institutions. It should be noted that this chapter draws on some of those cases. On another note, while presenting the concept of a global state, Cain's (2010) analysis of IFIs is similar to those of scholars of crimes of globalization. Drawing on the case of Trinidad and Tobago, Cain attributes increases in instrumental crimes (e.g. property crimes) and self-assertive crimes (e.g. crimes of violence) to policies mandated by IFIs. More generally, Cain suggests that, on a global scale, the increase in highly indebted countries, heightened levels of poverty, privatization of natural resources and state-held entities, reduced social services, and other recognized structurally negative mandated outcomes can, on many levels, be attributed to IFI policies, making them criminogenic in their effect.

Literature from ecological studies has also examined the issue of natural resources and environmentally degrading activities that are located within the international political economy (Rice, 2009). This includes the recognition that organizational and institutional mechanisms at the international level can be catalysts of this process. There is also "widespread recognition that structural adjustment and external debt force many developing nations to increase their natural resources exports to developed nations" (Bello, Cunningham, and Rau, 1999; Downey, Bonds, and Clark, 2010).

As noted by Downey, Bonds, and Clark (2010, p. 2): "One set of institutions that facilitate resource extraction activities are international trade and finance institutions such as the World Bank, International Monetary Fund (IMF), and World Trade Organization (WTO).". They also acknowledge that IFIs have multiple negative impacts on individuals, societies, and the environment (Bello *et al.*, 1999; Wallach and Woodall, 2004).

Although the body of literature on environmental, green, ecological, or conservation criminological research does address globalization in general and the connection to environmental harm, there is sparse, to no, attention paid directly to the role of IFIs in the promotion of a "globalized" world and environmental harms (White, 2010). There are direct and indirect acknowledgements of the role of IFIs and environmental harms, although no specific thorough analysis has been provided. For example, White (2003, p. 498) notes that:

> The activities of international financial institutions like the World Bank (as well as individual firms and companies) are re-dressed in ways that convey

the message that "sustainable development" is happening, and that global power-brokers are doing what needs to be done to protect the environment. This belies actual environmental harms perpetrated by many of these institutions and by specific businesses that, cumulatively, are doing great damage to the global environment.

As White (2003, p. 497) suggests, the links between capital and a state are manifested in coinciding ideological and financial agendas "regarding the privatization and commodification of nature"; the same can be said of IFIs and global capital interests.

Although there has been no specific focus linking the harms as crimes of globalization with the body of literature on environmental crimes, there are similar themes in some of the cases as noted above. Likewise, none of the crimes of globalization literature has focused specifically on the facilitation of environmental crimes such as open-pit mining by international finance institutions. It is our hope that this chapter begins to fill that gap and instigates a broader discourse on crimes of globalization, or the role of IFIs, in the production and sustainment of environmental crimes.

2 Open-pit mining and international finance institutions

> Mining is a critically important yet challenging sector and [the International Finance Corporation] IFC has a role to play in supporting responsible companies that will bring jobs, related infrastructure and government revenues to Africa.
> (Andrew Gunther, IFC's Senior Manager of Infrastructure and Natural Resources in Africa and Latin America, cited in Davenport, 2011)

Over the past decade, IFIs have "actively promoted and financed the liberalization of the hydrocarbon and mining sectors of national economies across the globe," stating that the "public-private collaborations among governments, IFIs and multinational corporations (MNCs) will enhance social well-being by eradicating poverty, promoting sustainable forms of economic development, protecting the environment and advancing the rights of indigenous peoples" (Sawyer and Gomez, 2008). While such statements are firmly grounded in IFIs' neo-liberal ideology of development and open markets, more often than not they remain unchallenged within the institutions and the promotion of resource extraction continues to escalate (see Appendix A for a list of country resource extraction supported by IFIs under the World Bank transparency initiative). The majority of resource extraction projects are funded through the World Bank Group arm, the International Finance Corporation (IFC), which is the largest global development institution focused exclusively on the private sector. This is the case with the mining projects as well. Consider that projects such as the Ahafo mine, Ghana included a $75 million investment loan (A equity loan) and a $10 million secured loan (B loan) to Newmont.[1] Likewise, the Simandou mine, Guinea, included an investment of a $35 million loan to Rio Tinto and a $15 million equity loan to Nyota for the Tulu Kapi mine, Ethiopia (International Finance Corporation, 2013b). Another current project is a $12 billion investment to develop a copper and gold mine at Oyu Tolgi, in the Southern region of Mongolia. The latter project is said to be "a cornerstone of Mongolia's economic development as the country strives to eradicate poverty and emerge as a middle-income country" (International Finance Corporation, 2012b). In May 2013, the IFC announced a Can$5 million investment in Unigold Incorporated for gold and base metal exploration for the Neita project in the Dominican Republic for a "future development plan," stating that the "IFC will work with the company to ensure that exploration and any subsequent mine development is carried out in an environmentally and socially sustainable manner" (International Finance Corporation, 2013a). While perhaps a well-intended statement, the development and operation of open-pit mining and resource extraction has not been associated with environmental or social sustainability. Prior to discussing case-specific examples of the direct facilitation of IFIs and environmental harms caused by open-pit mining, we provide a brief overview of the processes of open-pit mining.

3 Open-pit mining

There are various means by which mining extraction occurs and this is dependent on the type of natural resource that is being sought. Generally, they are ore deposits including but not limited to copper, gold, silver, coal, and nickel. The process of beginning a mining project starts with the initial exploration. This first phase includes clearing wide areas of vegetation and, in some cases, large indigenous populations. If enough natural resource is detected, the second phase of preparing the site and its development begins. This includes creating or using access roads and other infrastructure supports for large equipment to be brought in. Open-pit mining "is a type of strip mining in which the ore deposit extends very deep in the ground, necessitating the removal of layer upon layer of overburden and ore" (Environmental Law Alliance, 2010, p. 4). Due to the depth of these mines, a pit is created that extends below the groundwater table, requiring water to be pumped out of the pit, often creating a pit lake when the mining project ends. In some cases, water is needed to generate other processes of mining, where nearby lakes, rivers, and streams are tapped, often leading to shortages of water and impacting the ecological order.

In the process of open-pit mining, large quantities of waste rock are extracted in order to get to the desired mineral ore. For example, when mining copper,

---

1 When an IFC loan includes financing from the market through the B Loan structure, IFC retains a portion of the loan for its own account (the "A Loan" or equity), and sells participations in the remaining portion to participants in the market (the "B Loan").

99 tons of waste material needs to be removed for every one ton of copper. For gold, far more waste results as "almost three tonnes of ore is needed to produce enough gold for one typical wedding band" (Safe Drinking Water Foundation, 2013). Open-pit mining is believed to be the most environmentally harmful of all forms of resource extraction. To further elucidate these harms, we draw on several examples where IFIs – the IFC in particular – have promoted and financed a significant portion of the mining projects that have resulted in devastating environmental conditions.

4 Ghana[2]

The Newmont Mining Corporation was awarded a loan of US$125 million in January 2006 to develop the first Ahafo open-pit gold mine (Ahafo South) in a heavy agricultural region northwest of Ghana's capital, Accra. To get to the production level, Newmont "established a mill, waste rock disposal facilities, water storage facility, tailings storage facility, environmental control dams, haul roads and other mine infrastructure" (Owusu-Koranteng, 2010). Newmont currently operates four open-pit mines at Ahafo with the reserves contained in 11 constructed pits. Production of the fourth pit, Amoma, started in October 2010 (Newmont, 2013). The project covers:

> 774 square kilometres which comprises the overall mining license. The open pits are the most visible land disturbance but account for only 14% of the total land use. Stockpiles and waste dumps account for 35%, water and tailings reservoirs 34% and facilities, roads and other infrastructure 17%.
> (Kapstein and Kim, 2011, p. 51)

Beyond the social and economic harms, including the displacement of 10,000 indigenous persons, the environmental harms are numerous. There are normal environmental impacts and harms that result from open-pit gold mining, beginning with the destruction of the environment at the mine site, vast craters, and damage to the surrounding ecological system. Toxic mine drainage is commonly associated with gold mining. The process of digging up the rock can set off chemical reactions that produce a lot of acid-generating sulfides and leach toxic metals such as sulfuric acid and arsenic which can run off into lakes, streams, and rivers, posing serious risk to fish and other life forms dependent on the water outlets. Mine drainage is a common problem. Once the process of extracting the gold from the ore begins, there is also the issue of mercury through the roasting process or dousing the ore in cyanide that can result in nitrates being produced which can contaminate water. Gold tailing ponds, such as the four at the Ahofa mine site, are "chock-full of contaminants such as arsenic, antimony,

---

2 We selected Ghana as the primary case study due to the fact that it, along with South Africa, is the world's largest producers of gold.

residual cyanide and mercury. These tailings can stay toxic for centuries" (Rastogi, 2010, p. 1).

Specifically to the Ahofa mine, Newmont planned for cyanide to be discharged into specifically made tailing ponds (where the material that is left over once the ore has been processed is held) without a cyanide kill process, thus allowing residual cyanide at levels above water quality. As a result, seepage into groundwater occurs. While claiming the process of photo degradation would kill the cyanide, they failed to acknowledge that this form of degradation is only effective at or near the surface of the pond. The waste rock facilities were constructed with low permeability materials (Levit and Chambers, 2005) and the use and diversion of water storage dams has resulted in a loss for the surrounding indigenous population and the natural flow of the ecological order. As noted in the environmental assessment by the Center for Science and Public Participation, "water withdrawal for mine activities is discussed primarily in terms of water needed by the mine for its operations ... [not] the impact of withdrawal on natural resources and non-mine consumptive uses (such as drinking water, agriculture, etc.)" (Levit and Chambers, 2005, p. 18).

Over the course of the past seven years, since the initial onset of the first mine development process began, the mine has had two known cyanide leaks, with the largest occurring in October 2009, causing mass environmental harms by poisoning local water supplies and killing scores of fish (No Dirty Gold, 2010). There have been two floods that occurred from the Control Dam 2 (ECD 2), one in September 2007 that was the result of the spillway being opened and the other in July 2010. The sewage disposal at the Newmont operation has also been a concern because of the overflow of sewage into a stream and river, causing pollution in the River Subri, affecting the communities of Ahunukrom, Kwaku Addaikrom, Akorongo, and Kwameduanekrom as well as the general ecological system.

Despite this, Newmont continues to expand with additional mines in Ghana, namely the Akyem project that is centrally located in a forest reserve in the Birim North District of the Eastern Region of Ghana. The mine, when complete, will destroy roughly "340 acres of tropical forest along with a fourth of the forest left in the Ajenjua Bepo Forest Reserve" (Cardhoff, 2011, p. 1). Given the location, the potential for environmental harms that often result from mines – acid drainage, water contamination with heavy metals and cyanide that can leak, and the impact on the local and global biodiversity – raises serious concerns about the commitment to the environment over profit and free markets.

Although we have discussed the environmental (potential and real) impact and harms related to Newmont's mining projects, we point out that this is not specific to one corporation; it is an endemic problem that extends to all open-pit mining projects.

Consider the Tarkwa gold mine in the Wassa West District of Ghana, funded by the IFC and operated by Gold Fields Ghana, where another large environmental disaster occurred when large amounts of mine waste went into the Asuman River (2003), contaminating it with cyanide and other heavy metals (see also Rothe and Friedrichs, 2014). In this case, nearly all forms of life in the river and its branches died, including local birds that drank from the water. Further, these instances of spills leave residue that could potentially remain for decades, posing long-term environmental and health issues. These are but a few of the numerous examples of environmental harms as a result of mining projects funded and promoted by the IFC in Ghana. Consider the total gold extraction that has occurred over the course of the past nearly three decades:[3]

Gold thousand ounces	1985	1990	1995	2000	2001
	300	541	1,709	2,315	2,336

These numbers now stand at:

Gold million ounces	2010	2011	2012
	2.97	3.6	4.2

5 Summary

As evidenced by Appendix A, these projects and subsequent harms are not limited to Ghana; they stretch across the globe, predominantly in the least economically and politically empowered countries in relation to those that hold the greatest stake and power in IFIs. So why, given the environmental impact, do IFIs continue to promote and finance open-pit mining? The following section provides a theoretically driven discussion in an effort to shed some light on the contradiction posed by the stated goal of supporting only those environmentally sustainable projects that lead to eradication of poverty versus the social, economic, and environmental harms caused by the mining industry in collaboration with IFIs.

6 Discussion

The importance of the economy cannot be overstated in the context of addressing crimes of globalization. The earliest version of political economy theory emphasized the relation between the economic system of production with the government and law. This was later revised and expanded to include the international political economy (and international relations). The emphasis here, while broadened, remains on the relations between economic systems and politics within a country and between countries (Underhill, 2000). Specifically, the concern is with the ways political forces, including those of IFIs, shape broader systems through

---

3 Sources: World Bank Operations Evaluation Department (2003) for data in the first box and Modern Ghana (2013) for the current data in the latter box.

economic interactions and how the economy interacts with these political structures (IFIs in the case at hand) (Oatley, 2010). Given the emphasis on the relationship between politics and the economy, one should consider that the global paradigm that is embedded in the ideology that private sector-led development and open markets are the engine of economic recovery in developing countries undergirds IFIs' practices, policies, and organizational culture (as will be discussed more fully below). Additionally, the World Bank Group and the IMF operate under the marked political influence of certain countries, the holders of the majority votes. This is true for the IFC as well where the political decision-making or approving the funding of various projects is based on votes per stocks held, including veto rights (see Table 6.1).

States' influences and pressures play a role in motivating IFIs to continue to push, promote, and finance resource extraction at the behest of corporate and state interests.

Moreover, states' priorities are directed towards private ownership policies for companies within their own territory. As previously pointed out, "[p]olitics has always influenced the advice offered by the IMF and World Bank ... World Bank projects are sometimes covertly shaped by pre-existing agreements for contracts between large companies backed by powerful governments and borrowers" (Woods, 2006). As noted by Mackenzie (2006, p. 168):

> [T]he relationship between favorable outcomes for financiers and corporations in developed nations is not a case of simple string pulling in respect of puppet institutions. There is some level of influence that may be characterized as fairly direct: corporate lobbying, the bare threats and other less obvious coercive political tactics employed by developed nations in negotiations, and at root the power of veto given to the U.S. in relation to the IMF and the World Bank.

Given the dialectic and mutual relationship between the major powers and IFIs, such political pressure can easily translate into decision-making not in the interest of indigenous populations, host countries, or the environment (Rothe, 2010a, 2010b, 2010c; Rothe and Friedrichs, 2014).

Consider also the connection between IFIs and the United Nations Framework Convention on Climate Change that established the Green Climate Fund (hereafter referred to as the Fund) in 2010 and the potential impact on resource extraction and environmental harms. The Fund was created to promote low-emission, climate-resilient development projects. The World Bank is heavily intertwined with the Fund in that it is the interim trustee, managing the Fund's financial assets, and is being considered the long-term trustee, accredited with being the implanting entity of the Fund. That would mean it would determine the allocation of resources and activities. Even at the initial stages of the Fund development, the World Bank Group staff has played a central role in guiding the decisions the Fund board should make and the structure of votes allocated. As

Table 6.1 Subscriptions to capital stock of the International Finance Corporation

Country	Number of shares	Amount (in United States dollars)
Australia	2,215	2,215,000
Austria	554	554,000
Belgium	2,492	2,492,000
Bolivia	78	78,000
Brazil	1,163	1,163,000
Burma	166	166,000
Canada	3,600	3,600,000
Ceylon	166	166,000
Chile	388	388,000
China	6,646	6,646,000
Colombia	388	388,000
Costa Rica	22	22,000
Cuba	388	388,000
Denmark	753	753,000
Dominican Republic	22	22,000
Ecuador	35	35,000
Egypt	590	590,000
El Salvador	11	11,000
Ethiopia	33	33,000
Finland	421	421,000
France	5,815	5,815,000
Germany	3,655	3,655,000
Greece	277	277,000
Guatemala	22	22,000
Haiti	22	22,000
Honduras	11	11,000
Iceland	11	11,000
India	4,431	4,431,000
Indonesia	1,218	1,218,000
Iran	372	372,000
Iraq	67	67,000
Israel	50	50,000

Country	Number of shares	Amount (in United States dollars)
Italy	1,994	1,994,000
Japan	2,769	2,769,000
Jordan	33	33,000
Lebanon	50	50,000
Luxembourg	111	111,000
Mexico	720	720,000
Netherlands	3,046	3,046,000
Nicaragua	9	9,000
Norway	554	554,000
Pakistan	1,108	1,108,000
Panama	2	2,000
Paraguay	16	16,000
Peru	194	194,000
Philippines	166	166,000
Sweden	1,108	1,108,000
Syria	72	72,000
Thailand	139	139,000
Turkey	476	476,000
Union of South Africa	1,108	1,108,000
United Kingdom	14,400	14,400,000
United States	35,168	35,168,000
Uruguay	116	116,000
Venezuela	116	116,000
Yugoslavia	443	443,000
Total	100,000	100,000,000

Source: International Finance Corporation, 2012c.

stated by Lidy Nacpil (cited in Osuna, 2013, p. 3), the regional coordinator of the Jubilee South Asia-Pacific Movement on Debt and Development:

> The World Bank has been at the forefront of financing fossil-fuel projects that have exacerbated the climate crisis. It is now an ironic contradiction that this same institution that has greatly contributed to the climate crisis is to be entrusted with funds that promise to address the very same problem it helped to create in the first place.

Profit remains a highly motivating factor, for IFIs, the IFC in particular, as well as for the major "donors" and their multinational, transnational corporations. This becomes an important factor in the pressures and pulls for goal attainment as increased levels of income provide motivation to continue lending practices as it is profitable and with little to no risk for the stakeholders. As we noted previously, the culture of an organization has an impact on individual-level decision-making and organizational policies (organizational theory) (see also Rothe and Friedrichs, 2013; Friedrichs and Rothe, 2012). Once an organizational culture exists, it becomes institutionalized, making it far more difficult to alter shy of a major institutional transformation. As organizational theorists point out, organizational cultures and goals remain intact even as employees are replaced. This is of particular importance as the organizational goals of the global directive of the IFC is to "reduce poverty and improve people's lives" (Sarin et al., 2006, p. 1). There appears, however, to be a considerable disjuncture between the benefits of IFC investment in gold mining as conceptualized by the IFC and the reality experienced by the communities affected.

The IFC argues that continued investment in gold mining produces government revenues, and it is these revenues that lead to "economic growth and poverty reduction" (Sarin et al., 2006, p. 2). This is accomplished through job creation, social investment from corporations in the communities impacted by the mining, and general improvements in the way the private sector conducts business. These benefits are touted as being "spillover 'development' benefits from mining" (Sarin et al., 2006, p. 2). These benefits are then supported by an annual report from the IFC providing aggregate data on their overall contribution to development (International Finance Corporation, 2012a). The data presented in these reports indicate that the IFC-supported mining is quite successful. For example, in their 2005 Annual Report on Oil, Gas and Mining, the IFC reported a 122 percent return on its investment in oil, gas, and mining, accounting for 7.4 percent of the institution's total net financial portfolio (International Finance Corporation, 2005). However, these same reports do not provide project-level data, so it is impossible to accurately assess the actual impact of each of the IFC's investments, and there is no way to determine how each project has affected communities, the environment, and poverty reduction, as none of these factors can be fiscally averaged annually (Sarin et al., 2006).

Furthering the disjuncture between the institutional goal of the IFC and the realities of gold mining are some of the institution's own reports on the effects of mining. For example, consider the previously mentioned IFC-approved loan of $125 million to mining company Newmont Mining Corporation for use at the Ahafo gold mine in Ghana. The initial displacement of over 10,000 people was not addressed by the IFC and long-term solutions were not provided to the communities impacted. Additionally, little was done by either the private sector involved in the project or the IFC to address the loss and damage to the land suffered by the local community, or the loss of livelihood as experienced by those who were displaced and the environmental damage committed (Sarin et al., 2006).

Furthermore, in a report by the World Bank's independent evaluation unit, the gain to Ghana from the IFC mining project was directly questioned, as "the costs to local communities often exceeded the benefits they receive[d]" (World Bank Operations Evaluation Department, 2003). Although this report argued that the mining had increased income disparities by increasing the economic burden on the poor and unemployed in the mining areas (World Bank Operations Evaluation Department, 2003), the language of the IFC relating to the project's success was vastly different. The IFC reported that, based on "attracting private capital and strengthening sector management capabilities" (Liebenthal, Michelitsch, and Tarazona, 2005, p. 68), as well as "improving environmental awareness" (Liebenthal et al., 2005, p. 70), the project was a substantial success. It appears that the global discourse of development masks the dominant motivator for these projects, that of profit for investors, and ironically it is this same factor (profit) that is being used to measure project success.

Factors noted above come into contradiction with external pressures for IFIs to pay particular attention to the issue of environmental sustainability in its "journey" to eradicate poverty. This results in both real and symbolic efforts while simultaneously safeguarding the organizational goals and ideologies that undergird its actions.

One cannot dismiss two other aspects driving IFIs' support for resource extraction at the expense of the environment: states' monetary systems that are based on gold and "us," the consumers. In the later part of the nineteenth century, the growth of a culture of consumerism orientated the markets towards mass marketing and the consumption of goods. Due to the surplus production of goods resulting from the rise of a global capitalist economy, there has been a change in culture towards consumerism for the purposes of increasing consumption. This has transformed goods previously considered luxuries into necessities that have been available to more and more people (Robbins, 2010). In the US, as well as other places in the world, this has created an ideology of consumerism that dominates all aspects of people's lives, including defining who they are through the provision of social definitions of worth and success (Shah, 2003). As a consequence, certain items have become associated with status and worth, such as expensive cars, brand-name clothing, and jewelry (Robbins, 2010), including gold.

Recent statistics from the World Gold Council indicated that the demand for gold for jewelry was up 12 percent for the first fiscal quarter of 2013 (January–March). The total worth of the gold provided for jewelry totaled US$28.9 billion, setting a record high (World Gold Council, 2013a). The World Gold Council also reports that there are three dominant markets for gold jewelry: India, China, and the US. The US gold jewelry market is dominated by "gifting" with 77 percent of brides accepting a marriage proposal with gold jewelry (World Gold Council, 2013b). The dominant justification for the continued mining for gold is the notion that there is a need to keep up with market demand (Blumen, 2009). This, however, is untrue as approximately 50 to 100 times the amount of gold produced through mining is kept in stockpiles – 52 percent of which is held as jewelry. One of the reasons for the stockpiles is that gold is considered to be both a monetary asset and a commodity. For the most part, gold cannot be destroyed, meaning that all of the gold that has been mined still exists in some form across the globe and theoretically at any time these stockpiles can be mobilized (World Gold Council, 2016).

All of the broader structural conditions noted above, coupled with the organizational ideology, goals, and structure, come together to produce a criminogenic environment where crimes of globalization can flourish, including that of environmental degradations.

7 Concluding discussion

We began this chapter by attempting to situate crimes of globalization with environmental crimes by drawing on the examples of IFI promotion and support for resource extraction. Namely, our focus has been on open-pit gold mining that has caused and continues to cause significant social, economic, and environmental harm while claiming to be environmentally sensitive and supporting sustainable development. We have highlighted how the broader political economy and neo-liberal economic agenda has been the driving force behind the escalation and continuation of open-pit mining. However, we also noted that the demand for gold (and other natural resources) by governments and general consumers continues to support the broader economic drives, reifying rather than contesting IFIs' (and, in particular, the IFC's) policies. Given the push of IFIs for resource extraction, environmental crimes of this magnitude will continue while states, corporations, and general consumers of the product benefit at the cost of the environment and the most vulnerable populations. This will have long-term effects and costs, while few profit at the expense of the environment and of the continuation of the subjugation of the most vulnerable populations.

A broader acknowledgement by civil society members, non-governmental organizations, and scholars of the issues and problems related to international financial institutions policies and practices can be seen as a move forward. However, the needed changes within the organizational structures of these institutions that drive the motivational forces and policies linked to these environmental crimes are not likely to occur without a broader shift in the current neo-liberal ideology that undergirds the culture and practices of the international financial institutions. Such a shift would need to include the general consumer population's awareness of their fetishisms for these natural resources as well as a shift of prioritization of products and purchases. Additionally, with the strong discourse of "development" and "poverty reduction" that "legitimizes" IFI support and funding of projects that result in massive environmental harms, an additional challenge emerges: deconstructing the discourse used to justify these crimes of globalization.

These are significant challenges when we think in terms of policy to address this critical but under-examined area of crimes of globalization – the role of IFIs and environmental crimes. While it may seem futile or utopic to consider a potential global change where neo-liberal agendas do not dictate the policies of the IFIs and where "true" sustainable projects aimed at improving local populations' lives and ending starvation and lack of healthcare are prioritized, it is a necessary conversation.

Bibliography

Bello, W.F., Cunningham, S., and Rau, B. (1999). *Dark Victory: The United States and Global Poverty*. Oakland, CA: Pluto Press.

Blumen, R. (2009, 14 August). Does gold mining matter? *Ludwig von Mises Institute*. Available at http://mises.org/daily/3593 (accessed January 13, 2017).

Cain, M. (2010). Crimes of the global state. In F. Brookman, M. Maguire, H. Pierpoint, and T. Bennett (eds), *Handbook on Crime* (pp. 801–824). Portland, OR: Willan Publishing.

Cardhoff, S. (2011, 24 March). Newmont planning to advance Akyem mine project in Ghana Forest Reserve. Earthworks. Available at www.earthworksaction.org/earthblog/detail/newmont_planning_to_advance_akyem_mine_project_in_ghana_forest_reserve#.UdrHMvXD9D9 (accessed January 13, 2017).

Davenport, J. (2011, 9 February). IFC earmarks $300m for African mining investments over 3 yrs. *Mining Weekly Online*. Available at www.miningweekly.com/print-version/ifc-earmarks-300m-for-african-mining-investments-over-3-yrs-2011-02-09 (accessed January 13, 2017).

Downey, L., Bonds, E., and Clark, K. (2010). Natural resource extraction, armed violence, and environmental degradation. *Organization and Environment*, 23, 417–445.

Environmental Law Alliance. (2010). *Guidebook for Evaluating Mining Projects EIA*, Eugene, OR: Environmental Law Alliance Worldwide.

Extractive Industries Transparency Initiative. (2013, 1 July). EITI reports, EITI: Extractive Industries Transparency Initiative. Available at http://eiti.org/countries (accessed January 13, 2017).

Ezeonu, I. (2008). Crimes of globalization: Health care, HIV and the poverty of neoliberalism in Sub-Saharan Africa. *International Journal of Social Inquiry*, 1, 113–134.

Ezeonu, I., and Koku, E. (2008). Crimes of globalization: The feminization of HIV pandemic in Sub-Saharan Africa. *The Global South*, 2, 112–129.

Friedrichs, D., and Friedrichs, J. (2002). The World Bank and crimes of globalization: A case study. *Social Justice*, 29, 3–36.

Friedrichs, D., and Rothe, D.L. (2012). Crimes of globalization as a criminological project: The case of international financial institutions. In F. Packes (ed.), *Globalization and the Challenge to Criminology* (pp. 45–63). London: Routledge.

International Finance Corporation. (2005). *IFC, Annual Portfolio Performance Review – FY 05*. Washington, DC: The World Bank.

International Finance Corporation. (2012a). *Annual Report 2012*. Washington, DC: International Finance Corporation. Available at www.ifc.org/wps/wcm/connect/2be4ef804cacfc298e39cff81ee631cc/AR2012_Report_English.pdf?MOD=AJPERES (accessed January 13, 2017).

International Finance Corporation. (2012b). Environmental and social review summary. *International Finance Corporation*, July 1, 2013. Previously available at http://ifcext.ifc.org/ifcext/spiwebsite1.nsf/ProjectDisplay/ESRS29007.

International Finance Corporation. (2012c). *Articles of Agreement (As Amended through June 27, 2012)*. Washington, DC: International Finance Corporation.
International Finance Corporation. (2013a, 30 May). IFC makes its first investment in Dominican Republic mining sector through Unigold. *Yahoo! Finance*. Previously available at http://finance.yahoo.com/news/ifc-makes-first-investment-dominican-130000446.html.
International Finance Corporation. (2013b). *IFC Global Mining*. International Finance Corporation, July 1, 2013, Available at www.ifc.org/wps/wcm/connect/434c0a0049a5f8cda3d0e3a8c6a8312a/IFC+Mining+Overview.pdf?MOD=AJPERES (accessed January 13, 2017).
Kapstein, E., and Kim, R. (2011). *The Socio-Economic Impact of Newmont Ghana Gold Limited*. Haarlem: Stratcomm Africa.
Levit, S.M., and Chambers, D. (2005). *Environmental and Social Impact Assessment: Ahafo South Project*. Bozeman, MT: Center for Science in Public Participation.
Liebenthal, A., Michelitsch, R., and Tarazona, E. (2005). *Extractive Industries and Sustainable Development: An Evaluation of World Bank Group Experience*. Washington, DC: The World Bank.
Mackenzie, S. (2006). Systematic crimes of the powerful: Criminal aspects of the global economy. *Social Justice*, 33, 162–182.
Modern Ghana. (2013, 26 March). Ghana gold production climbs 17% in 2012. *MG Modern Ghana*. Available at www.modernghana.com/news/454977/1/ghana-gold-production-climbs-17-in-2012.html (accessed January 13, 2017).
Newmont. (2013). Beyond the mine: The journey towards sustainability. Newmont Mining Corporation, July 1, 2013. Available at http://sustainabilityreport.newmont.com/2014/overview/documents.php (accessed February 3, 2017).
No Dirty Gold. (2010). Wassa District Ghana: Ahafo Mine. Nodirtygold.org, January 21, 2010. Available at www.nodirtygold.org/wassa_district_ghana.cfm (accessed January 13, 2017).
Oatley, T. (2010). Political institutions and foreign debt in the developing world. *International Studies Quarterly*, 54, 175–195. Available at http://ghanaweb.com/mobile/wap.small/news.article.php?ID=197006 (accessed January 13, 2017).
Osuna, A.R. (2013). The World Bank and the Green Climate Fund: "An ironic contradiction"? Bretton Woods Project, June 20, 2013. Available at www.brettonwoodsproject.org/art-572645 (accessed January 13, 2017).
Owusu-Koranteng, D. (2010, 8 November). 15 killed in course of Newmont Ahafo Mine operations. Available at www.ghanaweb.com/GhanaHomePage/NewsArchive/15-killed-in-course-of-Newmont-Ahafo-Mine-operations-197006 (accessed February 3, 2017).
Rastogi, N.S. (2010, 21 September). Production of gold has many negative environmental effects. *The Washington Post*. Available at www.washingtonpost.com/wp-dyn/content/article/2010/09/20/AR2010092004730.html (accessed January 13, 2017).
Rice, J.T. (2009). The transnational organization of production and uneven environmental degradation and change in the world economy. *International Journal of Comparative Sociology*, 50, 215–236.
Robbins, R. (2010). *Global Problems and the Culture of Capitalism*. New York, NY: Pearson.
Rothe, D.L. (2010a). Facilitating corruption and human rights violations: The role of international financial institutions. *Crime, Law and Social Change*, 53, 457–476.
Rothe, D.L. (2010b). Dragon rising: The international financial institutions and China's aid policy on weakened states. In W. Chambliss, R. Michalowski, and R. Kramer (eds), *State Crime in a Globalized Age* (pp. 152–169). Cullompton: Willan Press.
Rothe, D.L. (2010c). International financial institutions, corruption and human rights. In M. Boersma and H. Nelen (eds), *Corruption and Human Rights* (pp. 177–197). Antwerp: Intersentia.

Rothe, D.L. and Friedrichs, D. (2013). Controlling crimes of globalization: A challenge for international criminal justice. In W. de Lint, M. Marmo, and N. Chazal (eds), *Crime and Justice in International Society* (pp. 246–266). London: Routledge.

Rothe, D.L. and Friedrichs, D. (2014). *Crimes of Globalization*. Abingdon: Routledge.

Rothe, D.L., Mullins, C.W., and Sandstrom, K. (2009). The Rwandan Genocide: International finance policies and human rights. *Social Justice*, 35, 66–86.

Rothe, D.L., Muzzatti, S., and Mullins, C.W. (2006). Crime on the High Seas: Crimes of globalization and the sinking of the Senegalese ferry Le Joola. *Critical Criminology: an International Journal*, 14, 159–180.

Safe Drinking Water Foundation. (2013). Mining and water pollution. Safewater.org, July 1, 2014. Available at www.safewater.org/PDFS/resourcesknowthefacts/Mining+and+Water+Pollution.pdf (accessed January 13, 2017).

Sarin, R., Relsch, N., Kalafut, J., and Slack, K. (2006). The World Bank Group's gold mining operations: Tarnished gold: Mining and the unmet promise of development, September 2006. Available at www.earthworksaction.org/files/publications/Tarnished Gold.pdf (accessed January 13, 2017).

Sawyer, S., and Gomez, E.T. (2008). Transnational governmentality and resource extraction: Indigenous peoples, multinational corporations, multilateral institutions and the state. Identities Conflict and Cohesion, Programme Paper 13, United Nations Research Institute for Development.

Shah, A. (2003, 14 May). Creating the consumer. Global Issues: Social, Political, Economic and Environmental Issues That Affect Us All. Available at www.globalissues.org/article/236/creating-the-consumer (accessed January 13, 2017).

Stanley, E. (2009). *Torture, Truth and Justice: The Case of Timor-Leste*. New York, NY: Routledge.

Underhill, G.R.D. (2000). State, market, and global political economy. *International Affairs*, 76, 805–824.

Wallach, L., and Woodall, P. (2004). *Whose Trade Organization: A Comprehensive Guide to the WTO*. New York, NY: New Press.

White, R. (2003). Environmental issues and the criminological imagination. *Theoretical Criminology*, 7, 483–506.

White, R. (2010). Globalisation and environmental harm. In R. White (ed.), *Global Environmental Crime: Criminological Perspectives* (pp. 20–36). Portland, OR: Willan Publishing.

Woods, N. (2006). *The Globalizers in Search of a Future: Four Reasons Why the IMF and World Bank Must Change, and Four Ways They Can*. Washington, DC: Center for Global Development.

World Bank Operations Evaluation Department. (2003). *Evaluation of the World Bank Group's Activities in the Extractive Industries: Background Paper, Ghana Case Study*. Washington, DC: The World Bank.

World Gold Council. (2013a). Investment: Demand and supply statistics. World Gold Council, July 1, 2013. Available at www.gold.org/investment/statistics/demand_and_supply_statistics (accessed January 13, 2017).

World Gold Council. (2013b). Jewelry. World Gold Council, July 1, 2013. Available at www.gold.org/jewellery/markets/us (accessed January 13, 2017).

World Gold Council. (2016). Gold supply. Available at www.gold.org/supply-and-demand/supply (accessed February 3, 2017).

Wright, W., and Muzzatti, S. (2007). Not in my port: The "death ship" of sheep and crimes of agri-food globalization. *Agriculture and Human Values*, 24, 135–144.

Appendix A

Table 6.2 Countries included in the World Bank extraction industry transparency initiative reports

Country name	Years covered	Sectors covered
Afghanistan	2008	Mining
Afghanistan	2009	Mining
Afghanistan	2010	Mining
Albania	2009	Oil, Mining
Albania	2010	Oil, Gas, Mining
Azerbaijan	2003	Oil, Gas
Azerbaijan	2004	Oil, Gas
Azerbaijan	2005	Oil, Gas
Azerbaijan	2006	Oil, Gas
Azerbaijan	2007	Oil, Gas
Azerbaijan	2008	Oil, Gas
Azerbaijan	2009	Oil, Gas, Mining
Azerbaijan	2010	Oil, Gas, Mining
Azerbaijan	2011	Oil, Gas, Mining
Burkina Faso	2008	Mining
Burkina Faso	2009	Mining
Burkina Faso	2010	Mining
Cameroon	2001	Oil, Gas
Cameroon	2002	Oil, Gas
Cameroon	2003	Oil, Gas
Cameroon	2004	Oil, Gas
Cameroon	2005	Oil, Gas
Cameroon	2006	Oil, Gas, Mining
Cameroon	2007	Oil, Gas, Mining
Cameroon	2008	Oil, Gas, Mining
Cameroon	2009	Oil, Mining
Cameroon	2010	Oil, Mining
Central African Republic	2006	Mining
Central African Republic	2007	Mining
Central African Republic	2008	Mining
Central African Republic	2009	Mining
Central African Republic	2010	Mining
Chad	2007	Oil, Gas, Mining
Chad	2008	Oil, Gas, Mining
Chad	2009	Oil, Gas, Mining

Table 6.2 (continued)

Country name	Years covered	Sectors covered
Chad	2010	Oil, Gas, Mining
Chad	2011	Oil, Gas, Mining
Côte d'Ivoire	2006	Oil, Gas
Côte d'Ivoire	2007	Oil, Gas
Côte d'Ivoire	2008	Oil, Gas, Mining
Côte d'Ivoire	2009	Oil, Gas, Mining
Côte d'Ivoire	2010	Oil, Gas, Mining
Côte d'Ivoire	2011	Oil, Gas, Mining
Democratic Republic of Congo	2007	Oil, Gas, Mining
Democratic Republic of Congo	2008	Oil, Gas, Mining
Democratic Republic of Congo	2009	Oil, Gas, Mining
Democratic Republic of Congo	2010	Mining, Oil, Gas
Gabon	2004	Oil, Gas
Gabon	2005	Oil, Gas, Mining
Gabon	2006	Oil, Gas
Gabon	2007	Oil, Gas
Gabon	2008	Oil, Mining
Gabon	2009	Oil, Gas, Mining
Gabon	2010	Oil, Gas, Mining
Ghana	2004	Mining
Ghana	2005	Mining
Ghana	2006	Mining
Ghana	2007	Mining
Ghana	2008	Mining
Ghana	2009	Mining
Ghana	2010	Mining, Oil, Gas
Ghana	2011	Mining, Oil, Gas
Guinea	2005	Mining
Guinea	2006	Mining
Guinea	2007	Mining
Guinea	2008	Mining
Guinea	2009	Mining
Guinea	2010	Mining
Indonesia	2009	Oil, Gas, Mining, Other
Iraq	2009	Oil
Iraq	2010	Oil, Gas
Kazakhstan	2005	Oil

Country name	Years covered	Sectors covered
Kazakhstan	2006	Oil, Gas, Mining
Kazakhstan	2007	Oil, Gas, Mining
Kazakhstan	2008	Oil, Gas, Mining
Kazakhstan	2009	Oil, Gas, Mining
Kazakhstan	2010	Oil, Gas, Mining
Kazakhstan	2011	Oil, Gas, Mining
Kyrgyz Republic	2004	Mining
Kyrgyz Republic	2005	Mining
Kyrgyz Republic	2006	Mining
Kyrgyz Republic	2007	Mining
Kyrgyz Republic	2008	Mining
Kyrgyz Republic	2009	Mining
Kyrgyz Republic	2010	Mining, Oil, Gas
Kyrgyz Republic	2011	Mining, Oil, Gas
Liberia	2008	Oil, Mining, Other
Liberia	2009	Oil, Mining, Other
Liberia	2010	Oil, Mining, Other
Liberia	2011	Oil, Gas, Mining, Other
Madagascar	2007	Mining
Madagascar	2008	Mining
Madagascar	2009	Mining
Madagascar	2010	Oil, Gas, Mining
Mali	2006	Mining
Mali	2007	Mining
Mali	2008	Mining
Mali	2009	Mining, Oil
Mali	2010	Mining
Mauritania	2005	Oil, Mining
Mauritania	2006	Oil, Mining
Mauritania	2007	Oil, Mining
Mauritania	2008	Oil, Mining
Mauritania	2009	Oil, Mining
Mongolia	2006	Mining
Mongolia	2007	Mining
Mongolia	2008	Oil, Mining
Mongolia	2009	Oil, Mining
Mongolia	2010	Oil, Mining
Mongolia	2011	Mining
Mozambique	2008	Gas, Mining

Table 6.2 (continued)

Country name	Years covered	Sectors covered
Mozambique	2009	Oil, Gas, Mining
Mozambique	2010	Oil, Gas, Mining
Niger	2005	Mining
Niger	2006	Mining
Niger	2007	Mining
Niger	2008	Mining
Niger	2009	Mining
Niger	2010	Oil, Gas, Mining
Nigeria	1999	Oil, Gas
Nigeria	2000	Oil, Gas
Nigeria	2001	Oil, Gas
Nigeria	2002	Oil, Gas
Nigeria	2003	Oil, Gas
Nigeria	2004	Oil, Gas
Nigeria	2005	Oil, Gas
Nigeria	2006	Oil, Gas
Nigeria	2007	Oil, Gas
Nigeria	2008	Oil, Gas
Nigeria	2009	Oil, Gas
Nigeria	2010	Oil, Gas
Nigeria	2011	Oil, Gas
Norway	2008	Oil, Gas
Norway	2009	Oil, Gas
Norway	2010	Oil, Gas
Norway	2011	Oil, Gas
Peru	2004	Oil, Gas, Mining
Peru	2005	Oil, Gas, Mining
Peru	2006	Oil, Gas, Mining
Peru	2007	Oil, Gas, Mining
Peru	2008	Oil, Gas, Mining
Peru	2009	Oil, Gas, Mining
Peru	2010	Oil, Gas, Mining
Republic of the Congo	2004	Oil, Gas
Republic of the Congo	2005	Oil, Gas
Republic of the Congo	2006	Oil, Gas
Republic of the Congo	2007	Oil, Gas
Republic of the Congo	2008	Oil, Gas

Country name	Years covered	Sectors covered
Republic of the Congo	2009	Oil, Gas
Republic of the Congo	2010	Oil, Gas
Republic of the Congo	2011	Oil, Gas
Sierra Leone	2006	Mining
Sierra Leone	2007	Mining
Sierra Leone	2008	Mining, Oil, Gas
Sierra Leone	2009	Oil, Gas, Mining
Sierra Leone	2010	Oil, Gas, Mining
Tanzania	2009	Oil, Gas, Mining
Tanzania	2010	Oil, Gas, Mining
Timor-Leste	2008	Oil, Gas
Timor-Leste	2009	Oil, Gas
Timor-Leste	2010	Oil, Gas
Timor-Leste	2011	Oil, Gas
Togo	2010	Mining, Oil, Other
Togo	2011	Mining, Oil, Other
Yemen	2005	Oil, Gas
Yemen	2006	Oil, Gas
Yemen	2007	Oil, Gas
Zambia	2008	Mining
Zambia	2009	Mining
Zambia	2010	Mining

Source: Extractive Industries Transparency Initiative, 2013

Chapter 7

Learning lessons from deepwater disasters: common ground in oil exploration in Brazil and the United States

Daniel Jacobs and Marcelo Varella

1 Introduction

Brazil and the United States – two of the richest, biggest, and most populated countries in the world – share common ground when it comes to oil exploration.[1] Both nations have vast oil reserves, including in deepwater far from their coastlines, that have profound geopolitical implications. In Brazil, the oil might serve as a strong catalyst for economic development. In the United States, the oil has begun to provide long-awaited energy independence and security. In both countries, as in others, the oil presents formidable sustainability challenges.

At present, the U.S. is more advanced than Brazil in both oil exploration and environmental protection. The U.S. oil industry has explored at home and abroad since 1860. Federal law provides a relatively strong framework to guard against pollution. Nonetheless, as the 2010 BP oil disaster in the Gulf of Mexico illustrates, the United States could serve both as a positive and negative model for Brazil (and other countries).

In 2012, Brazil marked its ascension as the sixth largest economy in the world, surpassing the United Kingdom.[2] The country's economic success can be attributed in part to oil exploration. Investment in technology, particularly in national oil production technologies, has created a dynamic economy and increased the number of multinationals interested in oil exploration in Brazil. New discoveries have transformed Brazil from an oil importer to an exporter.

A corresponding commitment to regulating oil exploration and protecting the environment, however, has not occurred in Brazil. The statutory framework remains weak, and is not structured well enough to respond to the risks presented by oil exploitation on the continental shelf.

---

1 Portions of this chapter written by Professor Jacobs have been excerpted and adapted from his book *BP Blowout: Inside the Gulf Oil Disaster* (Washington, DC: Brookings Institution Press, 2016). All rights reserved.
2 Charles Riley, "Brazil's economy tops United Kingdom's," *CNN Money*, March 7, 2012. Available at http://money.cnn.com/2012/03/07/news/economy/brazil-gdp-united-kingdom (accessed January 13, 2017).

No stranger to accidents from oil exploration off its coast, Brazil recently experienced its first major environmental problem with deepwater oil production on the continental shelf. In 2011, an accident at a Chevron drilling platform released thousands of barrels of oil. The Chevron accident, albeit of much smaller scale than the BP accident, highlights weaknesses in the Brazilian legal framework and institutional emergency response capacity – weaknesses that may well remain unresolved in the near future.

Such accidents demonstrate the need for both industrialized countries, such as the U.S., and emerging global economies, such as Brazil, to institute regulatory reforms designed to minimize the likelihood of such events in the future. In emerging economies like Brazil, fast-paced industrialization and technological advances are often not equally matched by corresponding development in the environmental protection legal and regulatory framework. Conversely, countries like the United States, with a longer tradition of environmental regulation, need to ensure that oversight and enforcement are sufficiently rigorous that industry acts more responsibly in the future.

The analysis is divided into two parts. The first part will focus on Brazil's legal framework, describe recent advances in Brazil's offshore oil exploration, and present a foundation for understanding the extent to which such exploration is subject to environmental protection precepts under the Brazilian legal system. We look at the application of Brazilian law to oil exploration on the continental shelf, especially on the pre-salt layer beyond territorial waters. We then use the recent Chevron accident as a case study to illustrate some of the deficiencies in Brazilian environmental protection with regard to oil and gas production.

In the U.S. portion, we take the converse approach – that is, we use a case study, namely the BP oil disaster in the Gulf of Mexico, to examine failures in the U.S. model of offshore oil exploration. We look at the underlying root causes of the disaster, as well as its legal aftermath. In the process, we discuss flaws in American oversight of offshore oil exploration. Drawing on criminological theory, we then examine means to promote greater industry compliance. In particular, we apply the tenets of penology to propose a more rigorous enforcement regime.

With the benefit of the lessons provided by the American experience (and hindsight), Brazil can minimize the chances of a BP-like disaster in its waters. But, it can do more. Brazil has the opportunity to positively influence global norms and institutions through a more proactive and responsible approach to offshore drilling. Whether in the U.S., Brazil, or other countries, we conclude that governments and companies share the responsibility for ensuring better protection of the environment.

2 Oil exploration in Brazil

Brazil launched national oil production in the 1930s. Several foreign companies were allowed by the government to engage in oil exploration. In 1953, the federal government nationalized oil production, excluding all foreign companies and creating state-owned Petróleo do Brasil S.A. (Petrobras). Petrobras eventually become a publicly traded company controlled by the federal government.[3] Following sweeping democratic reforms that began in Brazil in 1989, the administration of President Cardoso reopened national oil exploitation to foreign companies in 1993.[4]

In 2003, after substantial increases in investment, Petrobras and foreign companies discovered new reserves in various parts of the country, predominantly on the continental shelf.[5] These discoveries resulted in rapidly expanded production. In 2006, oil production in Brazil surpassed domestic demand for the first time, and exports could thus increase.[6] In 2015, Brazil exports crude oil and some derivatives, but continues to import gasoline and other oil products.

In 2007, the national landscape of oil development changed profoundly. Petrobras discovered massive oil reserves in the deepwater (pre-salt layer) off its coast.[7] At this point in time, no country had produced oil from such depths (5,000–8,000 meters) below the ocean and 180 miles offshore. The pre-salt oil layer extends about 500 miles from the state of Santa Catarina to the state of Espírito Santo, inside the exclusive economic zone.[8] New finds have been discovered recently throughout the area. More than 35 billion barrels were confirmed in 2015. If estimates of 50–80 billion barrels of oil and gas are confirmed, Brazil will become the sixth largest possessor of oil and gas reserves, after Saudi Arabia, Iran, Iraq, Kuwait, and the EAU.[9]

---

3 Petrobras is one of the oldest state-owned national oil companies worldwide. In August 2000, Petrobras issued US$4.3 billion in an IPO in Brazil and NYSE, not only to institutional investors but also to individuals; more than 400,000 Brazilians and many international investors bought shares. (See Andrea Goldstein, *Universia Business Review* 98 [2010]).

4 Celso Fernando Lucchesi, Petróleo, 12 (33) *Estudos Avançados* 1998, p. 3.

5 See art. 76 of the United Nations Convention on the Law of the Sea, which provides the legal definition of continental shelf and the criteria by which a coastal state may define its outer limits. In particular, pursuant to paragraph 1 of this provision, the continental shelf of a coastal state can be defined as the submerged natural prolongation of the land territory of that state. It comprises the seabed and subsoil of the submarine areas that extend beyond its territorial sea to the outer edge of the continental margin, or to a distance of 200 nautical miles where the outer edge of the continental margin does not extend up to that distance.

6 Alessandra Aloise de Seabra, Gilberto Passos de Freitas, Marcus Polette, Angel del Valls Casillas, A promissoraprovíncia do pré-sal, 7 (1) *RevistaDireito GV* 2 (2011).

7 The pre-salt layer is located on the continental shelves off the coast of Africa and Brazil has approximately 2000–3000 meters depth.

8 Under the United Nations Convention on the Law of the Seas, every coastal country has an Economic Exclusive Zone (EEZ). The EEZ normally includes 200 nautical miles (370 kilometers) from the country's coastal baseline. The domestic territory, where states have legal jurisdiction, goes to 12 nautical miles, but the monopoly on the economic exploitation of the sea and seabed goes far beyond, to 200 nautical miles. Countries can request an extension of the EEZ under some circumstances, according to the United Nations Commission on the Limits of the Continental Shelf (CLCS) rule.

9 www.reuters.com/article/iea-outlook-brazil-idUSL5N0IX3EE20131112 (accessed January 13, 2017).

Various experts have argued that extracting oil from the pre-salt area would be impossible since the costs would be prohibitive and the technology does not yet exist. To make production viable, Petrobras would have to raise more than US $220 billion through an initial public offering (IPO).

Moreover, Brazil had to change its legal frameworks governing oil exploration, both in terms of investment and environmental protection.[10] Until the pre-salt discoveries, Brazil had a favorable legal framework to encourage foreign investment in oil exploitation. Brazil formerly awarded legal concessions to foreign companies for offshore production. Petrobras had opened itself to foreign investment, and around 60% of its capital belonged to foreign investment funds. The Brazilian government decided, in 2010, to recapitalize the enterprise in an open process and expanded its role in administering the process. In exchange for a number of shares, the national government awarded Petrobras the right to extract five billion barrels of oil, which increased the company's market value. It was the largest sell-up in capital markets history, $64.5 billion.[11] Other investors could also buy shares during this process. The Brazilian government shares increased to 47.8% of the total capitalization of the company, giving the government control over company decisions.[12]

Since the pre-salt layer was confirmed as an important reserve, the Brazilian congress has altered the legal framework affecting its exploration. Following greater involvement by the federal government in the company, Petrobras must participate directly in at least 30% of any exploration project. Each and every company (national or foreign) has to create a partnership with Petrobras.[13] The new legal framework increased government royalties on new oil contracts and gave Petrobras a greater role in oil exploitation.

After corruption scandals involving Petrobras and its lack of financial capability to participate in all exploration projects, on November 29, 2016, the Brazilian Congress published a new law (Law no. 13.365) to provide Petrobras with the preemptive right to behave as an operator and hold a minimum interest of 30 percent in the consortiums formed for the exploration of blocks tendered under the production sharing regime, but not as an obligation to participate.

The Brazilian government created a national fund financed by royalties and other profits from oil to promote investments mainly in education but also in environmental protection, science, and technology throughout the country. Royalties go directly to a national fund for long-term investment in these areas and it is forbidden to employ these financial resources in any other area. There is a general expectation that these resources will be used to combat deforestation and climate change, and ensure the protection of the sea itself.

10 Veja.com. Perguntas e respostas. Pré-sal. Available at http://veja.abril.com.br/ida de/exclusivo/perguntas_respostas/pre-sal (accessed January 13, 2017).
11 See www.reuters.com/article/2010/09/03/us-petrobras-idUSTRE6821FX20100903 (accessed January 13, 2017).
12 See www.investidorpetrobras.com.br/pt/governanca-corporativa/capital-social (accessed January 13, 2017).
13 Brazilian Law 12.351, of December 22, 2010, art. 10, I, c.

The legal framework for all drill sites outside the pre-salt area remained the same. Many foreign companies, including the following, had already initiated production in Brazil, with Petrobras and newly created Brazilian companies: Anadarko, Devon, Exxon-Mobil, BG group, Petrogal, Repsol, Shell, Encana, SK, and UK Gas Company.[14]

Offshore production today represents 94.3% of Brazil's national oil production and 75.8% of national gas production.[15] Foreign enterprises such as Peregrino, Statoil, Ostra, and Shell control some of the most productive drill sites. Petrobras could develop a technology to exploit the pre-salt layer. However, production of pre-salt reserves increased to 600,000 barrels per day, although it is growing faster than all other sources.[16] The massive investments in pre-salt reserves show how important deepwater oil production will become in the next few years. It also portends many challenges.

To sum up, companies are investing very large financial resources, and they are using a technology never used before in the world, in an area outside the criminal jurisdiction of the state, with great potential for environmental impact. At the same time, oil is considered indispensable for the country's development. This formidable scenario underlines the importance of a robust legal framework to avoid serious disasters.

3 The Brazilian model of oil exploration

As noted, Brazil's major investments in offshore oil exploration in the pre-salt area mobilized domestic actors as well as global corporations. The legal and institutional frameworks governing oil production, however, remained largely static.

The main legal instrument for oil exploitation in Brazil is law No. 9,966 of April 28, 2000 (hereinafter "the Brazil Law on Oil"). The law has its origins in the International Convention for the Prevention of Pollution from Ships (MARPOL 73/78);[17] the International Convention on Civil Liability for Oil Pollution Damage of 1969, renewed in 1992; and the International Convention on Oil Pollution Preparedness, Response, and Co-operation of 1995. These documents delineate four levels of risk to marine ecosystems: high, medium, moderate, and low.

Every platform must have the necessary equipment to deal with oil accidents. The specifications of the required equipment depend on a technical study, based on the dimensions and location of the platform, the methods of operational control, the qualifications and number of people, and the time schedule for

---

14 Agência Nacional do Petróleo. Anuário estatístico brasileiro do petróleo, gás natural e biocombustíveis, 2015. Available at www.anp.gov.br/?pg=78136&m=&t1=&t2=&t3=&t4=&ar=&ps=&1449057255726 (accessed January 13, 2017).
15 Ibid.
16 Ibid.
17 *International Convention for the Prevention of Pollution from Ships* (MARPOL 73/78), adopted November 2, 1973, entered into force October 2, 1983. 12, I.L.M. 1319 (1973). The Marpol Convention only entered into force in December, 31, 1985, and it is a combination of the 1973 and 1978 texts.

implementation of the project.[18] The standards set up prohibitions against pollution, reporting requirements, and obligations for public and private companies to institute plans to avoid marine pollution.

Analysis of the engineering aspects of oil exploitation and the safety of operations must be approved by the National Agency for Oil, Gas, and Biofuels (ANP) and carried out prior to implementation. Some aspects are also controlled by the Navy, which must certify the conformity of platforms with respect to navigation safety, storage capacity, and accident prevention.

The Brazilian system is based on a command and control model. It imposes penalties, and government employees control every platform personally. Statutes require that each platform have a plan appropriate to its particular characteristics. Government personnel must control every detail. The Brazilian Institute of Environmental Protection (IBAMA) and the ANP must supply personnel to all sites to oversee all details of extraction and production.

The Brazilian Law on Oil necessitates the publication of a national contingency plan to be negotiated and enacted by ANP in cooperation with environmental agencies. Unfortunately, as of May 2015, after 12 years of deliberation, no plan has yet been approved. Discussions continue, particularly after the BP accident in the Gulf and the Chevron accident in Brazil (both will be discussed later in this chapter), but no law or principles have yet been agreed.[19]

Moreover, Brazil lacks regulations to protect sensitive areas such as high-biodiversity marine ecosystems. Article 28 of the law on oil exploration requires that the government delineate protected areas where oil exploitation, transport, and associated pollution are prohibited. However, the Brazilian government has yet to accomplish these geographic delineations, and after 12 years no process exists to develop regulations for such areas.

The following case study involving Chevron can be viewed as an early warning sign of the vulnerabilities of the Brazilian system.

4 Institutional problems: a case study of Chevron

The Chevron accident occurred 40 miles offshore, outside the Brazil pre-salt area, off the Rio de Janeiro State coast.[20] The well was being drilled at 1,200 meters of water, a depth theoretically more controllable than any at the deeper pre-salt layer. Petrobras reported a large oil release on November 8, 2011, and, using a remotely operated vehicle, discovered seven cracks in the seabed, the largest 1,000 feet long.[21] The total oil spilled was about 4,600 barrels.

18 Art. 5. of the Law 9.966, of 2000.
19 Interview with the Manager of Operational Safety of the Brazilian National Oil and Gas Agency, December 2012.
20 Chevron has a concession on this oil platform with Petrobras (Contract number 48000.003896/97-20).
21 Report of Petrobras, attached to the Case no. 02000.002345/2011-4.

The National Institute for Environmental Protection (analogous to the U.S. Environmental Protection Agency) and the ANP ordered Chevron to immediately begin executing its contingency plan. The plan had been formulated by Chevron and was previously approved by Brazil's national environmental agencies as a prerequisite for obtaining the concession and initiating oil production.[22]

Although Chevron had identified in its contingency plan the equipment it would use to respond to such an event, that equipment was not positioned in Brazil, but rather in the United States, too far away for timely transport to the scene. Consequently, Chevron was unable to control the discharge, which was estimated by IBAMA at 3,000 barrels.[23] In March 2012, Chevron identified the second oil spill two miles far from the first one, and much smaller.[24]

Petrobras was the first to identify the oil spill and start a contingency plan. Since Chevron did not have the equipment, the spill grew larger than it should have. Petrobras spent $748,423 in remedial measures and Chevron spent $173,934,000 to contain the oil.[25] Chevron argued that a single company normally does not have available equipment for its contingency plan on every platform. To reduce costs, it is common to share these facilities with other oil companies in the same area.[26] The authorities judged that the investment in prevention was too low to avoid considerable risks. In 2011, Petrobras, for example, invested only 0.022% of its budget in environment protection and only 0.092% in 2012.[27]

The IBAMA imposed on Chevron a penalty of US$22 million – the maximum penalty under the Brazilian law.[28] The ANP imposed an additional penalty of US $12 million.[29] Chevron appealed the first fine to the Brazilian judiciary, which nullified the penalty, but agreed to pay the second.[30] The two main charges against the company were that it did not possess the equipment required by the contingency plan and that it had edited the images of the cracked seabed obtained by the remote operational vehicle.

22 See above n. 13.
23 See above n. 13.
24 Rio de Janeiro. 20th Division – Environmental and cultural heritage. Conduct adjustment term document among the Federal Prosecution Service and Chevron Brazil Upstream Frade LTDA. Chevron Latin America Marketing Llc and Transocean Brazil Ltda, with the intervention of the National Agency of Petroleum, Natural Gas and Biofuels (ANP) and the Brazilian Institute of Environment and Renewable Natural Resources (IBAMA) (hereinafter TAC – Chevron).
25 Tribunal de Contas da União. TC 037.197/2011-8, p. 13.
26 Ibid.
27 Tribunal de Contas da União. TC 037.197/2011-8, p. 18.
28 http://g1.globo.com/rio-de-janeiro/noticia/2011/11/ibama-multa-chevron-em-r-50-milhoes-por-vazamento-no-rj-diz-minc.html (accessed January 13, 2017). Chevron paid R$42.8566.010 because it anticipated the payment. TAC – Chevron, p. 11.
29 Chevron paid R$25.592.000,00 because it benefited from a discount of 30%, paying the amendment in advance. TAC – Chevron, Para. 10.
30 http://veja.abril.com.br/noticia/economia/chevron-paga-multa-referente-a-vazamento-de-frade (accessed on January 13, 2017).

A few months later, before the investigation came to a close, a second oil leak occurred at the same drill site. As in the first instance, the pressure used in extraction was greater than the seabed soil could support and cracks developed in the soil, allowing oil to escape.

According to a report by IBAMA,[31] the accident was the result of several mistakes made by Chevron: failure to calculate the real conditions of exploitation, imprecise measurements of potential risks, failure of the contingency plan, omission of information, failure to clean the ocean after the oil leak, and failure to control the whole exploitation process. The contingency plan had been formulated on the basis of a much smaller-scale extraction project and was unrealistic for the actual explored site. It seems that the plan was prepared for other areas and reused by Chevron.

A second investigation involving Petrobras and Chevron, carried out by the ANP, concluded that (1) several units in operation had not gone through audits by the Operational Safety Management System (SGSO); (2) no preliminary inspection of the platforms or instruments had been carried out to confirm the existence and the condition of critical elements of safety of the plant at the time of approval of the Operational Safety Documentation (DSO); and (3) the incident investigations did not cover all regulations required, and the results were not widely disseminated as required.[32]

Chevron suspended all its activities in Brazil, and its executives left the country until mid-2012, when the company requested permission to reinitiate extraction activities at the same production site. On April 2013, production restarted; it was intensified in March 2014.[33]

The Federal Prosecutors Office initiated two lawsuits against Chevron and the two companies responsible for platform operations and the contingency plan – Transocean and Halliburton. The first action was for civil damages. The second was for criminal sanctions, requesting $10 billion in damages[34] and the imprisonment of the 17 Chevron employees responsible for the failures leading to the disaster. The Criminal Court of Rio finally rejected the criminal lawsuit on February 20, 2013.

Chevron defended itself on the grounds that the accident had occurred outside Brazilian territory.[35] As determined by the United Nations Convention on the Law of the Seas (UNCLOS), there are three zones with differing legal status: the

---

31 Brazilian National Institute for Environment. Nota Informativa 01//12 CPEG/DILIC/IBAMA. Available at www.mma.gov.br/port/conama/processos/DC218947/Parecer IBAMA.pdf (accessed January 13, 2017).
32 Tribunal de Contas da União. TC 037.197/2011-8, p. 11.
33 www.chevron.com.br/negocios/exploracao-producao-petroleo/campo-frade.aspx (accessed January 13, 2017).
34 The real amount was R$20 billion, approximately US$10 billion in 2013. Petition is available at http://s.conjur.com.br/dl/acao-civil-publica-chevron-mpf.pdf (accessed January 13, 2017).
35 See above n. 19.

territorial ocean, the contiguous zone, and the exclusive economic zone. The territorial ocean starts at the normal shoreline and extends outward 12 nautical miles. The contiguous zone extends to 24 nautical miles. The exclusive economic zone, where most Brazilian oil production occurs, extends 200 nautical miles from shore. In situations in which the continental shelf extends more than 200 nautical miles from shore, the exclusive economic zone extends the same distance, up to 350 nautical miles, though only on the seabed.

Within the exclusive economic zone, a coastal state has the sovereign right to explore and extract natural resources, living or not. It also has jurisdiction to protect and preserve marine environments there.[36] However, there is no criminal competence in the area.

In the Chevron case, the Federal Court of Rio de Janeiro ruled that it lacked jurisdiction because the accident occurred outside Brazilian territory (in the economic zone) and transferred the process to the state justice of Rio de Janeiro. This seems to be one of the major challenges of the exploitation in the pre-salt layer in Brazil. Since the zone lies beyond domestic jurisdiction, Brazil has a monopoly on exploitation, but has no criminal and civil jurisdiction. The Federal Prosecutor's Office appealed this decision.[37]

In September 2013, Chevron entered into an agreement with the Federal Prosecutors Office, IBAMA, and ANP to pay almost US$48 million to invest in preventive and precautionary measures to improve IBAMA monitoring capacity to prevent new oil spills.[38] Chevron compromised in other areas as well: to implement the emergency plan; to maintain two boat facilities to prevent oil spills and other damages, integrated with an automatic infrared maritime system to detect oil on the sea, with ROV images; to install a climate station with wind sensors; and to implement multiple sea sensors with output available to IBAMA. The criminal lawsuit continues independently of this agreement.

The Brazilian Court of Accounts carried out a second audit regarding Petrobras' responsibility for the accident. Petrobras was the subject of an important corruption scandal in 2013, but it had no link with the Chevron accident. Regarding the Chevron oil spill, Petrobras transferred responsibility for oil prospecting to Chevron. According to Brazilian law, Petrobras would be mutually responsible for all damages, independently of fault. However, the joint operating agreement between Petrobras and Chevron states that in case of gross negligence or wilful misconduct, Chevron alone is responsible for the damages. Thus, in the Chevron case, the company accepted that it would pay all fines alone.[39] Nonetheless, the Brazilian Court of Auditors decided that Petrobras should improve its contingency plan as an economic measure since the IBAMA started to close

---

36 See art. 56 of United Nations Convention on the Law of the Sea.
37 There was no decision at the time of writing this chapter. However, the first decision will probably be confirmed.
38 R$95.160.000,00. TAC – Chevron.
39 Tribunal de Contas da União. TC 037.197/2011-8, p. 4–5.

multiple platforms due to lack of safety, an outcome more expensive than implementing safety plans.⁴⁰

5 The BP oil disaster in the Gulf: lessons for Brazil

Like the Chevron accident, the BP accident occurred in deepwater, and was preventable. Both of the accidents can be attributed in part to actions and inactions on the part of the government and the company. On April 20, 2010, an explosion occurred at a BP oil well site known as "Macondo" in the Gulf of Mexico, resulting in 11 deaths, and the subsequent discharge of an estimated 3.2 million barrels of oil. Most of the oil gushed uncontrolled into the Gulf over the course of the next three months, viewable around the world on television via live video feed from the wellhead at some 18,000 feet below the surface of the water.

In his Oval Office address to the nation on June 15, 2010, President Obama described the situation as "the worst environmental disaster America has ever faced."⁴¹ He implicitly put the disaster on the same plane as the fight against terrorism when he alluded to Al-Qaeda, and referred to "the battle we're waging against an oil spill that is assaulting our shores and our citizens."⁴²

As they move towards their shared ambition of becoming one of the largest oil producers in the world, both Brazil *and* Petrobras should take heed of the lessons of the BP disaster and of the government and corporate failures that served as precursors to it.

5.1 The root causes of the disaster

What caused the worst environmental disaster in American history? Human error. BP made a series of blunders that constitute "gross negligence," according to the federal judge that heard the civil case.⁴³

---

40 Testimony of Magda Maria de Regina Cambriard, director of ANP, to the Congress (CPI no. 302, destinada a aputurar irregularidades envolvendo a empresa Petróleo Brasileiro S/A). See also: www19.senado.gov.br/sdleg-getter/public/getDocument?docverid=d85766a1-ffd0-4aa0-9cbd-99a5730e6290;1.0 (accessed January 13, 2017).
41 www.whitehouse.gov/the-press-office/remarks-president-nation-bp-oil-spill (accessed January 13, 2017).
42 Ibid.
43 In re: Oil Spill by the Oil Rig "Deepwater Horizon" in the Gulf of Mexico, on April 20, 2010, This Document Applies To: No. 10-2771, In re: The Complaint and Petition of Triton Asset Leasing GmbH, *et al.* and No. 10-4536, United States of America v. BP Exploration & Production, Inc., *et al.* 21 F. Supp.3d 657, 674 (E.D. La. 2014) [Hereinafter, "Court's Phase I Opinion."]. As used herein, "BP" refers to the company writ large, to include its various corporate forms or "family of companies" as Chief Judge Vance described in her order accepting BP's guilty plea in the criminal case. Reasons for Accepting Plea Agreement, No. 12-292, (E.D. La.) (January 29, 2013). At the civil trial, Lamar McKay, the current worldwide second-in-command of BP, testified that BP has several hundred subsidiaries around the world. Trial Transcript. Day Three, p. 595.

Deepwater drilling is by definition high risk. The deeper water presents higher risk partly because the pressure increases with depth (as any scuba diver would know). And this wasn't just deep water, it was ultra-deep water. The wellhead was one mile below the surface of the ocean, and the bottom of the well was another two miles down.

Despite the inherent danger of this type of offshore drilling, over and over again BP made decisions that made the venture substantially riskier than it had to be. Among the worst of these bad decisions were the following three, covered in detail in an opinion by the federal judge in the civil case against BP: (1) BP cut safety corners in drilling the well, violating federal regulations in the process. (2) After completing the drilling, BP rushed to close the well, making many mistakes in the process. (3) BP ignored final test results showing that the well had not in fact been properly plugged.[44]

1. As the well drilling neared completion at over 18,000 feet, BP decided to go still deeper. The decision to go the last 100 feet, according to a drilling expert who testified at trial, was "one of the most dangerous things [he] had ever seen in [his] 20 years experience" and "totally unsafe."[45]

2. After BP had finished drilling the well (the exploration phase), it set about plugging it temporarily with cement, so that the *Deepwater Horizon* could move to its next job. BP's plan was for another rig to eventually take its place for the lucrative oil production phase. At the point that drilling was complete on April 9, 2010, BP was $60 million over budget and 54 days behind on the well. And, the dollar figure went up by a $1 million each day that the *Deepwater Horizon* remained at the well.[46] Perhaps a drop in the bucket for one of the world's richest companies, which in the first quarter of 2010 reported profit of more than $6 billion.

In a combination of haste, recklessness, and lack of professionalism, BP made major mistakes in plugging the well. The most significant of these seems to have been in using the wrong methods to ensure that the cement was properly applied in all of the right places. As a result, the cement casing essentially had holes in it, through which oil, other fluids, and gas could penetrate. It was only a matter of time before they did.[47]

BP had repeatedly ignored red flags during the cement job. One senior operational manager in Houston had been callously uninterested when alerted to them: "John, I've got to go to dance practice in a few minutes. Let's talk this afternoon," he wrote in an e-mail.[48] That follow-up conversation did not take place.

3. Finally, and perhaps most critically, BP inexplicably ignored all-important well seal test results that came in around 7.55pm. These clearly showed that there

---

44 Court's Phase I Opinion at 674–691.
45 Ibid. at 674.
46 Ibid.
47 Ibid. at 691.
48 Trial transcript, Phase 1, Day 1, p. 76 and Trial Exhibit 1694.

was pressure on the drill pipe, indicating fluids were moving dangerously through the casing. As one expert would later testify, this so-called negative pressure test was a "pass–fail" test, and BP had failed.[49] Nevertheless, BP declared the test and the cement job a success.

Those very test results had been reported in a phone call to the BP senior engineer in Houston. But, incredibly enough, he did not order further troubleshooting and testing despite thinking at one time that the cement design was so poor that it would result in a "shittie" job.[50] BP's Accident Investigation Report conveniently omitted any reference to this critical phone call. The Report also concluded that "[t]he investigation team has found no evidence that the rig crew or well site leaders consulted anyone outside their team about the pressure abnormality," a statement the Court later found to be "patently false."[51]

The Court found that "BP's decision to drill the final 100 feet was the initial link in a chain that concluded with the blowout, explosion, and oil spill," a decision that the Court said "was motivated by profit."[52] The botched cement job was a subsequent link.[53] And the misinterpretation of the negative pressure test was the final link.[54] The Court concluded that BP employees had acted "recklessly" with regard to the negative pressure test, and that BP "had committed a series of negligent acts or omissions" that together constituted "gross negligence" and "wilful misconduct" under the Clean Water Act.[55]

5.2 BP's history

In addition to civil liability for the accident, BP bore criminal responsibility for it. When BP formally entered its guilty plea in the criminal case, history was made in some respects but not others. Corporations are routinely charged with crimes in the United States, including environmental crimes. But it is relatively rare for a company to be charged with a homicide; only in the last few decades have such cases been brought in the U.S.[56]

---

49 Ibid. at 685.
50 Ibid. at 699.
51 Ibid.
52 Ibid. at 674–675.
53 Ibid. at 699.
54 Ibid. at 703.
55 Ibid. at 794–795.
56 As of 2011, only 15 states had prosecuted corporations for manslaughter or criminally negligent homicide. See Note: Corporate Criminal Liability for Homicide: A Statutory Framework, 61 Duke L. J. 123, 133. In one of the first such cases, the State of Indiana prosecuted Ford Motor Company in 1979–80 for reckless homicide after three high school girls died in the fiery inferno that ensued when the 1973 Ford Pinto in which they were traveling was rear-ended on a highway. The indictment charged that Ford had been reckless in delaying the recall of the vehicle, long known to it to have an unsafe fuel tank. See William J. Maakestad, "*State v. Ford Motor Co.:* Constitutional, Utilitarian and Moral Perspectives, 27 St. Louis U. L. J. 857 (1983).

The federal criminal charges brought against BP as a result of the disaster in the Gulf were neither the first environmental crimes to which BP had pled guilty, nor the first time it had been charged criminally for the deaths of workers at one of its facilities. Indeed, during Congressional investigations into the blowout, Congressman (now Senator from Massachusetts) Ed Markey, who chaired a House Subcommittee that investigated the disaster, linked BP's past record to the disaster it caused in the Gulf:

> When the culture of a company favors risk-taking and cutting corners above other concerns, systemic failures like this oil spill disaster result without direct decisions being made or tradeoffs being considered. What is fully evident, from BP's pipeline spill in Alaska and the Texas city refinery disaster, to the Deepwater Horizon well failure, is that BP has a long and sordid history of cutting costs and pushing the limits in search of higher profits.[57]

Similarly, when, in January 2013, Chief U.S. District Judge Sarah Vance in New Orleans accepted BP's record $4 billion guilty plea deal, she expressly noted that "the BP family of companies has a history of deficient safety management."[58] Addressing the record criminal penalty, the judge wrote: "If past is prologue, only a sentence several orders of magnitude more severe than any previously imposed on any BP company will be sufficient to achieve adequate deterrence and protect the public from future misconduct by BP."[59]

Another record was set in early July 2015, when BP entered into a post-trial settlement in principle to resolve its civil liability to the U.S. Government. BP agreed to pay an additional $20 billion.

Given BP's history, does the prospect of even such record high monetary penalties sufficiently deter it (and other oil companies) from irresponsible conduct? This question will be explored in the next section of this chapter.

5.3 Government oversight failures

The BP disaster represents multiple failures in terms of public policy. Central among these was that the oil industry largely controlled its regulator at the Interior Department, the Minerals Management Service (MMS). MMS was created in 1982 under Interior Secretary James Watt not so much with a mandate to regulate offshore drilling as with a mandate to promote it.[60] As history

---

57 www.markey.senate.gov/GlobalWarming/mediacenter/pressreleases_2008_id=0334.html (accessed January 13, 2017).
58 See "Reasons for Accepting Plea Agreement," U.S. v. BP Exploration and Production, Inc., Criminal Action No. 12-292 (E.D. La., 1/29/13) at 5.
59 Ibid. at 6.
60 See Peter Jan Honigsberg, "Conflict of interest that led to the Gulf Oil Disaster," 41 *Environmental Law Reporter* 10414 (2011).

would prove, those objectives do not go hand in hand. Rather, they represent an inherent conflict of interest, as one law professor has observed.[61]

Indeed, the Presidential Commission that investigated the accident concluded that the underlying regulatory structure was fatally flawed:

> Federal efforts to regulate the offshore oil and gas industry have suffered for years from cross-cutting purposes, pressure from political and industry interests, a deepening deficit of technical expertise, and severely inadequate resources available to the government agencies tasked with the leasing function and regulation.[62]

One reason for the regulatory failures, according to the Commission, was what it described as the "dominant role" of the American Petroleum Institute (API), the oil industry's trade and lobby group, in industry standard-setting.[63] In a classic example of what is known in public administration circles as "capture" of the regulator, Interior historically has largely relied on API to make the rules governing the industry.[64] "[T]he inadequacies of the resulting federal standards are evident in the decisions that led to the Macondo well blowout," the Commission concluded.[65]

The limited government oversight of oil exploration can be seen in the paper trail that emerged once the well had blown out. BP's lengthy Initial Exploration Plan for the well was submitted in February 2009. In the section entitled "Blowout Scenario," BP wrote that "A scenario for a potential blowout of the well from which BP would expect to have the highest volume of liquid hydrocarbons is not required for the operations proposed in this EP."[66] It took Interior just six weeks to approve the plan. BP's permit application to actually drill was submitted in March 2009. It took Interior less than four weeks to approve it. These relatively quick turn-around times do not suggest intensive review for a very complicated and potentially dangerous project. On the contrary, MMS granted a "categorical exclusion" to BP for the well. This essentially meant that the agency had waived a full environmental impact assessment of the effect of drilling.

BP's official Oil Spill Response Plan described the various species of wildlife that supposedly could be affected by an accident in the Gulf. Tellingly, some of the species identified in the plan (such as sea lions, sea otters, and walruses) exist

---

61 Ibid.
62 National Commission Report to the President (January 2011) at 1, 250.
63 Ibid.
64 Ibid. at 225.
65 Ibid.
66 BP Exploration and Production, Inc., Initial Exploration Plan, Mississippi Canyon Block 252, February 2009, p. 2-1. Available at www.eenews.net/assets/2010/06/02/document_gw_09.pdf (accessed February 14, 2017).

not in Gulf waters but in Alaskan waters.[67] Interior also gave this flawed plan its usual rubber stamp approval.

What has become clear is that both the regulator and the company were simply going through the motions perpetuating a façade of oversight. Once the well exploded on April 20, 2010, the veneer vanished as millions of barrels of oil hemorrhaged into the sea.

6 Reforming the oil industry and the government

Fatal explosions on oil rigs have continued to occur in the Gulf of Mexico, where oil production is expected to climb to a record of nearly 2 million barrels per day by the end of 2017. In November 2015, the Justice Department brought criminal charges for a 2012 accident off the Louisiana coast that killed three workers. Although the explosions since 2010 thus far have had limited environmental impact, is it only a matter of time before a disaster of BP magnitude strikes again – either in Brazilian or American waters? The best answer is one a good lawyer often gives: "It depends."

In American waters, it depends partly on what the oil industry and government do to change the *status quo* that produced the BP disaster. The consumer protection legend and one-time Presidential candidate Ralph Nader famously declared that automobiles are "unsafe at any speed." Similarly, offshore drilling is inherently risky, and deepwater drilling all the more so. The likelihood of another disaster is directly proportionate to what is done to minimize that risk.

6.1 Industry

Drawing on the lessons of the BP disaster, the Presidential Commission made recommendations for improving the safety of offshore drilling industry-wide. The Commission called for formal industry self-policing, with the creation of a private sector oversight body akin to what exists in the nuclear power industry. The proposal was not adopted. Instead, in 2011, the oil industry founded the Center for Offshore Safety, which seems to function primarily as a virtual informational clearinghouse of sorts, and by all indications is a toothless far cry from what the Commission had in mind.

Although it declined to collaborate on a means of self-governance that could help prevent another incident like the BP blowout, the oil industry has made a significant joint investment (reportedly $1 billion) to ensure that it will not get caught flatfooted if another major accident does happen. Ten major companies are members of the Marine Well Containment Company (MWCC), which is said to be ready with equipment, manpower, and knowhow to address the next catastrophe in the Gulf. MWCC also assists companies in obtaining drilling permits. Another 16 lesser-known companies (that claim to extract half of the oil and gas

---

67 Commission Report (n. 63 above) at 84 (noting this type of cookie-cutter plan was not at all unique to BP).

annually in the Gulf) are members of a similar consortium known as the Helix Well Containment Group (HWCG).

Although not one of the original four founding companies of MWCC, BP is now a member. More importantly perhaps, BP claims to be taking major precautions so that it will not need to call upon MWCC's resources. Timed for effect around the fifth anniversary of the disaster, in spring 2015, BP released a heavily aired TV commercial pitching how it had become a safer company. Like its other advertising, this one featured an actual BP employee. "What happened here five years ago changed us," he proclaims after speaking of toughened safety standards, increased training and monitoring, and greater authority to employees to stop jobs they consider unsafe. "Committed to America and a safer BP," reads the message at the end. Perhaps so. Only time will tell.

6.2 Government

Highlighting the public policy failures of the BP disaster, the Presidential Commission called for sweeping reform of how the federal government regulates the oil industry. The Commission proposed new laws and major bureaucratic changes to improve oversight of offshore drilling. The Commission's recommendations for the Interior Department included creating a new regulatory agency, an entirely new risk management-based approach to regulation, increased expertise, greater reliance on consultants, heightened focus on safety, better reporting, and improved standards.

Given the magnitude of the disaster and the ongoing threat, there has yet to be effective reform, and change has been slow in coming. The MMS has been rebranded into two separate entities: the Bureau of Ocean Energy Management (BOEM) now handles the permitting function and the Bureau of Safety and Environmental Enforcement (BSEE) took on the policing function. However, the reorganization seems to be largely a case of putting old wine into new bottles. For example, the BSEE did not issue new well control regulations until April 2016, six years after the disaster. Those regulations will be phased in over several years. In July 2016, BOEM and BSEE finally announced more stringent safety and environmental regulations for Arctic Ocean drilling.[68]

The Commission, which was disbanded after issuing its official report in January 2011, was so dissatisfied with the lack and pace of reform that its original seven members took it upon themselves to issue additional reports. In April 2012 and 2013, on the second and third anniversaries of the disaster, the former Commissioners assessed the progress made since their January 2011 report.[69] In 2012, they warned:

68 Bureau of Ocean Energy Management, "Interior Issues Final Regulations to Raise Safety & Environmental Standards for Any Future Exploratory Drilling in U.S. Arctic Water," press release July 7, 2106.
69 Oil Spill Commission Action, "Assessing Progress: Implementing the Recommendations of the National Oil Spill Commission" (2012); Oil Spill Commission Action, "Assessing Progress: Three Years Later" (2013) [hereinafter "Assessing Progress"].

The risks will only increase as drilling moves into deeper waters with harsher, less familiar environmental conditions. Delays in taking the necessary precautions threaten new disasters, and their occurrence could, in turn, seriously threaten the nation's energy security.[70]

In each of those years, the former Commissioners were most critical of Congress for failing to enact legislation. In 2012, they gave Congress a "D."[71] In 2013, Congress got a "D+." It seems incapable of overcoming its state of perpetual gridlock, rebuffing the oil industry lobby, and mustering the political will to pass effective new laws.

Notwithstanding its makeover, the Interior Department seemingly remains incapable of playing the role of effective regulator. A 2012 report by the General Accountability Office (GAO), the investigatory wing of the U.S. Congress, which assessed reform in the Interior Department found:

> Interior continues to face challenges following its reorganization that may affect its ability to oversee oil and gas activities in the Gulf of Mexico. Specifically, Interior's capacity to identify and evaluate risk remains limited, raising questions about the effectiveness with which it allocates its oversight resources … It also continues to face workforce planning challenges, including hiring, retaining, and training staff.[72]

A 2016 report by the Chemical Safety Board, a relatively obscure but respected government body that investigated the disaster, also found inadequate regulatory improvements.[73] The Board warned: "[A] culture of minimal regulatory compliance continues to exist in the Gulf of Mexico and risk reduction continues to prove elusive."

Even the head of BSEE, a retired Navy Admiral, agreed. When interviewed shortly after the fifth anniversary of the BP explosion in 2015, he candidly said: "I'm not confident the problem is solved."[74] This comment is especially troubling given the 36% increase in deepwater drilling in the Gulf of Mexico during the preceding four-year period.[75]

70 Assessing Progress, 2102, p. 2.
71 Assessing Progress, 2012, p. 5.
72 U.S. GAO, "Interior's Reorganization Complete, but Challenges Remain in Implementing New Requirements" Report 1-423 (July 2012).
73 U.S. Chemical Safety Board, "The U.S. Chemical Safety Board's Investigation into the Macondo Disaster Finds Offshore Risk Management and Regulatory Oversight Still Inadequate in Gulf of Mexico." April 13, 2016, available at www.csb.gov/the-us-chemical-safety-boards-investigation-into-the-macondo-disaster-finds-offshore-risk-management-and-regulatory-oversight-still-inadequate-in-gulf-of-mexico (accessed January 13, 2017).
74 J. Dlouhy, "Q&A: Top regulator sees offshore safety as a work in progress." *Houston Chronicle*, May 6, 2015.
75 Statement of Abigail Ross Hopper, Director, Bureau of Ocean Energy Management, before the House Committee on Natural Resources, Subcommittee on Energy and Mineral Resources, March 17, 2015.

As these reviews suggest, effective government oversight has yet to occur. And, unfortunately, it is unlikely to materialize even if all of the Commission's well-intended recommendations were to be fully implemented. Although various components of the Interior Department can be reorganized and rebranded to an extent, history has proven that the agency simply cannot be pitted against an industry as powerful as the oil industry.[76] It is a classic David and Goliath mismatch. Moreover, the government and the law routinely have trouble keeping up with technology, and Interior is known as a technological backwater. Relying on the agency to oversee the oil industry is simply a leap of faith, unless it is far better supported by Congress and the Executive.

6.3 Reform

Whether in the United States, in Brazil, or elsewhere, companies should be incentivized to act more responsibly by upping the ante of irresponsible behavior at the corporate level. Mitt Romney, while running for President in 2012, famously declared that corporations are people, a view also recently embraced by the U.S. Supreme Court. Just as people can lose privileges when they abuse them, so should corporations.

Compare, for example, one of the most fundamental privileges that most citizens take for granted: a driver's license. When the privilege to drive is abused, it is terminated, either temporarily or permanently. Indeed, not just drug and alcohol impairment, but even relatively minor motor vehicle offenses such as the failure to pay a ticket can result in the suspension of a license. Or, at a much more serious level, compare the "three strikes" laws in many states. Repeat criminal offenders lose the privilege of living in society – that is, they are imprisoned for life – after having committed three serious felonies.

Why should the privilege of extracting minerals in the ocean be treated any differently? Why not suspend a company's permit to drill for oil when the privilege has been abused, and ultimately revoke it after repeated violations? Permits could be withdrawn for a single well, the leasehold, a particular region, deepwater drilling, or all of a nation's waters.

Permanent revocation could mirror the three-strike laws that apply to serious recidivists. Just as when a common criminal pays the ultimate price (short of death) after three serious felonies, an oil company that has committed three serious environmental felonies should be permanently banned from operating, if not in all of the country's waters, at least in the region where the felonies have occurred.

---

76 The Presidential Commission emphasized that the federal government does not lack authority to regulate oil drilling. Rather: "The root problem has instead been that political leaders within both the Executive Branch and Congress have failed to ensure that agency regulators have had the resources necessary to exercise that authority, including personnel and technical expertise, and, no less important, the political autonomy needed to overcome the powerful commercial interests that have opposed more stringent safety regulation." Commission Report (n. 63 above) at 67.

Such treatment fulfills the three classic purposes of punishment taught in criminological theory: (1) deterrence; (2) incapacitation; and (3) just desserts. To apply the three theories: (1) if a company knew that it could lose its permit to operate if its conduct was sufficiently bad, theoretically, it would have a greater incentive to act responsibly; (2) suspending or revoking a permit is the functional equivalent of incapacitating the company – that is, by removing the threat of future bad conduct; and (3) a company that has acted egregiously in the pursuit of money deserves punishment that deprives it of money.

BP seems to have perceived accidents as a *cost of doing business*. Given its massive profits, that strategy might have made financial sense in all but the worst-case scenarios such as resulted from the blowout in the Gulf. With the recent decline in oil prices, however, oil companies can less afford to pay the extraordinary costs of a large-scale accident, providing an added incentive to prevent one. But just imagine the incentive that would be provided if companies were to associate accidents with a *loss of business*. In 2014, BP reported extracting the equivalent of 252,000 barrels of oil daily in the deepwater Gulf.[77] With oil averaging $93 per barrel that year, a company producing at that level would be risking losing roughly $23.5 million per day in revenue. That is a cost it presumably would not be willing to bear, given how lucrative drilling is in the Gulf. Companies understand money. It is hard to think of a greater deterrent, even at lower oil prices.

Such an approach also tracks free market principles. If a transgressing company loses its privilege to operate in a given region and forfeits its leases, other companies can move in. This scenario serves to instill a competitive advantage to operating responsibly.

7 Conclusion

The United States' worst environmental disaster provides a host of lessons, not just for BP and the oil industry in the U.S. and elsewhere but for business in general. The central lesson is that a business must genuinely strive to be sustainable, in the economic, environmental, and social senses. The BP disaster serves as a $62 billion wake-up call reinforcing that proposition.

It is axiomatic that offshore oil drilling is inherently risky, especially in deep water.[78] Perhaps one of the most important lessons for Brazil to learn from the BP oil disaster in the Gulf, then, as it permits expanded drilling into the deep water of its pre-salt find, is that it must insist on the maximum controls possible to minimize the inevitable risk.

To that end, first and foremost, Brazil must have in place a legal framework that serves as a sufficient deterrent to irresponsible corporate behavior and

---

77 www.bp.com/en_us/bp-us/what-we-do/exploration-and-production.html (accessed January 13, 2017).
78 See Commission Report (n. 63 above) at 218, 224–225.

adequately punishes violators. Companies with poor records should lose their permits to drill.

Second, a robust legal framework must be supported through a stringent regulatory environment, one that rigorously monitors compliance and enforces regulations designed to protect workers, public health, and the environment.

Third, it is important to recognize that the command and control model, even at its strongest, has its limitations. Thus, Petrobras – and any other company given the privilege to drill in Brazilian waters – should independently take primary responsibility for perpetuating a culture that puts the paramount premium on safety and environment. Petrobras has for some time portrayed itself as being sustainable.[79] But then, so did BP. Petrobras should set – and hold itself – to the highest standards.

Although the revenues from oil exploration may be a blessing in terms of Brazil's ongoing efforts to reduce its poverty level, the oil is, at the same time "a curse," as Dilma Rousseff said on more than one occasion. Brazil needs to put in place a structure that will maximize the potential for the oil to be a blessing, not a curse. Unless and until it is confident that it has such a structure in place, it should not permit Petrobras (or any other company) to expand drilling in its waters.

Brazil may well have an opportunity to become one of the world's leaders in oil production. In the process of moving towards that goal, it can also avail itself of the opportunity of doing a better job than the US in protecting its people and its environment, and, concomitantly positively influence global norms and institutions.

Bibliography

Agência Nacional do Petróleo. (2015). *Anuário Estatístico Brasileiro do Petróleo, Gás Natural e Biocombustíveis*. Available at www.anp.gov.br/?pg=78136&m=&t1=&t2=&t3=&t4=&ar=&ps=&1449057255726 (accessed January 13, 2017).

Aloise de Seabra, A., Passos de Freitas, G., Polette, M., Del Valls Casillas, A., (2011). A promissoraprovíncia do pré-sal. *RevistaDireito GV*, 7(1), 2.

BP. (2009, February). Exploration and Production, Inc., Initial Exploration Plan, Mississippi Canyon Block 252.

BP. (n.d.). Exploration and Production. Available at www.bp.com/en_us/bp-us/what-we-do/exploration-and-production.html (accessed January 13, 2017).

Brazilian Law 12.351, of December 22, 2010.

Brazilian National Institute for Environment. Nota Informativa 01//12 CPEG/DILIC/IBAMA. Available at www.mma.gov.br/port/conama/processos/DC218947/Parecer IBAMA.pdf (accessed January 13, 2017).

Bureau of Safety and Environmental Enforcement. (2015, February). Voluntary confidential near-miss reporting system. IADC Health, Safety, Environment and Training

---

[79] See "The Greening of Petrobras," *Harvard Business Review* (2009).

Conference (presentation). Available at www.bsee.gov/sites/bsee.gov/files/public-comm ents/bsee/iadc-near-miss-february-2015.pdf (accessed January 13, 2017).

Chevron Brasil. (n.d.). Operação no Campo Frade. Available at www.chevron.com.br/ negocios/exploracao-producao-petroleo/campo-frade.aspx (accessed January 13, 2017).

de Azevedo, J.S.G. (2009, March). The greening of Petrobras. *Harvard Business Review*. Available at https://hbr.org/2009/03/the-greening-of-petrobras (accessed January 13, 2017).

Dlouhy, J. (2015, 6 May). Q&A: Top regulator sees offshore safety as a work in progress. *Houston Chronicle*. Available at www.houstonchronicle.com/business/energy/conferenc es/article/Top-regulator-sees-offshore-safety-as-work-in-6247567.php (accessed January 13, 2017).

Goldstein, A. (2010). The emergence of multilatinas: The Petrobras experience. *Universia Business Review*, 98–111.

Honigsberg, P.J. (2011). Conflict of interest that led to the Gulf Oil Disaster. *Environmental Law Reporter News & Analysis*, 41, 10414–10418.

International Convention for the Prevention of Pollution from Ships (MARPOL 73/78), adopted 2 November 1973, entered into force 2 October 1983. 12, I.L.M. 1319 (1973).

Lucchesi, C.F. (1998). Petróleo. *Estudos Avançados*, 12(33), 17–40.

Maakestad, W.J. (1983). *State v. Ford Motor Co.*: Constitutional, utilitarian and moral perspectives. *St. Louis University Law Journal*, 27, 857–880.

Markey, E. (2010, November 8). Markey statement on BP Spill Commission hearing. Available at www.markey.senate.gov/GlobalWarming/mediacenter/pressreleases_ 2008_id=0334.html (accessed January 13, 2017).

National Commission on the BP Deepwater Horizon Oil Spill and Offshore Drilling. (2011, January). Report to the President, Deep Water – The Gulf Oil Disaster and the Future of Offshore Drilling. Available at https://www.gpo.gov/fdsys/pkg/GPO-OIL-COMMISSION/pdf/GPO-OILCOMMISSION.pdf (accessed April 2017).

Oil Spill Commission Action. (2012). *Assessing Progress: Implementing the Recommendations of the National Oil Spill Commission*. Available at http://oscaction.org/wp-content/uploads/ OSCA-Assessment-report.pdf (accessed April 10, 2017).

Oil Spill Commission Action. (2013). *Assessing Progress: Three Years Later*. Available at http:// oscaction.org/wp-content/uploads/FINAL_OSCA-No2-booklet-Apr-2013_web.pdf (accessed April 10, 2017).

Reuters. (2010, 3 September). Petrobras to sell $ 65 billion stock in record offer. Available at www.reuters.com/article/2010/09/03/us-petrobras-idUSTRE6821FX20100903 (accessed January 13, 2017).

Reuters. (2013, 12 November). Brazil set to become major global oil supplier. Available at www.reuters.com/article/iea-outlook-brazil-idUSL5N0IX3EE20131112 (accessed January 13, 2017).

Riley, C. (2012, 7 March). Brazil's economy tops United Kingdom's. *CNN Money*. Available at http://money.cnn.com/2012/03/07/news/economy/brazil-gdp-united-kingdom (accessed January 13, 2017).

The White House, Office of the Press Secretary. (2015, 15 June). Remarks by the President to the Nation on the BP Oil Spill. Available at www.whitehouse.gov/the-press-office/ remarks-president-nation-bp-oil-spill (accessed January 13, 2017).

U.S. Government Accountability Office. (2012, July). Interior's Reorganization Complete, but Challenges Remain in Implementing New Requirements (Report 12–423).

Washington, DC: Author. Available at www.gao.gov/assets/600/593110.pdf (accessed January 13, 2017).

Veja.com. (2012, 27 September). Chevron paga multa de 35 milhões referente a vazamento de óleo no Campo de Frade. VEJA. Available at http://veja.abril.com.br/noticia/econom ia/chevron-paga-multa-referente-a-vazamento-de-frade (accessed January 13, 2017).

Veja.com. (2009, September). Perguntas e respostas: Pré-sal. VEJA. Available at http://veja. abril.com.br/idade/exclusivo/perguntas_respostas/pre-sal (accessed January 13, 2017).

Court cases

Tribunal de Contas da União. TC 037.197/2011-8, p. 13.

Re: Oil Spill by the Oil Rig "Deepwater Horizon" in the Gulf of Mexico, on April 20, 2010, Re: The Complaint and Petition of Triton Asset Leasing GmbH, *et al.* and No. 10-4536, United States of America v. BP Exploration & Production, Inc., *et al.* 21 F. Supp.3d 657, 674 (E.D. La. 2014)

U.S. v. BP Exploration and Production, Inc., Criminal Action No. 12-292 (E.D. La., 1/29/13).

Chapter 8

Toxic ships, environmental crimes, and the North–South discourse

Jona Razzaque

1 Introduction

Notwithstanding the presence of the Basel Convention on the Control of Transboundary Movements of Hazardous Wastes and their Disposal,[1] the movement of hazardous waste has grown globally in the form of dumping of toxic and electronic waste, relocation of ship-breaking industries, and even in the form of recycling of hazardous waste. A substantial proportion of toxic waste exports go to countries outside Europe, including Asian and African countries. Waste treatment in these countries usually occurs in the informal sector[2] without any government intervention, causing significant environmental pollution and health risks for local people. The focus of this chapter is the relocation of ship-breaking industries from the North to the South.[3] The chapter will examine the relevance of environmental crime in managing the health and environmental problems associated with ship-breaking industries, as well as the effectiveness of the remedies under national regulatory mechanisms and the efficiency of regulatory standards and remedies at the international level that deal with the hazardous movement of toxic ships.

The toxic trade issue reveals a deep chasm between developed and developing countries as large quantities of waste are exported to the developing world which lacks capacity to dispose of it safely or to recycle it in an environmentally safe manner. The toxic trade regime, as the discussion below highlights, is weak in integrating environmental principles such as common-but-differentiated responsibility, the precautionary principle, and the polluter pays principle. The movement of hazardous and toxic waste to developing countries happens due to a

---

1 Basel Convention on the Control of Transboundary Movements of Hazardous Wastes and their Disposal 1989, 1673UNTS 126 (adopted 22 March 1989; entered into force 5 May 1992).
2 For example, waste collected by individuals or small entrepreneurs.
3 In this chapter, "ship breaking" means the final disposal or recycling of ships containing hazardous materials. The terms "North" and "South" distinguish wealthy industrialized nations (e.g. the member states of the European Union) from their generally less prosperous counterparts in Asia, Africa, and Latin America (i.e. the South).

combination of factors, including the weakness of regulatory measures, the illegal waste trade, and the lack of will on the part of some of the poorer developing countries.[4] The disproportionate capacity of developing countries leads to environmental injustice in the South. At the same time, the developed countries' high standards of recycling make the ship-breaking activities expensive for shipping companies. For example, the European Union (EU) Regulation on the shipment of waste[5] implements the requirements of the Basel Convention, including the provisions of the Basel Ban Amendment prohibiting the export of hazardous waste both within the EU, and between the Member States and third countries. Another EU Regulation,[6] considered in section 4 below, aims to facilitate the ratification of the Hong Kong Convention[7] and to ensure that hazardous waste from such ship recycling is subject to environmentally sound management. The crucial nature of ship recycling is voiced by the European Commission:

> [I]n 2009, more than 90% of EU-flagged ships were indeed dismantled outside the OECD, mostly in South Asia (India, Pakistan and Bangladesh) through the so-called 'beaching' method and with significant environmental and health impacts.[8]

This beaching[9] method puts workers "at great risk, both acute and chronic, proper containment of hazardous materials is impossible, and the part of hazardous materials that is taken out separately is not treated adequately."[10] For instance, out of 140 waste shipments that IMPEL inspected, 68 (49%) of these breached EU rules and the majority of these shipments were destined for

---

4 This is discussed in section 2 of this chapter. Also see: Zada Lipman, Trade in hazardous waste: Environmental justice versus economic growth, Basel Action Network. http://ban.org/library/lipman.htm
5 Regulation (EC) No 1013/2006 on Shipment of Waste (Consolidated version); Regulation (EU) No 660/2014 of 15 May 2014 amending Regulation (EC) No 1013/2006 regarding the strengthening of Member States' inspection systems.
6 Regulation (EU) No 1257/2013 of the European Parliament and of the Council of 20 November 2013 on ship recycling and amending Regulation (EC) No 1013/2006 and Directive 2009/16/EC.
7 The Hong Kong International Convention for the Safe and Environmentally Sound Recycling of Ships, 2009.
8 European Commission, Proposal for a Regulation of the European Parliament and of the Council on Ship Recycling, Executive Summary of the Impact Assessment accompanying the document, Brussels, 23.03.2012, SWD (2012) 45 final, COM 2012 118 final, p. 2.
9 Beaching is a process whereby ships are driven as close as possible to a beach during high tide and deliberately grounded on the mudflats near the beach or shallow water. They are cut apart vertically into very big parts using manual labour.
10 Carl Schlyter, Report on the proposal for a regulation of the European Parliament and of the Council on ship recycling, A7-0132/2013, European Parliament Committee on the Environment, Public Health and Food Safety, p. 69.

developing countries.[11] According to the European Commission,[12] the reasons for this non-compliance include: lack of recycling capacity in the OECD, in particular for the largest ships; fierce and unfair competition between recyclers in the major recycling states in South Asia (Bangladesh, India, and Pakistan) and competitors with higher technical standards (EU, Turkey, China); current legislation in recycling states that is not adapted to the specificities of ships as it is still difficult to identify when ships turn into waste; and ships escaping legal obligations by adopting a flag of convenience from a state with less strict environmental standards.

There is no doubt that the EU ship-recycling regulation has transnational impacts as it deals with recycling of ships in developing countries. What are the legal responses in these ship-breaking countries? These developing countries, in many instances, lack financial and technical capacity to comply with the provisions of multilateral environmental agreements such as the Basel Convention. Also, there are substantive[13] weaknesses as well as procedural[14] flaws in the compliance mechanisms of the Basel Convention.[15] Without the enabling conditions of participation and cooperation, compliance mechanisms are not implemented adequately by the developing countries. Weak remedies[16] structure with the lack of provisions on sanction, compensation, or retaliation creates further problems for compliance with the Basel Convention.[17] If the purpose of remedy in environmental law is to provide redress to victims, implement obligations, promote restoration, reinforce the rule of law, and encourage sustainable development, the remedies offered under the toxic waste trade regime fail to achieve these objectives. Indeed, remedies against non-compliance of regulations must be adequate to encourage effective implementation of treaty obligations. The expectation is that the compensation and suspension of environmental obligations should be available as

11 European Union Network for the Implementation and Enforcement of Environmental Law (IMPEL), IMPEL-TFS Seaport Project II: International Cooperation in Enforcement Hitting Illegal Waste Shipments (Brussels: European Union Network for the Implementation and Enforcement of Environmental Law, 2006).
12 European Commission, Proposal for a Regulation of the European Parliament and of the Council on Ship Recycling, Executive Summary of the Impact Assessment accompanying the document, Brussels, 23.03.2012, SWD (2012) 45 final, COM 2012 118 final, pp. 2–3.
13 These substantive weaknesses are identified in section 3.1 of this chapter.
14 For example, lack of participation of the developing countries during negotiation and in the implementation of the MEA provisions.
15 The Basel Convention: Mechanism for Promoting Implementation and Compliance. Celebrating a Decade of Assistance to Parties. Secretariat of the Basel Convention, December 2011, pp. 11–12.
16 "Remedy is the means by which the violation of a right is prevented, redressed, or compensated." Remedies can be by act of the injured parties (e.g. retaliation), by operation of law, by agreement between parties (e.g. arbitration), and by judicial remedies (e.g. litigation). Black's Law Dictionary, 2nd edition, http://thelawdictiona ry.org/remedy/#ixzz2l64KjAYT
17 Daniel Bodansky, *The Art and Craft of International Environmental Law* (Harvard University Press, 2011) chapter 11, 225.

remedies against non-compliance. While there are provisions on compliance, reporting, and review mechanisms which seek to ensure that parties report and monitor compliance, remedies remain weak if these provisions are breached.[18] A number of major incidents of dumping in African countries led to the adoption of the Basel Convention in 1989; however, the remedies it provides remain ineffective.[19]

Is there any role for criminal law in the movement of toxic ships regime? The Basel Convention includes the right of parties to prohibit the import of hazardous wastes and the minimization of both the generation of hazardous wastes and transboundary movements.[20] There are broad obligations to prevent pollution due to hazardous waste, minimize consequences to human health and the environment, and manage waste in an environmentally sound manner. Article 4(3) establishes that "illegal traffic in hazardous wastes or other wastes is criminal." Similarly, the Bamako Convention[21] closely followed the structure of its Basel counterpart. It applied a common commitment "to prohibit the import of all hazardous wastes, for any reason, into Africa from non-Contracting Parties" and any import in contravention of the ban would be "deemed illegal and a criminal act."[22] At the national level, penalties may "include fines, suspension of a licence, seizure of profits or forfeiture of proceeds, reimbursement of costs for the seizure, storage or detention of wastes, payment of the costs associated with the environmentally sound disposal of the wastes, detention and prison."[23] At the same time, successful prosecution of toxic trade crime needs "cooperation between multiple agencies, both nationally and internationally," and bring together "different enforcement approaches and varying levels of available powers (such as for entering premises, seizing goods and taking samples, and detaining or arresting suspects)."[24]

The toxic ship trade is an "environmental crime"[25] as it has an impact on human health and causes damage to the environment. For example, INTERPOL's Environmental Crime Programme's scope includes all environmental crime areas,

---

18 P. Sands and J. Peel. *Principles of International Environmental Law* (New York: Cambridge University Press, 2012), Chapter 5.
19 Chukwuka Eze, The Probo Koala Incident in Abijan Côte d'Ivoire: A Critique of the Basel Convention Compliance Mechanism, *Eighth International Conference on Environmental Compliance and Enforcement (INECE 2008)*, pp. 354–356. www.inece.org/library/show/57964f9b7ce59
20 Article 4 of the Basel Convention.
21 Bamako Convention on the Ban of the Import to Africa and the Control of Transboundary Movement and Management of Hazardous Wastes within Africa 1991, 30 ILM 773 (entered into force 22 April 1998).
22 Article 4(1).
23 Basel Convention, Instruction manual for the legal profession on the prosecution of illegal traffic (UNEP, 2012) paragraph 53, p. 25.
24 Ibid. Paragraph 11, p. 9.
25 According to UNEP, environmental crime is "the violations or breaches of national environmental laws and regulations that a State determines to be subject to criminal penalties under its national laws and regulations." Paragraph 7, p. 8.

including illegal trafficking of hazardous wastes. INTERPOL has linked pollution crimes with organized crime and stated that:

> The far-reaching impacts of environmental crime underscore the importance of adequate sentencing for such crimes. In order to deter environmental crime effectively, sentences, including incarceration and monetary penalties, must exceed the economic advantage gained by the defendant as a result of its non-compliance. Sentences must also be high enough to at least cover the costs of mitigating the damage inflicted.[26]

With these issues in mind, this chapter first considers the problems associated with the movement of toxic ships from developed to developing countries (section 2) and underscores the ineffectiveness of the regulatory mechanisms at the national level. Second, it examines the international and regional standards regulating the movement of toxic ships under the Basel Convention and the Hong Kong Convention. This section assesses the effectiveness of the international standards to manage the disposal of toxic ships in developing countries (section 3). Third, it explores the efficiency of remedies available at the international level including various criminal law tools (section 4 and 5). Fourth, in conclusion, it offers some recommendations and considers complementary tools available to protect the affected people and the environment (section 6).

2 Toxic ships and developing countries

Currently, the global ship-breaking industry dismantles more than 1,000 large ocean-going ships, such as container ships, bunkers, oil and gas tankers, and passenger ships, each year in order to recover steel and other valuable metals or recyclable items.[27] Nearly all ship-recycling activities are concentrated in five countries: the three South Asian countries (Bangladesh, India, and Pakistan), China, and Turkey. Further capacity is available in North America (US, Canada, Mexico) and within the EU (e.g. Denmark, Belgium, and the UK). The EU represented 2.2% of the total share in 2012 with 28 dismantled ships.[28] According to a report,[29] 365 end-of-life ships were sent by European-based shipping

---

26 Advocacy Memorandum, Arguments for Prosecutors of Environmental Crimes, Interpol Pollution Crimes Working Group, Penalties Project, 5 June 2007, p. 2.
27 NGO Shipbreaking Platform, Pakistan Shipbreaking Outlook: The Way Forward for a Green Ship Recycling Industry – Environmental, Health and Safety Conditions (2013). www.shipbreakingplatform.org/shipbrea_wp2011/wp-content/uploads/2013/10/SDPI-NSP-Pakistan-Position-Paper-For-Printing.pdf
28 Ibid. The remaining 1% – mostly single ships – was dismantled in Bahrain, the Dominican Republic, Mexico, Ecuador, Indonesia, the Philippines, Canada, and Ukraine.
29 This report was produced by the Shipbreaking Platform, an NGO coalition. The list was compiled using Lloyd's List, Intermodal, Robin des Bois reports, Equasis, and

companies[30] to South Asia in 2012. The top four European shipping companies that sent ships to be scrapped in South Asia are based in Greece, Germany, the UK, and Norway respectively. Bangladesh, India, and Pakistan are the three countries which have the greatest number of ships scrapped every year. In these countries, the ship-breaking yards employ unskilled and unprotected workers who manually handle poisonous chemicals and are exposed to the risk of explosion while dismantling old ships. According to the UN Special Rapporteur,[31]

> [t]he methods of ship dismantling currently followed in South Asian shipbreaking yards often fail to comply with generally accepted norms and standards aimed at ensuring the protection of the environment from the adverse effects caused by the discharge of hazardous wastes and products that may be present on end-of-life vessels … End-of-life ships are rarely pre-cleaned before their arrival on the shores of South Asia, and most of the shipbreaking yards do not have any containment to prevent pollution of soil, air, and marine and freshwater resources, nor the technology needed to ensure the environmentally safe management and disposal of hazardous wastes and materials. In addition to causing a long-term adverse effect on the environment, the current methods of ship dismantling also adversely affect local communities surrounding the shipbreaking facilities, which often rely on agriculture and fishing for their subsistence.

In recent years, global ship scrapping has increased at an alarming rate due to the accelerated phase-out of single hull tankers, the economic crisis, and a major overcapacity of the global fleet.[32] Ship owners decide to sell end-of-life ships for scrapping as it is economically profitable and there are demands for scrap steel. The increase in the ship-breaking business is due to the fact that ship owners are required to modernise their fleet to increase their efficiency and comply with environmental standards.[33] For ship owners, low labour and compliance costs for

 other relevant sources. This list is not exhaustive. www.shipbreakingplatform.org/platform-report-european-ships-sent-to-south-asia-in-2012
30 Greek ship owners sent 167 ships, or nearly half of all ships sent by European ship owners in 2012. German ship owners sent 48 ships followed by ship owners from the UK (30 ships), Norway (23 ships), Cyprus (13 ships), Bulgaria (8 ships), Denmark (6 ships), and the Netherlands (5 ships). The rest was sent by ship owners based in Estonia (3 ships), Sweden (3 ships), Lithuania (2 ships), Belgium (2 ships), Romania (2 ships), Latvia (1 ship), and Poland (1 ship).
31 Okechukwu Ibeanu, *Report of the Special Rapporteur on the adverse effects of the Movement and dumping of toxic and dangerous products and wastes on the enjoyment of human rights*, U.N. Doc. A/HRC/12/26 (July 15, 2009).
32 European Commission, Proposal for a Regulation of the European Parliament and of the Council on Ship Recycling, Executive Summary of the Impact Assessment accompanying the document, Brussels, 23.03.2012, SWD (2012) 45 final, COM 2012 118 final, pp. 13–23.
33 NGO Shipbreaking Platform, Pakistan Shipbreaking Outlook: The Way Forward for a Green Ship Recycling Industry – Environmental, Health and Safety Conditions (2013), p.7. www.shipbreakingplatform.org/shipbrea_wp2011/wp-content/uploads/

environmental protection, low standards of hazardous waste management, and workers' health and safety in the importing countries offer an economically cost-effective solution. In South Asia, rapid economic growth leads to a growing demand for steel and the scrap steel recovered in the ship-breaking yards is sold in domestic markets in South Asia and, in some instances, the scrap steel can also be re-exported, for example, to the EU.

The key actors in the ship-breaking industries are the ship owners based in the developed countries, the ship-breaking yards based in the developing countries, and, in some cases, the cash buyers or brokers who buy the ship before its last voyage and deliver the ship to the scrap yard. While these non-state actors play a crucial role in the ship-breaking industries, what obligations do states have to ensure that the ship-breaking industry is clean and safe? The Basel Convention,[34] the Bamako Convention, and the Hong Kong Convention[35] adopted the precautionary approach. The Bamako Convention adopted a low threshold and referred to a threat that "may cause harm to humans and the environment."[36] Applying the "common-but-differentiated responsibility" principle to the toxic ship trade, there is a duty owed by the developed countries as they take a greater part in generating this toxic ship. This principle arises in the Basel Convention and in the EU regulation.[37] For example, the Basel Convention takes into account the "limited capabilities of the developing countries to manage hazardous wastes and other wastes."[38] This concern underscores the distributive injustice because the shipping companies, brokers, and the financial institutions (e.g. commercial banks) funding these ship-breaking activities are reaping the benefits of the low-cost recycling process while causing damage to human health and the environment. Moreover, this is an example of social injustice as the ship-breaking activities of the developed countries have caused irreparable damage to the poor communities of the South.[39] The toxic ship trade is also an example of corrective injustice as the victims of this waste trade bear enormous environmental and social costs and may not be able to bring a claim against the ship-exporting developed countries.

2013/10/SDPI-NSP-Pakistan-Position-Paper-For-Printing.pdf. Okechukwu Ibeanu, (n. 31, above).
34 Guiding Principles, Draft strategic framework 2012–2021 for the implementation of the Basel Convention, OEWG-VII/1: Strategic framework for 2012–2021.
35 Preamble, Hong Kong Convention.
36 Article 4(3)(f) of the Bamako Convention.
37 Preamble, Basel Convention. Preamble, para. 7, EU Regulation 1257/2013 on ship recycling.
38 Preamble. Basel Convention.
39 Okechukwu Ibeanu, *Report of the Special Rapporteur on the adverse effects of the Movement and dumping of toxic and dangerous products and wastes on the enjoyment of human rights*, U.N. Doc. A/HRC/12/26 (15 July 2009).

Indeed, the conditions prevailing at the many ship-breaking yards in South Asian countries adversely affect the enjoyment of several human rights, including the right to life, the right to the highest attainable standard of physical and mental health, and the right to safe and healthy working conditions. Noting this, the UN Human Rights Council has identified ship breaking as a new form of waste trafficking and stated that end-of-life ships should be considered hazardous waste.[40]

> Ship breaking activities expose workers to a wide range of workplace activities or conditions which may cause death, permanent or temporary disabilities, injuries, ill-health and occupational diseases ... Long-term exposure to hazardous substances and wastes protection may also lead to serious or irreversible work-related diseases, including lung diseases, several forms of cancer and asbestos-related illnesses ... Health and safety legislation is often not applicable to ship breaking activities, due to the fact that it is not recognized as an industry in some countries, and this leaves workers in ship breaking yards in a particularly vulnerable situation. Furthermore, when national labour standards are applicable, they are rarely enforced due to corruption of law enforcement officials and the lack of effective inspection mechanisms ... In Bangladesh, for example, neither the yard owners nor public authorities appear to collect statistical data about deaths and disabilities caused by accidents at ship breaking yards.[41]

3 International standards and the movement of toxic ships

The international standards of the toxic trade regime are found in the Basel Convention, the Hong Kong Convention, International Labour Organization (ILO) recommendations,[42] International Maritime Organization (IMO) Guidelines,[43] the Rotterdam Convention,[44] and the Stockholm Convention.[45]

---

40 Okechukwu Ibeanu, *Report of the Special Rapporteur on the adverse effects of the Movement and dumping of toxic and dangerous products and wastes on the enjoyment of human rights*, U.N. Doc. A/HRC/12/26 (July 15, 2009) at para. 19. www2.ohchr.org/english/bodies/hrcouncil/docs/12session/A-HRC-12-26_E.pdf
41 Ibid. Paragraphs 21, 22 and 23, 28.
42 ILO, "Safety and Health in Shipbreaking: Guidelines for Asian Countries and Turkey" (2004), http://ilo.org/safework/info/standards-and-instruments/codes/WCMS_107689/lang-en/index.htm. Also see: ILO, Occupational Safety and Health Convention 1981 (No. 155); ILO, Convention on a Promotional Framework for Occupational Safety and Health 1987 (No. 187).
43 See the list of IMO Guidelines: www.basel.int/Implementation/ShipDismantling/TechnicalGuidelines/tabid/2767/Default.aspx
44 Rotterdam Convention on the Prior Informed Consent Procedure for Certain Hazardous Chemicals and Pesticides in International Trade (adopted on 10 September 1998; entered into force on 24 February 2004).
45 Stockholm Convention on Persistent Organic Pollutants, 22 May 2001, 2256 U.N.T. S. (adopted on 22 May 2001; entered into force on 17 May 2004).

These instruments integrate the precautionary principle and the proximity principle,[46] and the essence of these principles is found in environmentally sound management (ESM). Informed largely by the understanding that such wastes should be disposed of as close to their source of origin as possible, ESM encompasses minimizing waste generation and enhancing the capacity of Member States to manage effectively and safely the hazardous wastes in their jurisdiction. The crux of the arrangement is that the country with capacity will be prohibited from exporting to a country with weak economic and regulatory frameworks for safe waste management.

3.1 The Basel Convention

The Basel Convention (BC) applies to the transboundary movement of hazardous waste, prohibits unauthorized transportation or disposal of hazardous wastes, and creates an obligation for Member States to follow prior informed consent (PIC) procedure.[47] This Convention also covers end-of-life ships containing hazardous materials.[48] The exporting country is under an obligation to re-import or otherwise arrange to dispose of a ship with hazardous substances on board if it arrives or is going to arrive in a country without prior consent.[49] However, where a ship started a journey as a ship and not as a waste, PIC procedure will not be relevant.[50] Also, if a ship is sold for recycling once the ship is outside the EU or on the high seas, Basel obligations do not apply as it is difficult to identify the state of export.[51]

The Basel Convention allows transboundary movement of wastes if they are "required as a raw material for recycling or recovery industries in the State of import."[52] Exporting end-of-life ships from developed to developing countries for recycling can be said to be illegal only if the exporting country knows that the

---

46 According to the proximity principle, "disposal of hazardous wastes must take place as close as possible to their point of generation, recognising that economically and environmentally sound management of some wastes will be achieved at specialised facilities located at greater distances from the point of generation." UNEP/Secretariat of the Basel Convention, The Basel Convention: A Global Solution for Controlling Hazardous Wastes, United Nations New York and Geneva, May 1997, 12.
47 Articles 4(1)(c), 4(2)(f).
48 In October 2004, the Basel COP affirmed that end-of-life ships may be a waste and thus controlled by the Basel Convention (Decision VII/26). In October 2011, COP-10 decision reaffirmed this view and called on all Parties and all organs of the Basel Convention to continue to assist countries in applying the Basel Convention as it relates to ships (Decision X/17).
49 Article 9(2).
50 Saiful Karim, Environmental Pollution from the Shipbreaking Industry: International Law and National Legal Response, *Georgetown International Environmental Law Review* (2010) vol. 22, 185.
51 Article 2(10): State of export is defined as the state "from which a transboundary movement of waste is planned to be initiated or is initiated."
52 Article 4(9)(b).

importing country will not recycle the end-of-life ship in an environmentally sound manner and does not have the capacity to handle the hazardous substances.[53] Although there have been a number of capacity-building initiatives,[54] developing countries – primarily the waste importers – are unable to comply with their obligations in relation to procedures, monitoring, and verification for ESM due to technical or financial constraints. In 1995, the Parties to the COP adopted the Amendment to the Basel Convention (the Ban Amendment) which prohibits the export of hazardous wastes for final disposal and recycling/recovery operations from countries listed in Annex VII of the Convention (Liechtenstein, EU, and OECD Member States) to non-Annex VII countries.[55] Until the Basel Ban Amendment comes into effect, there is no direct legal ban on exporting hazardous wastes from developed to developing countries. Although it has yet to enter into force, it has influenced regional and national legislation relating to waste management.[56]

A Protocol on Liability and Compensation of the Basel Convention was adopted in 1999.[57] The objective of the Protocol is "to provide a comprehensive regime for liability and adequate and prompt compensation for damage resulting from the transboundary movement of hazardous wastes and other wastes and their disposal, including illegal traffic."[58] However, all ratifications to date are by developing countries. The Protocol imposes strict liability for "damage" on the person who "notifies" the proposed shipment; depending on the circumstances, this could be the State of export, generator, or exporter.[59] These persons are required to carry insurance, bonds, or other financial guarantees to cover their

53 CIEL, Shipbreaking and the Basel Convention: Analysis of the Level of Control Established under the Hong Kong Convention (Washington DC, 2011), pp. 20–21. www.shipbreakingplatform.org/shipbrea_wp2011/wp-content/uploads/2011/12/CIEL-on-Basel-IMO-compairson.pdf
54 See, for example, Basel Convention, *Technical Guidelines for the Environmentally Sound Management of the Full and Partial Dismantling of Ships* (2003), www.basel.int/Portals/4/Basel%20Convention/docs/meetings/sbc/workdoc/techgships-e.pdf.; Secretariat of the Basel Convention, The Global Programme for Sustainable Ship Recycling (2008). www.basel.int/Default.aspx?tabid=2770
55 It states: "Each Party listed in Annex VII shall prohibit all transboundary movements of hazardous wastes which are destined for operations according to Annex IV A, to States not listed in Annex VII." UNEP, Third meeting of the Conference of the Parties to the Basel Convention on the Control of Transboundary Movements of Hazardous Wastes and their Disposal, Geneva, UNEP/CHW.3/35, 28 November 1995.
56 For example, Regulation (EC) No 1013/2006 of the European Parliament and of the Council of 14 June 2006 on shipment of waste, Official Journal L 190, 12/7/2006.
57 Protocol on Liability and Compensation for Damage Resulting from Transboundary Movements of Hazardous Wastes and their Disposal 1999, UN Doc UNEP/CHW.1/WG/1/9/2 (adopted 10 December 1999; not in force).
58 Protocol, Article 1.
59 "Notifier" is the person who notifies under Article 6 of the Convention and Protocol Article 4. This duty of notification relates to the prior informed consent procedure.

liability.[60] Damage for which compensation is available is confined to loss of life, personal injury, or damage to property. Pure environmental damage (that is, damage to the environment *per se* and to natural resources) is not covered unless it results in loss of income or from measures taken to reinstate the environment.[61] Fault-based liability targets the person who causes damage through failing to comply with the Convention, or by his "wrongful intentional, reckless or negligent acts or omissions."[62] The Protocol does not impose any financial limits for fault-based liability, but does set minimum financial limits for strict liability depending on the tonnage involved.[63] As the Protocol has not come into force, the strict or fault-based liability regime is not operationalized.

In the absence of any liability and compensation mechanism, one possible way forward is to empower the Compliance Committee to enforce compliance, to impose fines and suspensions, and to name and shame through the publicizing of breaches that could act as a deterrent. Multilateral initiatives could be beneficial to detect and monitor illegal trafficking in hazardous wastes. For example, in 2013, Demeter III, a global customs operation by customs officers from 44 countries, conducted over five weeks, confiscated more than 7,000 metric tonnes of illegal waste.[64]

3.2 Hong Kong Convention

The Hong Kong Convention (HKC)[65] imposes a general obligation on the parties "to prevent, reduce, minimize and, to the extent practicable, eliminate accidents, injuries and other adverse effects on human health and the environment caused by Ship Recycling."[66] To ensure that these goals are met, state parties must "enhance ship safety, protection of human health and the environment throughout a ship's operating life."[67] The Convention takes a cradle-to-grave approach, which is much needed for the environmentally sound disposal of end-of-life ships.[68] It declares that states may take more stringent measures consistent with

60 Protocol, Article 14(1).
61 Protocol, Article 2 (2)(c).
62 Protocol, Article 5.
63 Protocol, Annex B.
64 World Customs Organization, Tons of illegal waste seized under Operation Demeter III, Brussels, 20 January 2014. www.wcoomd.org/en/media/newsroom/2014/janua ry/tons-of-illegal-waste-seized-under-operation-demeter-iii.aspx
65 Hong Kong International Convention for the Safe and Environmentally Sound Recycling of Ships, opened for signature 1 September 2009, IMO Doc. SR/CONF/ 45 (19 May 2009) (not in force). Minimum 15 states sign or ratify, minimum 40% of gross tonnage, minimum ship recycling volume 3% of gross tonnage. Initiated by the IMO but will need to be ratified by the major flag and recycling states in order to enter into force and start producing effects.
66 Article 1(1).
67 Article 1(1).
68 CIEL, supra, pp. 23–26. www.shipbreakingplatform.org/shipbrea_wp2011/wp-con tent/uploads/2011/12/CIEL-on-Basel-IMO-compairson.pdf

international law with respect to safe and environmentally sound recycling of ships.[69] However, the HKC does not criminalize the act of illegal transfer of waste.

There are some key differences between the HKC and the Basel Convention (BC) regarding the scope, standards, and enforcement mechanisms. For example, unlike the BC, the HKC does not include the actual waste treatment downstream of the dismantling yard; furthermore, the HKC does not provide for inspections of the recycling yards, and does not rule out beaching. The HKC has introduced an optional procedure for prior approval of a ship-recycling plan[70] and this procedure is different from the PIC procedure. The HKC is silent regarding the status of any ship arriving at the recycling facility of a country without PIC. Furthermore, in contrast to the BC, the HKC does not call for *ex-ante* authorization of recycling yards, and does not impose a duty on states to re-import illegally transferred waste. Also, the HKC does not apply to government ships if they are on "government non-commercial service."[71] However, parties are required to adopt appropriate measures so that government ships act in a manner consistent with the Convention. By contrast, the Basel Convention and the EU Waste Shipment Regulation do not exclude government ships.[72]

So far, none of the ship-breaking countries in South Asia has signed or acceded to the Convention, and only two of the 15 ship-owning countries have ratified it.[73] The provisions of the HKC highlight the divergence among the ship owners, the ship-exporting countries, and ship-breaking countries.

First, the HKC includes requirements for ships such as having an Inventory of Hazardous Materials (IHM) or an International Ready for Recycling Certificate prior to recycling[74] as well as reporting requirements.[75] The ship-recycling facilities need to be authorized by the competent authorities that the Convention requests Member States to establish,[76] and are required to implement a ship-recycling plan that covers worker safety and training, protection of human health and the environment, roles and responsibilities of personnel, emergency response, and systems for monitoring, reporting, and record-keeping.[77] It proposes several types of surveys including an initial survey, periodic survey, additional survey, and a final survey.[78]

69 Article 1(2).
70 Article 16(6), Annex, reg. 9.4.
71 Article 3(2).
72 Refer to the Clemenceau Case (2005) where the French government decided to send the French aircraft Clemenceau to India in order to be dismantled. The Conseil d'Etat of France held that the transport must be arranged in compliance with the Basel Convention, as implemented by the European Waste Shipment Regulation, irrespective of the use of the ship as a military aircraft carrier.
73 Norway ratified the Convention in June 2013. France ratified the Convention on 2 July 2014.
74 Article 8.
75 Annex, reg. 23.
76 Annex, reg. 8.1, reg. 16.
77 Annex, reg. 8.4.
78 Annex, reg. 10.1

The key purpose of these surveys is to verify that the IHM required by the Convention is correct and well maintained. However, the shipping industry argues that the system of periodic survey will be difficult to comply with and unreasonably burdensome.[79]

Second, inspection and verification of the inventory must be in accordance with the guidelines developed by the IMO.[80] The inventory must specify that the ship complies with the green shipbuilding requirements of the Convention. Although the Convention provides for minimizing the waste on board, there is no provision for pre-cleaning of hazardous substances in the structure of the ship, except a conditional requirement for oil tankers.[81] While the feasibility of such pre-cleaning has been questioned from an economic and safety angle,[82] according to some ship-breaking countries, such pre-cleaning of hazardous substances can save financial cost and time.[83]

Third, under the HKC, a recycling facility preparing to receive a ship for recycling has to notify its government and provide all necessary information.[84] It requires each party to ensure that ship-recycling facilities that operate under its jurisdiction are duly authorized and inspected.[85] It also requires each party to exchange information regarding its recycling facilities with the IMO and other parties.[86] It outlines the control, authorization, management of hazardous materials, emergency response, and reporting procedures for ship-recycling facilities.[87] It applies to "ships entitled to fly the flag of a Party" as well as to "Ship Recycling Facilities operating under the jurisdiction of a Party."[88] The HKC imposes an obligation on both flag states and recycling states to take appropriate action for compliance with the Convention by their ships and recycling facilities.[89] It also imposes on the parties a general obligation of "effective implementation of, compliance with, and enforcement of the Convention" and also of "encourag[ing] the continued development of technologies and practices" for ship recycling.[90] The Convention specifically imposes an obligation on the states to enact the necessary domestic legal framework to ensure that ship-recycling facilities

79 IMO, MEPC, 54th Session, Recycling of Ships: Proposal for a New Legally Binding Instrument on Recycling of Ships, para. 11, IMO Doc. MEPC 54/3/11 (January 27, 2006) (submitted by ICS, BIMCO, INTERTANKO, INTERCARGO, IPTA, WNTI). http://merchantmarine.financelaw.fju.edu.tw/data/IMO/MEPC/54/MEPC%2054-3-11.pdf
80 Article 8.
81 Annex, reg. 8.3.
82 European Commission Directorate General Environment, Ship Dismantling and Precleaning of Ships (June 2007). Final report, p. 93. http://ec.europa.eu/environment/waste/ships/pdf/ship_dismantling_report.pdf
83 CIEL, supra, p.55.
84 Annex, reg. 24(2).
85 Article 6.
86 Article 7.
87 Annex, regs. 15–23.
88 Article 3(1).
89 Article 4.
90 Articles 1(3), 1(4).

operating under their jurisdiction comply with regulations and standards set out by the Convention.[91] The national legal framework also must ensure that recycling facilities are designed, constructed, and operated in a safe and environmentally sound way. Recycling facilities also must develop a "ship-specific Ship Recycling Plan" in consultation with the ship owner.[92] It will undoubtedly be a big challenge in terms of cost, capacity, and technology for the developing countries' ship-recycling facilities to comply with these provisions.

Although the implementation of the HKC – especially some of its measures such as the environmental design of the ship, comprehensive IHM for the whole operational life of a ship, survey and certification requirements, authorization of ship-recycling facilities, notification and reporting requirements, dissemination of information, inspection, and regulatory enforcement for violations – could contribute to improving the environmental, health, and human rights performance of ship breaking, the HKC's scope is limited. Examples of these limitations include excluding whole categories of ships from the application of the legal regime (e.g. government-owned non-commercial ships and warships as well as ships under 500GT). Furthermore, although the HKC covers the recycling of ships, it fails to monitor the hazardous waste-processing facilities further downstream. This is of particular concern for developing countries as inadequate management of residues, leakage, and emissions after the recycling process has been completed can cause severe damage to human health and the environment. In addition, it does not contain a provision for a ship – recycling fund or other financing mechanism to assist ship recycling facilities largely situated in developing countries.

4 European Union, dismantling of toxic ships, and environmental crime

The Basel Convention and the Ban Amendment's requirements are now almost systematically circumvented due to the mobility of ships and the ease with which they can move from one jurisdiction to another or outside all national jurisdictions (e.g. on the high seas).[93] Thus, in 2013, the EU agreed on a new Ship Recycling Regulation[94] that aims to reduce the negative impacts linked to the recycling of EU-flagged ships in the global South. The Regulation is based on the

---

91 Annex, reg. 15(1).
92 Annex, reg. 9.
93 Explanatory Memorandum, point 1.1. European Commission, Proposal for a Regulation of the European Parliament and the Council on ship recycling, COM(2012) 118 final, 2012/0055 (COD), 23 March 2012.
94 Regulation (EU) No. 1257/2013 of the European Parliament and of the Council of 20 November 2013 on ship recycling and amending Regulation (EC) No 1013/2006 and Directive 2009/16/EC, 10.12.2013, OJ L330/1.

EU competence for legislative actions as regards the "Environment."[95] Its purpose is "to prevent, reduce, minimise and, to the extent practicable, eliminate accidents, injuries and other adverse effects on human health and the environment caused by ship recycling."[96] The Regulation exempts ships from the scope of existing EU Regulation on the shipment of waste "in order to avoid duplication."[97] There are some concerns that the 2013 Regulation does not provide an equivalent level of protection as is provided for by the BC as it allows the export of end-of-life ships for recycling under certain conditions to developing countries.[98] The EU has ratified the Basel Ban Amendment.[99] Conversely, the Regulation allows the export of ships considered hazardous waste to non-OECD countries, subject to the Basel Convention. Thus, the EU is under an obligation to refrain from any action that would defeat its object and purpose.[100]

Designed to implement the HKC, the regulation applies to large commercial ships flying the flag of the EU Member States and to ships flying the flag of the third country calling at EU ports. The Regulation sets out a number of requirements for the facilities willing to recycle European ships. It contains provisions on the control of hazardous materials;[101] on the preparation for the ship's recycling and on the actual recycling of the ship[102] including surveys of the ship;[103] and on the contracts between the owner of the ship and a ship recycling facility.[104] These requirements are stricter than under the HKC[105] and allow the European Commission to set up a European List of compliant ship-recycling facilities in which EU-flagged ships can be dismantled.

Under the Regulation, the European ship owners will have to ensure that each end-of-life ship is prepared for recycling. They will have to provide the necessary information about the ship to the recycling facility, notify the intention to recycle the ship to the relevant administration, provide an updated IHM, and minimize the amount of cargo residues, remaining fuel oil, and ship-generated wastes remaining on board. Finally, they will have to provide a "ready for recycling"

---

95 Article 192(1) of the Treaty on the Functioning of the European Union.
96 Article 1 of the EU Regulation 1257/2013.
97 Paragraph 10, Article 26 and 27 of the EU Regulation 1257/2013.
98 Ludwig Krämer, The Commission Proposal for a Regulation on ship recycling, the Basel Convention and the protection of the environment (Legal Analysis, 4 November 2012). www.shipbreakingplatform.org/shipbrea_wp2011/wp-content/uploads/2012/12/Legal-Analysis-of-EC-proposal_Ludwig-Kramer_FINAL-1.pdf
99 Basel Convention Ban Amendment, Status of Ratifications, www.basel.int/Implementation/LegalMatters/BanAmendment/tabid/1484/Default.aspx
100 Ludwig Krämer, supra.
101 Articles 4 and 5.
102 Articles 6 and 7.
103 Articles 8, 10, and 11.
104 Article 9.
105 Article 16(1) of the Hong Kong Convention. The EU is not a party to the Hong Kong Convention. The European Council Decision of 14 April 2014 (2014/241/EU) authorized member states to ratify or accede to Hong Kong Convention, "for the parts falling under the exclusive competence of the Union." Article 1, OJEU L128/45.

certificate. Both EU and non-EU ships would also have to carry an IHM when calling at ports in the EU.[106] According to the European ship owners, the mandatory contract requirements including the obligation to take back the ship prior to the start of the recycling or after the start of the recycling increase risk and liability, and lead to an unfair liability regime between the recycling facilities and the ship owners.[107] The organizations representing ship owners added that "the reporting and enforcement process concentrates almost solely on the role of the ship owners, and this unfairly introduces excessive liabilities simply in the interests of affording Europe control on the recycling of EU flagged ships."[108]

In order to be included in the European List, any ship recycling facility irrespective of its location will have to comply with a number of requirements.[109] Prior to any recycling of a European ship, the ship recycling facility, a large number of which are based in the developing countries, will have to develop a ship recycling plan based on the information provided by the ship owner. The plan will contain information about the ship essential for its safe and sound treatment, and thus will facilitate the work of the ship recycling facility. European ships will undergo surveys verifying compliance of the IHM with the requirements of the Regulation. The Commission will assess the applications received from the ship recycling facilities located in third countries and, for facilities located in the EU Member States, it will be done by national authorities.[110]

There are several concerns regarding the enforceability and effectiveness of the new Regulation as many fear that it will have limited impact.[111] One major concern regarding the enforceability of the regulation is linked to the competitiveness of EU-flagged ships.[112] Concerns are raised as to the appropriateness of regional measures in the current situation as the HKC is not yet in force and the possible consequences of "flag out" by ship owners who would try to circumvent the 2013 Regulation and continue beaching of the ship.[113] The shipping industries are concerned about the restrictive requirements (e.g. downstream waste treatment facilities for the protection of human health and the environment) on ship

---

106 Article 5 of the EU Regulation 1257/2013.
107 ICS, ESCA, BIMCO, INTERTANKO, Commission Proposal for a New Regulation On Ship Recycling, 13/12/2012. www.ecsa.eu/files/EU_Ship_Recycling_Regulation_Joint_Industry_letter_Final_v13_12_2012.doc
108 Ibid.
109 Article 13.
110 Articles 14 and 15 of the EU Regulation 1257/2013.
111 Ida Karlsson, New EU Rules "Fail" against Shipbreaking Dangers, *Inter Press Service* (17 July 2013). www.ipsnews.net/2013/07/new-eu-rules-fail-against-shipbreaking-dangers
112 European Parliament/Legislative Observatory, Debate in Council, 2012/0055 (COD), 25/10/2012. www.europarl.europa.eu/oeil/popups/summary.do?id=1231927&t=e&l=en
113 CIEL, Legality of the EU Commission Proposal on Ship Recycling (December 2012). www.shipbreakingplatform.org/shipbrea_wp2011/wp-content/uploads/2013/01/CIEL-legal-opinion-on-EU-Ships-Proposed-Regulation-12-Dec-2012.pdf

recycling facilities both within and outside the EU.[114] According to the Shipbreaking Platform:

> In 2012, three quarters of European owned ships broken on the beaches of South Asia were registered under non-EU flags such as Panama, Liberia and Bahamas. With the new Regulation being a further incentive to flag out, ships still registered under a flag of an EU Member State at end-of-life is likely to decline.[115]

As a consequence, this Regulation may not improve the unsustainable ship recycling practices.

Indeed, the compliance with the Regulation will require adequate funding. EU-flagged end-of-life ships will only be allowed to be recycled in those ship-recycling facilities that comply with Regulation standards. As these facilities can be situated in any EU or non-EU country, the European ship recyclers will have to compete with, for instance, facilities situated in developing countries. Without financial incentives, European ship recyclers fear that they would not be able to attract business. One proposal to create an EU fund to subsidise safe recycling of the EU ships was rejected by the European Parliament.[116] According to the shipping industries, the anti-competitive financial mechanism to fund environmentally sound ship recycling will have an adverse effect on their business activities.[117] However, the preamble of the Regulation proposes to apply the polluter pays principle and

> assess the feasibility of establishing a financial mechanism applicable to all ships calling at a port or anchorage of a Member State, irrespective of the flag they are flying, to generate resources that would facilitate the environmentally sound recycling and treatment of ships without creating an incentive to out-flag.[118]

---

114 ICS, ESCA, BIMCO, INTERTANKO, Commission Proposal for a New Regulation on Ship Recycling, 13/12/2012. www.ecsa.eu/files/EU_Ship_Recycling_Regulation_Joint_Industry_letter_Final_v13_12_2012.doc

115 NGO Shipbreaking Platform, Press Release – EU Bans Breaking of Ships on Beaches: NGOs Call on a Financial Incentive to Ensure Effective Implementation of New EU Ship Recycling Regulation (22 October 2013). www.shipbreakingplatform.org/press-release-eu-bans-breaking-of-ships-on-beaches

116 According to Schlyter, "The fund was supported by all the political groups, but then the parliament voted it down after strong lobbying from ship owners and EU ports. The ports claimed that the arrangement would result in over 100 percent increase in fees, which is not true." Ida Karlsson, New EU Rules "Fail" against Shipbreaking Dangers (17 July 2013). www.ipsnews.net/2013/07/new-eu-rules-fail-against-shipbreaking-dangers

117 ICS, ESCA, BIMCO, INTERTANKO, Commission Proposal For A New Regulation On Ship Recycling, 13/12/2012. www.ecsa.eu/files/EU_Ship_Recycling_Regulation_Joint_Industry_letter_Final_v13_12_2012.doc

118 Paragraph 19 of the EU Regulation 1257/2013.

Outside the EU, China launched a financial incentive for ship recycling in 2013.[119] Although it will be interesting to see whether other ship-breaking countries promote a national incentive mechanism towards ship recycling, it is, however, too early to assert that the example from China is an indication of a general trend.

Efficient audit of the inventory and regular inspection of recycling facilities remain prerequisites for sustainable ship recycling. The shipping industry formally committed in 2009 to establish inventories for new and existing ships[120] – unfortunately, only a few ship owners adhered to this commitment. According to Patrizia Heidegger, the Executive Director of the NGO Shipbreaking Platform:

> To ensure that the Regulation has a positive impact on improving ship recycling practices globally the European Commission needs to make sure that the listed facilities are properly audited and certified to guarantee Environmentally Sound Management (ESM) of hazardous waste.[121]

For the developing countries, there is an urgent need to develop adequate technical guidance on the requirements for ship-recycling facilities and for the certification and auditing of ship-recycling facilities outside the EU.

5 Criminalization of the toxic ship trade

Illegal traffic of hazardous wastes is an "environmental crime"[122] – therefore, any criminal prosecution of illegal traffic in hazardous and other wastes aims to

---

119 Ship Breaking Platform, NGOs Publish 2013 List of Toxic Ship Dumpers: German and Greek Shipping Companies Amongst the World's Worst, Press Release, 3 February 2014. www.shipbreakingplatform.org/press-release-ngos-publish-2013-list-of-toxic-ship-dumpers-german-and-greek-shipping-companies-amongst-the-worlds-worst

120 *Guidelines on Transitional Measures for Ship-owners Selling Ships for Recycling, In Preparation for the entry into force of the IMO Hong Kong International Convention for the Safe and Environmentally Sound Recycling of Ships* (October, 2009). www.ilo.org/wcmsp5/groups/public/—ed_protect/—protrav/—safework/documents/publication/wcms_117945.pdf.
Also see: European Parliament, Draft Report on the proposal for a regulation of the European Parliament and of the Council on ship recycling, COM(2012)0118 -C7-0082/2012-012/0055(COD), Committee on the Environment, Public Health and Food Safety (2009–2014). 20/11/2012. Rapporteur: Carl Schlyter.

121 NGO Shipbreaking Platform, Press release – EU Bans Breaking of Ships on Beaches: NGOs Call on a Financial Incentive to Ensure Effective Implementation of New EU Ship Recycling Regulation (22 October 2013). www.shipbreakingplatform.org/press-release-eu-bans-breaking-of-ships-on-beaches/

122 Environmental crime has been defined as meaning "the violations or breaches of national environmental laws and regulations that a State determines to be subject to criminal penalties under its national laws and regulations." UNEP Guidelines on Compliance with and Enforcement of Multilateral Environmental Agreements, 2001, available at www.unep.org/delc/Portals/119/UNEP.Guidelines.on.Compliance.MEA.pdf

protect communities and the environment from the harmful consequences of the toxic trade. For a ship owner dealing with toxic ships, evasion of regulations lowers costs and opens up markets that might otherwise be unavailable, even though that activity is in contravention of international and regional law. Indeed, the dispute between India and Denmark regarding the Danish ship *Riky* [123] underscores the problem with weak regulatory approaches and enforcement of legal standards. The ship was registered in St. Vincent and the Grenadines, but when the ship, which contained asbestos, was sold, it was docked in Denmark. When departing Denmark, the owner of the ship informed Danish authorities that the ship had been sold for service in the Middle East as a cargo ship. After leaving Danish waters, the ship was sent to India to be dismantled. Denmark, as the state of export, wanted to re-import the ship, but India declined. The ship was dismantled in India in contravention of the Basel Convention as well as the Indian Supreme Court's Guidelines on ship recycling.[124]

In order to bring toxic trade of ships within the realm of environmental crime,[125] there are several issues that need to be determined. First, the national law dealing with criminalization of toxic trade of ships needs to be clear and complete in line with the Basel Convention (or regional legal framework), and provide rules and consequences in case of violation of these rules. In some instances, it may be difficult to show that the waste is hazardous, especially when it is mixed with non-hazardous waste, which can create additional complexities with regard to criminal prosecution.

Second, the alleged offence may fall under the scope of several national laws; it may be a violation of domestic environmental legislation or criminal law (such as forgery, fraud, false statement, money laundering, bodily harm, and property damage). Related charges could also be taken into consideration: for example, theft, assault, criminal damage, falsification of records, or conspiracy or even corporate manslaughter may all have a bearing on the case. Furthermore, the criminal activity of toxic waste trade may be part of organized crime activities so prosecution may be based on the national legislation implementing the UN Convention against Transnational Organized Crime.[126]

Third, it is necessary to identify the scope of application of criminal sanctions *ratione personae*. Anybody involved in the illegal transboundary movement of toxic

---

123 European Commission Directorate General Environment, Ship Dismantling and Pre-cleaning of Ships Final report, June 2007. http://ec.europa.eu/environment/waste/ships/pdf/ship_dismantling_report.pdf
124 *Research Foundation for Science and Technology and Natural Resources Policy v Union of India* (14 October 2003) Writ Petition (civil) 657 of 1995 (India Supreme Court).
125 There are also administrative sanctions and civil measures available at the national level. Article 12 of the Convention and the Protocol on Liability and Compensation for Damage Resulting from Transboundary Movements of Hazardous Wastes and Their Disposal.
126 United Nations Convention against Transnational Organized Crime, adopted by General Assembly resolution 55/25 of 15 November 2000. www.unodc.org/unodc/treaties/CTOC

waste can potentially be prosecuted: the generator, the exporter, the importer, the individuals completing the paperwork (e.g. freight forwarder, broker), and the disposer. The application of national offences and penalties to the various actors involved in a transboundary movement will need to be set out in the national legal framework.[127] The national law may also specify whether charges should be brought against a legal entity (a business or a corporate body), an individual, or both.

Fourth, in the transnational context characterizing ship-breaking activities, the difficulty of applying criminal law extraterritorially poses further challenges. Thus, national law would need to clarify the extraterritorial application of criminal law. Certainly, the challenges remain with the principle of territorial sovereignty as it prevents direct extraterritorial regulations to close illegal ship-dismantling yards in developing countries.[128] However, noting the global environmental and human rights impacts of such ship-dismantling activities, regulatory provisions (for instance, the EU's regulation) on inspection, surveys, and PIC procedure must be clearly established at the national level. However, this type of national or regional law with extraterritorial jurisdiction is not new as examples can be found in the EU Renewable Energy Directive[129] and EU Food Hygiene Regulation.[130] For instance, the EU Regulation asks the ship-recycling facilities situated in the ship-breaking countries (i.e. mostly developing countries) to develop a ship-recycling plan based on the information provided by the ship owner. This plan will include information on "any preparatory work, such as pre-treatment, identification of potential hazards," "the establishment, maintenance and monitoring of the safe-for-entry and safe-for-hot work conditions for the specific ship," and "type and amount of hazardous materials and of waste to be generated by the recycling of the specific ship."[131]

Fifth, the choice of forum plays a role while bringing a case of illegal toxic waste trade. The jurisdiction of a country under which a suspected case of illegal traffic has the best chances of leading to a conviction is also a factor that may be taken into account before bringing a case to court. For instance, in South Asia, there is very little use of criminal law[132] to prosecute environmental crime. In

---

127 For information on UK law regulating import and export of waste, see Environment Agency, Guidance on Waste: Import and Export: www.gov.uk/importing-and-exporting-waste
128 Thomas Ormond, Enforcing EU environmental law outside Europe? The case of ship dismantling. *Environmental Law Network International* (2009) No. 1. www.elni.org/elnireview-archive.0.html
129 Articles 17, 18, and 19. Directive 2009/28/EC of the European Parliament and of the Council of 23 April 2009 on the promotion of the use of energy from renewable sources and amending and subsequently repealing Directives 2001/77/EC and 2003/30/EC.
130 EU Regulation 852/2004 on the on the hygiene of foodstuffs requires food business operators to implement and maintain hygiene procedures based on HACCP (Hazard Analysis Critical Control Point) principles.
131 Article 7 of the EU Regulation 1257/2013.
132 Jona Razzaque, *Public Interest Environmental Litigation in India, Pakistan and Bangladesh* (Kluwer, 2004), chapters 4 and 5.

England and Wales, the Environment Agency would always require a decision to prosecute to be made, and guidance on enforcement and sanctions is provided by the Agency to demonstrate its approach which is used when considering whether an enforcement response is necessary to achieve the desired outcome (i.e. compliance).[133] There is some discretion regarding the most appropriate route to be taken in the prevailing circumstances, which may or may not result in a decision to prosecute in the courts. A warning, a caution, or prosecution are all available remedies.[134]

The 2013 Regulation includes provisions on penalties and access to justice and enforcement. However, some of these issues are already covered by the EU Directive on Environmental Crime[135] and the Directive establishes criminal penalties for illegal waste shipments which can be applicable if this 2013 Regulation is violated.[136] Specific measures on penalties are left to Member States following the subsidiarity rule whereby Member States have the authority to establish penalties and determine the rules on enforcement action.[137] The Regulation envisages the application of the polluter pays principle and "[t]he penalties provided for shall be effective, proportionate and dissuasive."[138] As the criminal law enforcement agencies can hardly cope with the complexity, ideology, and dynamics of environmental regulations,[139] crime related to ship recycling is likely to create additional difficulties.

6 Challenges and complementary mechanisms

The weak regulatory framework to tackle the toxic ship trade in developing countries means there are inadequate human and financial resources for customs authorities, inadequate training opportunities for customs officials, weak

---

133 For information on UK law regulating import and export of waste, see Environment Agency, Guidance on Waste: Import and Export: www.gov.uk/importing-and-exporting-waste
134 Environment Agency, *Cracking down on Waste Crime*, Waste Crime Report 2012–13 (October 2013). www.gov.uk/government/uploads/system/uploads/attachment_data/file/288604/LIT_8776_956402.pdf; Environmental Services Association Education Trust, *Waste Crime: Tackling Britain's Dirty Secret* (March 2014). www.esauk.org/esa_reports/ESAET_Waste_Crime_Tackling_Britains_Dirty_Secret_LIVE.pdf
135 Directive 2008/99/EC of the European Parliament and of the Council of 19 November 2008 on the protection of the environment through criminal law, OJ L328/28, 06.12.2008.
136 Article 30 of the EU Regulation 1257/2013: The Commission shall assess which infringements of this Regulation should be brought under the scope of Directive 2008/99/EC and shall report on its findings by 31 December 2014 to the European Parliament and to the Council and, if appropriate, accompany it by a legislative proposal.
137 Paragraph 17 and Article 22 of the EU Regulation 1257/2013.
138 Article 22(1) of the EU Regulation 1257/2013.
139 David C. Fortney, Thinking outside the "black box" tailored enforcement in environmental criminal law, 81 *Texas Law Review* (2003), pp. 1609–1635.

laboratory facilities in countries' major ports, and lack of capacity to prosecute and punish environmental crimes by, *inter alia*, organizing appropriate training opportunities for judges and prosecutors.[140] Regulatory failures or gaps may arise in the form of inadequate clarity over what constitutes ownership of (and responsibility for) waste. Waste-related regulations may not apply to waste brokers and supply chains may escape direct regulatory control.[141] Absence of clear and comprehensive legislation as well as vague definition and classifications of hazardous waste and weak liability regimes facilitate the perpetration of environmental crime in relation to toxic waste trade.

For instance, while the environmental impact assessment (EIA) needs to be conducted for ship-breaking industries in Bangladesh and Pakistan, this is not always happening in practice.[142] The NGOs have brought cases in national courts of India[143] and Bangladesh[144] alleging the lack of enforcement of national constitutional, environmental, EIA, and labour laws in ship-dismantling yards. The Basel Convention has been used as a litigation strategy to protect human health and the environment. For example, in India, the Supreme Court has issued a decision that detailed general requirements for ship-recycling facilities.[145] In Bangladesh, the Supreme Court ordered the government to frame rules to stop entry of toxic ships into Bangladesh.[146] There is no doubt that the weak

---

140 Okechukwu Ibeanu, Report of the Special Rapporteur on the adverse effects of the movement and dumping of toxic and dangerous products and wastes on the enjoyment of human rights, 2 September 2010. www.shipbreakingplatform.org/shipbrea_wp2011/wp-content/uploads/2012/08/UN-special-rapporteur-mission-to-India-report-January-2010.pdf
141 Nicholas Dorn, StijnVan Daele and Tom Vander Beken, Reducing Vulnerabilities to Crime of the European Waste Management Industry: the Research Base and the Prospects for Policy, *European Journal of Crime, Criminal Law and Criminal Justice* (2007) Vol. 14, Issue 1, 23–36, 31.
142 Maria Sarraf, Frank Stuer-Lauridsen, Milen Dyoulgerov, Robin Bloch, Susan Wingfield, and Roy Watkinson, The Ship Breaking and Recycling Industry in Bangladesh and Pakistan (2010). Report No 58275-SAS. http://siteresources.worldbank.org/INTPOPS/Publications/22816687/ShipBreakingReportDec2010.pdf
143 *Research Foundation for Science and Technology and Natural Resources Policy v Union of India* (14 October 2003) Writ Petition (civil) 657 of 1995 (India Supreme Court); *Research Foundation for Science and Technology and Natural Resources Policy v Union of India* (2007) SC 890. Legal challenge to Adani's ship recycling project (2014) www.recyclinginternational.com/recycling-news/8045/research-and-legislation/india/legal-challenge-adani-039-s-ship-recycling-project
144 *Bangladesh Environmental Lawyers Association (BELA) v Bangladesh and others.* (2009) High Court Division, Writ Petition 7260 of 2008. Judgment on 05.03.2009 & 17.03.2009. Judgment of this case is available at www.belabangla.org/public-interest-litigation
145 *Research Foundation for Science v Union of India*, Writ Petition No. 657 of 1995,judgment delivered Sep. 6, 2007 (India) (unreported), http://ec.europa.eu/environment/waste/ships/pdf/indian_order2007.pdf
146 *Bangladesh Environmental Lawyers Association v Bangladesh* (Writ Petition No. 3916 of 2006) Judgment delivered July 6, 2006 (Bangladesh Supreme Court, High Court

enforcement of law leads to evasion of legal standards. For example, enforcement becomes difficult when hazardous waste is mixed with non-hazardous wastes. At the same time, new standards in relation to recycling (as seen above in the EU) increase waste management and compliance costs, as well as corruption. To avoid increasing costs, waste operators may assess the risks involved in avoiding the costs and take recourse to misrepresentation and illegal dumping. Thus, low wages, weak economies, and ineffective controls become attractive to hazardous waste exporters as profit maximization remains the key goal.

At the international level, the inefficiency and inadequate enforcement of the toxic ship trade regime leads to environmental injustice with devastating impacts on the environment and health of the poorest people of the South. Thus, complementary mechanisms (e.g. self-regulation) may play a role to strengthen the regulatory framework.

As funding for the ship-breaking industries is crucial, it is necessary that funding institutions play a responsible role. The OECD report showed the heavy involvement of commercial banks to fund companies actively involved in ship-dismantling industries.[147] According to a report on Bangladesh:

> A ship breaker typically buy [sic] a ship to be scrapped for around 4–10 million dollars depending on the size and quality of the ship. The purchase of a ship is often done through a middleman, who links the local buyers with the international sellers. The ship breaker takes a loan in a local bank often with a high interest rate, and the full loan is repaid in six months time when the ship is completely ripped apart and all the scrap is sold to international and national buyers. Outdated and scrapped ships, which previously where [sic] a liability, is now a great asset.[148]

The social responsibility of companies and financial institutions (e.g. commercial banks) is integrated in various international and regional codes of conduct – primarily from concerns about the transnational conduct of companies or financial institutions, and their abuse of human and environmental rights.[149] Both public and private actors are involved in initiating codes of conduct on a range of topics through soft or informal instruments.[150] For example, codes developed by

---

Division) [MTAlfaship Case]. M.T Enterprise case (2008) [Writ Petition no. 7260 of 2008].
147 OECD Council Working Party on Shipbuilding (WP6), *The Shipbuilding Industry in Turkey*, September 2011. www.oecd.org/turkey/48641944.pdf
148 Young Power in Social Action, Overview of Ship Breaking in Bangladesh. www.shipbreakingbd.info/overview.html
149 For a general overview, see OECD, Codes of Corporate Conduct: Expanded Review of their Contents (Working Paper on International Investment No 2001/6, May 2001).
150 Examples of such Codes and Guidelines can be found in http://recyclingships.blogspot.co.uk/p/un-convention-guidelines-and-regional.html

multi-stakeholders[151] (e.g. Equator Principles, OHSAS 18001[152]) complement the codes created by the relevant UN agencies, regional bodies, or business entities targeting good corporate practice and benchmarks.[153] As part of the Equator Principles,[154] it is possible for commercial banks[155] to exclude ship-breaking industries from funding activities.[156] Commercial banks funding the ship-breaking industries can play a role in ensuring that ship-dismantling activities are conducted in a safe and environmentally sound manner.[157]

In a way, these initiatives are emanations of a free market philosophy and neoliberal ideology that aim to fill the regulatory vacuum created by weak international and national laws regulating business actors.[158] The voluntary guidelines or standards target responsible business conduct (including employment and industrial relations, human rights, environment, and information disclosure), consumer interest, competition, and taxation, as well as combat bribery and corruption. The ISO standards on ship-recycling management systems (e.g. 30000 series,[159] 14000 series[160]), industry codes of practice on

---

151 Examples of multi-stakeholders initiatives include Ethical Trading Initiative, Social Accountability 8000 (SA8000), Clean Clothes Campaign, Fair Wear Foundation, the Fair Labour Association, Workers Rights Consortium, Roundtable on Sustainable Palm Oil, and the Forest Stewardship Council.
152 Occupational Health and Safety Assessment Series. www.ohsas-18001-occupational-health-and-safety.com/what.htm
153 Jona Razzaque, Corporate Responsibility in Tackling Environmental Harm: Lost in the Regulatory Maze? *Australasian Journal of Natural Resources Law and Policy*, (2013), vol. 16, issue 2, 197–231.
154 The Equator Principles (EP) is a credit risk management framework for determining, assessing, and managing environmental and social risk in project finance transactions. The Equator Principles apply globally, to all industry sectors and to four financial products: (1) project finance advisory services, (2) project finance, (3) project-related corporate loans, and (4) bridge loans.
155 Equator Principles, Members and Reporting. www.equator-principles.com/index.php/members-reporting
156 ING, Environmental and Social Risk Framework, ESR Exclusion Policy (2012), p. 7. ABN AMRO sustainability report (2012), p. 23.
157 See, for instance, ABN AMRO sustainability report (2012), p. 23.
158 For a discussion of the weaknesses of national and international mechanisms, see Steven R. Ratner, Corporations and Human Rights: A Theory of Legal Responsibility, *Yale Law Journal* (2001), Vol. 111, No. 3, 443; Amanda Perry-Kessaris, Corporate Liability for Environmental Harm, in Malgosia Fitzmaurice, David M. Ong and Panos Merkouris (eds), *Research Handbook on International Environmental Law* (Edward Elgar Publishing, 2010) pp. 361–78.
159 These standards specify requirements for a management system to enable a ship recycling facility to develop and implement procedures, policies, and objectives in order to be able to undertake safe and environmentally sound ship recycling operations in accordance with national and international standards. www.iso.org/iso/catalogue_detail.htm?csnumber=51244
160 The ISO 14000 family addresses various aspects of environmental management. It provides practical tools for companies and organizations looking to identify and

ship recycling,[161] and industry self-regulation measures, such as the DEMOLISHCON,[162] are relevant. For instance, the DEMOLISHCON prescribes that the Notice of Readiness shall be accompanied by an inventory in the form recommended by the Industry Code of Practice on Ship Recycling, and the inventory should provide an estimate of all potentially hazardous or contaminating materials or substances on board the ship, inherent in its structure, or as an integral part of the machinery and/or equipment at the time of the sale.[163] However, the standard form of inventory exonerates the ship owners and any of their representatives from liability as a result of errors or omissions on their part in completing the inventory. Certainly, multi-stakeholder initiatives with their different functions (e.g. certification, disclosure of information, dialogues) and actors have the potential to raise human rights and environmental standards beyond the existing domestic law.

A collaborative approach between state and non-state actors encourages the development of a smart mix of regulations supporting companies to improve their green credentials; a participatory approach directs multi-stakeholders towards improved engagement and inclusion; the push toward a self-regulatory approach with an emphasis on good corporate governance underscores the need for external monitoring mechanisms; and a more outcome-focused approach to litigation puts an emphasis on enforcement and compliance. There are several concerns regarding multi-stakeholder initiatives. Examples from the ship-recycling market highlight the concerns about the availability of independent monitoring, the diversity of certification schemes, and standards. In order to make these multi-stakeholder initiatives more effective, there is a need to build trust among, for instance, the flag states, ship owners, ship-breaking companies, and brokers, and to encourage these actors to be actively involved in the creation of standards and guidelines.

Based on the foregoing discussion on the ship-recycling trade, the North–South dimension on trade injustice is evident. A justice-based approach to the toxic ship trade requires redress of the North–South economic disparities by curtailing Northern double standards while giving Southern countries the flexibility to develop their policy space to comply with international obligations, foster the capacity that promotes environmentally friendly ship-recycling practices, and

control their environmental impact and constantly improve their environmental performance.
161 This Code was produced in 2001 by the Industry Working Party on Ship Recycling established under the coordination of ICS. Available at http://archive.basel.int/ships/docs/08e.pdf
162 DEMOLISHCON is a Standard Contract for the Sale of Vessels for Demolition and Recycling introduced by the Baltic and International Maritime Council (BIMCO). A sample form of that contract can be found at http://archive.basel.int/ships/docs/10e.pdf
163 See: provisions of clause 7. BIMCO, Explanatory Notes to DEMOLISHCON (Standard Contract for the Sale of Vessels for Demolition and Recycling (2003).https://www.bimco.org/Chartering/Clauses_and_Documents/Documents/Sale_and_Purchase/DEMOLISHCON/Explanatory_Notes_DEMOLISHCON.aspx

provide adequate funding that encourages transition to sustainable ship-recycling trade. It is necessary to remove the complexities to allow the nexus of law enforcement, administrative controls, industrial self-regulation, and independent monitoring to work in complete harmony. Developed and developing countries need to collaborate on initiatives that encourage the dismantling of corporate domination in the toxic waste trade and promote effective monitoring and enforcement of regulatory mechanisms.

Bibliography

Bamako Convention on the Ban of the Import to Africa and the Control of Transboundary Movement and Management of Hazardous Wastes within Africa 1991, 30 ILM 773 (entered into force 22 April 1998).
Basel Convention on the Control of Transboundary Movements of Hazardous Wastes and their Disposal 1989.
BIMCO, Explanatory Notes to DEMOLISHCON (Standard Contract for the Sale of Vessels for Demolition and Recycling) (2003).
Bodansky, D. (2011). *The Art and Craft of International Environmental Law*. Cambridge, MA: Harvard University Press.
CIEL. (2011). Shipbreaking and the Basel Convention: Analysis of the Level of Control Established under the Hong Kong Convention. Washington, DC: CIEL, pp. 20–21. Available at www.shipbreakingplatform.org/shipbrea_wp2011/wp-content/uploads/ 2011/12/CIEL-on-Basel-IMO-compairson.pdf (accessed 14 January 2017).
CIEL. (2012). Legality of the EU Commission proposal on ship recycling. Washington, DC: CIEL Available at www.shipbreakingplatform.org/shipbrea_wp2011/wp-content/ uploads/2013/01/CIEL-legal-opinion-on-EU-Ships-Proposed-Regulation-12-Dec-2012. pdf (accessed 14 January 2017).
Directive 2009/28/EC of the European Parliament and of the Council of 23 April 2009 on the promotion of the use of energy from renewable sources and amending and subsequently repealing Directives 2001/77/EC and 2003/30/EC, OJ L 140, 5.06.2009, 16–62.
Directive 2008/99/EC of the European Parliament and of the Council of 19 November 2008 on the protection of the environment through criminal law, OJ L328/28, 06.12.2008.
Dorn, N., Daele, S.V., and Vander Beken, T. (2007). Reducing vulnerabilities to crime of the European waste management industry: the research base and the prospects for policy. *European Journal of Crime, Criminal Law and Criminal Justice*, 14, 1, 23–36.
Environment Agency. (2013). Cracking down on Waste Crime, Waste Crime Report 2012–2013. Available at www.gov.uk/government/uploads/system/uploads/attachm ent_data/file/288604/LIT_8776_956402.pdf (accessed 14 January 2017).
Environmental Services Association Education Trust. (2014). Waste Crime: Tackling Britain's Dirty Secret. Available at www.esauk.org/esa_reports/ESAET_Waste_Crime_Ta ckling_Britains_Dirty_Secret_LIVE.pdf (accessed 14 January 2017).
European Commission, (2007). Ship Dismantling and Pre-cleaning of Ships, Final report. Directorate General Environment.
European Commission, Proposal for a Regulation of the European Parliament and of the Council on Ship Recycling, Executive Summary of the Impact Assessment accompanying the document, Brussels, 23.03.2012, SWD (2012) 45 final, COM 2012 118 final.

European Commission, Proposal for a Regulation of the European Parliament and the Council on ship recycling, COM(2012) 118 final, 2012/0055 (COD), 23 March 2012.
European Parliament. (2012). Draft Report on the proposal for a regulation of the European Parliament and of the Council on ship recycling, COM(2012)0118–C7-0082/2012-012/0055(COD), Committee on the Environment, Public Health and Food Safety (2009–2014). Rapporteur: Carl Schlyter.
European Union. (2006). Network for the Implementation and Enforcement of Environmental Law (IMPEL), IMPEL-TFS Seaport Project II: International Cooperation in Enforcement Hitting Illegal Waste Shipments. Brussels: European Union Network for the Implementation and Enforcement of Environmental Law.
Eze, C. (2008). The Probo Koala Incident in Abijan Côte d'Ivoire: A critique of the Basel Convention Compliance Mechanism, *Eighth International Conference on Environmental Compliance and Enforcement*. INECE, pp. 354–356. Available at www.inece.org/library/inece-conferences/featured-articles-from-the-8th-conference-proceedings/show/57964f9b7ce59 (accessed 6 February 2017).
Fortney, D.C. (2003). Thinking outside the "black box": Tailored enforcement in environmental criminal law. *Texas Law Review*, 81, 1609–1635.
Hong Kong International Convention for the Safe and Environmentally Sound Recycling of Ships, opened for signature Sep. 1, 2009, IMO Doc. SR/CONF/45.
Human Rights Council. (2009). Report of the Special Rapporteur on the adverse effects of the Movement and dumping of toxic and dangerous products and wastes on the enjoyment of human rights, Ibeanu O., U.N. Doc.A/HRC/12/26.
Human Rights Council. (2010). Report of the Special Rapporteur on the adverse effects of the movement and dumping of toxic and dangerous products and wastes on the enjoyment of human rights. Ibeanu O., Addendum. Mission to India. UN Doc. A/HRC/15/22/Add.3.
ICS, ESCA, BIMCO, INTERTANKO, Commission Proposal for a New Regulation on Ship Recycling, 13/12/2012. Available at www.ecsa.eu/files/EU_Ship_Recycling_Regulation_Joint_Industry_letter_Final_v13_12_2012.doc (accessed 14 January 2017).
ILO. (1981). Occupational Safety and Health Convention (No. 155).
ILO. (1987). Convention on a Promotional Framework for Occupational Safety and Health 1987 (No. 187).
ILO. (2004). Safety and Health in Shipbreaking: Guidelines for Asian Countries and Turkey.
International Maritime Organisation, MEPC, 54th Session, *Recycling of Ships: Proposal for a New Legally Binding Instrument on Recycling of Ships*, IMO Doc. MEPC 54/3/11 (Jan 27, 2006).
International Chamber of Shipping. (2009). Guidelines on Transitional Measures for Shipowners Selling Ships for Recycling, in Preparation for the entry into force of the IMO Hong Kong International Convention for the Safe and Environmentally Sound Recycling of Ships.
INTERPOL Pollution Crimes Working Group. (2007). Arguments for Prosecutors of Environmental Crimes', Advocacy Memorandum (Penalties Project, 5 June). Available at https://www.interpol.int/Media/Files/Crime-areas/Environmental-crime/Advocacy-Memorandum-%E2%80%93-Arguments-for-Prosecutors-of-Environmental-crimes-2007/ (accessed April 2017).
Karim, S. (2010). Environmental pollution from the shipbreaking industry: International law and national legal response. *Georgetown International Environmental Law Review*, 22, 185–240.
Karlsson, I. (2013, 17 July). New EU rules 'fail' against shipbreaking dangers. *Inter Press Service*. Available at www.ipsnews.net/2013/07/new-eu-rules-fail-against-shipbreaking- dangers

Kramer, L. (2012, 4 November). The Commission Proposal for a Regulation on ship recycling, the Basel Convention and the protection of the environment (Legal Analysis).
Lipman, Z. (2011). Trade in hazardous waste: Environmental justice versus economic growth, Basel Action Network. Available at http://archive.ban.org/library/lipman.htm (accessed 6 February 2017).
NGO Shipbreaking Platform. (2013). Pakistan Shipbreaking Outlook: The Way Forward for a Green Ship Recycling Industry – Environmental, Health and Safety Conditions (2013). Available at www.shipbreakingplatform.org/shipbrea_wp2011/wp-content/uploads/2013/10/SDPI-NSP-Pakistan-Position-Paper-For-Printing.pdf (accessed 14 January 2017).
NGO Shipbreaking Platform. (2013). Press Release – EU Bans Breaking of Ships on Beaches: NGOs Call on a Financial Incentive to Ensure Effective Implementation of New EU Ship Recycling Regulation (22 October 2013). Available at www.shipbreakingpla tform.org/press-release-eu-bans-breaking-of-ships-on-beaches (accessed 16 January 2017).
NGO Shipbreaking Platform. (2014). Press Release – NGOs Publish 2013 List of Toxic Ship Dumpers: German and Greek Shipping Companies Amongst the World's Worst, 3 February 2014.
OECD Council Working Party on Shipbuilding (WP6). (2011, September). *The Shipbuilding Industry in Turkey*. Available at www.oecd.org/turkey/48641944.pdf (accessed 16 January 2017).
OECD. (2001, May). Codes of corporate conduct: Expanded review of their contents. Working Paper on International Investment No 2001/6.
Ormond, T. (2009). Enforcing EU environmental law outside Europe? The case of ship dismantling. *Environmental Law Network International*, 1. Available at www.elni.org/elnir eview-archive.0.html (accessed 16 January 2017).
Perry-Kessaris, A. (2010). Corporate liability for environmental harm. In M. Fitzmaurice, D.M. Ong, and P. Merkouris (eds), *Research Handbook on International Environmental Law* (pp. 361–378). Cheltenham: Edward Elgar Publishing.
Protocol on Liability and Compensation for Damage Resulting from Transboundary Movements of Hazardous Wastes and their Disposal 1999, UN Doc UNEP/CHW.1/WG/1/9/2 (adopted 10 December 1999; not in force).
Ratner, S.R. (2001). Corporations and human rights: A theory of legal responsibility. *Yale Law Journal*, 111, 3, 443–545.
Razzaque, J. (2004). *Public Interest Environmental Litigation in India, Pakistan and Bangladesh*. The Hague: Kluwer Law International.
Razzaque, J. (2013). Corporate responsibility in tackling environmental harm: Lost in the regulatory maze? *Australasian Journal of Natural Resources Law and Policy*, 16, 2, 197–231.
Regulation 852/2004 on the on the hygiene of foodstuffs requires food business operators to implement and maintain hygiene procedures based on HACCP (Hazard Analysis Critical Control Point) principles.
Regulation (EC) No 1013/2006 of the European Parliament and of the Council of 14 June 2006 on shipment of waste, Official Journal L 190, 12/7/2006.
Regulation (EU) No. 1257/2013 of the European Parliament and of the Council of 20 November 2013 on ship recycling and amending Regulation (EC) No 1013/2006 and Directive 2009/16/EC, 10. 12. 2013, OJ L330/1.
Regulation (EU) No 660/2014 of 15 May 2014 amending Regulation (EC) No 1013/2006 regarding the strengthening of Member States' inspection systems.
Rotterdam Convention on the Prior Informed Consent Procedure for Certain Hazardous Chemicals and Pesticides in International Trade 1998.

Sands, P., and Peel, J. (2012). *Principles of International Environmental Law* (3rd edn). New York, NY: Cambridge University Press.

Sarraf, M., Stuer-Lauridsen, F., Dyoulgerov, M., Bloch, R., Wingfield, S., and Watkinson, R. (2010). Ship breaking and recycling industry in Bangladesh and Pakistan. Report No 58275-SAS. Available at http://siteresources.worldbank.org/INTPOPS/Publications/22816687/ShipBreakingReportDec2010.pdf (accessed 16 January 2017).

Secretariat of the Basel Convention. (2008). The Global Programme for Sustainable Ship Recycling. Available at www.basel.int/Default.aspx?tabid=2770 (accessed 16 January 2017).

Secretariat of the Basel Convention (2011). The Basel Convention: Mechanism for promoting implementation and compliance. Celebrating a decade of assistance to parties.

Secretariat of the Basel Convention. (2003). Technical Guidelines for the Environmentally Sound Management of the Full and Partial Dismantling of Ships. Basel Convention series/SBC No. 2003/2.

Stockholm Convention on Persistent Organic Pollutants, 22 May 2001, 2256 U.N.T.S.

UNEP (2001). Guidelines on compliance with and enforcement of multilateral environmental agreements. Available at www.unep.org/delc/docs/Portals/119/UNEP.Guidelines.on.Compliance.MEA.pdf (accessed 6 February 2017).

UNEP (1995). Amendment to the Basel Convention, Third meeting of the Conference of the Parties to the Basel Convention on the Control of Transboundary Movements of Hazardous Wastes and their Disposal, Geneva, UNEP/CHW.3/35.

UNEP (2012). Basel Convention: Instruction manual for the legal profession on the prosecution of illegal traffic.

United Nations Convention against Transnational Organized Crime, 15 November 2000. Available at www.unodc.org/documents/treaties/UNTOC/Publications/TOC%20Convention/TOCebook-e.pdf (accessed 6 February 2017).

World Customs Organization. (2014, 20 January). Press Release –Tons of illegal waste seized under Operation Demeter III. Available at www.wcoomd.org/en/media/newsroom/2014/january/tons-of-illegal-waste-seized-under-operation-demeter-iii.aspx (accessed 16 January 2017).

Court cases and related files

Bangladesh Environmental Lawyers Association v Bangladesh (Writ Petition No. 3916 of 2006) Judgment delivered July 6, 2006 (Bangladesh Supreme Court, High Court Division) [MTAlfaship Case]. M.T Enterprise case (2008) [Writ Petition no. 7260 of 2008].

Bangladesh Environmental Lawyers Association (BELA) v Bangladesh and others. (2009) High Court Division, Writ Petition 7260 of 2008. Judgment on 05.03.2009 & 17.03.2009. Available at www.belabangla.org/public-interest-litigation (accessed 16 January 2017).

Research Foundation for Science and Technology and Natural Resources Policy v Union of India (14 October 2003) Writ Petition (civil) 657 of 1995 (India Supreme Court)

Research Foundation for Science v. Union of India, Writ Petition No. 657 of 1995, judgment delivered September 6, 2007 (India) (unreported). Available at http://ec.europa.eu/environment/waste/ships/pdf/indian_order2007.pdf (accessed 16 January 2017).

Research Foundation for Science and Technology and Natural Resources Policy v Union of India (2007) SC 890. Legal challenge to Adani's ship recycling project (2014). Available at www.recyclinginternational.com/recycling-news/8045/research-and-legislation/india/legal-challenge-adani-039-s-ship-recycling-project (accessed 16 January 2017).

Part III

Forging socio-legal solutions to environmental harms: lessons from around the world

Chapter 9

Determining the public interest in environmental enforcement, sanctioning and prosecution

Anne Brosnan

1 Introduction

In this chapter we will consider the principles behind enforcement activity undertaken by the Environment Agency in England and whether the complex matrix of penalty principles and public interest considerations it espouses serve to bring about real environmental benefits from enforcement decisions.

In particular we will look at the use of civil or administrative sanctions and how decisions are made in relation to these, and how public interest factors underlie enforcement decision making across the whole regulatory spectrum.

Public interest is most closely defined in relation to the decision whether or not to prosecute an offence. In every case where there is sufficient evidence to justify criminal proceedings, prosecutors must consider whether a prosecution is required in the public interest. In short, a prosecutor must be satisfied that there are public interest factors tending against prosecution which outweigh those in favour. In some cases the prosecutor may be satisfied that the public interest can be properly served by offering the offender the opportunity to have the matter dealt with by an out-of-court disposal rather than bringing a prosecution. This test therefore embodies a socio-legal approach to the decision as to when prosecution proceedings are appropriate.

The extension of enforcement options by the introduction of administrative sanctions has introduced new principles and issues to decision making and we will consider the extent to which this framework is underpinned by similar or related public interest considerations.

2 Background

The Environment Agency (EA) administers and supervises the regulatory regime for environmental protection in England. It is a non-departmental public body, answerable to Parliament through the Secretary of State for Environment Food and Rural Affairs. Its functions are extensive including pollution control, waste regulation, management of water resources, flood and coastal risk management, fisheries, conservation and navigation. It is not the sole regulatory body for the environment; some aspects of environmental protection fall within the jurisdiction of Natural England and some to local authorities.

The EA has extensive functions not only as a regulator but also as an environmental operator (principally in the area of flood and coastal risk management), as a monitor of the state of the environment and as an advisor to government. The central regulatory mechanism for environmental protection is the environmental permit, although low-risk operations may be specifically exempted from regulatory control. Compliance is monitored by the EA against permits and the terms of qualifying exemptions. Enforcement may be contemplated for breaches of permits and exemptions and where illegal activity takes place wholly outside of the regulatory regime.

The underlying purpose of the regulatory framework is to secure compliance with environmental legislation debated and enacted by Parliament. As a starting point, and in socio-legal terms, public interest can therefore be characterised in the terms of such legislation and any supporting statutory guidance issued by government. Regulators may issue their own guidance as to the manner in which they will exercise their powers and duties, but this must be in accordance with the legislative and statutory framework.

3 Exercise of statutory powers and duties

In carrying out its functions the EA, as a creature of statute,[1] must have regard to its statutory powers and duties and any directions and statutory guidance issued by the Secretary of State.

The EA's principal aim is set out in section 4 of the Environment Act 1995: to carry out its functions so as to contribute to the objective of achieving sustainable development.[2] It has a number of other complementary and subsidiary duties, most notably managing the risk to people and property from flooding, conservation, augmentation of water resources and water quality, and the regulation of major industry and waste operations so as to prevent harm to human health and the environment.[3] The EA has a number of public statements detailing how it will go about its functions. The most important of these is its Corporate Plan entitled 'Creating a Better Place' approved by its Board, which sets out a number of themes, including acting to reduce climate change and its consequences, protecting and improving water, land and air, working with people and communities to create better places and working with business and other organisations to use resources wisely.

4 Generic statutory duties and the Regulators' Code

There are generic statutory duties placed upon regulators which impinge upon their day-to-day activities. An example is section 21 of the Legislative and

---

1 Environment Act 1995
2 Section 4 Environment Act 1995
3 Sections 5–10 Environment Act 1995

Regulatory Reform Act 2006 which requires regulators to have regard to the principles of transparency, accountability, proportionality and consistency in the exercise of their functions. It requires also that regulatory activities should be targeted only at cases in which action is needed.

As a non-economic regulator, the EA is also bound by the Regulators' Code when devising and implementing regulatory policies and systems.[4] This code was reissued by government in July 2013. It establishes how non-economic regulators should interact with those they are regulating.

It states that regulators should:

- carry out their activities in a transparent way that helps those they regulate comply and grow;
- design simple and straightforward ways to engage with and hear the views of those they regulate;
- base their regulatory activities on risk and share information about compliance and risk;
- ensure clear information, guidance and advice is available to help those they regulate meet their responsibilities.

The very recent Deregulation Act 2015 imposed an important new duty on regulators. The duty to have regard to the desirability of promoting economic growth (the 'growth duty') is accompanied by a power enabling the Secretary of State to issue statutory guidance to those exercising non-economic regulatory functions ('regulators') as to how the duty may be discharged. The Deregulation Act 2015 provides that those who are subject to the growth duty must have regard to the guidance when carrying out their regulatory functions.

It emphasises that regulators exist primarily to protect people or to achieve other social or environmental outcomes. The growth duty removes uncertainty about whether regulators are able to respond to economic concerns. It clarifies that growth is an important factor to be taken into account in the delivery of protections. The duty requires that economic growth is a factor to be taken into account alongside regulators' other statutory duties. Draft Guidance has been issued by government to regulators suggesting that how protection of economic growth ranks against existing duties is a judgment only a regulator can and should make. However, it explicitly states that the instigation and conduct of prosecution proceedings are excluded from the growth duty. It is unfortunately too early to measure the real impact of this new duty on the EA's actions in relation to environmental protection.

In relation to the exercise of its regulatory functions, the EA has published an Enforcement and Sanctions Statement (ESS) and Guidance (ESG) detailing how it will go about its regulatory activities.

4 Regulators' Code made pursuant to section 23 of the Legislative and Regulatory Reform Act 2006

5 Enforcement and Sanctions Statement (ESS)

In the ESS, the EA states that it believes in firm but fair regulation and sets out its commitment to principled regulation. It affirms its adherence to the Regulators' Code and the Macrory Penalty Principles.[5] In undertaking enforcement activities, the EA adheres to principles of:

- transparency as to how it operates and what those who are regulated may expect;
- consistency of approach;
- targeting of enforcement action in accordance with risk;
- proportionality in the application of the law and in securing compliance; and
- accountability for actions taken by way of enforcement.

The EA states that provision of clear advice and guidance will be its main approach to securing legislative compliance. However, securing compliance through other, more rigorous, enforcement powers including civil sanctions and prosecution is also important, where guidance has proved ineffective or is inappropriate.

The Macrory Penalty Principles derive from the work undertaken by Professor Richard Macrory in his report of 2006 on Regulatory Justice, building on the work of the earlier Hampton Review.[6] These Penalty Principles state that any enforcement and sanctions activity should:

- aim to change the behaviour of the offender;
- aim to eliminate any financial gain or benefit from non-compliance;
- be responsive and consider what is appropriate for the particular offender and regulatory issue, which can include punishment and the public stigma that should be associated with a criminal conviction;
- be proportionate to the nature of the offence and the harm caused;
- aim to restore the harm caused by regulatory non-compliance where appropriate; and
- aim to deter future non-compliance by changing offenders' behaviour.

These principles reflect a socio-legal approach to offending which takes into account the wider societal value of enforcement and what it seeks to achieve, rather than simply concentrating on punishment and deterrence. Both the Hampton and Macrory reviews attempted to revise the approach to regulatory enforcement, including environmental law enforcement, by considering the

---

5 Richard Macrory, *Regulatory Justice: Making Sanctions Effective*, The Macrory Review, November 2006. http://webarchive.nationalarchives.gov.uk/20121212135622/http://www.bis.gov.uk/files/file44593.pdf

6 Sir Philip Hampton, *Reducing Administrative Burdens: Effective Inspection and Enforcement*, The Hampton Report, HM Treasury, London, March 2005.

outcomes that regulation seeks to achieve and the extent to which these can be realised without unnecessary bureaucracy and administrative burdens.

6 Enforcement and Sanctions Guidance

In its ESG, which is a more detailed exposition of the manner in which it will approach individual enforcement decisions, the EA states its commitment to Outcome Focussed Regulation. It sets out the range of enforcement options available and indicates how it will determine the most appropriate response or responses. Such response(s) should be designed to achieve the environmental outcomes most appropriate to the case under consideration. The outcomes considered are the need:

- to stop offending;
- to restore and/or remediate;
- to bring under regulatory control; and
- to punish and/or deter offending behaviour.

A context for enforcement action rather than an outcome in itself is the need to bring about a level playing field for operators – that is, ensuring that legitimate operators are not disadvantaged by operators undercutting them by reducing costs at the expense of the environment. As mentioned earlier, enforcement decisions must also be taken with regard to the growth duty recently established by the Deregulation Act 2015.

Within the ESG, the Agency has identified the Public Interest Factors that it will take into account in deciding on appropriate enforcement action. These are:

- **Intent:** Offences that are committed deliberately, recklessly or with gross negligence are more likely to result in prosecution. Where an offence is committed as a result of an accident or a genuine mistake, this is more likely to result in the use of advice and guidance, warning or civil sanction as alternatives to prosecution, reflecting the hierarchy of enforcement options available.
- **Foreseeability:** Where the circumstances leading to the offence could reasonably have been foreseen, and no avoiding and/or preventative measures were taken, the response will normally be to impose a sanction beyond advice and guidance or the use of a warning.
- **Environmental effect:** The response will address the potential and actual harm to people and the environment. Reference will be made to the Agency's Common Incident Classification and Compliance Classification Schemes.
- **Nature of the offence:** Where the offending impacts on the EA's ability to be an efficient and effective regulator. For instance, where staff are obstructed, where the Agency is targeting a particular type of offending or where it is provided with false or misleading information, it will normally prosecute.

- **Financial implications:** Where legitimate business is undercut, or where profits are made or costs are avoided such as costs saved by not obtaining a permit, this will normally lead to the imposition of a civil penalty or prosecution. This will include offences motivated by financial gain.
- **Deterrent effect:** The need to bring about deterrence is included as an important public interest factor. Prosecutions, because of the stigma attached, may be appropriate even for lesser offences where they might contribute to a greater level of overall deterrence.
- **Previous history:** The degree of offending and/or non-compliance (including site-specific offending or generic failures by the offender) will be taken into account. Enforcement responses will normally be escalated where previous sanctions have failed to achieve the desired outcome.
- **Attitude of the offender:** Where the offender has a poor attitude towards the offence and/or is uncooperative with the investigation or remediation, this will normally mean that the Agency will tend to consider a prosecution or a civil penalty. Conversely, where the offender provided details of an offence voluntarily through a self-reporting mechanism, this will be taken into account in deciding whether an alternative sanction or advice and guidance will suffice.
- **Personal circumstances:** The personal circumstances of an offender will be taken into account – for example, serious illness, mental capacity or age. Where costly remediation is involved, then the offender's ability to pay may also be taken into account.

7 Enforcement and regulatory position statements

The EA has adopted regulatory position statements for certain low-risk permitted activities. A regulatory position statement (RPS) sets out how the Agency intends to regulate a particular activity for a set period of time (i.e. until regulations are brought in, reviewed or changed). Most regulatory position statements specifically relate to waste issues where the requirement for a permit is considered disproportionate to the activity. Some position statements allow an operator to carry out an activity without having an environmental permit or exemption, provided that they adhere to the position's rules and do not cause harm to the environment or human health. Compliance with the requirements of an RPS will enable the activity to be carried on outside of regulatory control. There is no requirement for an operator to inform the Environment Agency that they are operating under an RPS.

8 The Code for Crown Prosecutors

The Agency's ESG expressly states that where it is decided that a criminal sanction is appropriate, the case will be considered in accordance with the Code for

Crown Prosecutors (the Code)[7] before a prosecution is commenced. The Code, however, already underpins more broadly the Agency's ESG, which draws upon factors expressly set out in earlier versions of the Code, in setting out public interest factors which it will take into account in decision making.

The ESG indicates that the formal decision-making process set out by the Code will be followed. This is a two-part test before proceedings are commenced: that there is evidential sufficiency to pass the threshold for embarking upon a prosecution and that such a prosecution is in the public interest.

The Code was reissued in January 2013. It sets out the general principles to be applied when making decisions about prosecutions. The Code is issued primarily for prosecutors in the CPS, but other prosecutors follow it either through convention or because they are required to do so by law. The Code states that each case must be considered on its own facts and on its own merits, but that there are general principles that apply in every case. It exhorts decision makers to act impartially and with integrity to secure justice for victims, witnesses, defendants and the public. Prosecutors are required to ask themselves a series of questions around evidential sufficiency and then public interest.

The evidential test requires that there is sufficient evidence so that an objective, impartial and reasonable jury or bench of magistrates or judge hearing a case alone, properly directed and acting in accordance with the law, is more likely than not to convict a defendant of the charge alleged. A case which does not pass the evidential stage must not proceed no matter how serious or sensitive it may be.

The public interest factors to be taken into account within the Code are:

- seriousness of offence;
- culpability of suspect;
- circumstances of and harm caused to the victim;
- age of the suspect – there are additional considerations for children and young persons;
- impact on community;
- proportionality;
- protection of sources (of information).

These factors (which in strict terms apply only to prosecution decisions) are worthy of further examination as they undoubtedly have an impact upon wider decisions on environmental enforcement. The wording of these factors influences the EA's interpretation of its own slightly more specialised public interest criteria.

---

7 The Code for Crown Prosecutors, January 2013, available at www.cps.gov.uk/publications/code_for_crown_prosecutors

9 A comparison of public interest factors

9.1 Seriousness

The Code requires decision makers to consider the seriousness of a case. The EA has a well-established system for the assessment of the seriousness of environmental incidents, its Common Incident Classification Scheme or CICS. This scheme allows for the categorisation of incidents depending on their impact or potential impact upon air water or land. It couples this assessment of seriousness with the need for EA response and then provides a categorisation of the incident, Category 1 being the most serious, Category 3 the least serious but substantiated incident and Category 4 being an unsubstantiated report. There is a parallel scheme for the assessment of regulatory breaches, the Compliance Classification Scheme, which assesses the seriousness of breaches of environmental permits from regulated premises.

Seriousness is judged by the EA in accordance with these classification schemes. However, the EA may put forward a further view of the seriousness of an offence for the purposes of sentencing based on its initial assessments, as refined by its investigation, for the purposes of the sentencing court (see below) based upon a combination of harm, including risk of harm, and culpability.

9.2 Culpability

The Code looks generically at culpability. Culpability is assessed by the investigating officer having regard to the circumstances of the offence, but the officer is expressly directed, by the EA exposition of public interest factors, towards the foreseeability of the incident, the intent of the offender and the history of the offender. It is worth examining these in more detail. Where the circumstances leading to the offence could reasonably have been foreseen, and no avoiding and/or preventative measures have been taken, a more serious view of the incident will be taken. Case law[8] in the environmental jurisdiction allows for offenders to be convicted of offences where the actual cause of the incident may have been the intervening act of a third party on a strict liability basis and so foreseeability and a failure to take preventative measures may become important considerations for sentence.

Similarly, an incident may arise from the deliberate actions of an offender or by reason of recklessness, negligence or by accident. The investigative process is vital to collect evidence upon which to establish the true basis of an offence. For some strict liability offences, intent may not be necessary to establish guilt but it will always be relevant as a factor in deciding the appropriate enforcement response including whether or not to prosecute and in due course, where relevant the appropriate sentence.

---

8 *Empress Car Company (Abertillary) Ltd v National Rivers Authority HL*, 22 January 1998, [1998] 2 WLR 350.

9.3 Victims

The Code expressly refers to the circumstances of, and the harm caused to, the victim. The EA guidance on Public Interest factors does not expressly use the term 'victim' but it has an analogous consideration of environmental effect. This may be because environmental offences do not always have victims in the accepted sense of the word. The victim of an environmental crime may be a landowner whose premises are subject to an illegal deposit of waste, possibly hazardous waste, or a fishing club whose income is reduced because of a major fish kill associated with water pollution.

The criminal justice system is not yet entirely comfortable with the wider consideration of victim to include some expression of the intrinsic value of the environment itself. In environmental terms, the victim may be the fish that are killed in a water pollution incident, birds that are oiled or a sensitive invertebrate community that is damaged or degraded by pollution. The environment is sadly sometimes thought of as a nebulous green entity, obviously deserving of protection in some unspecified way, but having value only as used, enjoyed and perceived by man. The socio-legal considerations are essentially distilled to 'use considerations' and the extent to which financial value can be attributed to these. Accordingly, the natural value of a river for its own sake or a pure unpolluted aquifer holding groundwater which may have accumulated over many thousands of years seems only capable of being valued in terms of its uses for man, for watering cattle, for recreation or for drinking and supplying to homes and hospitals.

The Code states: 'The greater the vulnerability of the victim, the more likely it is that a prosecution is required.' As Professor Ludwig Kramer states,[9] the environment does not have a voice and to that extent may be considered to be a victim without any other recourse or right of action and hence especially vulnerable.

The Environment Agency is currently implementing a scheme to protect the interests of victims and to provide for a Victims' Right to Review for certain prosecution decisions. The definition of victim is construed so as to provide for some leeway around *locus standi*, bearing in mind that the UK is a signatory to the Aarhus Convention and its requirements for access to justice in environmental matters.

9.4 Impact on the community

The Code requires decision makers to have regard to the impact of offending behaviour on the community. It suggests that this is an inclusive term and is not restricted to communities defined by location. But what is the community in environmental terms? This factor can be loosely correlated with the EA criteria of environmental effect as part of the CICS classification which looks at effects on

---

9 L. Kramer, 1992, presentation 'Report on Proceedings of INECE Second International Conference on Environmental Enforcement,' Budapest, Hungary 1992, Conference Closing remarks.

human health, amenity value, agriculture, commerce and property. If the impact on the community is to be assessed, it might be argued that one should include all those who benefit from a clean environment locally, regionally and even nationally. However, this criterion does not capture intrinsic environmental worth or natural capital, the concept of protecting the environment purely for its own sake. The EA may consider this in its decision making but this may not be reflected in the decision making of outside bodies, the courts and the tribunal service. It will be interesting to see how this factor is interpreted by the courts in the event of challenge.

9.5 Age and personal circumstances

Within the Code, 'age of offender' is the only criterion which is specifically identified as relevant to public interest. The Code explicitly deals with offenders under the age of 18 years and urges caution in assessing the public interest in prosecuting juveniles. It restates the principal aim of the youth justice system: to prevent offending by children and young persons and refers to the United Nations 1989 Convention on the Rights of the Child. The EA criteria recognise and go somewhat beyond this, stating that a first offence by a juvenile will not normally result in a prosecution. Additionally, the EA guidance specifically includes reference to serious illness and ability to pay as relevant personal circumstances. Ability to pay is expressed in terms of financial penalty or a requirement to perform costly remediation.

Additionally, the EA guidance includes attitude of the offender as relevant. Where the offender has a poor attitude towards the offence and/or is uncooperative with the investigation or remediation, this will normally mean that a more serious view of the offending behaviour is taken. Conversely, where there is self-reporting, this will be taken into account when deciding on appropriate action. There is therefore a comprehensive assessment of mitigating factors peculiar to the offender and the facts of the case forming part of the assessment of public interest.

The history of the offender is also specifically identified as a relevant consideration by the EA. Where previous warnings or sanctions have been used to deal with offending or risk of offending but have failed to encourage a behaviour change and prevent a repeat of the offending, it is more likely that an escalated response will be adopted.

9.6 Proportionality

The new factor of proportionality makes explicit reference to the issue of cost. Regulators are exhorted to have regard to the cost of proceedings with regard to the likely outcome. Thus, cases should be prioritised and those cases pursued which are likely to secure the most effective outcomes. The EA's CICS scheme is designed to allow for categorisation and subsequent prioritisation of offences. The

EA has a stand-alone cost–benefit duty under s39 Environment Act 1995, although this has never been considered to apply to individual decision making in prosecutions. Also, the issue of proportionality is not limited to cost; as per the Macrory Penalty Principles, the response should be proportionate to the nature of the offence and the harm caused.

9.7 Protection of sources

The protection of information sources, particularly human information sources, is generally not an issue in environmental crime. Pollution incidents tend to be reported by many individuals and come to the attention of the Agency through numerous channels, including members of the public, the police and local authorities. Anonymous complaints are accepted by the EA but as a matter of policy the Agency does not use covert human intelligence sources under RIPA.[10]

9.8 Other public interest considerations

Whilst the new Code has embraced the government's approach of less is more in terms of guidance, the EA guidance, which predates this, provides a more detailed exposition of those matters which are stated to be relevant considerations. This element of the guidance touches upon those factors which might make an offence a more serious offence of its type and conversely what incidents might be considered minor. Minor offences are stated to be those where there is no environmental impact, and advice and guidance will be the normal enforcement response in such cases.

The EA guidance states that in cases involving overt criminality, gross negligence or reckless behaviour, or where the seriousness of an offence requires that it be heard in a public forum, it will normally choose to prosecute.

EA guidance goes beyond the generic statements of the Code and sets out some very specific responses which can be anticipated in environmental cases. It suggests that there will be a presumption towards prosecution, subject to a consideration of public interest factors, where:

- the offending has been intentional, reckless or grossly negligent or involves outright criminal activity;
- the offending has created serious harm (or has the potential to cause such harm) to the environment or to people;
- there has been large-scale and protracted non-compliance with regulatory provisions;
- our staff have been subject to harassment, alarm, distress or fear of violence;
- intentionally, recklessly or wilfully making a false or misleading statement or record;

10 Regulation of Investigatory Powers Act 2000

- we have been obstructed in our duties and this obstruction has prevented the investigation of potentially criminal activity or an offender had impersonated an Environment Agency officer; or
- where an offender has failed to comply with a Stop Notice.[11]

It is plain that public interest factors underpin the assessment of appropriate response across all of the EA's activities including additionally now the imposition of administrative or civil sanctions.

10 Civil sanctions under the Regulatory Enforcement and Sanctions Act 2008

Since January 2011 the Environment Agency has been able to impose civil or administrative sanctions pursuant to the Environmental Civil Sanctions (England) Order 2010 and the Regulatory Enforcement and Sanctions (RES) Act 2008. This was a ground-breaking development in terms of regulation, moving, both under the influence of the Macrory Review and the government's commitment to cost reduction and deregulation, from the usual criminal justice style approach in England and Wales based around criminal law to a much wider, less punitive, range or hierarchy of sanctions. This was an important departure for both the Environment Agency and its regulated community.[12] Although the order was made in April 2010, the EA spent some time putting together its policy and procedures for the application of the new sanctions. The order provides that the EA has power to impose small Financial Monetary Penalties (FMPs), Compliance and Restoration Orders either on their own or coupled with a Variable Monetary Penalty (VMP). There is power additionally to impose a Stop Notice to require that operations are ceased where there is significant risk of serious harm and an offence has been or is being committed. It was anticipated that VMPs would form the largest part of the activity in relation to administrative sanctions but, in fact, because of the complexity of the calculation for a VMP this has proved not to be the case.

The availability of civil sanctions has allowed the EA to approach outcome-focused regulation with a much wider array of options to secure compliance. Minor offences can be dealt with by FMPs which are limited to £300 for companies and £100 for individuals. Compliance and Restoration notices secure environmental compliance where more formal proceedings are not considered necessary, and a VMP allows the regulator, in theory, to impose a fine upon an operator up to £250,000 per offence without recourse to the courts.

There is a very high test to be met before an administrative sanction can be imposed. Not only must the regulator be satisfied that an offence has been

---

11 Environment Agency, Enforcement and Sanctions – Guidance (LIT 5551, Version 4, 2015) at p. 14. Available at www.gov.uk/government/uploads/system/uploads/attachment_data/file/468315/LIT_5551.pdf
12 Environmental Civil Sanctions (England) Order 2010, SI 2010 No. 1157

committed, a test beyond that required for the commencement of criminal proceedings under the Code for Crown Prosecutors, but it must be established that it is not necessary or desirable in the public interest to bring criminal proceedings. A full assessment of all public interest factors is therefore essential in deciding that a diversion away from the criminal courts is appropriate.

11 Enforcement Undertakings

The big success so far in the EA's use of civil sanctions has been the development of Enforcement Undertakings (EUs). This is a sanctioning option whereby a wrongdoer can, without admission of guilt, offer to put right his offending behaviour, to make a financial payment to any party affected by his wrongdoing and to put in place measures to ensure that the failure cannot be repeated. These measures, usually coupled with a payment of the EA's costs and a payment to an environmental charity, will expunge the wrongdoer's liability and will be accepted in lieu of any further enforcement action so long as the undertaking is complied with.

Unusually, because this is a form of reverse regulation, with the offer of reparation originating with the offender, public interest considerations only arise in terms of the Agency's decision whether to accept the offer. That decision must be rational and reasonable within Wednesbury principles[13] and both proportionate and fair in accordance with Human Rights legislation.[14] Considerations for determining the acceptance of an EU are set out in the EA's ESG which includes and references similar public interest criteria across both criminal and civil regimes. These principles apply to other non RES Act civil sanctions in relation to any discretion which arises.[15]

Additionally, under the direct scrutiny and supervision of its Executive Directors, the EA has developed a set of internal consistency guidelines to enable consistent decision making in relation to offers of Enforcement Undertakings. An Enforcement Undertaking will rarely be considered appropriate in a case where the incident giving rise to harm in the Category 1 or Category 2 range involves deliberate or reckless offending.[16] To ensure behaviour change, any offer needs to make clear the appropriate level of commitment to achieving and maintaining environmental compliance within a corporate structure. The offender will be asked to demonstrate in their offer that any payment to a third party meets the

---

13 *Associated Provincial Picture Houses Ltd v Wednesbury Corporation* [1948] 1KB 223, 229–30
14 Human Rights Act 1998
15 Environment Agency Enforcement and Sanctions Guidance, page 13
16 Assessment of Environmental breaches is undertaken in accordance with the EA's Common Incident Classification scheme and Compliance Classification Scheme for Regulated Industry. Category 1 harm is the most serious categorisation and Category 4 the least serious. Seriousness of an incident is assessed by the harm and risk of harm involved and the need for EA response.

objectives that the breached legislation is trying to achieve – that is, any charity identified must have clear links to a relevant environmental improvement.

The use of EUs, which was originally limited to some smaller specific regimes, was only recently extended, in April 2015, to the Environmental Permitting regime, the EA's core regulatory mechanism. So it is to be anticipated that the jurisprudence around Enforcement Undertakings and sufficiency of restorative measures will be expanded rapidly over the next couple of years, particularly as this will be running parallel to the EA's experience of prosecuting under the new Sentencing Guideline (see below). It will be important that there is some relationship between the two regimes so that an EU is not seen to be a means of 'buying off' the regulator so as to avoid prosecution. There will remain a body of cases where prosecution is necessary to meet the public interest and seriousness of a matter, but there may be cases – for example, those of lesser culpability and harm, for first-time or one-off offenders – where a prosecution is not necessary in the public interest. In these cases an EU may be acceptable, provided the quantum of the EU is sufficient to meet the objectives of the regime and ensure true reparation.

The Environment Agency has now been using civil sanctions for nearly five years and has developed its thinking as to how civil sanctions fit within its hierarchy of enforcement responses. These are seen to sit below the most serious of offences which are deserving of prosecution for reasons of transparency, accountability and to retain the credibility of the regime. EUs have proved to be extremely valuable and have provided greater scope for negotiation and dialogue between the Agency and its regulated community. In the Producer Responsibility regime, which concerns packaging waste, negotiations have been led by the compliance scheme managers who have developed a degree of expertise in advising their scheme members on the appropriate quantum of EU offers. This will not of course be the case for the wider environmental permitting regime where there are fewer representative bodies such as trade associations and these have a looser relationship with their members. It is to be anticipated that challenges and jurisprudence around the use of EUs may therefore arise from interaction with the major players such as the water undertakers and larger waste companies.

12 Independence in regulatory decision making

Recent cases have stressed the need for independence in decision making by regulators other than the Crown Prosecution Service and the quality of enforcement policy needed, and have cast light on the interpretation of public interest considerations. The first of these is the case of *R v A* [2012] EWCA Crim 434. Here, Lord Judge CJ upheld prosecutorial discretion and made it clear that, provided the exercise of a prosecutorial discretion has been conscientiously undertaken, the only question for the court is whether the substantive offence has been committed or not. He stated that the decision whether or not to prosecute, in most cases, requires a judgment to be made about a multiplicity of interlocking circumstances. Therefore, even if it can be shown that in one respect or another, part or parts of the relevant guidance or policy have not been adhered to, it does not follow that there would inevitably be an abuse of process. It remains open to the prosecution in an individual case, for good reason, to disapply its own policy or guidance. Only in cases of misconduct or oppression or where there has been unreasonable disregard for or unjustified or inexplicable disapplication of existing prosecutorial policy is the exercise of prosecutorial discretion liable to be impugned by the courts.

However, this general approach was balanced by restatement of the need for prosecutorial independence and objectivity, particularly in cases where prosecutors are co-located with those involved in the investigation of offences. The first of these cases is *Moss & Son Ltd v Crown Prosecution Service* [2012] EWHC 3658 (Admin). This case concerned the employment, by a dairy, of a dairy herdsman through an unlicensed gang master which was operating in breach of the relevant regulations, in that it was paying the herdsman less than the minimum agricultural wage. The dairy operator challenged the decision to prosecute as an abuse of process in that it was arbitrary and outside of the prosecuting authority's policy as to how and when prosecutions would be instigated. The court refused a stay and this decision was upheld on appeal.

The Lord Chief Justice, Lord Thomas, stated that a failure to follow and apply a prosecution policy would not of itself give rise to a stay on the grounds of abuse of process. More had to be proved; the defendant must establish misconduct or oppression (as set out in more detail in the case of *ex parte Bennett* [1994] 1 AC 42). The court said:

> It is of some importance that the principles in A can be applied to all prosecutorial decisions. For that and other constitutional reasons, there should be clear arrangements which ensure that decisions on prosecution policy and the decision to prosecute are made by persons who can exercise their judgment entirely independently of the Executive Government or Executive Agency.

And then in the case of *R (Barons Pub Co Ltd) v Staines Magistrates Court* [2013 EWHC] 898, judicial review was sought of a decision to prosecute a company for breaches of food hygiene legislation. The application alleged a failure, by the prosecuting local authority, to follow a prosecution policy in the form of a statutory code of practice issued by the Secretary of State for the Environment Food and Rural Affairs. The application was refused. The court indicated that proof of oppression in the sense described in Bennett and other cases would be essential if an abuse of process application was to succeed. In a case where a policy has been considered but wrongly applied, some degree of oppression above and beyond the ordinary consequences of initiating a prosecution would have to be shown. The Lord Chief Justice commented, obiter, that any prosecution policy should be reviewed by or on behalf of the DPP to ensure that it formed part of a coherent and logical approach to prosecution to be adopted by all prosecutors.

13 Sentencing considerations

It is worth looking at how environmental offences are sentenced to see whether and how the factors identified as relevant considerations for determining public interest are taken into account by sentencing courts and whether there is anything that the courts are looking at which decision makers are not, earlier on in proceedings, and whether any matters fall by the wayside.

In July 2014, the Sentencing Council of England and Wales issued a Guideline on the Sentencing of Environmental Offences.[17] This was informed by a public consultation on the issue, where views were sought from the public, members of the judiciary, legal practitioners and individuals within the criminal justice system as to the right approach to sentencing. Concern had been widely expressed that fines for environmental offences were too low. The societal value of the environment and concerns as to its degradation led to the eventual guideline for sentencers which identifies harm, risk of harm and culpability as the starting points for assessing seriousness and sentencing environmental offences. The factors that should be taken into account on sentencing are wholly analogous to the public interest factors discussed earlier. For example, under the issue of harm, the courts are asked to consider the nature of the pollutant and its ability to cause substantial adverse effect or to be noxious, widespread or pervasive with long-term health implications. These considerations would equally form part of the earlier public interest assessment of environmental effect. Courts are also asked to consider the degree of interference with other lawful activities due to the offence. This would seem to point towards maintaining the level playing field for operators within the regulatory regime but may also be intended to look at the socio-economic aspects of a large-scale environmental incident such as the explosion at the Buncefield Oil Terminal in Hertfordshire in December 2015 when an oil storage facility serving Heathrow airport sustained a catastrophic spillage and ignition. In that case the socio-economic aspects of the resultant explosion were estimated (in the resulting civil proceedings) to be approximately £1 billion.[18] This would form part of the earlier public interest assessment for the EA under financial implications.

There is an innovative approach to sentencing in the Guideline, whereby corporate offenders are classified according to size. Offenders which are companies, partnerships or bodies delivering a public or charitable service are expected to provide comprehensive accounts for the last three years, to enable the court to make an accurate assessment of their financial status. The court is then required to focus on the organisation's annual turnover or equivalent to reach a starting

---

17 Sentencing Council, Environmental Offences, Definitive Guideline, July 2014, available at www.sentencingcouncil.org.uk/publications/item/environmental-offences-definitive-guideline
18 *R v Total (UK) Ltd, Hertfordshire Oil Storage Ltd (HOSL), TAV Engineering Ltd, Motherwell Control Systems (2003), and Ltd & British Pipeline Agency Ltd, 2010* – St Albans Crown Court (Unreported); for further details see https://cdn.harper-adams.ac.uk/document/profile/150716-Health-and-Safety-Casebook—1837-to-2014502355.pdf

point for a fine. There are four tables of starting points and ranges: one for large organisations, one for medium organisations, one for small organisations and one for micro-organisations. 'Very large organisations' are outside of the tariff in the guidance but recent case law has suggested that very large penalties are appropriate.[19]

The Guideline states that the level of fine should reflect the extent to which the offender fell below the required standard. The fine should meet, in a fair and proportionate way, the objectives of punishment, deterrence and the removal of gain derived through the commission of the offence; it should not be cheaper to offend than to take the appropriate precautions. It allows some degree of leeway to the sentencing court as to the eventual penalty based on any aggravating or mitigating features present and other considerations.

The aggravating and mitigating features which are detailed within the Guideline do not add wholly new considerations to the public interest factors already described but they do spell out the importance of some aspects of these. For example, the general heading of 'History of offending' is extended to encompass the statutory aggravating feature of previous convictions[20] and an offence committed whilst on bail. Other aggravating features include obstruction of justice and, for an individual, an offence committed whilst on licence. As these factors would be considered aggravating features by a court, their presence at the decision-making stage should properly be weighed in the balance in terms of public interest. These would be considered as part of the history of offending and seriousness of the offence.

Mitigating features also play a role in enforcement decisions as part of the public interest assessment. It is not for a decision maker to usurp the role of the court, but they should have regard to those features which both the Code and the Sentencing Council have indicated that courts should consider as properly reducing seriousness or reflecting personal mitigation. These will be part of the earlier assessment of the personal circumstances of the offender. The table of aggravating and mitigating features is reproduced below and it should be noted how closely these features mirror the previously described public interest criteria.

Factors increasing seriousness

Statutory aggravating factors:

Previous convictions, having regard to a) the nature of the offence to which the conviction relates and its relevance to the current offence; and b) the time that has elapsed since the conviction

Offence committed whilst on bail or on licence

Other aggravating factors include:

History of non-compliance evidenced by receipt of warnings by regulator

---

19 *R v Sellafield Ltd & R v Network Rail Infrastructure* [2014] EWCA Crim 49
20 Criminal Justice Act 2003, s 143 (2)

Location, for example, offence near housing, schools, livestock or environmentally sensitive sites

Repeated incidents of offending or over an extended period of time, where not charged separately

Deliberate concealment of illegal nature of activity

Ignoring risks identified by employees or others

Established evidence of wider/community impact

Offence committed for financial gain

Breach of any order

Obstruction of justice

Factors reducing seriousness or reflecting personal mitigation:

No previous convictions or no relevant/recent convictions

Remorse

Evidence of steps taken to remedy problem

Compensation paid voluntarily to remedy harm caused

One-off event not commercially motivated

Little or no financial gain

Effective compliance and ethics programme

Self-reporting, co-operation and acceptance of responsibility

Good character and/or exemplary conduct

Mental disorder or learning disability, where linked to the commission of the offence

Serious medical conditions requiring urgent, intensive or long-term treatment

Age and/or lack of maturity where it affects the responsibility of the offender

Sole or primary carer for dependent relatives[21]

14 Conclusion

It is plain that similar public interest factors arise at various stages of the enforcement process. The decision as to what is the most appropriate enforcement response, a decision to divert a matter out of the criminal process by way of administrative sanction, and any eventual sentencing decision all take into account fundamental socio-legal principles about what the criminal process seeks to achieve, how the seriousness of an incident can be objectively measured, and how to assess what enforcement action is in the public interest.

The regulator's responsibilities, as set out by statute, guidance and codes of practice, are all intended to secure a just and fair outcome. For environmental offending, that means an outcome which properly provides justice to the complainant, the defendant, any qualifying victim or third party, and the environment itself, however represented, if at all. The Criminal Procedure Rules set out the

---

21 Sentencing Council, Environmental Offences, Definitive Guideline, July 2014, available at www.sentencingcouncil.org.uk/publications/item/environmental-offences-definitive-guideline

overriding objective of the just and fair determination of criminal proceedings, where these are underway. This includes fairness to all parties, acquitting the innocent and convicting the guilty, recognising the rights of defendants, respecting the interests of witnesses and victims, and dealing with cases efficiently and expeditiously.

However, for environmental offences there are significant additional wider issues in play, such as recognising the desirability of restoration, giving credit to opportunities taken to make reparation, particularly if this happens very soon after the incident giving rise to environmental damage, and an offender's commitment to measures which will enhance and protect the interests of victims, the community and the environment itself. Public interest considerations may be influenced by the size and scale of preventative measures which have been overborne by the unforeseeability or remoteness of an event which was not guarded against and occasionally the preference of those affected by a pollution incident to allow a matter to proceed by way of undertaking rather than prosecution. These are important considerations for those involved in decision making and must be approached carefully on a case-by-case basis. On occasions fine judgments must be made as to where the public interest lies, but it is to be hoped that at all stages the guiding principles described above will be of assistance.

There is now a much wider and more diverse spectrum of tools available to secure compliance with environmental legislation in the UK. The previous emphasis on hard enforcement and criminal prosecution has been supplanted by a more complex, outcome-focused regime. The decision as to which enforcement option is most appropriate is now driven by consideration of case-specific factors which are assessed against the established public interest methodologies. Whilst criminal prosecution is likely to remain the final strand of environmental protection, other more interventionist approaches are being used to secure compliance such as on-site advice and guidance and the service of enforcement notices. Civil sanctions, which may include the payment of lesser financial penalties, or involve softer enforcement mechanisms such as EUs, are designed to bring about a change in operator behaviour, and it may be a finely balanced question as to which is most appropriate in any given case. It remains to be seen how the balance plays out between each in terms of securing the best environmental outcomes. However, it is clear that there is now a much more sophisticated matrix of enforcement options, subject to public interest decision making. The new options place a considerable degree of discretion and power in the hands of the regulator, and much effort will need to go into demonstrating objectivity and independence by decision makers and establishing and maintaining the highest standards of quality oversight and scrutiny of decision making. The Environment Agency is committed to ensuring that this remains the case.*

* This chapter discusses law and policy as at May 2016. A review of the Environment Agency's enforcement documentation is anticipated during Summer 2017 involving public consultation.

Bibliography

Criminal Justice Act 2003.
Environment Act 1995, Chapter 25.
Environment Agency Enforcement and Sanctions Guidance.
Environmental Civil Sanctions (England) Order 2010, SI 2010 No. 1157.
Hampton, P. (2005). *Reducing Administrative Burdens: Effective Inspection and Enforcement*. London: HM Treasury.
Human Rights Act 1998.
Macrory, R. (2006). *Regulatory Justice: Making Sanctions Effective*. London: HM Treasury. Available at http://webarchive.nationalarchives.gov.uk/20121212135622/http://www.bis.gov.uk/files/file44593.pdf (accessed 6 February 2017).
The Code for Crown Prosecutors. Available at www.cps.gov.uk/publications/code_for_crown_prosecutors (accessed 6 February 2017).
Kramer, L. (1992). Report on proceedings of INECE Second International Conference on Environmental Enforcement. Budapest, Hungary. Closing remarks. Available at www.inece.org/2ndvol2/closing%20kramer.pdf (accessed 6 February 2017).
Regulation of Investigatory Powers Act 2000.
Regulators' Code made pursuant to section 23 Legislative and Regulatory Reform Act 2006.
Sentencing Council, Environmental Offences Definitive Guideline, July 2014. Available at www.sentencingcouncil.org.uk/wp-content/uploads/Final_Environmental_Offences_Definitive_Guideline_web1.pdf (accessed 6 February 2017).

Court cases

Associated Provincial Picture Houses Ltd v Wednesbury Corporation [1948] 1KB 223, 229–30.
Empress Car Company (Abertillary) Ltd v National Rivers Authority, HL January [1998] 2 WLR 350.
R v Total (UK) Ltd, Hertfordshire Oil Storage Ltd (HOSL), TAV Engineering Ltd, Motherwell Control Systems (2003) Ltd & British Pipeline Agency Ltd, 2010, (Unreported). see commentary at https://cdn.harper-adams.ac.uk/document/profile/150716-Health-and-Safety-Casebook—1837-to-2014502355.pdf (accessed 6 February 2017).
R v Sellafield Ltd & R v Network Rail Infrastructure [2014] EWCA Crim 49.

Chapter 10

The legal and social context of wildlife trafficking

Tanya Wyatt

1 Introduction

Wildlife trafficking or the illegal wildlife trade has been an environmental, animal welfare and criminal concern for many years, but only recently has it begun to truly capture the attention of governments and the international community. As concern has grown, so have the efforts to combat it. Yet how best to tackle a crime where human, animal, environmental and economic interests collide? This chapter explores how a legal approach, predominantly through the Convention on the International Trade in Endangered Species of Wild Fauna and Flora (CITES), to combating wildlife trafficking overlooks harm to people and animals. This is done by investigating the negative impacts of criminal law on people's livelihoods and cultural traditions. Additionally, the chapter investigates the absence of criminal law that recognizes the harm and abuse to the environment and animals that is inherent in wildlife trafficking. Finally, the chapter will give an example of an approach where a combined socio-legal solution (one that takes into account both social and legal concerns) may provide guidance on ways forward in other situations where wildlife trafficking needs to be stopped.

2 The legal context – the Convention on the International Trade in Endangered Species of Wild Fauna and Flora

CITES, founded in 1975, is the main international instrument for wildlife trade. As such, it provides the global framework in which wildlife trade takes place and therefore will be described in some detail. It is a voluntary agreement to govern all the global sales of wildlife in such a way to ensure the sustainability of the trade. The 180 member countries track and then report the amount of trade and illegal activity to the Secretariat in Geneva (CITES, 2015c). Each country establishes a Management Authority to oversee the permit process (which is briefly detailed below) and a Scientific Authority to determine the survival status of species that are traded and then how many individuals can be traded (CITES, 2015c). Depending upon that status and other negotiations between members, species can be listed on one of three appendices. The appendices reflect the potential for overexploitation and extinction and require different permits to accompany the trade. Appendix I are species which are highly endangered and have limited circumstances under which they can be traded. For instance, trading of endangered rhinoceros for breeding or scientific research would be allowed. In this case, to be legal the trade needs an export permit indicating that the country from which the wildlife is leaving has determined the trade is non-detrimental and therefore allowed and an import permit indicating the country that is receiving the wildlife has agreed. For those species facing less of a threat of overexploitation and extinction, they are listed in Appendix II. These species are subject to trade quotas limiting the number of individuals allowed to be traded. For these transactions, there must be an export permit. Appendix III is not used that often in comparison. It essentially provides official recognition that a species may be heading towards Appendix II status.

As of October 2013 there are 5,592 non-human animals listed in the CITES appendices – 630 Appendix I, 4,827 Appendix II, and 135 Appendix III (CITES, 2015a). Additionally, there are 29,905 plant species – 301 Appendix I, 29,592 Appendix II, and 12 Appendix III (CITES, 2015a). This means there are 35,497 species monitored by the Convention and 931 of those face the possibility of extinction. It is estimated that there are several million species on the planet and that only 15 percent are believed to have been discovered (Sweetlove, 2011). Even so, there is a significant number of species threatened with extinction largely because of trade. The non-human animals traded are amphibians, birds, fish, invertebrates, mammals and reptiles. The plants are the range of cacti, orchids, shrubs, trees, vascular and non-vascular plants. As mentioned, the listing of a species on to one of the CITES appendices is determined not only by the species' survival status, but also by a process of negotiation. Member countries vote to list species on the different appendices. As the last Conference of the Parties[1] in 2013 demonstrated, the threat to species is not the only consideration. Japan and China had been actively blocking the protection of shark and manta ray species despite populations that are severely decreasing (Carrington, 2013). Carrington (2013) reports a delegate at the Conference admitting the involvement of economic and political interests, as well as cultural concerns, since shark fin soup is a traditional wedding dish. Another example of political and cultural conflict within CITES negotiations could be seen in regard to a proposed ban on the trade of polar bear products. In 2013 a motion was made to end the trade of all items made from polar bear. EU countries have agreed to vote the same way on CITES proposals, so when Denmark (of which Greenland is a territory where polar bear hunting still takes place) opposed the ban on economic and cultural grounds, all members voted against it or abstained (Dale-Harris, 2013). Both of these examples are evidence of the nexus of environmental, animal welfare and economic conflicts in the wildlife trade.

1 The Conference of the Parties is the meeting of all members and committees that takes place every three years.

Each of the member countries as signatories to the Convention agree that they will bring their national legislation in line with CITES provision. In terms of criminal laws, this means they agree to prohibit trade in specimens in violation of the Convention, penalize such trade and confiscate illegally traded or possessed wildlife (CITES, 2015b). CITES monitors how well member countries are implementing such legislation. Based upon their performance, countries are placed into one of three categories. Category 1 countries are thought to generally meet the requirements for implementation (CITES, 2015b). There are 87 Category 1 countries (CITES, 2014). Category 2 countries generally do not meet all of the requirements and Category 3 countries generally do not meet some of the requirements (CITES, 2015b). Those countries and territories in Categories 2 and 3 have action plans to improve their implementation and therefore meet the standards of Category 1. These action plans vary in urgency and priority based upon how long the country has been a member – more than 20 years, between 20 and five years and less than five years. For instance, Belize is listed as a priority as it has been a member since 1981 and is a Category 3 country (CITES, 2014). Laws to meet the implementation requirements have now been drafted with the help of the CITES Standing Committee and the next step is for the legislation to be submitted (CITES, 2014). The above shows that a purely legal approach has its limitations. In this case, it is because the necessary and required criminal statutes to enforce and punish wildlife trafficking, although agreed to by 180 countries, have not been brought into practice by nearly 100 of those signatories.

The legal trade is worth billions of dollars annually and includes millions of individual wildlife (CITES, 2015c). The profits support numerous businesses, industries and individual people, which rely on wildlife for part, if not all, of their livelihood. Wildlife is also engrained in cultural traditions. Both of these will be discussed in terms of how a legal approach to governing wildlife trafficking can negatively impact upon these. This will be followed by consideration of the lack of animal welfare within such an approach.

2.1 Human livelihood

The businesses, industries and people linked to the wildlife trade depend upon a healthy environment, stable wildlife populations and access to these populations to support their activities. The United Nations Environment Program (UNEP, 2007) estimates that half of the world's jobs are linked to fisheries, forestry and agriculture. In regard to a healthy environment and stable wildlife populations, the illegal wildlife trade can threaten both of these through the loss of biodiversity from poaching and harvesting and the introduction of invasive species and/or disease through unmonitored smuggling. These can damage the health of marine environments, forests and agricultural areas and in turn the industries that rely on them. The illegal wildlife trade as a source of these environmental threats has a connection to the economic well-being of industry, governments and individuals. In order to maintain a healthy environment with viable populations of species, governments have and do limit industry's and individual people's access to wildlife. This too impacts human livelihoods.

Limiting access to wildlife often comes in the form of legislation prohibiting hunting, collecting and trade of wildlife. This is the approach taken by CITES, where member countries protect, through national law, the species that are listed in the appendices. In the most extreme cases, this may alter entire industries. As an example, in the 1800s both species of sturgeon in the United States, the Atlantic and the Shortnose, were sought after for their meat and caviar (Sweka, Mohler and Millard, 2006). The pressure on the sturgeon populations was so intense that by the 1900s the populations had severely declined and fishing was greatly reduced (Sweka et al., 2006). The Shortnose sturgeon was listed in the Endangered Species Preservation Act in 1967 (American Museum of Natural History, 2010). By 1980 the Atlantic sturgeon was again being commercially fished, but this only lasted until 1996. A moratorium was put in place on both commercial and recreational fishing of sturgeon (Sweka et al., 2006). A thriving industry was similarly destroyed in New Zealand. When the Europeans invaded in the 1830s, the native Kauri trees were pervasively logged, causing a massive decline in their population (Terra Nature, 2003). Only 1 percent of the original forests survive after all of the local construction, exporting of logs, clearing for agriculture and fires (Terra Nature, 2003). Although timber remains an important industry in New Zealand, Kauri trees were protected in 1973, so can no longer be logged (Terra Nature, 2003). These examples are proof of alterations to industries through legal means. The sturgeon industry ceased to operate after the species were overexploited and thus in need of protection. The Kauri trees, a native hardwood that could have provided a unique product, are off limits because they too were overexploited to the point where the species needed legal protection to survive. Both of these cost people their jobs as well as damaging the environment.

In addition to employment, people are reliant on the environment in other ways. The environment directly supports rural villagers and other populations of people living in the area or nearby. Legislation protecting that environment and the wildlife may mean a loss of income, but may also mean a loss of resources to build shelter and a loss of a food source to feed their families. This potentially will impact upon people's health and where they are able to live. In places like Indonesia, where it is believed tens of millions of people directly depend on the forests for their livelihoods (Four Corners, 2002), creating national parks and nature reserves that protect forests and non-human animals can have far-reaching implications for the livelihoods of those people in proximity to these areas. There are further examples of this from all over the world. For instance, in Malawi when Liwonde National Park was created in the 1970s little consideration was given to the natural resource use and needs of the local people (BirdLife International, 2011). This has led to resentment and lack of incentive for those people to support the park or the conservation efforts (BirdLife International, 2011). Similarly, in India in order to protect the endangered Western Tragopan (a brightly feathered pheasant native to the Himalaya), human pressure on its habitat is strictly minimized (Chhatre and Saberwal, 2005). This means restrictions on grazing of livestock and plant collecting, traditional activities for the local people. These are just a few snapshots of the many conflicts like this that are taking place around the globe.

2.2 Cultural traditions

People's consumption and relationship with wildlife is more than just as a source of income, sustenance or shelter. Wildlife for many communities has cultural meaning that is preserved through long-standing historic traditions. Again, when legal provisions block access to wildlife, this has human implications – in this instance on the cultural traditions of people, and often indigenous communities. In particular, legal bans on certain wildlife may affect people's demand for what have been categorized as processed commodities, traditional medicines and food, consumption of which may in part be driven by cultural practices (Wyatt, 2013b).

Much of the wildlife that is consumed is processed into products for purchase. This means that the wildlife are manufactured into objects and often these objects have a cultural significance (Wyatt, 2013b). This category of processed commodities includes a range of species and their derivatives. Timber for manufacture into furniture, decorations, houses and so forth, and fur from mammals for clothing, rugs and carpets are just two examples. As evident from these two examples, a fairly substantial transformation takes place to turn the wildlife into a product, and skilled workers and craftspeople undertake the work. Both of these examples too have an element of cultural tradition to their consumption. For example, fur and animal skins have been made and used by numerous aboriginal tribes. If international legal protection were given to fur-bearing mammals without an exception for indigenous people, it would impact upon this traditional practice. For example, in the proposed polar bear ban referred to earlier, currently indigenous tribes can hunt polar bears, but this would have changed and thus changed the people's ability to use the fur and other parts (Dale-Harris, 2013).

The consumption of traditional medicines is similar to the above processed commodities in regard to historical traditions. Traditional medicine "refers to the knowledge, skills and practices based on the theories, beliefs and experiences indigenous to different cultures, used in the maintenance of health and in the prevention, diagnosis, improvement or treatment of physical and mental illness" (World Health Organization, 2013). For wildlife trade and trafficking, the demand for ingredients to make and use traditional medicines mostly comes from China and Southeast Asia. There is the long-held cultural belief that non-human animals and plants taken from the wild have specific properties. These properties impart traditional medicines with their healing ability (Drury, 2009). So specific treatments made from wild individual non-human animals or plants will have special properties as opposed to the same treatment made from the same wildlife raised in captivity. So even though bear bile, used mainly for treating arthritis, is available from legal farms in Far East and Southeast Asia where bile is collected from caged bears and then made into medicine, there are those who will still seek out bile from illegally caught wild bears (World Society for the Protection of Animals, 2015). The legal approach, in this case protecting bears from hunting and poaching, comes into conflict with human cultural tradition to use their parts as medicines. Even with a farmed alternative, which has its own animal welfare implications, and with the availability of a synthetic version of bile as well, the consumption of wild bears' bile is ongoing and resilient to criminalization.

As with processed commodities and traditional medicines, the species of wildlife in demand for food are diverse. The consumption is also diverse ranging from the demand for 'exotic' foods such as bear paws and whale to luxury foods like caviar and truffles. There is also routine consumption of wildlife that is prevalent and local to certain regions. This was, until recently, the case with pangolins – a scaly mammal found in Southeast Asia and Africa. In Southeast Asia, historically they have been an item on menus in wildlife meat restaurants. But as Pantel and Anak (2010) report, they have become so popular to eat (as well as their scales being used in traditional medicines) that their survival is threatened. In parts of Africa, traditional reliance on bushmeat similarly can place pressure on endangered and threatened wildlife populations. Bushmeat is the term used to describe wildlife taken for food (Bushmeat Crisis Task Force, 2009b). The term originates from Africa, where the forest is referred to as the 'bush', but is also used to describe the same practice in Asia and South America (Bushmeat Crisis Task Force, 2009b). There are two aspects to bushmeat consumption that highlight its cultural nature. The first is that bushmeat is smuggled to diaspora communities in the West, where communities still insist on eating traditional foods (Bushmeat Crisis Task Force, 2009a). Cane rats, for instance, have been found for sale in a London market near African diaspora communities (Lynn, 2012). The second aspect is that, like traditional medicines, consumption of wildlife meat is sometimes justified in terms of wild meat having better flavor or that the wildlife will impart their strengths to the person eating them (Momii, 2002). The person consuming the wild meat then takes on the essence of that wildlife, like the strength of a tiger (Momii, 2002). As in the previous two contexts, legal restrictions that ban the hunting of wildlife for food can be met with resistance since they conflict with cultural and historic traditions.

The presence or absence of a historically engrained culture for the consumption of specific wildlife has a significant role to play in the success of criminalization of hunting and collecting of that species. The use of some processed commodities, traditional medicines and food for different groups of people has persisted within their culture for generations. Ivory carving takes place throughout China and Southeast Asia, traditional medicines also have a long history there, and in some countries in Africa bushmeat is a part of people's diet. What culture means for efforts to combat wildlife trafficking is that a purely legal approach will be met with resistance. For example, despite rapidly decreasing numbers of some of wildlife consumed in these ways, such as rhinos and pangolins, the demand for these wildlife products continues. Despite public campaigns in consumption countries by the World Wildlife Fund (WWF) and other NGOs to obey the law or save the environment and the wildlife, demand continues. This supports the idea that a singular legal approach to stop wildlife trafficking will not be completely successful and must be combined with other methods, as will be discussed later. First, however, further oversights of a legal approach are detailed – that of non-human animal welfare and harm.

2.3 Animal welfare

Historically, criminal law and related civil and administrative regulations have adopted human-centric definitions of crime and harm. This means that non-human animals are defined as property and not victims in their own right (Beirne, 1999), and that the environment and plants have largely been ignored. Yet there are numerous cases where non-human animals suffer and are injured in spite of recognition by the law. Wildlife trade and trafficking are no exception, and CITES is no different from other legal provisions in its anthropocentric foundation. As it is a trade treaty that is meant to sustain the utilization of wildlife as a resource, it is probably not surprising that it has no specific welfare requirements. The Management Authority of the member country is tasked "to minimize the risk of injury, damage to health and cruel treatment" for 'live specimens' that are being cared for, handled, prepared, held, shipped and/or transported (CITES, 1973, p. 3). They are also expected to set up a rescue center to look after the welfare of confiscated specimens (CITES, 1973). These are all fairly vague terms and subject to interpretation. It does mean the capturing and harvesting at the initial phase or the rearing of captive-bred wildlife, which is an allowed exception under CITES, has no oversight in terms of animal welfare. The member state may enact such provisions, but it is not part of the required implementation of the Convention. However, as demonstrated below, the entire journey from capture to being sold holds potential for harm and abuse in both the legal and illegal trades.

Most non-human animals that fuel the legal and illegal trades must be kidnapped (captured) from their habitat. If they are being made into a product of some sort – medicine or commodity – or eaten, clearly they have to be killed. Other wildlife must be farmed, which can be a source of suffering and injury in itself. If livestock farming of domestic animals is used as a comparison, then it is clear that the conditions captive non-human animals are kept in and the practices that they are subjected to may be traumatic and harmful. For example, in pig farming pigs are kept indoors without access to dirt or mud. This disrupts the pigs' natural behaviors (Wyatt, 2014). This combined with overcrowding and close quarters means the pigs act out by biting each other. Rather than addressing the root cause of the behavior, unnatural living conditions, the pigs have their tails removed to prevent the most severe injuries. Numerous non-human animals (or humans) all living together creates toxic amounts of feces. In the case of pig farms, the noxious gasses harm not only the pigs, but also the farmers and the surrounding environment (Wyatt, 2014). Captive breeding of wildlife, as seen also through bear bile farms (World Society for the Protection of Animals, 2015), is not likely to improve upon the conditions for captive non-human animals or the practices that harm them.

To capture wildlife alive, a variety of tactics are used including nets, snares, pits and leg-traps. Being caught in any of these ways causes stress for the wildlife and holds the potential for injury. All of these methods entail the trafficker having to come back and check the trap for captured wildlife, so further suffering takes place while the wildlife struggles in the trap trying to free themselves. Depending upon how long they wait to be collected, they can also suffer from lack of food and water and exposure to either heat or cold. For those being consumed as food or a product, they undergo the ultimate form of injury – they are killed. This may happen immediately – for instance, for those wildlife consumed as bushmeat, the trap will kill them. Guns and bows and arrows are of course used to hunt wildlife as well. Some, though, are subjected to cruel forms of death, such as pangolins which are sometimes boiled alive to be made into soup (Pantel and Anak, 2010). When some rhinos are poached, they are only tranquilized. Their horns are then sawn off while they are alive and then they are left to die from shock or blood loss (Milliken and Shaw, 2012). Sharks are caught, their fins cut off and then they are tossed back into the ocean. Most of them die a slow painful death (Humane Society International, 2013). How wildlife is caught or killed is not an aspect of CITES, so both the legal and illegal trades harm the wildlife.

In both the legal and illegal trades, wildlife that remains alive must contend with being transported. In the case of the illegal trade, this most likely means being hidden in order to be smuggled to the final destination. Although legal trade takes place in the open, there are welfare concerns that should be addressed. Stress and therefore some level of trauma appear to be inevitable when non-human animals are transported on modern modes of transportation, such as flying. This is due to increased levels of fear stemming from the novelty of the experience (Grandin, 1997). Grandin (1997) documented increased levels of cortisol, a stress hormone, even in cattle that had been trained to enter the squeeze chute to be loaded on to trucks. Presumably, for non-habituated wildlife the stress would be the same if not greater. Smuggling adds further complications because of the need for secrecy. This increases the likelihood that the transportation will involve injurious and harmful conditions. The exception to this would be where the illegal wildlife is being smuggled using fraudulent or forged paperwork that makes it appear legal. In this case, the laundered wildlife appears to be a legitimate trade and is therefore transported like any other legal wildlife. However, as mentioned, this does not remove the possibility for harm. Non-human animals are sometimes shipped in containers that may be too small for them or which are overcrowded and have too many individuals in the container (Wyatt, 2013a). As an example, even in Europe where there are regulations stipulating welfare for non-human animals during transportation, there are still violations. Turtles legally imported into the UK have been found shipped in food containers that were then packed into a large wooden crate with other boxes full of reptiles. The inspection found there were too many turtles in the smaller containers so that each of them did not have their own space to stand (Wyatt, 2013a). Furthermore, plane and ship voyages can be lengthy. Conditions in the cargo hold of planes or ships may mean significant temperature fluctuations and discomfort. The wildlife must also deal with the lack of food and water, the darkness and the loud noise. Again, these are the potential injuries and stress caused when the transportation is legal.

When the non-human animal must be completely hidden, the transportation is even more harmful. In order to hide a live non-human animal, the animal often needs to be sedated or subdued in some fashion. For example, Wyatt (2011) found that smuggled raptors are often tranquilized while they are smuggled and in some cases have their eyelids sewn shut to try to make them calm. All of the birds of prey are swaddled. They are then usually stuffed into tubes and then hidden in suitcases or compartments on various transportation methods (Lyapustin, 2006). These conditions contribute to the estimate that only 10 percent of birds smuggled live to reach their final destination (Lyapustin, 2006). The conditions for smuggling other wildlife such as reptiles and mammals are similar (Wyatt, 2013b).

The harm, injury, suffering and death through all parts of the wildlife trade provide evidence that, either legal or illegal, there are non-human animal welfare concerns. By only employing a legal approach to combating wildlife trafficking, the element of animal welfare is invisible. This is due to the predominantly anthropocentric foundation of the majority of legal systems. As discussed below, incorporation of concerns beyond only those captured by criminal law holds the potential to improve the efforts to curb this injurious crime. This is not only in terms of animal welfare, but, as argued above, to ensure sustainable environments and human livelihoods as well.

3 A combined socio-legal approach to combat wildlife trafficking

Efforts to legally protect the environment and wildlife from trafficking often take the form of national parks, which include hunting and foraging restrictions. This cuts off people's access to wildlife. There are exceptions to national parks, such as creation of nature conservancies which go beyond only legal considerations. Namibia, in southern Africa, is often given as an example of a place where legal provisions and community input and concerns are inseparable. Their socio-legal approach to protecting the environment and wildlife has been very successful in terms of human livelihoods as demonstrated below. The legal protection for the environment is human-centered and is guaranteed in the Constitution. Article 95, Promotion of the Welfare of the People, states in section 1 that the government will promote policies aimed at

> maintenance of ecosystems, essential ecological processes and biological diversity of Namibia and utilization of living natural resources on a sustainable basis for the benefit of all Namibians, both present and future; in

particular, the Government shall provide measures against the dumping or recycling of foreign nuclear and toxic waste on Namibian territory.

(Namibian Government, 1990)

Ecosystems, their services, biological diversity and natural resources must be preserved for the use of living and future generations of Namibians. This provides the legal foundation, then, for conservation policy throughout the country. Conservation, particularly of wildlife, is important for Namibia as it has unique landscapes and charismatic mega fauna, such as black rhinoceros, cheetahs, desert elephants, giraffes, leopards, lions and zebras (WWF, 2011), several of which are endangered. Alpert (1996) notes that poaching for feathers, horns, ivory and skins had reduced the wildlife populations in Namibia by 90 percent by the mid-1990s. Not only is the conservation environmentally important, but it is also economically important because of the possibility of ecotourism and the supporting service industry.

Upon independence from South Africa in 1990, Namibia took a progressive approach to conservation by ensuring that the benefit from, and management of use of, wildlife was given to local people (Boudreaux and Nelson, 2011). This was partly inspired by the historical context of wildlife management in the country. The white commercial farmers, who owned the land they farmed, had been given incentives to protect wildlife on that land (Alpert, 1996). Wildlife in these areas appeared to decrease less than in other areas. At the same time, those who did not own land and could not afford hunting licenses – usually black citizens – were known to help commercial poachers (Alpert, 1996). Presumably, this was to reap some benefit from the wildlife that was denied to them. A new approach was then taken to address both conservation and social justice. This manifested as a nationwide community-based natural resource management program supported by a variety of international governments and non-governmental organizations like WWF's Living in a Finite Environment (LIFE). These organizations sought to aid in the testing of a revolutionary idea that viewing wildlife as an asset makes it worth saving for present and future use (WWF, 2015). There are now more than 50 local conservancies and the program is expanding to community forests (Boudreaux and Nelson 2011). Community-based natural resource management is thus a merging of the conservation of nature with economic empowerment of all rural people. As Bandyopadhyay *et al.* (2004) relate, the basic foundation for these initiatives is that if communities are given the authority and control over wildlife resources, they will manage them well and protect them because they will profit from them.

The situation in Namibia provides proof that this is true. Boudreaux and Nelson (2011) found that both rural incomes and human capital are rising. Bandyopadhyay *et al.* (2004) also discovered that households partaking in the conservancies saw an increase in cash income, non-cash rewards and/or community-level benefits, such as access to improved schools, hospitals and infrastructure. Their findings indicate the poorest people may not necessarily receive the most benefit, but also that the more elite or well-off in the communities were not disproportionately benefiting either. This is significant as an argument against community-based initiatives is that power can get predominantly captured by traditional hierarchies, further marginalizing the poor (Bandyopadhyay et al., 2004). In fact, Namibia's approach is considered by some to be one of the most successful programs to legally empower the poor in recent times, since local people now have regular chances to make decisions and participate in the conservancy meetings (Boudreaux and Nelson, 2011). This is formalized as the conservancies must establish voluntary membership. Then, from these members, a management committee is chosen. The committee then drafts a constitution, which will be legally recognized, that sets out the management of wildlife in the conservancy as well as how the benefits from the wildlife will be shared amongst the members (Boudreaux and Nelson, 2011) As part of this, they must negotiate with neighboring conservancies or private land owners the borders of their conservancy (Boudreaux and Nelson, 2011).

In regard to the second aspect of community-based natural resource management, there has been significant increase of a range of wildlife species in Namibia on the conservancies (Boudreaux and Nelson, 2011; WWF, 2011). Hoof stock numbers such as springbok, oryx and zebra have risen from nearly zero to "52,000, 25,000 and 15,000 respectively in 2008" (NACSO, 2010, p. 17). Elephant numbers are also on the rise from 100 to 1,000, probably due in large part to the decrease in poaching and the improved management of wildlife–human conflict that takes place in shared spaces (NASCO, 2010).

That is not to say there are not criticisms or problems with community-based natural resource management programs. Even in Namibia, where the conservancies appear widespread and have international recognition, Bandyopadhyay et al. (2004) found that less than a quarter of residents knew about the conservancies. They suggest an awareness-raising campaign may be warranted in order for more people to take part and therefore benefit from the conservancies. The local people are financially benefiting as well as gaining skills from participation in the conservancies, but Boudreaux and Nelson (2011) point out that there are still tensions regarding land tenure. For example, although the communities control the conservancies, the government still owns the land. Additionally, the land is still communal, so not only is there the conservancy committee, but there also is the communal land board. This board has a traditional composition of elders and other community members. The interests of the communal land board and the conservancy may not always align and there is no clarity as to which group's decision may have priority over the other's decision (Boudreaux and Nelson, 2011). In regard to human capital and skills, there is also the worry that donor and development aid to help train and enhance the capacity of local people to govern and run businesses will not always be there to support this program, and more needs to be done to enable local people to become self-sufficient (Boudreaux and Nelson, 2011). As mentioned, although there has been some improvement in the management of wildlife–human conflict, 50 percent of residents surveyed reported they had experienced damage to their crops or loss of livestock from wildlife (Bandyopadhyay et al., 2004). Some conservancies have tackled this through compensation programs for damage or loss, but it does remain an ongoing challenge (Boudreaux and Nelson, 2011). An added complication is that the Ministry of Environment and Tourism has control over threatened and endangered species as well as those that may come into conflict with people. The ministry also is in charge of setting the quotas for hunting of this wildlife (Boudreaux and Nelson, 2011). This is in compliance with CITES implementation, where a national authority must oversee listed species. As the conservancies do not always agree with the quotas set (too few leads to less revenue) or the handling of cases of wildlife–human conflict (Boudreaux and Nelson, 2011), this is a source of friction.

The consideration of the social aspects of wildlife in the context of Namibia, though not without its flaws, goes a long way in addressing the problems discussed earlier of a purely legal approach to the combating of wildlife trafficking. Giving the local communities oversight of the wildlife does seem to help the wildlife survive as well as support the livelihoods of the people. What is not evident from the above example is the issue of animal welfare. Further research would need to be undertaken to ascertain if the hunting provisions of the government and the conservancy takes into account the suffering and injury of the wildlife. The extra attention given in Namibia to wildlife–human conflicts, however, does indicate a concern for the well-being of both the people and the wildlife.

4 Conclusion

Wildlife trafficking will not be reduced if a purely legal approach is taken. This is partly because legislation is rarely fully implemented, leaving places where the crime will still take place, and not always enforced – again providing a gap for criminal activity to happen. That nearly 100 countries have not fully implemented CITES is evidence that a strictly legal approach can fall short. Additionally, legal approaches will also not be fully successful because they fail to consider the human element to the crime. This chapter has specifically focused on the human livelihood and cultural aspects and how these link to some wildlife trafficking. If a resource or cultural object is suddenly taken from a community through a legal ban on the use or consumption of wildlife, it is likely the people will not adhere to the restriction. Other provisions need to be put in place in conjunction with bans. This may be alternative livelihood programs, educational campaigns about the environmental consequences of wildlife consumption or limitations rather than bans. Key, however, is the involvement of local communities in these decisions as well as their participation in their implementation and governance. In this way communities and wildlife can benefit from conservation. A legal approach may also leave out the welfare of the wildlife, as is the case with CITES. In a holistic program that takes into account the well-being of human communities alongside the conservation of the environment, it seems possible to also integrate the well-being of the wildlife. If we are to sustainably consume and use wildlife, there should also be consideration to do so in a humane manner. Efforts that combine legal statutes with social and environmental elements stand the best chance of curbing a complex crime like wildlife trafficking.

Bibliography

Alpert, P. (1996). Integrated conservation and development projects. *Bioscience*, 46(11), 845–855.
American Museum of Natural History. (2010). Quantifying the relative abundance of juvenile Atlantic Sturgeon, Acipenser oxyrhychus, in the Hudson River. Available at www.amnh.org/learn-teach/young-naturalist-awards/winning-essays/2010/quanti fying-the-relative-abundance-of-juvenile-atlantic-sturgeon-acipenser-ox yrhychus-in-the-hudson-river (accessed 17 January 2017).
Bandoyopadhyay, S., Humavindu, M., Shyamsundar, P., and Wang, L. (2004). Do households gain from community-based natural resource management? An evaluation of community conservancies in Namibia. World Bank Policy Research Working Paper No. 3337. Washington, DC: World Bank.
Beirne, P. (1999). For a nonspeciesist criminology. *Criminology*, 37(1), 117–147.
BirdLife International. (2011). Involving local communities in the management of Liwonde National Park in Malawi. Presented as part of the BirdLife State of the world's birds website. Available at http://datazone.birdlife.org/sowb/casestudy/involving-local-communities-in-the-management-of-liwonde-national-park-in-malawi (accessed 6 February 2017).
Boudreaux, K., and Nelson, F. (2011). Community conservation in Namibia: Empowering the poor with property rights. *Economic Affairs*, 31(2), 17–24.
Bushmeat Crisis Task Force. (2009a). Smuggling dangerous delicacies: Island woman tried to import monkey and antelope parts; she also faces unrelated assault charges. Available at www.bushmeat.org/node/75 (accessed 17 January 2017).
Bushmeat Crisis Task Force. (2009b). What is the bushmeat crisis? Available at www. bushmeat.org/bushmeat_and_wildlife_trade/what_is_the_bushmeat_crisis (accessed 17 January 2017).
Carrington, D. (2013, 11 March). Five shark species win protection against finning trade. *The Guardian*. Available at www.theguardian.com/environment/2013/mar/11/shark-sp ecies-greater-protection-finning (accessed 17 January 2017).
Chhatre, A., and Saberwal, V. (2005). Political incentives for biodiversity conservation. *Conservation Biology*, 19(2), 310–317.
Convention on the International Trade in Endangered Species of Wild Fauna and Flora (CITES). (1973). Text of the Convention. Available at http://cites.org/sites/default/files/eng/disc/CITES-Convention-EN.pdf (accessed 17 January 2017).
Convention on the International Trade in Endangered Species of Wild Fauna and Flora (CITES). (2014). Status of legislative progress for implementing CITES. Available at http://cites.org/sites/default/files/eng/prog/Legislation/CITES-NLP-status-Annex.pdf (accessed 17 January 2017).
Convention on the International Trade in Endangered Species of Wild Fauna and Flora (CITES). (2015a). The CITES Species. Available at http://cites.org/eng/disc/species. php (accessed 17 January 2017).
Convention on the International Trade in Endangered Species of Wild Fauna and Flora (CITES). (2015b). National laws for implementing the Convention. Available at http://cites.org/eng/legislation (accessed 17 January 2017).

Convention on the International Trade in Endangered Species of Wild Fauna and Flora (CITES). (2015c). What is CITES? Available at http://cites.org/eng/disc/what.php (accessed 17 January 2017).

Dale-Harris, L. (2013). Why joint European votes are bad for wildlife. *Spiegel Online*, 21 March. Available at www.spiegel.de/international/europe/vote-against-polar-bears-evidence-of-growing-eu-bloc-vote-problem-a-890064.html (accessed 6 February 2017).

Drury, R.C. (2009). *Identifying and Understanding Consumers of Wild Animal Products in Hanoi, Vietnam: Implication for Conservation Management*. Doctor of Philosophy Thesis, University College London. Available at http://eprints.ucl.ac.uk/16275/1/16275.pdf (accessed 17 January 2017).

Four Corners. (2002). Consequences of illegal logging. ABC Net. Available at www.abc.net.au/4corners/content/2002/timber_mafia/resources/resources_consequences1.htm (accessed 17 January 2017).

Grandin, T. (1997). Assessment of stress during handling and transport. *Journal of Animal Science*, 75(1), 249–257.

Humane Society International. (2013). Shark finning. Available at www.hsi.org/issues/shark_finning (accessed 17 January 2017).

Lyapustin, S. (2006). The smuggling of falcons of the Far East – A threat to the existence of rare birds. *Preservation of Bioresources*, March, 89–100. (In Russian.)

Lynn, G. (2012, 17 September). Cane Rat meat 'sold to public' in Ridley Road Market. BBC News. Available at www.bbc.co.uk/news/uk-england-london-19622903 (accessed 17 January 2017).

Milliken, T. and Shaw, J. (2012). *The South Africa – Viet Nam Rhino Horn Trade Nexus: A Deadly Combination of Institutional Lapses, Corrupt Wildlife Industry Professionals and Asian Crime Syndicates. A TRAFFIC Report*. Johannesburg: TRAFFIC.

Momii, M. (2002). *A Comparative Study of Wildlife Law in the UK and Japan and the Differences in Cultural Context*. Doctoral Thesis, University of Kent.

Namibian Association of CBNRM (Community based natural resource management) Support Organizations (NACSO). (2010). *Namibia's Communal Conservancies: A Review of Progress and Challenges in 2009*. Windhoek: NACSO.

Namibian Government. (1990). The Constitution of the Republic of Namibia. Available at www.orusovo.com/namcon (accessed 17 January 2017).

Pantel, S. and Anak, N.A. (2010). *A Preliminary Assessment of Sunda Pangolin Trade in Sabah. A TRAFFIC Report*. Petaling Jaya, Malaysia: TRAFFIC.

Sweetlove, L. (2011). Number of species on Earth tagged at 8.7 million. *Nature*, 23 August 2011. Available at www.nature.com/news/2011/110823/full/news.2011.498.html (accessed 17 January 2017).

Sweka, J.A., Mohler, J. and Millard, M.J. (2006). *Relative Abundance Sampling of Juvenile Atlantic Sturgeon in the Hudson River*. Lamar, PA: U.S. Fish & Wildlife Service – Northeast Fishery Center.

Terra Nature. (2003). Kauri Logging. New Zealand Ecology: Big Trees. Available at www.terranature.org/kauriLogging.htm (accessed 17 January 2017).

United Nations Environment Program (UNEP). (2007). *Global Environment Outlook 4*. Nairobi, Kenya: UNEP.

World Health Organization (WHO). (2013). Traditional and complementary medicines. Available at www.who.int/topics/traditional_medicine/en (accessed 17 January 2017).

World Society for the Protection of Animals (WSPA). (2015). Bear bile industry. Previously available at www.wspa-international.org/wspaswork/bears/bearfarming/default.aspx (accessed 28 April 2015).

World Wildlife Fund. (2011). Namibia: How communities led a conservation success story. Available at http://wwf.panda.org/who_we_are/history/50_years_of_achievements/stories/?200002/namibia-how-communities-led-a-conservation-success-story (accessed 17 January 2017).

World Wildlife Fund. (2015). WWF on the ground in Namibia. Available at http://wwf.panda.org/what_we_do/where_we_work/project/projects_in_depth/life (accessed 5 May 2015).

Wyatt, T. (2011). The illegal raptor trade in the Russian Federation. *Contemporary Justice Review*, 14(2), 103–123.

Wyatt, T. (2013a). The local context of wildlife trafficking: The Heathrow Animal Reception Centre. In D. Westerhuis, R. Walters and T. Wyatt (eds), *Emerging Issues in Green Criminology: Exploring Power, Justice and Harm* (pp. 108–126). Basingstoke: Palgrave Macmillan.

Wyatt, T. (2013b). *Wildlife Trafficking: A Deconstruction of the Crime, Victims and Offenders*. Basingstoke: Palgrave Macmillan.

Wyatt, T. (2014). A criminological exploration of the industrialisation of pig farming. *Internet Journal of Criminology: Special Issue on Green Criminology*. Online: www.internetjournalofcriminology.com, 12–28.

Chapter 11

Eco-crime and green activism

Reece Walters

> Each week at least two people are being killed for taking a stand against environmental destruction. Some are shot by police during protests, others gunned down by hired assassins. As companies go in search of new land to exploit, increasingly people are paying the ultimate price for standing in their way.
> (Global Witness, 2015, p. 1)

1 Introduction

The involvement of citizens in environmental activism has been pivotal to the progression and development of environmental policies and regulation (Clifford and Edwards, 2012). Environmental movements are becoming central in the identification, detection, and prevention of environmental crime. Their resources, technologies, data bases, and personnel are increasingly utilized by law enforcement agencies to police, regulate, and prosecute both organized and localized environmental crime. The advent and mobilization of activist movements for prevention and regulation of organized environmental crime is arguably what Habermas referred to as a style of participatory democracy or more specifically the 'revival of the public sphere'. Social movements respond to a passive and compliant citizenry by constructing a counter discourse that is harnessed through action, and mobilized as truth (Habermas, 1991). Here, environmental activism, through technology and networks of action, local alliances, as well as appeals to citizens and officials, elevates the social movement to a reliable and reputable status that is inculcated into government and regulatory structures. Environmental activism becomes not mere representative democracy but participatory democracy with both a visible presence and impact. As such, with public and political integration, it becomes a new and important form of environmental governance. The momentum created by environmental movements is, to quote Foucault, a source of mobilized power. He argued that 'innovation no longer occurs through parties, syndicates, bureaucracies, politicians. It consists of an individual, moral concern.' For Foucault, coordinated and concerned citizens who coalesce and form alliances of collective concern become accepted and relied upon as alternative knowledges or regimes of 'truth'. Such grassroots endeavours are powerful innovations capable of influencing governing authorities and commercial enterprises (Foucault, 1979, p. 23).

As this chapter will discuss, green activists have formed important networks in environmental law enforcement and are increasingly drawn upon by official agencies for intelligence. On the other hand, environmental or green activism has become a threat to corporate and governing elites that seek power and profit through the exploitation of natural resources. It is widely known that environmental activists have long been the targets of corporate spying, police infiltration, and state espionage (Lubbers, 2012). As such, the plight of those seeking to protect and preserve the environment through vocal and direct public action has been both risky and dangerous. The opening quotation attests to the perils of contemporary green activism, but also highlights the intrinsic power and impact of those who resist capitalism and environmental despoliation. The international NGO Global Witness reported that between 2002 and 2013, a total of 908 environmental activists were killed across 35 countries with only ten reported convictions (Lakhani, 2014). It concludes that two environmental activists are killed every week, stating: 'Many of those facing threats are ordinary people opposing land grabs, mining operations and the industrial timber trade, often forced from their homes and severely threatened by environmental devastation' (Global Witness, 2014, p. 4).

This chapter examines the role of environmental activism in preventing, exposing, and regulating eco-crime. It seeks to understand the dynamics of the environmental protest movement and why green activists are increasingly the targets of corporate and state intervention, while also being relied upon as quasi-state agents of environmental law enforcement. In doing so, this chapter draws on original fieldwork conducted at the Faslane Peace Camp, the world's longest-running anti-nuclear demonstration that has been stationed on the Clyde in Scotland continuously since 1981.

2 Eco-crime, green criminology and environmental movements

The term 'eco-crime' is often preferred over 'environmental crime' when exploring state and corporate exploitations of the environment (Walters, 2010). It encapsulates a range of different acts, not all of which are illegal in all jurisdictions. This term covers legal and government dominated terminology of 'environmental crime' which is often used to define specific disorder-type offences and thus fails to acknowledge the social, cultural, and economic consequences experienced by people who are the victims of acts that damage the environment. In contrast, an important dimension of 'eco-crime' is recognition that the 'environment' includes impacts on both human and non-human species. The term 'eco-crime' has its origins in social movements and within the lexicon of green activism. It seeks to identify and resist the harms caused by the powerful and governing elites who manipulate the environment for personal or political gain (see Walters, 2011; Westra, 2004) As Jeffrey Reiman (1979) has succinctly argued in his classic text

The Rich Get Richer and the Poor Get Prison, 'the more likely it is for a particular form of crime to be committed by middle- and upper-class people, the less likely it is that it will be treated as a criminal offence' (Carribine *et al.*, 2004, p. 77).

The use of 'eco-crime' is an attempt to redress this imbalance and cast light on the unethical and harmful acts of the powerful. This chapter argues that the term 'eco-crime' is better able to encapsulate existing legal definitions of environmental crime as well as sociological analyses of those environmental harms not necessarily specified by law (Walters, 2010). The term also permits analyses that transcend national borders. When eco-crime is contextualized within notions of harm, we can observe a broadening of the gaze beyond legal terrains to include discourses on risk, rights, and regulation. As a result, eco-crime extends existing definitions of environmental crime to include licensed or lawful acts of ecological degradation committed by states and corporations. Harmful environmental actions committed in pursuit of free trade or progress are 'attacks on the human person' that deprive civilians (notably the poor and marginalised) from the social, cultural, and economic benefits of their environment (Westra, 2004). Hence, the term 'eco-crime' is widely adopted and endorsed within protest movements because it positions environmental harms within broader notions of social justice and exclusion. This is consistent with the objectives of a green criminology, an evolving set of critical narratives seeking to shift political and legal discourses to recognize and inculcate acts of environmental harm and exploitation (Lynch and Stretesky, 2014). Or as Natali (2010) has noted, green criminology 'encompasses those dimensions of damage, injustice and social harm often neglected by criminal law and by the criminal justice system' (cited in South and Brisman, 2013a, p. 3).

The criminal justice system 'neglects' or fails to process actions not reflected in criminal statutes. As such, agents of the state are not routinely involved in the prevention and prosecution of those harmful environmental acts beyond legal definitions and thus outside official regulatory regimes. Moreover, insufficient resources and limited political will often impede the identification and prevention of environmental offences. For White and Heckenberg (2014, p. 228), green activists provide an increasingly important environmental law enforcement role, stepping 'into the breach, exposing instances of ecological and species harm, providing details of poor regulation and enforcement practices, and contributing both formally and informally to crime reduction and prosecution processes'. There are emerging examples of environmental activism combining with international policing instruments to combat organized environmental crime (White, 2011). We are witnessing international conferences and workshops focused on environmental crime where law enforcement officials are collaborating with green activists and policymakers to enhance knowledge and improve detection and prevention strategies (EJOLT, 2014). Both Interpol and Europol have actively engaged with NGOs to seek solutions to expanding networks of transitional environmental crime. Such initiatives include the Interpol Environmental Crimes Committee, which focuses on training, data collection, and enforcement of pollution and wildlife crimes (UNEP, 2011). It implements an 'intelligence-led policing' model which emphasizes 'operational partnerships'. In 2010, during the UN's International Year of Biodiversity, Interpol's General Assembly passed a resolution that would witness 188 national law enforcement agencies collaborate with organizations such as the World Bank and environmental movements; this initiative promises a substantial increase in policing resources to reduce organized environmental crime (Environment News Service, 2010; Interpol, 2011). In Italy, for example, organized environmental crime is not only being addressed or tackled by senior political officials and government administrators of policing agencies; they all play a part, but the real difference is being made through Legambiente. This non-governmental agency, established in 1980, is a left-wing environmental activist organization with 115,000 active members across 45 offices. With the use of its technologies, databases, and local intelligence, Legambiente has not only played an important public education role about organized crime, but has also been instrumental in tightening waste disposal regulations and in the prosecutions of mafia personnel. In a similar fashion to the ecomafia[1] having a public identity in Italy, Legambiente are widely thought of as a form of 'eco police' (Walters, 2013). This environmental organization, with its roots in the anti-nuclear movement, 'represents the United Nations Environment Programme for Italy, and is one of the leading members of the European Environmental Bureau'. In 2015, Legambiente described its values and initiatives thus:

> We denounce any abuse to the detriment of ecosystems, the indiscriminate use of resources, pollution. We fight against nuclear power, in favor of renewable energy and clean. We are against GMOs. We propose new lifestyles in order to live in harmony with the environment around us. We protect the artistic and cultural heritage of the territories. We offer educational programs in schools to grow generations informed and aware. We struggle against all forms of discrimination and social injustice, we promote the values of solidarity and peace.
>
> (Legambiente, 2015)

As Stretesky and Knight (2013) state, there are 263 environmental NGOs, similar in mission and purpose to Legambiente, operating across 48 countries.

There have been several international and regional environmental crime prevention initiatives in recent years, all of which highlight and involve the input of green activists (Nurse, 2011) In 2007 signatory countries to the United Nations Millennium Development Goals agreed to 'ensure environmental stability', though, *inter alia*, targeting and preventing organized environmental crime

---

1 The term 'ecomafia' emerged in the mid-1980s to describe mafia-related monopolies of domestic and industrial waste industries in the United States (see Block and Scarpetti, 1985). It has since been used to describe the mafia's corrupt control and domination of waste and property development activities in Italy (see Edmondson and Carlisle, 2003). The term is sometimes used more broadly to describe organized environmental criminal activity (see Walters, 2013).

(United Nations, 2007). The proceeds of organized environmental crime are laundered through legitimate and legal commercial activities. As a result, the Financial Action Task Force[2] now officially recognizes environmental crime as inextricably associated with money laundering. The Asian Regional Partners Forum on Combating Environmental Crime (ARPEC) was set up in 2005, and continues to play an active role in coordinating enforcement endeavours in the Asia Pacific region, an area renowned for trade in illicit wildlife. One important initiative, the Partnership Against Transnational Crime through Regional Organized Law Enforcement, has witnessed significant increases in wildlife seizures through coordinated policing and information exchange (UNODC, 2017). Moreover, in July 2011, eight signatory countries to the Lusaka Agreement on Co-operative Enforcement Operations Directed at Illegal Trade in Wild Fauna and Flora (which was the brain-child of Wildlife Law Enforcement Officers from eight Eastern and Southern African countries) met to increase enforcement resources to prevent wildlife crime (ARC, 2011). All of these recent international taskforces involve the intelligence of green activists not only as the 'eyes and ears' of operational activities but as partners in identifying and preventing transnational environmental crime. In a similar fashion to the successful involvement of citizen environmental activism in the historically progressive regulation of environmental crime in the United States (Clifford and Edwards, 2012), the above international approaches expressly rely upon organizations such as Greenpeace, Endangered Species International, Environmental Investigation Agency, Environmental Justice Foundation, Legambiente, and the World Wide Fund for Nature, just to mention a few, to combat global organized environmental crime. Environmental movements are becoming central in the identification, detection, and prevention of environmental crime. As mentioned above, their resources, technologies, networks, and personnel are increasingly utilized by law enforcement agencies to police, regulate, and prosecute organized environmental crime.

The overall impact of green activist organizations, to date, in combatting environmental harm is succinctly described by Stretesky and Knight (2013, p. 178) as 'advocacy and operations work'. Through an analysis of over 200 environmental NGOs, they identify the ways in which green activist movements positively prevent environmental harm, notably through direct operations that aid the enforcement and prosecution of eco-crime; through the monitoring of illegal and harmful environmental practices; and by educating the public of the importance of environmental sustainable practices. They provide numerous examples of

2 The Financial Action Taskforce (FATF) 'is an inter-governmental body established in 1989 by the Ministers of its Member jurisdictions. The objectives of the FATF are to set standards and promote effective implementation of legal, regulatory and operational measures for combating money laundering, terrorist financing and other related threats to the integrity of the international financial system. The FATF is therefore a "policy-making body" which works to generate the necessary political will to bring about national legislative and regulatory reforms in these areas' (FATF, 2015).

the ways in which such objectives and actions have influenced and shaped environmental regulations in various countries.

I shall return to some of these issues later. For now it is useful to examine the issues raised above including both the perils and prospects of green activism through a detailed examination of an ongoing green activist peace camp. The purpose of this discussion is to identify the dynamics and impacts of a green activist group and the ways in which they are capable of influencing political decision-making and reducing environmental harm. The location of this example is the longest continuous environmental demonstration in history, namely the Faslane Peace Camp in Scotland. I visited the camp on two occasions and attended two demonstrations outside the gates of the UK Government's Faslane Nuclear Naval Base.

3 Scotland's Faslane Peace Camp

3.1 Origins and development

On 12 June 1982, the Faslane Peace Camp was founded adjacent to the UK Government's Faslane Nuclear Submarine Military Base on the Clyde River in Argyll and Bute, Scotland. The naval base is Britain's nuclear deterrent and contains four submarines, with one on patrol at all times. Each submarine carries up to eight nuclear warheads and 16 missiles. Each warhead has the explosive power equivalent of eight times the bomb that destroyed Hiroshima (Royal Navy, 2015).

The peace camp has been occupied since its inception and, as such, is recognized as the longest continuously active demonstration in the world. Its beginnings emerged during times of political conservatism and war in the UK and against a media backdrop of criticism and denigration as described by one of its founding members:

> [E]stablished in Autumn 1981 ... it subsequently found itself operating against a backdrop of the jingoism of the Falklands War, and the Tory resurgence which that episode occasioned. Undermined by attacks from the English gutter press reacting in part to the 'women only' nature of the action ... the Camp nevertheless managed to expand.
>
> (Dunion, 1984, p. 2)

The political temperature in Scotland in the early 1980s and for the past three decades has, however, been very different from its southern neighbour. Scotland continues to push for independence from the UK and recent national elections that appointed an unprecedented number of Scottish National Party members to Westminster attests to the separate identity and culture that exists in northern Britain (Kerr, 2015). Politicians of all political persuasions have been opposed to a nuclear naval base in Scotland's backyard. The Faslane Nuclear Naval Base is funded by Westminster (the UK Government) to the tune of $2 billion per year and the positioning of atomic weapons on the Clyde River outside Glasgow has always attracted both united public and political opposition in Scotland. This bipartisan support has often been witnessed at peace camp demonstrations where politicians of the Scottish Parliament, and members of the public, routinely participate in marches and protests outside the front gates of the naval base. Indeed, some of the earliest protesters at the peace camp have subsequently become elected politicians and local councillors.

Scotland has a long tradition of anti-nuclear protesting. It successfully resisted the establishment of a nuclear base in northern Scotland in the early 1960s due to the Direct Action Committee against Nuclear War, a non-violent social movement of nuclear disarmament established in 1957. For the activists at Faslane, the peace camp has been a continuous protest against nuclear war and the nuclear arms race. It remains committed to this endeavour; however, it now pursues peaceful resistance through direct protest actions as well as an educative role through public speaking and community outreach.

The camp has relied upon the donations of supporters and throughout the years has been gifted a single-decker bus, several caravans, a bicycle-powered washing machine, a wood-fired stove and regular food parcels, tools, and building materials. The camp currently occupies a 100-metre-long space on the edge of the A814, near Helensburgh, about a mile from the front gate of the nuclear naval base.

3.2 Residence and governance

During the past 33 years there have been hundreds of activists occupying the peace camp from countries all over the world. On average the residents stay for 2–4 months but many have remained for years. At the time of my second visit to the camp in September 2013 there were 12 occupants on site from five countries ranging in age from four to 35. The four-year-old was born at the camp and her mother had been back and forth to the camp from southern England for over 15 years. There are backpackers from Europe, university students from the UK, and long-term or professional activists. All residents are politically engaged with in-depth historical and contemporary knowledge of the nuclear disarmament movement. They are also very well versed on the policies and activities of the UK Ministry of Defence. The biographies and activities of occupants have been well documented. Since 2011 the camp has operated an excellent website at faslanepeacecamp. wordpress.com that provides abundant information about actions, strategies, and residents. The occupants take up residence for various reasons: to prevent the spread and use of nuclear arms; to provide a visible resistance to atomic war and the use of nuclear weapons as a military deterrent; to connect with past activists, share experiences, and learn; and to educate those yet 'to be radicalized'. Irrespective of the motive, one consistent message emerging from the narratives of residents is that their participation in the Faslane Peace Camp has changed their lives and had given them the strength to overcome past hardships and the confidence to seek new challenges (Zelter, 2008).

There are a set of agreed upon rules at the peace camp: no alcohol in communal areas; no violence; no new residents unless they are prepared to commit to a minimum two-week stay; all camp residents contribute to 'chores' (cooking, cleaning, shopping, vegetable gardening, firewood, maintenance); everyone protests; no one pays fines; and everyone works on camp projects (building, letter writing, clothes making, flyers, banners, community outreach, updating the website) – the camp is a hive of ongoing activity. The Faslane Peace Camp website identifies the standards expected of all potential residents:

> Making sure the Peace Camp is a safe environment for all participants and visitors is everyone's responsibility. By being here, you agree to uphold a minimum standard of behaviour which is respectful of others and their comfort and safety. In particular, the following will not be tolerated at any time: Violence, or threats of violence; Drug- or alcohol-induced aggression; Sexual assault or harassment. Additionally, you are asked not to consume alcohol or other drugs in shared spaces. Anyone who cannot or will not make this agreement is asked to leave.
>
> (Faslane Peace Camp, 2015)

The above camp rules are strictly adhered to. The camp is watched on a daily basis by the local police and any illicit conduct by residents may serve as justifiable grounds for all residents to be removed and the camp closed.

When 'serious' decisions are to be made about camp or protest policy, the residents defer to the 'veterans' – those original members who, while no longer occupants, maintain a close and ongoing interest in the protest movement as well as the activities of the Faslane peace demonstration. Such members, now in their fifties and sixties, serve as 'elders' with institutional memory and jurisprudential-like knowledge of historical camp precedence. They are both 'law' and 'lore' in a symbolic sense, with no legal power but substantial moral influence. Their guidance is intermittently sought on such matters as building a community centre to educate school children on the dangers of nuclear weaponry or on potential legal challenges to government decisions on the increased use of truck convoys to transport atomic missiles.

3.3 Police and community relations

The occupants of the peace camp have experienced a mixed relationship with local officials and community members. In 1998, the local council sought to have the residents evicted from their protest site on the grounds that the protesters were operating business-like activities. In Scotland, trespass laws do not exist unless a person or persons are causing a nuisance or obstruction. Given that this ground could not be established, the local government sought to have the activists evicted and their camp dismantled on the premise that their activities were akin to an illegal business. However, this was dismissed by the local sheriff who 'was given a standing ovation when he rose to leave the bench' (Page, 1998). Subsequent eviction threats by 'conservative' local authorities have not materialized due to anticipated exorbitant legal fees. As a result, the camp remains. In recent years it has secured council permits to have up to seven caravans on site; as such, in the eyes of many local authorities it is considered a 'permanent site' for anti-nuclear demonstration.

There is a visible police presence at the camp on a daily basis. The police officers usually park adjacent to the camp for an hour. They sometimes enter the camp and are usually friendly, knowing the residents by name. Interestingly, the same police officers who arrest camp residents at demonstrations often attempt to access camp personnel for intelligence regarding wanted local criminals, always to no avail. The camp residents describe their relationship with the police as 'cordial' and are clear that their camp is not a 'hideout' for those escaping the law, nor is it a shelter for the homeless. Interestingly, throughout the years, camp residents have been 'courted' by military and police personnel and pro-nuclear politicians in convivial and friendly ways. Such approaches have often been met with suspicion and have sometimes been seen as a diplomatic attempt to curb activity and resistance. There have also been several instances of 'spying' where residents or potential residents claiming to be students have been suspected of being police officers or private security personnel – discussed further below.

The camp's relationship with the local community has always been mixed. There are several hundred local residents employed at the naval base as cleaners, caterers, nurses, plumbers, etc., and the ideology of the peace camp to close the military facility is seen as a direct threat to their livelihoods. The activists have often experienced verbal abuse from residents during protests and also day-to-day activities. The camp's response is educate, to be open to school visits, to speak at local events, and to enter into dialogue with the local community. Throughout the years, as camp members have continued to liaise, debate, and educate local residents, the relationship with the community has gradually improved. It has long been argued by the anti-nuclear movement that the annual costs of the naval base, as mentioned above to be $2 million, would go a long way to compensating and redeploying its non-military personnel should it be closed.

3.4 Actions and observation

The peace campers are involved in a range of environmental actions, often joining with other groups, in united endeavours. Throughout the years they have been invited to parliament to give testimony, they have appeared in courts of law to provide expertise, they have regularly been reported in various forms of media – all resulting in changes to the ways in which the Ministry of Defence transports its weaponry, conducts its drills and operational exercises, hires its staff, and implements its health and safety regulations. Moreover, the Faslane Peace

Camp has been instrumental in mobilizing politicians of all ideological persuasions in opposition to nuclear military technologies as well as dismantling the military base on the Clyde River. The peace campers do not own or use sophisticated technologies or datasets to map and track the activities of the Ministry of Defence. They rely on networks of collective concern and their daily observations and research. Some of their activities that have resulted in arrests have demonstrated the poor security at the nuclear naval base. One such action recently involved entering the base and seeing how close they could get to a nuclear missile. One of the demonstrators reported:

> I am amazed and disturbed by the accessibility of the UK's top defence site. Up to eighty nuclear warheads are often stationed here, along with several nuclear reactors. We thought we could get in, but not that we would be arrested within metres of nuclear materials.
>
> (Faslane Peace Camp, 2014)

The activists expose the fraught and poor security of one of the world's most extensive nuclear military sites. They have also documented the injuries to base staff, the accidents at sea, and the mechanical problems with the nuclear submarines – claims that are often denied by the Ministry of Defence but often supported with photographic and video evidence. The camp protesters have also documented the road accidents involving unmarked military convoys transporting nuclear missiles from Reading in England to the naval base on the Clyde – a distance of over 350 miles that requires a seven-hour journey through civilian towns. For years the MoD has hired non-military personnel to drive trucks carrying atomic weapons through British towns, often at night and during poor weather. The camp residents have documented evidence of accidents where drivers have lost control and careered off the road crashing into fields, or when the convoys have got lost, or blown tires exceeding speed limits. Such knowledge has been broadcast by camp activists to Scottish residents and has been instrumental in garnering broader public and political support.

4 Environmental activists – eco-warriors or eco-terrorists?

Green criminology is an intellectual enterprise that moves 'beyond the narrow boundaries of traditional criminology and draws together political and practical action to shape public policy' (South, 2010, p. 242). Such diverse and multidisciplinary narratives include the voices and experiences of resistance movements and those directly involved in environmental activism. Theories in new movements and radical social change assert that occupations and protest groups have become a key platform for informing and shaping future political projects (Fominaya, 2014). Throughout the past decade the voices of social movements have been influential in mobilizing public and political support. The Occupy movement, the Arab Spring, and the anti-war movement have had a significant impact on political, foreign, and trade policy as well stirring widespread media and public debate. Within environmental or conservation movements there have been noticeable protests and political backlash on genetically modified food, oil spills, the trafficking in protected wildlife, and illegal logging – to mention just a few issues. These protests have been met with corporate resistance and, as mentioned above, acts of violence. When environmentalism threatens corporate profit or political power, it is often met with state intervention. However, 'eco power crimes' committed by those in positions of political and corporate influence are able 'to control the effects of their actions and to conceal (or negotiate) their criminal nature' (Ruggiero, 2013, p. 262). In such circumstances green activists and their networks of knowledge become a threat and not an intelligence resource.

The environmental movements that seek to blockade or forestall transnational trade are often labelled and targeted as threats to safety and fiscal prosperity. Indeed, activists, when damaging or trespassing on property, have in recent years been swiftly constructed and criminalized by state power as both terrorists and threats to national security. For example, the FBI defines eco-terrorism as 'the use or threatened use of violence of a criminal nature against innocent victims or property by an environmentally-oriented, subnational group for environmental-political reasons, or aimed at an audience beyond the target, often of a symbolic nature' (Jarboe, 2002). Interestingly, the state usage of terms such as eco-terrorists is confined to the highly developed industrialized nations. Green activists in the majority world are at the greatest risk of personal violence; in the developed world, they are at risk of prosecution. Within countries such as the US and the UK, the imperatives of a strong military presence, for example, are often presented by governments as paramount to global security. For Stretesky and Knight (2013), environmental NGOs are not evenly distributed across those nations most exploited for their flora and fauna. For them, the advancement of capital accumulation has meant that those wealthy advanced neo-liberal societies have witnessed the lion's share of environmental advocacy. The poor and highly indebted nations, notably in the global South, are not well represented by coordinated and influential environmental organizations.

That said, in advanced capitalist societies eco-crime and environmental harms are subsidiary to free trade and national security. As a result, green activists who resist and actively protest against nuclear technologies, pollution, animal experimentation, war, and genetic developments in the affluent rich Western nations are much more likely to be targeted as eco-terrorists. In doing so, these protesters are opposing the justified and legitimated 'legal' actions of powerful democratic elites and, therefore, are not welcome partners in the fight against environmental crime but are threats to capital accumulation and vested interests of Western power. As such, they are systematically spied upon, infiltrated, and monitored as the enemy within. This process of labelling and regulation serves to demonstrate what Bachrach and Baratz (1970, p. 43) referred to as the 'mobilisation of bias'. They describe this as 'a set of predominant values, beliefs, rituals, and institutional procedures ("rules of the game") that operate systematically and consistently to the benefit of certain persons and groups at the expense of others'. In relation to nuclear military technologies and trade-related activities that exploit and damage the environment, 'those who benefit are placed in a preferred position to defend and promote their vested interests' (p. 43).

As mentioned in the above case study, green activists often refer to cost savings when safer and more environmentally technologies are adopted. Corporations and governments often report how regulatory requirements to be 'cleaner' and 'greener' will bring added costs to the consumer, or, as Lukes (2005, p. 21) observed, 'the securing of compliance through the threat of sanction'. In this case, rising consumer costs, reductions in productivity, unemployment, and loss of economic prosperity are all presented as the consequences of promoting environmental interests above commercial ones. However, nowadays, 'green business' is an important component of most corporate vision. It is here that we observe what Nye (2004, p. 5) refers to a 'soft power', or 'an ability to shape the preferences of others'. For Parmar and Cox (2010), it is a form of ambassadorial power based on persuasion, charm, and diplomacy. The large polluting corporations in the oil, power, and automotive industries and the industries experimenting on animals for new pharmaceuticals have used this approach effectively to bring favour with consumers, governments, and foreign markets. Here the promises of wealth and healthy living are presented through environmentally friendly images and language. The advertising and promotion slogans of such industries capture international rhetoric in environmentalism to create green images of corporate innovation.

As discussed above, green activists also find themselves part of an emerging environmental crime prevention strategy. However, I would argue that this occurs more often with eco-crimes committed within local municipalities by residents and small businesses in highly developed countries, and for the purposes of detecting and preventing transnational organized environmental crime, within developing and highly indebted countries. This point requires further expansion and deliberation. Throughout the past decade it has been widely reported that 'Environmental crime is currently one of the most profitable forms of criminal activity and it is no surprise that organized criminal groups are attracted to its high profit margins' (Banks et al., 2008, p. 2). The 'environment' is big business for organized crime. The United Nations Environment Programme, for example, estimates that organized crime syndicates earn in the region of US$20–30 billion from environmental crimes (Nellemann, 2012). Such earnings come at substantial social, economic, and environmental expense for communities, their livelihoods, and habitats. Indeed, organized environmental crime is identified by the UN as a key factor in the impoverishment, displacement, and violent conflicts of millions of people, notably in developing societies. The theft of biodiversity and the demise of animal species and habitats have resulted not only in financial loss but in the increase of 'environmental refugees', people dislocated and forced to migrate due to loss of livelihoods (Walters, 2013). It is within these volatile contexts that local green activists living in South America and Asia are not only the targets of violence by corrupt government officials and corporate entities, but also 'partners' with institutional organizations such as Interpol for eco-crime prevention purposes.

For many, understanding and responding to the complexities of organized environmental crime requires an examination of the networks of corruption that facilitate criminal markets. Such analyses require 'joined up thinking' across various transnational government and non-government agencies (Elliot, 2009). Notwithstanding the importance of this network-type analysis, it must be recognized that policies of free trade governed by principles of market regulation provide the contexts for organized environmental crime to flourish. The role of green criminologists must be to unpack and disentangle the ways that policies and practices of legitimate trade facilitate the opportunities and activities of organized environmental criminal networks. In the United States, the illegal trafficking in wildlife continues to accelerate at an alarming rate, and has caused the State Department to establish a Coalition Against Wildlife Trafficking comprising government, protest groups, and corporate partners to address an industry of organized crime (United States Department of State, 2011). The Wildlife Conservation Society in New York continues to emphasize the seriousness of the issue, stating, 'We are rapidly losing big, spectacular animals to an entirely new type of trade driven by criminalized syndicates, and the world is not yet taking it seriously' (Coghlan, 2011).

Such state and non-government transnational crime prevention initiatives in highly developed advanced liberal democracies are increasingly common. However, it must be remembered that organized environmental crime continues to flourish because of trade and market demand. Affluent European and North American countries that actively promote international environmental treaties to preserve and protect natural heritage provide the markets for organized crime syndicates to dispose of their illegal merchandise (Walters, 2013). The green activists protecting rainforests in their native South American countries are those environmentalists most at risk of violence and death. They are protecting natural resources that are often illegally pirated and sold 'legally' in markets in the UK, Australia, and the US. The use of indigenous and protected woodlands in Peru or Indonesia are often illegally harvested and sold for house building and gardening in Western nations. The dynamics of free-trade economies permit the contexts and circumstances for organized crime to flourish, in doing so victimizing entire populations in poorer and undeveloped countries (South and Brisman, 2013c).

5 Conclusion

The ongoing role of green activists within the detection and prevention of eco-crime is complicated and contentious. In highly developed advanced liberal societies they are held in both suspicion and, at times, confidence by governing authorities. However, when their activities jeopardize the fiscal prosperity of governments and transitional corporations, they are the targets of surveillance and prosecution. Green activists in the majority world face greater peril. They seek to protect their natural habitats within hostile and corrupt contexts that place them in material danger. It is clear that the environment has become a target of big business. It is both a business and resource to be protected and conserved. The priorities of trade and preservation are often in conflict. As White (2011) notes, environmental harm is often publicly and politically accepted as necessary for maintaining economic growth and social well-being. As a result, it is essential to inculcate discourses in political economy to analyze and understand the ways in which notions of harm, risk, and justice are mediated between publics, government policy, and corporate and agricultural practice. While trade continues to assert an international priority within the landscapes of global economics and fiscal prosperity, organized eco-crime takes advantage of growing markets. As a result, movements of environmental activism emerge as the new front in the detection of harm and mobilization of resistance. Such voices must continue to be central to future green criminological perspectives that seek environmental, ecological, and species justice.

Bibliography

African Regional Coverage. (2011). African governments discuss collaboration to combat poaching. Available at http://africasd.iisd.org/news/african-governments-discuss-collaboration-to-combat-po (accessed April 2017).

Bachrach, P., and Baratz, M. (1970). *Power and Poverty: Theory and Practice*. New York, NY: Oxford University Press.

Banks, D., Davies, C., Gosling, J., Newman, J., Rice, M., Wadley, J., and Walravens, F. (2008). *Environmental Crime: A Threat to Our Future*. London: Environmental Investigation Agency.

Block, A., and Scarpetti, F. (1985). *Poisoning for Profit: The Mafia and Toxic Waste in America*. New York, NY: William Morrow and Co.

Carrabine, E., Iganski, P., Lee, M., Plumer, K., and South, N. (2004). *Criminology: A Sociological Introduction*. London: Routledge.

Clifford, M. and Edwards, T. (2012) *Environmental Crime* (2nd edn). Burlington, MA: Jones and Bartlett Learning.

Coghlan, A. (2011, 2 August). Mob move into organised wildlife crime. *New Scientist*. Available at www.newscientist.com/article/dn20754-mob-move-into-organised-wildlife-crime.html (accessed 18 January 2017).

Dunion, K. (1984). Foreword. In: *Faslane: Diary of a Peace Camp*. Written by members of the Faslane Peace Camp. Edinburgh: Polygon Books.

Edmondson, G. and Carlisle, K. (2003). Italy and the eco-mafia. *Businessweek*. Available at www.bloomberg.com/news/articles/2003-01-26/italy-and-the-eco-mafia (accessed 20 February 2017).

Elliot, L. (2009). Combatting transnational environmental crime: Joined up thinking about transnational networks. In K. Kangaspunta and I. Marshall (eds), *Eco-Crime and Justice. Essays on Environmental Crime*. Turin: UNICRI.

Environmental Justice Organizations, Liabilities and Trade (EJOLT). (2014). Fighting environmental crime. Available atwww.ejolt.org/2014/11/fighting-environmental-crime-2 (accessed 18 January 2017).
Environment News Service. (2010). World's police unite for environmental crime crackdown. 16 November. Available at http://ens-newswire.com/2010/11/17/worlds-police-unite-for-environmental-crime-crackdown (accessed 20 February 2017).
Faslane Peace Camp. (2014, 21 March). Peace campers arrested on board nuclear sub. Press Release. Available at https://faslanepeacecamp.wordpress.com/2014/03/21/peace-campers-arrested-on-board-nuclear-sub (accessed 18 January 2017).
Faslane Peace Camp. (2015). Safer Spaces agreement. Available at https://faslanepeacecamp.wordpress.com/contact (accessed 18 January 2017).
Fominaya, C. (2014). *Social Movements and Globalization: How Protests, Occupations and Uprisings are Changing the World.* Hampshire: Palgrave.
Foucault, M. (1979). Truth and power: An interview with Michel Foucault. *Critique of Anthropology*, 4, 131–137.
Global Witness. (2014). *Deadly Environment: The Dramatic Rise in Killings of Environmental and Land Defenders.* Available at www.globalwitness.org/sites/default/files/deadly%20environment%20embargoed.pdf (accessed 18 January 2017).
Global Witness. (2015). *How Many More?* Available at www.globalwitness.org/campaigns/environmental-activists/how-many-more (accessed 18 January 2017).
Habermas, J. (1991). *The Structural Transformation of the Public Sphere: An Inquiry into a Category of Bourgeois Society.* Cambridge, MA: MIT Press.
Interpol. (2011). International Consortium on Combating Wildlife Crime. Available at www.interpol.int/Crime-areas/Environmental-crime/International-Consortium-on-Combating-Wildlife-Crime (accessed 20 February 2017).
Jameson, A. (2005, 17 February). Nuclear audit says Sellafield 'lost' 30kgs of plutonium. *The Times*, p. 1.
Jarboe, J. (2002). Domestic Terrorism Section Chief, Counterterrorism Division Federal Bureau of Investigation Before the House Resources Committee, Subcommittee on Forests and Forest Health Washington, DC February 12, 2002. Available at www.fbi.gov/news/testimony/the-threat-of-eco-terrorism (accessed 18 January 2017).
Kerr, A. (2015). Election 2015: SNP wins 56 of 59 seats in Scots landslide. BBC News. Available at www.bbc.com/news/election-2015-scotland-32635871 (accessed 31 July 2015).
Lakhani, N. (2014). Surge in deaths of environmental activists over past decade, report finds. Available at www.theguardian.com/environment/2014/apr/15/surge-deaths-environmental-activists-global-witness-report (accessed 18 January 2017).
Legambiente. (2015). What do we do. Available at http://translate.google.com.au/translate?hl=en&sl=it&u=http://www.legambiente.it/&prev=search (accessed 18 January 2017).
Lubbers, E. (2012). *Secret Manoeuvres in the Dark: Corporate and Police Spying on Activists.* London: Pluto Press.
Lukes, S. (2005). *Power: A Radical View* (2nd edn). Basingstoke: Palgrave.
Lynch, M., and Stretesky, P. (2014). *Exploring Green Criminology: Toward a Green Criminological Revolution.* London: Ashgate.
Natali, L. (2010). The big grey elephants in the backyard of Huelva, Spain. In R. White (ed.), *Global Environmental Harm: Criminological Perspectives* (pp. 193–209). Cullompton: Devon.

Nellemann, C. (2012). *Green Carbon, Black Trade: Illegal Logging, Tax Fraud and Laundering in the World's Tropical Forests*. United Nations Environment Program. Available at www.unep.org/pdf/RRAlogging_english_scr.pdf (accessed 18 January 2017).

Nurse, A. (2011). Policing wildlife: Perspectives on criminality in wildlife crime. *Papers from the British Criminology Conference*, 11, 38–53.

Nye, J. (2004). *Soft Power: The Means to Success in World Politics*. New York, NY: Public Affairs.

Page, C. (1998, 7 April). Peace camp joy as eviction bid is thrown out. *Scottish Daily Record*. Available at www.highbeam.com/doc/1G1-60263598.html (accessed 18 January 2017).

Parmar, I., and Cox, M. (eds) (2010). *Soft Power and US Foreign Policy: Theoretical, Historical and Contemporary Perspectives*. London: Routledge.

Reiman, J. (1979). *The Rich Get Richer and the Poor Get Prison: Ideology, Class and Criminal Justice*. New York, NY: Wiley.

Royal Navy. (2015). HMS Vanguard. Available at www.royalnavy.mod.uk/our-organisation/where-we-are/naval-base/clyde (accessed 18 January 2017).

Ruggiero, V. (2013). The environment and the crimes of the economy. In N. South and A. Brisman (eds), *Routledge International Handbook of Green Criminology* (pp. 261–271). London: Routledge.

South, N. (2010). The ecocidal tendencies of late modernity: Transnational crime, social exclusion, victims and rights. In R. White (ed.), *Global Environmental Harm: Criminological Perspectives* (pp. 228–247). Devon: Willan.

South, N., and Brisman, A. (2013a). Introduction. Horizons, issues and relationships in green criminology. In N. South and A. Brisman (eds), *Routledge International Handbook of Green Criminology* (pp. 1–23). London: Routledge.

South, N., and Brisman, A. (2013b). Critical green criminology. Environmental rights and crimes of exploitation. In S. Winlow and R. Atkinson (eds), *New Directions in Crime and Deviance* (pp. 99–111). London: Routledge.

South, N., and Brisman, A. (2013c). Resource wealth, power, crime and conflict. In R. Walters, D. Westerhuis, and T. Wyatt (eds), *Emerging Issues in Green Criminology: Exploring Power, Justice and Harm* (pp. 57–71). London: Palgrave.

Stretesky, P., and Knight, O. (2013). The uneven geography of environmental enforcement INGOs. In R. Walters, D. Westerhuis, and T. Wyatt (eds), *Emerging Issues in Green Criminology: Exploring Power, Justice and Harm* (pp. 173–196). London: Palgrave.

The Financial Action Taskforce. (2015). Who we are. Available at www.fatf-gafi.org/pages/aboutus (accessed 18 January 2017).

United States Department of State. (2011). Wildlife trafficking. Available at www.state.gov/e/oes/ecw/wlt (accessed 20 February 2017).

United Nations. (2007). *The Millennium Development Goals Report 2007*. Available at www.un.org/millenniumgoals/pdf/mdg2007.pdf (accessed 20 February 2017).

United Nations Environment Programme. (2011). *Division of Environmental Law and Conventions. Manual on Compliance with and Enforcement of Multilateral Environmental Agreements*. Nairobi: UNEP.

UNODC. (2017). Partnership Against Transnational crime through Regional Organized Law enforcement (PATROL). Available at www.unodc.org/southeastasiaandpacific/en/Projects/2009_04/Transnational_Crime.html (accessed 20 February 2017).

Walters, R. (2010). Eco crime. In J. Muncie, D. Talbot, and R. Walters (eds), *Crime: Local and Global*. Devon: Willan.

Walters, R. (2011). *Eco Crime and Genetically Modified Food*. London: Routledge.

Walters, R. (2013). Eco mafia and environmental crime. In K. Carrington, M.J. Ball, E. O'Brien, and J.M. Tauri (eds), *Crime, Justice and Social Democracy* (pp. 281–294). London: Palgrave MacMillan.

Westra, L. (2004). *Ecoviolence and the Law: Supranational Normative Foundations of Ecocrime*. Ardsley, NY: Transactional Publishers.

White, R. (2011). *Transnational Environmental Crime: Toward an Eco-Global Criminology*. London: Routledge.

White, R., and Heckenberg, D. (2014). *Green Criminology: An Introduction to the Study of Environmental Harm*. London: Routledge.

Zelter, A. (ed.) (2008). *Faslane 365: A Year of Anti-Nuclear Blockades*. Edinburgh: Luath Press.

Chapter 12

The criminalisation of the intentional destruction of cultural heritage

Ana Filipa Vrdoljak

1 Introduction

The Arch of Titus on the Via Sacra in Rome (Figure 12.1) was erected in 82 AD to commemorate the sacking of Jerusalem by the Roman Emperor Titus. The south panel depicts the procession of spoils from the Temple with the Menorah being carried in the centre of the relief. Hugo Grotius in *De jure belli ac pacis* (1625) noted that Titus Flavius Josephus, who served Titus during the siege of Jerusalem, argued that the Temple's destruction was 'in accordance with the law of war'.[1] This relief, which has survived two millennia, remains a powerful symbol of the deliberate destruction and pillage of the cultural heritage and subjection of a people. As the ancients acknowledged, such acts were integral to the conduct of war and belligerent occupation as a means of demoralising the enemy and accelerating their conquest.[2] However, since the nineteenth century and the earliest efforts to codify the laws and customs of war, the international community has sought to condemn such acts and hold the perpetrators to account. This chapter examines how modern international law is protecting World Heritage ('the cultural heritage of all humanity') by criminalising the intentional destruction of cultural heritage.

The permanent recording of the sacking of the Temple in Jerusalem, over and above the physical act of destruction itself, is telling. The intrinsic propaganda value was not lost on the conquered or the inhabitants of the conqueror. In the digital age of the twenty-first century, which has witnessed a proliferation of deliberate acts of destruction, damaging and pillaging of World Heritage sites and its broadcasting via social media and the Internet, this potential continues to be exploited. This chapter examines the evolving rationales for the intentional destruction of cultural heritage since the early twentieth century and international law's response to such acts. First, there is an analysis of its initial criminalisation with the codification of the laws and customs of war and their interpretation by the Nuremberg Tribunal in 1945 through to the jurisprudence of the

1 H. Grotius, *De jure belli ac pacis. Libri tres.* J.B. Scott (ed.) and F.W. Kelsey (trans.) (Oxford: Clarendon Press, 1925), p. 662.
2 Ibid., at pp. 658–661.

Figure 12.1 Arch of Titus, Rome, Italy
Source: iStock

International Criminal Tribunal for the former Yugoslavia and the International Criminal Court, The Hague. Next, I consider how these developments were extended to crimes against humanity and genocide which enabled deliberate, targeted destruction of cultural heritage to be viewed as intrinsic to gross violations of international humanitarian law and systematic abuses of human rights. Finally, I examine the transformative impact of the digital age on the deliberate destruction of World Heritage and the efforts of the international community, through the UN Security Council and UNESCO, to cooperate in curbing incitement and holding perpetrators to account for crimes against the common heritage of humanity.

2 War crimes

Modern international law has prohibited the deliberate seizure, destruction or damaging of cultural property from the first codifications of the laws and customs of war in the nineteenth century. These earliest efforts made clear that although cultural and religious sites and monuments, and works of art and science, may be bounded to the territory of a State, they attracted international protection because of their importance to all humanity, such acts constituted war crimes, and perpetrators of such acts would be held to account. These basic tenets have been reiterated repeatedly in successive multilateral instruments for over 150 years.

2.1 Codification and the Nuremberg Judgment

The destruction of Strasbourg's cathedral and library during the Franco-Prussian War of 1870–71 and the ensuing public outcry led to an international conference in mid-1874, which adopted the International Regulations on the Laws and Customs of War (Brussels Declaration).[3] Although it never entered into force, it contains the core elements of the protection of cultural property during armed conflict in place today.[4] It provides that during belligerent occupation, 'all seizure or destruction of, or wilful damage to, institutions dedicated to religion, charity and education, the arts and sciences', historic monuments, works of art and science should be *made subject of legal proceedings by the competent authorities*' (Article 8 (emphasis added)).

The first binding international obligations for the protection of cultural heritage related to the rules of war emerged from the series of international conferences held in 1899 and 1907.[5] The Regulations annexed to the Convention (II) with Respect to the Laws and Customs of War on Land (1899 Hague II Convention) and Convention (IV) respecting the Laws and Customs of War on Land (1907 Hague IV Convention)[6] were found to be customary international law and 'recognized by all civilized nations' by the International Military Tribunal (IMT) at Nuremberg in 1945.[7] A decade earlier, jurist Charles de Visscher noted that this immunity was granted because these objects and sites were 'dedicated to an ideal purpose'.[8] He added that 'international conventional law has established such acts as genuine violations of the law of nations, the perpetrators of which are marked out for collective repression by the signatory States'.[9] Under the Hague Regulations, during hostilities 'all necessary steps should be taken to spare, as far as possible, buildings dedicated to religion, art, science, or charitable purposes, historic monuments, hospitals, and places where the sick and wounded are collected' as long as they are not used for military *purposes*, marked with the distinctive sign, and have been notified to the enemy (Article 27). During occupation, the

---

3 G. Rolin-Jaequemyns, 'Essai complémentaire sur la guerre franco-allemande dans ses rapports avec le droit international', 2 *Revue de droit international* (1871) 288, at 302.
4 International Declaration concerning the Laws and Customs of War, 27 August 1874, not ratified, 1 *American Journal of International Law* (1907) vol.1(supp.), p. 96.
5 See M. Huber, 'La propriété publique en cas de guerre sur terre', *Revue Générale de Droit International Public* (1913), at 657.
6 Convention (II) with Respect to the Laws and Customs of War on Land and Annex, 29 July 1899, in force 4 September 1900, *American Journal of International Law* (1907), vol. 1(supp.), p. 129; and Convention (IV) respecting the Laws and Customs of War on Land, and Annex, 18 October 1907, in force 26 January 1910, *American Journal of International Law* (1907), vol. 1(supp.), p. 90.
7 International Military Tribunal, Nuremberg, 'Judgment', *American Journal of International Law* (1947) vol. 41, p. 172, at pp. 248–249.
8 C. De Visscher, 'International Protection of Works of Art and Historic Monuments', in Department of State Publication 3590, International Information and Cultural Series 8, reprinted in *Documents and State Papers* (June 1949), p. 821, at p. 828.
9 Ibid.

'property of the communes, that of religious, charitable, and educational institutions, and those of arts and science' is protected as private property with no reference to military necessity. Seizure, destruction or wilful damage to these institutions, historical monuments, works of art or science 'is forbidden', with violations '*to be made subject to legal proceedings*' (Article 56 (emphasis added)).

These prohibitions were tested with the widespread, deliberate destruction of cultural property during the First World War, especially on the Western Front, including Louvain University's library and Reims Cathedral.[10] The Preliminary Peace Conference of Paris of 1919 established the Sub-Commission III of the Commission on Responsibilities, which was instructed to investigate and make recommendations on the violation of the laws and customs of war perpetrated by Germany and her allies.[11] The draft list of war crimes it prepared included the 'wanton destruction of religious, charitable, educational and historic buildings and monuments'.[12] Unable to secure trials before an inter-Allied criminal tribunal, affected countries pushed for extradition of suspects to stand trial before their own national courts.[13] France sought extradition of several suspects for violations against cultural property;[14] however, these requests proved fruitless and they were tried *in absentia*.

During the Second World War, Allied Powers made successive announcements stating their intention to hold Axis nationals who had violated the laws and customs of war to account at the end of the conflict.[15] The Hague Regulations and work of the 1919 Commission proved vital in the indictment and prosecution of the Nazi and Axis war criminals. The jurisdiction of the IMT at Nuremberg covered violations of the laws and customs of war including 'plunder of public or private property, wanton destruction of cities, towns or villages, or devastation not justified by military necessity'.[16] The indictment of the major war criminals charged that part of their 'plan of criminal exploitation' included the 'destr[truction of] industrial cities, cultural monuments, scientific institutions, and property of all types in the occupied territories'.[17] Alfred Rosenberg had headed 'Einsatzstab Rosenberg', a programme involving the confiscation of cultural objects from private German

10 See P. Clemen, *Protection of Art during War* (Leipzig: E.A. Seeman, 1919).
11 *American Journal of International Law* (1947) vol. 14, p. 95 at pp. 114–115.
12 Ibid.
13 J. Horne and A. Kramer, *German Atrocities. 1914: A History of Denial*, (New Haven, CT: Yale University Press, 2001), Appendix, pp. 448–50.
14 Ibid.
15 See in particular, Declaration of the Four Nations on General Security (Moscow Declaration), 30 October 1943, *American Journal of International Law* (1944) vol. 38 (supp.), pp. 7–8.
16 Art.6(b) of the Charter of the International Military Tribunal, Nuremberg annexed to the Agreement by United Kingdom, United States, France and USSR for the Prosecution and Punishment of the Major War Criminals of the European Axis, 8 August 1945, 82 UNTS 279.
17 Count Three (War Crimes), Part E (Plunder of Public and Private Property), Indictment, in *Trial of the Major War Criminals before the International Military Tribunal, Nuremberg,*

collections and occupied territories.[18] The U.S. Prosecutor referred to 'the forcing of this treasure-house by a horde of vandals bent on systematically removing to the Reich these treasures which are, in a sense, the heritage of all of us'.[19] The IMT found that Rosenberg had directed that the Hague Regulations 'were not applicable to the Occupied Eastern Territories'; and that he was 'responsible for a system of organised plunder ... throughout the invaded countries of Europe'.[20] He was found guilty and sentenced to death. There were also examples covering the deliberate destruction of cultural property. For instance, the French Permanent Military Tribunal found a civilian guilty of a war crime for destroying a statue of Joan of Arc and a monument commemorating the First World War dead, on the order of a German official, in violation of Articles 46 and 56 Hague Regulations, the 1919 Commission List, and Article 257 of the French Penal Code.[21]

The Nuremberg Judgment proved influential in the codification efforts of UNESCO which led to the adoption of the Convention for the Protection of Cultural Property in the Event of Armed Conflict (1954 Hague Convention).[22] Its *travaux* noted that the Nuremberg Tribunal has 'introduced the principle of punishing attacks on the cultural heritage of a nation into positive international law'.[23] The Convention's preamble speaks of the universal importance of the cultural heritage:

> Being convinced that damage to cultural property belonging to any people whatsoever means damage to the cultural heritage of all mankind, since each people makes its contribution to the culture of the world;
> Considering that the preservation of the cultural heritage is of great importance for all peoples of the world and that it is important that this heritage should receive international protection ...[24]

For the first time there is reference to 'cultural heritage' rather than 'cultural property' in a multilateral instrument,[25] which emphasises its intergenerational importance. This aspect was reaffirmed by a resolution adopted at the first meeting of the High Contracting Parties to the Convention which noted that 'the purpose of the Convention ... is to protect the cultural heritage of all peoples for

14 November 1945–1 October 1946, (42 vols, Nuremberg: [s.n.], 1947–1949), vol. 1, at pp. 11–30.
18 L. Nicholas, *The Rape of Europa: The Fate of Europe's Treasures in the Third Reich and the Second World War* (London: Papermac, 1994).
19 *Trial of the Major War Criminals*, note 17, vol. IV, p. 81.
20 Nuremberg Judgment, note 7, p. 237.
21 Trial of Karl Lingenfelder, French Permanent Military Tribunal, Metz (judgment of 11 March 1947), in UNWCC, *Law Reports of Trials of War Criminals* (London: HMSO, 1949), vol. 9, p. 67.
22 14 May 1954, into force 7 August 1956, 249 UNTS 240.
23 UNESCO Doc.7C/PRG/7, Annex I, at p. 5.
24 1954 Hague Convention, PP2 and PP3.
25 UNESCO Doc.7C/PRG/7, Annex II, at p. 20.

future generations'.[26] The 'importance' of the protected cultural site or object is not determined exclusively by the State where it is located; rather, it extends to 'people'.[27] Also, the Convention applies to international and non-international armed conflicts.[28] In respect of international armed conflict, each of the parties to the conflict is bound by the Convention's obligations 'as a minimum' (Article 19 (1)). If one of the Parties is not a High Contracting Party, the treaty obligations remain binding on the High Contracting Parties and any other Party which declares that it accepts and applies the obligations (Article 18(3)). The *travaux* indicates that this is because of the 'moral obligation to respect the cultural property of an adversary not party to the Convention, such property belonging to the international community as well as the State concerned'.[29] Its application to non-international armed conflict is recognised in customary international law.[30] Also, the United Nations has stated that its peacekeeping forces observe the 1954 Hague Convention.[31]

The 1954 Hague Convention defines obligations for the safeguarding and respect of cultural property by the High Contracting Parties during peacetime, armed conflict and belligerent occupation. The obligation to respect arising during hostilities is engaged with the declaration of war or an armed conflict between two or more High Contracting Parties, even if not recognised as a state of war by one of them (Article 18).[32] It applies to total or partial occupation of the territory of the High Contracting Party even if there is no resistance. The obligation to respect includes respect for cultural property situated within one's *own* territory as well as the territory of other High Contracting Parties, by not using the property and its immediate surroundings for purposes that could expose it to destruction or damage (Article 4(1)). Second, they must not engage in any act of hostility against such property, with the obligation being waived if 'military necessity imperatively requires' (Article 4(2)). This qualifier was confirmed in the

---

26 UNESCO Doc.CUA/120, at p. 22. The draft recital had read: 'Being convinced that damage to cultural property results in a spiritual impoverishment for the whole of humanity': UNESCO Doc.7C/PRG/7, Annex II, at p. 20.
27 This definition is applied to the two Protocols to the Convention: see Art. 1, Protocol for the Protection of Cultural Property in the Event of Armed Conflict (First Hague Protocol), 14 May 1954, into force 7 August 1956, 249 UNTS 358; and Art. 1(b), Second Protocol to the Hague Convention for the Protection of Cultural Property in the Event of Armed Conflict (1999 Hague Protocol) 26 March 1999, into force 9 March 2004, 2253 UNTS 212.
28 Art. 19, 1954 Hague Convention; and Art. 22, 1999 Second Hague Protocol.
29 UNESCO Doc.7C/PRG/7, Annex I, at 5–6.
30 Prosecutor v Duško Tadić, Interlocutory Appeal on Jurisdiction Judgment, No IT-94-1-A, Appeals Chamber, ICTY, (2 October 1995), at 98 and 127.
31 Secretary-General's Bulletin on the Observance by UN Forces of International Humanitarian Law, 6 August 1999, UN Doc.ST/SGB/1999/13, para. 6.6.
32 The *travaux* notes that the obligation to respect 'means abstention from endangering cultural property and the arrangements which ensure its safeguarding, and abstention from prejudicing them': UNESCO Doc.7C/PRG/7, Annex, at p. 8.

Second Protocol (Article 6).[33] During belligerent occupation, the High Contracting Party as occupying power must cooperate with and support the competent national authorities in protecting the cultural heritage (Article 5, 1954 Hague Convention). The provision extends to informing insurgent groups of their obligation to respect cultural property.[34] Article 9 of the Second Protocol provides that the State Party must prevent and prohibit any illicit export, other removal, or transfer of ownership of cultural property;[35] archaeological excavations except when 'strictly required to safeguard, record or preserve' cultural property; and changes to the cultural property intended to hide or destroy 'cultural, historical or scientific evidence'. This protection afforded cultural heritage during occupation is augmented by the First Protocol concerning the removal and return of movable heritage.

The distinction made in the 1954 Hague Convention between general protection (Chapter I) and special protection (Chapter II of Convention and Regulations) is significant for the purposes of the prosecution of war crimes – that is, grave breaches of international humanitarian law. However, the criteria laid down for attracting special protection were so onerous that very few sites or properties were listed. By the late twentieth century, only one site (the Vatican) was nominated. Reiterating the obligation contained in the 1907 Hague Regulations, the 1954 Hague Convention requires High Contracting Parties to 'undertake to take, within the framework of their ordinary criminal jurisdiction, all necessary steps to prosecute and impose penal or disciplinary sanctions upon those persons, of whatever nationality' who commit or order to commit violations of its obligations (Article 28).[36] The provision's weak wording and subsequent failure of High Contracting Parties to enact enabling legislation was noted by a 1993 review of the 1954 Hague Convention.[37] Prepared in the shadow of the Yugoslav conflicts, its recommendations to address this limitation were realised in the Second Hague Protocol adopted in 1999.

2.2 Bombing of Dubrovnik, ICTY and 1999 Hague Protocol

The jurisprudence of the International Criminal Tribunal for the former Yugoslavia (ICTY) established in 1993 picked up where the Nuremberg Tribunal had left off almost a half century before. During the Yugoslav wars of the 1990s, the

---

33 P.J. Boylan, Review of the Convention for the Protection of Cultural Property in the Event of Armed Conflict (The Hague Convention of 1954), UNESCO Doc.CLT-93/WS/12 (1993), at p. 17.
34 See also Art. 32, Part VI of the 1956 UNESCO Recommendation on International Principles Applicable to Archaeological Excavations, in UNESCO, *Records of the General Conference, Ninth Session, New Delhi 1956: Resolutions*, (Paris: UNESCO, 1957), at p. 40.
35 Arts 11 and 12 of the Convention on the Means of Prohibiting and Preventing the Illicit Import, Export and Transfer of Ownership of Cultural Property, 14 November 1970, in force 24 April 1972, 823 UNTS 231.
36 The USSR had unsuccessfully proposed a more detailed provision borrowing from Article 146 of the Geneva Convention (IV) relative to the Treatment of Civilian Persons in Time of War of 1949: UNESCO Doc.CBC/DR/71, at p. 390.
37 Boylan, note 33, at p. 93.

combatants deliberately targeted the cultural and religious property of the opposing side, including World Heritage listed sites.[38] In response, the United Nations indicated that it would investigate and prosecute those responsible. The adoption of the ICTY Statute during the Yugoslav wars was intended to have punitive and deterrent objectives.[39] The relevant provision covering crimes against cultural property reflect the wording of Article 56 of the 1907 Hague Regulations, and not the 1954 Hague Convention and its Protocol, even though all belligerents were Parties.[40] Article 3(d) ICTY Statute covers war crimes including: '[S]eizure, destruction or wilful damage done to institutions dedicated to religion, charity and education, the arts and sciences, historic monuments and works of art and science.' Under this provision, it must be shown that the international or internal armed conflict existed and had a close nexus with the alleged acts.[41]

The most significant cases on this count pertain to the bombardment of the fortified city of Dubrovnik in early October 1991.[42] The leading cases involved Miodrag Jokić, a commander of the Yugoslav People's Army and responsible for the forces which attacked Dubrovnik on 6 October 1991, and Pavle Strugar, his superior found to have 'legal and effective control' over the forces in the area. When deciding which property falls within the protection afforded under Article 3(d), the tribunal has referenced definitions contained in conventions covering both during armed conflict and peacetime including the Convention concerning the Protection of the World Cultural and Natural Heritage (World Heritage Convention).[43] In *Strugar*, the Trial Chamber emphasised the Old Town's inscription on the World Heritage List. It noted that the List included 'cultural and natural properties deemed to be of outstanding universal value from the point of view of history, art or science' and a reasonable trier of fact could

---

38 See Report of the Secretary-General to the President of the UN Security Council, annexing the Interim Report of the Commission of Experts Established Pursuant to SC Res.780(1992), UN Doc.S/1993/25274 (9 February 1993); and M. Kéba M'Baye, Final Report of the United Nations Commission of Experts Established Pursuant to SC Res.780(1992), UN Doc. S/1994 674 (27 May 1994) Annex XI: Destruction of Cultural Property Report, 66–68, at pp. 285–297.

39 M. Frulli, 'Advancing the Protection of Cultural Property through the Implementation of Individual Criminal Responsibility: The Case-Law of the International Criminal Tribunal for the former Yugoslavia', *Italian Yearbook of International Law* (2005) vol. 15, p. 195, at p. 197.

40 Yugoslavia was a High Contracting Party to the 1954 Hague Convention and 1954 Hague Protocol, and after its dissolution the successor states have become parties: Croatia (1992), Slovenia (1992), Bosnia and Herzegovina (1993), Serbia (2001) and Montenegro (2007). Serbia (2002), Slovenia (2004), Croatia (2006) and Montenegro (2007) are Parties to the 1999 Second Protocol.

41 Prosecutor v Duško Tadić, Appeal Judgment, No IT-94-1-A, Appeals Chamber, ICTY (2 October 1995), at 66–70.

42 See C. Bories, *Les bombardements serbes sur la vieille ville de Dubrovnik: La protection internationale des biens culturels* (Paris: Pedone, 2005).

43 16 November 1972, into force 17 December 1975, 1037 UNTS 151.

conclude it came within the meaning of cultural property in Article 3(d).[44] With the *actus reus* element of Article 3(d), the ICTY considered customary law concerning attacks on cultural heritage. In *Strugar*, it emphasised that the cultural property's use rather than its location was determinative of loss of immunity.[45] The tribunal found it was presumed to enjoy the same general protection afforded to civilian objects, except where they had become military objectives because 'their nature, location, purpose or use make an effective contribution to military action and whose total or partial destruction, capture, or neutralisation, in the circumstances ruling at the time, offers a definite military advantage'.[46] For the *mens rea* requirement of this crime, it was necessary to show that the defendant committed the act wilfully – that is, deliberately or with reckless disregard for the substantial likelihood of the destruction or damage of a protected cultural or religious property.[47] The perpetrator must act with the knowledge that the object is cultural property. In *Strugar* this was established because Dubrovnik was on the World Heritage List; and in *Jokić* the tribunal found that the 1954 Hague emblem was manifestly visible at the relevant time.[48] In the sentencing phase for war crimes against cultural property, the tribunal has stated that 'this crime represents a violation of values especially protected by the international community'.[49] In *Jokić*, the Trial Chamber held that while 'it is a serious violation of international humanitarian law to attack civilian buildings, it is a crime of even greater seriousness to direct an attack on an especially protected site'.[50] A site once destroyed could not be returned to its original status.[51] Jokić was sentenced to seven years' imprisonment,[52] and Strugar for eight years.[53]

44 Prosecutor v Pavle Strugar, Rule 98bis Motion, No IT-01-42-T, Trial Chamber II, ICTY (21 June 2004), at 80–81; and Prosecutor v Miodrag Jokić, Trial Judgment, No IT-01-42/1-S, Trial Chamber I, ICTY (18 March 2004), at 49 and 51.
45 Prosecutor v Pavle Strugar, Trial Judgment, Chamber II, ICTY, No IT-01-42-T, (31 January 2005), at 310.
46 Prosecutor v Radoslav Brđanin, Trial Judgment, Case No IT-99-36-T, Trial Chamber II, ICTY (1 September 2004), at 596. The court also noted even non-State Parties to Additional Protocol I, including the United States, Turkey and India, recognised the customary law nature of Art. 52(2) Protocol Additional to the Geneva Conventions of 12 August 1949, and Relating to the Protection of Victims of International Armed Conflicts (Additional Protocol I), 8 June 1977, in force 7 December 1978, 1125 UNTS 3, during the diplomatic conference called for the Second Hague Protocol in 1999: at footnote 1509.
47 Ibid., at 599; and Prosecutor v Pavle Strugar, Appeals Judgment, No IT-01-42-A, Appeals Chamber, ICTY (17 July 2008), at 277–278.
48 Jokić, Trial Judgment, note 44 at 23 and 49; and Strugar, Trial Judgment, note 45, at 22, 183, 279, 327 and 329.
49 Jokić, Trial Judgment, note 44, at 46.
50 Ibid., at 53.
51 Ibid., at 52.
52 Confirmed on appeal: Prosecutor v Miodrag Jokić, Judgment on Sentencing Appeal, No IT-01-42/1-A, Appeals Chamber, ICTY (30 August 2005).
53 This sentence was reduced on appeal to seven and a half years' imprisonment: Strugar, Appeals Judgment, and pardoned by Decision of the President on the application

The Second Protocol to the 1954 Hague Convention, adopted in 1999, provides further detail concerning the obligation to prosecute violations of the laws and customs of war relating to cultural property. Parties to the Second Protocol must introduce domestic penal legislation (establishing jurisdiction and appropriate penalties) concerning serious violations occurring within their territory or perpetrated by nationals (Articles 15(2) and 16(1)).[54] Serious violations are defined as acts committed intentionally and in violation of the Convention or Second Protocol – namely, attacks on property under enhanced protection, using such property or its immediate surroundings in support of military action, extensive destruction or appropriation of cultural property covered by general protection, making such property the object of attack, and theft, pillage or misappropriation of property under general protection (Article 15(1)).[55] Universal jurisdiction must be established for the first three of these serious violations (Article 16(10)(c)). If a Party does not prosecute, it must extradite to a country that can and which meets minimum standards in international law (Articles 17 and 18).[56] Further, a Party may introduce legislative, administrative or disciplinary measures which suppress the intentional use of cultural property in violation of the Convention or Second Protocol (Article 21). The Committee for the Protection of Cultural Property in the Event of Armed Conflict's Guidelines for the Implementation of the 1999 Protocol require Parties to report on the implementation of these obligations, but to date it has not provided guidance on how this is to be done.[57]

2.3 Sacking of Timbuktu and the International Criminal Court

By the close of the twentieth century, international legal obligations prohibiting the deliberate destruction and pillage of cultural property were broadly

for pardon or commutation of sentence of Pavle Strugar, No IT-01-42-ES (16 January 2009).
54 See Report on the obligations of the Parties to implement Chapter 4 (Criminal Responsibility and Jurisdiction) of the Second Protocol, March 2012, available at www.unesco.org/new/fileadmin/MULTIMEDIA/HQ/CLT/pdf/Report-obligations-chapter4-en_20120306.pdf (accessed 19 January 2017).
55 The Summary Report of the Diplomatic Conference on the Second Protocol to the Hague Convention for the Protection of Cultural Property in the Event of Armed Conflict (June 1999) at 6, at 26 and 27 records that drafters intended this provision to be consistent with Art. 85, Additional Protocol I and the Rome Statute. However, serious concerns were raised about the initial draft particularly by the International Committee of the Red Cross (ICRC) which questioned the omission of intentional attacks and pillage as war crimes.
56 It also provides for grounds for refusal of extradition (political crimes or racial, religious, etc. motivations) and provision of mutual legal assistance: Arts 19 and 20.
57 Guidelines for the Implementation of the 1999 Second Protocol to the Hague Convention of 1954 for the Protection of Cultural Property in the Event of Armed Conflict, 22 March 2012, UNESCO Doc.CLT-09/CONF/219/3 REV.4, p. 28. The ICRC has prepared a Model Law for common law countries; see ICRC, *The Domestic Implementation of International Humanitarian Law: A Manual*, (Geneva: ICRC, 2013), Annex XVIII.

reaffirmed in the governing statutes of several international criminal tribunals. The Yugoslav wars and the ICTY Statute influenced the wording of the provisions relating to the war crime against cultural property in the Rome Statute for the International Criminal Court (ICC). It defines the war crime of 'intentionally directing attacks against buildings dedicated to religion, education, art, science or charitable purposes' and 'historical monuments'.[58] The first indictment by the ICC under these provisions arose in respect of the situation in Mali during 2012, under a warrant issued in September 2015.

In 2012, Mali requested that the ICC Prosecutor investigate and indict the perpetrators of attacks on religious and cultural sites including the World Heritage site in Timbuktu.[59] Pursuant to the principle of complementarity under the Rome Statute, Mali as a State Party has primary jurisdiction over war crimes committed on its territory or by its nationals; with the ICC exercising jurisdiction following a referral by a State Party which does not or cannot prosecute in its domestic courts or a referral from the UN Security Council (Article 13). Significantly, Mali's referral was made by the transitional government against rebel forces. In the days leading up to the referral, the ICC Prosecutor and the Security Council had noted the destruction of monuments in the World Heritage site in northern Mali with alarm. The ICC Prosecutor advised: 'Those who are destroying religious buildings in Timbuktu should do so in full knowledge that they will be held accountable and justice will prevail.'[60] The Security Council adopted Resolution 2056(2012) under Chapter VII of the UN Charter which '[c]ondemn[ed] strongly the desecration, damage and destruction of sites of holy, historic and cultural significance, especially but not exclusively those designated UNESCO World Heritage sites, including the city of Timbuktu'.[61] It stressed that such attacks violated Additional Protocol II of the 1949 Geneva Conventions and the Rome Statute, and that the perpetrators would be brought to justice.[62] The UN Secretary-General called on the Security Council to impose sanctions on the perpetrators of attacks on sites that are designated as 'part of the indivisible

---

58 Arts 8(2)(b)(ix) (international armed conflict) and 8(2)(e)(iv) (non-international), Rome Statute of the International Criminal Court (Rome Statute), 17 July 1998, into force 1 July 2002, 2187 UNTS 90.
59 M. Coulibaly, 'Referral under Article 14 ICC Statute from Malian Minister for Justice to ICC Prosecutor, 13 July 2012', available at www.icc-cpi.int/NR/rdonlyres/A245A47F-BFD1-45B6-891C-3BCB5B173F57/0/ReferralLetterMali130712.pdf (accessed 19 January 2017).
60 ICC Prosecutor's Statement on Mali, 1 July 2012, OTP Briefing, Issue #126, 20 June–3 July 2012, available at www.icc-cpi.int/NR/rdonlyres/B8B506C8-E2 DE-4FF5-A843-B0687C28AA6C/284735/OTPBriefing20June3July2012.pdf (accessed 19 January 2017).
61 SC Res.2056 on Peace and Security in Africa, 5 July 2012, UN Doc.S/RES/2056 (2012). This was reaffirmed in SC Res.2071 of 12 October 2012, UN Doc.S/RES/2071 (2012) and SC Res.2085 of 20 December 2012, UN Doc.S/RES/2085 (2012).
62 SC Res.2056(2012), paras 13 and 16.

heritage of humanity'.[63] The ICC Prosecutor found a *prima facie* case of war crimes including intentionally directing attacks against protected objects (Article 8 (2)(e)(iv) Rome Statute) whose 'value transcends geographical boundaries, and which are unique in character and are intimately associated with the history and culture of the people'.[64] She noted that the series of intentional attacks against nine of the 16 mausoleums and two of three great mosques in Timbuktu, on the World Heritage List since 1988, 'shocked the conscience of humanity'. The Prosecutor concluded: '[T]he destruction of religious and historical sites in Timbuktu appears grave enough to justify further action by the Court.'[65] On 26 September 2015, following the issue of a warrant for war crimes committed in Timbuktu between 30 June and 10 July 2012, Ahmad Al Mahdi Al Faqi was surrendered by Niger to the ICC.[66] He pleaded guilty and was sentenced in late 2016.

Subsequent Security Council resolutions on Mali affirmed the importance of justice and holding perpetrators to account for the peace process in the country through its cooperation with the ICC.[67] A 2014 resolution extended the mandate of the UN Multidimensional Integrated Stabilization Mission in Mali (MINUSMA) whose mandate included 'assist[ing] the Malian authorities, as necessary and feasible, in protecting from attack the cultural and historical sites in Mali, in collaboration with UNESCO'.[68] An Agreement on Peace and Reconciliation was signed by the Malian government and several armed rebel groups in mid-2015.[69] The Security Council resolution, acknowledging this agreement, reiterated earlier calls for Malian authorities to cooperate with the ICC and extended MINUSMA's mandate, including its support for cultural preservation.[70] Subsequently, the Security Council expressed alarm at ceasefire violations and the slow pace of MINUSMA's work.[71] Nonetheless, the Secretary-General also noted positively the work of UNESCO including the reconstruction of 14 mausoleums in Timbuktu.[72]

63 B. Ki-moon, Secretary-General's Remarks to the Security Council on Mali. Speech delivered at the UN Security Council, 8 August 2012, available at www.un.org/sg/statements/index.asp?nid=6232 (accessed 19 January 2017). See B. Ki-moon, Report of the Secretary-General on the situation in Mali, UN Doc. S/2012/894 (28 November 2012).
64 International Criminal Court Prosecutor (ICCP), Situation in Mali Article 53(1), Report, 16 January 2013, pp. 31 and 34.
65 Ibid., pp. 31–32.
66 ICC, Press Release: Situation in Mali, Ahmad Al Faqi Al Mahdi surrendered to the ICC on charges of war crimes regarding the destruction of historical and religious monuments in Timbuktu, 26 September 2015, Doc.ICC-CPI-2015926-PR1154.
67 SC Res 2164 of 25 July 2014, UN Doc.S/RES/2164 (2014).
68 SC Res 2164(2014), at para. 14(b).
69 SC Res 2227 of 29 June 2015, UN Doc.S/RES/2227 (2015).
70 SC Res 2227(2015), at para. 14(h).
71 Security Council Report, September 2015 Monthly Forecast: Mali, available at http://www.securitycouncilreport.org/monthly-forecast/2015-09/mali_18.php?print=true (accessed 19 January 2017).
72 Report of the Secretary-General on the situation in Mali, 22 September 2015, UN Doc.S/2015/732, at p. 12.

3 Crimes against humanity, cultural landscapes and human rights

For millennia, combatants have deliberately targeted the cultural property affiliated with their enemy during armed conflict and belligerent occupation. The Nuremberg Trials highlighted that the cultural patrimony of targeted cultural, religious and ethnic communities was intentionally damaged, destroyed or seized to persecute and ultimately eliminate them. Such acts were not confined to the theatre of war or occupation, but were perpetrated by States upon their own inhabitants. The extension of international criminal law to crimes against humanity and genocide has served as an important means of reinforcing that the targeted, intentional destruction of cultural property is intrinsic to gross and systematic abuses of human rights.

3.1 Persecution

In the mid-twentieth century, the atrocities of the Axis forces went beyond the established time and space parameters of existing international humanitarian law as defined by the Hague Regulations. They had occurred prior to the commencement of war and were often perpetrated by States against their own nationals within their own territory. Allied declarations reflective of the Hague Conventions made no reference to such acts. However, Article 6(c) of the London Charter extended the IMT's jurisdiction to encompass crimes against humanity including 'persecutions on political, racial or religious grounds in execution of or in connection with any crime within the jurisdiction of the Tribunal, whether or not in violation of the domestic law of the country where perpetrated'.[73] Count Four of the Nuremberg Indictment detailed how 'Jews [were] systematically persecuted since 1933 ... [Millions] of Jews from Germany and from the occupied Western Countries were sent to the Eastern Countries for extermination'.[74] The IMT held that confiscation and destruction of religious and cultural institutions and objects of Jewish communities amounted to persecution that was a crime against humanity.[75] The prosecution of crimes against humanity without reference to 'time and place and national sovereignty' reflected the Charter's centrality in the promotion of human rights.[76] Rosenberg was found guilty of crimes against humanity including the persecution of the Jews through acts such as the plunder of Jewish homes in the Occupied Eastern Territories.[77] Julius Streicher was also found guilty on Count

---

73 Agreement by the Governments of the United Kingdom, the United States of America, the Provisional Government of the French Republic and USSR for the Prosecution and Punishment of the Major War Criminals of the European Axis, signed and entered into force 8 August 1945, 82 UNTS 279.
74 Ibid.
75 Nuremberg Judgment, note 7, at pp. 243–247.
76 E. Schwelb, 'Crimes against Humanity', *British Yearbook of International Law* (1946) vol. 23, p. 178 at p. 181.
77 Nuremberg Judgment, note 7, at pp. 287–288.

Four for his role in the destruction of the Nuremberg synagogue in 1938 and incitement of the persecution and extermination of Jews as editor of the newspaper *Der Stürmer*.[78]

The international and hybrid criminal tribunals established under the auspices of the United Nations since the 1990s have invariably extended jurisdiction to the crimes against humanity of persecution.[79] The ICTY reopened the question of persecution as it related to cultural heritage. During the first years of the Yugoslav conflicts, the International Law Commission in its 1991 Report on the Draft Code of Crimes Against Peace and Security related persecution on social, political, religious or cultural grounds to 'human rights violations ... committed in a systematic manner or on a mass scale by government officials or by groups that exercise de facto power over a particular territory'.[80] It observed that the systematic destruction of monuments, buildings and sites of highly symbolic value for a specific social, religious or cultural group was persecution.[81] This definition included the suppression of language and religious practices, and detention of community or religious leaders. Under the ICTY Statute, crimes against humanity are covered by Article 5. This provision does not list acts against cultural property nor does it define 'persecution'. However, the ICTY has found the destruction or damaging of the institutions of a particular political, racial or religious group is a crime against humanity, namely persecution under Article 5(h).[82] Referring to the Nuremberg Judgment, the 1991 ILC Report and its own jurisprudence, the ICTY Trial Chamber in *Kordić and Čerkez* held that such destruction 'when perpetrated with the requisite discriminatory intent ... manifests a nearly pure expression of the notion of "crimes against humanity", for all humanity is indeed injured by the destruction of a unique religious culture'.[83] The tribunal affirmed that the attacks must be directed against a civilian population, be widespread or systematic and perpetrated on discriminatory grounds for damage inflicted to

78 Nuremberg Judgment, note 7, at pp. 294–295.
79 See Art. 3(h), Statute for the International Criminal Tribunal for Rwanda, SC Res.955 of 8 November 1994, UN Doc.S/RES/955(1994); Arts 7(1)(h) and 2(g), Rome Statute; Art. 2(h) Statute of the Special Court for Sierra Leone, 16 January 2002, into force 12 April 2002, 2178 UNTS 138; Art. 9 Agreement Between the United Nations and the Royal Government of Cambodia Concerning the Prosecution under Cambodian Law of Crimes Committed During the Period of Democratic Kampuchea, GA Res 57/228B of 22 May 2003, UN Doc.A/RES/57/228B (2003) Annex; and Art. 3 (Religious Persecution) and Art. 5 (Crimes Against Humanity including persecution) Law on the Establishment of Extraordinary Chambers in the Court of Cambodia for the Prosecution of Crimes committed during the period of Democratic Kampuchea, with the inclusion of amendments as promulgated on 27 October 2004, Doc.NS/RKM/1004/006.
80 Report of the International Law Commission on the Work of its Forty-Third Session, UN Doc.A/46/10/supp.10 (1991), at p. 268.
81 Ibid.
82 Prosecutor v Dario Kordić and Mario Čerdez, Trial Judgment, No IT-95-14/2-T (26 February 2001), at 207.
83 Ibid., at 206 and 207.

cultural property to qualify as persecution.[84] This requirement is intended to ensure that crimes of a collective nature are penalised because a person is 'victimised not because of his individual attributes but rather because of his membership of a targeted civilian population'.[85] Similarly, cultural property is protected not for its own sake but because it represents a particular group.

The ICTY has held that a vital element of crimes under Article 5 is that they are part of 'a widespread or systematic attack against a civilian population'.[86] Acts should not be examined in isolation but in terms of their cumulative effect.[87] The Trial Chamber found that an act must reach the same level of gravity as the other crimes against humanity enumerated in Article 5; however, such acts were not limited to those listed in Article 5 or elsewhere in the ICTY Statute, 'but also include the denial of other fundamental human rights, provided they are of equal gravity or severity'.[88] Persecution requires a specific additional *mens rea* element over and above that needed for other crimes against humanity, namely a discriminatory intent 'on political, racial or religious' grounds (not necessarily cultural).[89] Although the *actus reus* of persecution may be identical to other crimes against humanity, it was distinguishable because it was committed on discriminatory grounds.

3.2 Genocide

Several indictments brought before the ICTY for the deliberate destruction or damage of cultural property of religious or ethnic groups included counts of persecution and genocide. Such acts have been used to establish the *mens rea* of a defendant – that is, the discriminatory intent required for proving genocide and persecution. However, the targeting of cultural property may amount to *actus reus* in respect of the crime of persecution, but the ICTY has not included such acts *per se* within the definition of genocide under Article 4 of its Statute.

Two months after the Nuremberg Judgment, the UN General Assembly adopted the resolution on the Crime of Genocide (Genocide Resolution).[90] The Resolution states that genocide 'is a crime under international law', without

---

84 Prosecutor v Zoran Kupreškić and Others, Trial Judgment, Case No IT-95-16-T, Trial Chamber, ICTY (14 January 2000) at 544; and Prosecutor v Tihomir Blaškić, Trial Judgment, Case No IT-95-14-T, Trial Chamber, ICTY (30 March 2000), at 207.
85 Prosecutor v Duško Tadić, Opinion Trial Judgment, No IT-94-1-T, Trial Chamber, ICTY (7 May 1997), at 644.
86 Prosecutor v Radislav Krstić, Trial Judgment, Case No IT-98-33, Trial Chamber, ICTY (2 August 2001), at 535.
87 Kupreškić and Others, Trial Judgment, note 84, at 615.
88 Krstić, Trial Judgment, note 86, at 535; and Prosecutor v Radoslav Brđanin, Appeals Judgment, Appeals Chamber, ICTY (3 April 2007), at 296–297.
89 Blaškić, Trial Judgment, note 84, at 283; Krstić, Trial Judgment, note 86, at 480; and Kordić and Čerkez, Trial Judgment, note 82, at 211 and 212.
90 GA Res.96(I) of 11 December 1946, in UN, *Yearbook of the United Nations* (1946–47), at p. 255.

reference to a nexus to armed conflict.[91] Its preamble notes that genocide 'shocked the conscience of mankind [and] resulted in great losses to humanity in the form of cultural and other contributions represented by these groups'. Yet it goes on to define genocide as 'a denial of the right to existence of entire human groups, as homicide is the denial of the right to live for individual human beings'. The *travaux* of the Genocide Convention show that early drafts included the 'systematic destruction of historical or religious monuments or their diversion to alien uses, or destruction or dispersion of documents or objects of historical, artistic, or religious interest and of religious accessories' in the definition of genocide.[92] However, the only 'cultural' element in the definition of genocide of the Convention on the Prevention and Punishment of Genocide, which was adopted by the General Assembly in 1948, is the reference to the removal of children from the group (Article II).[93] This narrower definition of genocide has been repeatedly reaffirmed by the international community.[94]

Article 4 of the ICTY Statute contains the same definition of genocide as Article II of the Genocide Convention and does not require that the acts occur during an armed conflict. The acts must have been perpetrated with a specific intent (*dolus specialis*) – that is, 'to destroy, in whole or in part, a national, ethnic, racial or religious group as such'.[95] The ICTY has emphasised that there are two elements to the special intent requirement of the crime of genocide: (a) the act or acts must target a national, ethnical, racial or religious group;[96] and (b) the act or acts must seek to destroy all or part of that group. In the case of *Radoslav Krstić*, the defendant was charged with atrocities which took place during the fall of Srebrenica in 1995 and the ICTY Trial Chamber took the opportunity to re-examine the issue of whether acts directed at the cultural property of a group amounted to the international crime of genocide. It observed: '[O]ne may ... conceive of destroying a group through purposeful eradication of its culture and identity resulting in the eventual extinction of the group as an entity distinct from the remainder of the community.'[97] It added that, unlike genocide, persecution was not limited to the physical or biological destruction of a group but extended to include 'all acts designed to destroy the social and/or cultural bases of a group'.[98] The ICTY found that the drafters of the Genocide Convention

91 GA Res 96(I), para. 1.
92 Committee on the Progressive Development of International Law and its Codification, Draft Convention for the Prevention and Punishment of Genocide, prepared by the Secretariat, 6 June 1947, UN Doc.A/AC.10/42, draft Art. 3(e)
93 Art. 2(e), Convention on the Prevention and Punishment of the Crime of Genocide, UNGA Res 260A(III), 9 December 1948, in force 12 January 1951, 78 UNTS 277.
94 See Art. 2, ICTR Statute; Art. 6, Rome Statute; Art. 9, Statute of the Special Court for Cambodia; and Art. 4, Law on the Establishment of Cambodian Extraordinary Chambers.
95 Krstić, Trial Judgment, note 86, at 480.
96 Ibid., at 551–553.
97 Ibid., at 574.
98 Ibid., at 575.

expressly considered and rejected the inclusion of the cultural elements in the list of acts constituting genocide.[99] Indeed, it observed that despite numerous opportunities to recalibrate the definition of genocide, Article II of the Convention was replicated in the statutes of the tribunal for Rwanda, the 1996 Draft ILC Code of Crimes Against Peace and Security of Mankind[100] and Rome Statute. The Trial Chamber in *Krstić* found these developments had not altered the definition of genocidal acts in customary international law and felt confined by the principle of *nullum crime sine lege*. The Appeals Chamber in *Krstić* confirmed that the Genocide Convention and customary international law limited genocide to the physical or biological destruction of the group, noting with approval that 'the Trial Chamber expressly acknowledged this limitation, and eschewed any broader definition'.[101] Yet the Trial Chamber in *Krstić* used evidence of the destruction of the cultural and religious property of Muslims to prove the specific intent element of genocide. It found:

> [W]here there is physical or biological destruction there are often simultaneous attacks on cultural and religious property and symbols of the targeted group as well, attacks which may legitimately be considered as evidence of an intent to physically destroy the group.[102]

The Appeal Chamber pronounced that genocide was 'crime against all humankind' because the perpetrators 'seek to deprive humanity of the manifold richness its nationalities, races, ethnicities and religions provide'.[103]

The *Genocide* case brought by Bosnia and Herzegovina against Yugoslavia (later Serbia and Montenegro) before the International Court of Justice in 1993 concerned Yugoslavia's alleged violations of its obligations under the 1948 Genocide Convention. Unlike the cases before the ICTY which covered individual criminal responsibility, this action concerned the culpability of a State in respect of the international crime of genocide. Accepting that there was 'conclusive evidence of the deliberate destruction of the historical, cultural and religious heritage of the protected group',[104] the ICJ reaffirmed the ICTY's interpretation in *Krstić* that the definition of genocide had not evolved beyond Article II. It concluded that the destruction of the historical, religious and cultural heritage of a group only goes to proving the *mens rea* of the crime of genocide and not the *actus reus*.[105] In

---

99 Ibid., at 576.
100 Art. 17, Draft Code of Crimes Against the Peace and Security of Mankind, 51 UN GAOR Supp. (No 10) at p. 14, UN Doc.A/CN.4/L.532, corr. 1, corr. 3 (1996).
101 Prosecutor v Radislav Krstić, Appeals Judgment, Case No IT-98-33-A (19 April 2004) at 25.
102 Krstić, Trial Judgment, note 86, at 580.
103 Krstić, Appeals Judgment, note 101, at 36.
104 Application of the Convention for the Prevention and Punishment of the Crime of Genocide (Bosnia and Herzegovina v Serbia and Montenegro), ICJ, Judgment of 26 February 2007, at p. 344.
105 Ibid.

early 2015, in the *Genocide* case between Croatia and Serbia, the International Court reiterated this interpretation by stating that 'there was no compelling reason in the present case for it to depart from that approach'.[106]

4 Crime against the common heritage of humanity

From the deliberate destruction of the monumental Buddhas in Bamiyan, Afghanistan, by the Taliban in 2001 to the systematic and intentional destruction of successive World Heritage sites in Syria and Iraq in 2014–2015, the motivation for such acts by the perpetrators has evolved beyond solely demoralising the local populace of the territory where the sites are located. The digital age, and the Internet and social media with it, has proliferated and globalised the propaganda potential of such acts of destruction of cultural heritage. Often the monuments, sites and shrines are not directly related to the cultural and religious practices of present-day inhabitants; instead, they are evidence of the multilayered history and diversity of these sites. It is this cultural and religious diversity that the perpetrators find abhorrent and seek to expunge through such acts. The recording of these acts of destruction and their circulation on social and traditional media is designed to demoralise not only the local populace but the international community as a whole. Accordingly, the acknowledged universal importance of these sites and monuments to all humanity has increasingly elicited a coordinated response by intergovernmental organisations such as the United Nations and its agencies, including UNESCO, to hold the perpetrators to account.

4.1 Intentional destruction: UNESCO Declaration and Security Council Resolutions

The obligation to prosecute those engaged in acts of deliberate destruction of cultural property was reinforced in the twenty-first century with UN Security Council resolutions covering Iraq, Afghanistan and Syria, and UNESCO instrument covering the intentional destruction of cultural heritage. These resolutions take this obligation beyond the States Parties to the 1954 Hague Conventions and its Protocols, by articulating a legally binding obligation on all UN Member States to cooperate in preventing such acts and holding perpetrators to account.

The UNESCO Declaration concerning the Intentional Destruction of Cultural Heritage was adopted in response to the deliberate destruction of the monumental Buddhas in the World Heritage listed site of Bamiyan, Afghanistan, on 1 March 2001.[107] A month earlier, the Taliban had issued an edict requiring the

---

106 Application of the Convention for the Prevention and Punishment of the Crime of Genocide (Croatia v Serbia), ICJ, Judgment of 3 February 2015, para. 389.
107 UNESCO Declaration concerning the Intentional Destruction of Cultural Heritage, adopted by the General Conference of UNESCO at its 31st session, 17 October 2003.

destruction of all non-Islamic shrines in Afghanistan. Within days, the UN General Assembly denounced the 'deliberate ongoing destruction of these relics and monuments which belong to the common heritage of humankind'.[108] The UNESCO General Conference in November 2001 adopted a Resolution on Acts constituting a crime against the common heritage of humanity,[109] which called on Member States not party to the relevant conventions, including the 1954 Hague Convention and its Protocols and the 1972 World Heritage Convention, to join these 'in order to maximize the protection of the cultural heritage of humanity, and in particular, destructive acts'.[110] It reiterates that these obligations should guide 'governments, authorities, institutions, organizations, associations and individual citizens'.[111] It requested the Director-General prepare a draft convention on intentional destruction for adoption by the General Conference. The rationale contained in the preamble of the 1954 Hague Convention was reaffirmed by the Declaration concerning the Intentional Destruction of Cultural Heritage adopted by the UNESCO General Conference in 2003. It states in part:

> The international community recognizes the importance of the protection of cultural heritage and reaffirms its commitment to fight against its intentional destruction in any form so that such cultural heritage may be transmitted to the succeeding generations.[112]

The Declaration covers cultural heritage 'linked to a natural site', and acts occurring outside the theatre of war, and within the territory of a State. In support it invokes not only the 1954 Hague Convention, Additional Protocols I and II to the 1949 Geneva Conventions, 1899 Hague II and 1907 Hague IV Conventions, but the relevant provisions of the Rome Statute and the ICTY Statute and related jurisprudence.

The deliberate destruction of cultural heritage again became the focus of international attention in 2014 with atrocities committed by extremist groups, including Al Nusrah Front (ANF) and Islamic State of Iraq and the Levant (ISIL), in Iraq and Syria. The Security Council had called on all parties to 'immediately end all violence which has led to human suffering in Syria, save Syria's rich societal mosaic and cultural heritage, and take appropriate steps to ensure the protection of Syria's World Heritage Sites'.[113] It stressed that there was a need to 'end impunity for violations of international humanitarian law and abuse of

---

108 GA Res.55/243 on the Destruction of Relics and Monuments in Afghanistan, 9 March 2001, UN Doc.A/RES/55/243. The UN General Assembly had previously adopted resolutions 54/189 of 17 December 1999, PP4 and OP30, and 55/174 of 19 December 2000, PP4 and OP30.
109 31C/Res.26 of 2 November 2001.
110 31C/Res.26 of 2 November 2001, para. 1.
111 SC Res.26(2001), para. 3.
112 Intentional Destruction Declaration, para. 1.
113 SC Res.2139 of 22 February 2014, UN Doc.S/RES/2139(2014), PP8.

human rights' and bring those responsible to justice.[114] The Human Rights Council likewise expressed deep concern for the 'rampant destruction of monuments, shrines, churches, mosques, and other places of worship, archaeological sites and cultural heritage sites'.[115] It called on the Iraq government to investigate all alleged violations of international humanitarian law and abuses of human rights and 'prosecute the perpetrators of such attacks'.[116] Likewise, UNESCO's Executive Board, recalling the 2003 Declaration, noted that these acts 'damage the cultural heritage of all humankind' and could amount to war crimes under the Rome Statute.[117]

The Security Council adopted resolution 2199 of 12 February 2015 which condemned 'the destruction of cultural heritage in Iraq and Syria particularly by ISIL and ANF, whether such destruction is incidental or deliberate, including targeted destruction of religious sites and objects'.[118] The resolution was adopted pursuant to Chapter VII of the UN Charter and is therefore binding on UN Member States and takes precedence over any conflicting treaty obligations. In their Namur Call, the Committee of Ministers of the Council of Europe in April 2015 recorded that they 'deplor[ed] the deliberate destruction of cultural heritage ... which constitute[d] an impoverishment of the common heritage and incur[red] our collective responsibility with regard to future generations'.[119] It reinforced European cooperation on legal instruments such as those covering unlawful destruction of cultural heritage.[120] In a resolution on 'Saving the cultural heritage of Iraq' adopted in mid-2015, the General Assembly referenced the 1907 Hague Regulations, the 1949 Geneva Conventions, the 1954 Hague Convention and its Protocols, 1970 UNESCO Convention, 1972 World Heritage Convention, UN Convention against Transnational Organized Crime, and the UNESCO Declaration on the Intentional Destruction of Cultural Heritage, and 'resolved to stand up against attacks on the cultural heritage of any country as attacks on the common heritage of humanity as a whole'.[121] Yet the deliberate destruction

114 SC Res.2139(2014), para. 13. See also SC Res.2170 of 15 August 2014, UN Doc.S/RES/2170(2014), OP2 and 5.
115 HRC Res.S-22/1 of 1 September 2014, UN Doc.A/HRC/RES/2-22/1, PP6.
116 HRC Res.S-22/1(2014), PP5.
117 UNESCO Executive Board Item 31 Protection of Iraqi Heritage, Explanatory Note, 1 October 2014, UNESCO Doc.195EX/31, paras 6 and 8.
118 SC Res.2199 of 14 November 2014, UN Doc.S/2014/815, OP15. See also UNESCO Executive Board decision 196EX/29 Culture in conflict areas. UNESCO's role and responsibilities, 22 May 2015.
119 Committee of Ministers of the Council of Europe, The Namur Call, 23–24 April 2015.
120 See Recommendation No. R(96)R of the Committee of Ministers to Members States on the Protection of Cultural Heritage against Unlawful Acts, adopted 19 June 1996, references the Council of Europe's European Convention on Offences relating to Cultural Property, 1954 Hague Convention, 1970 UNESCO Convention and 1972 World Heritage Convention.
121 GA Res.69.281 on Saving the Cultural Heritage of Iraq, 28 May 2015, UN Doc.A/RES/69/281, PP2 and 4.

continued. On 4 September 2015, the Committee for the Protection of Cultural Property in the Event of Armed Conflict condemned the destruction of the temples of Baal Shamin and Bel, in Palmyra, built almost 2,000 years ago, and part of a World Heritage site.[122] It advised that this 'systematic destruction' was a violation of international law and possibly a war crime. It urged the international community 'to unite and intensify its efforts to confront this unprecedented situation, caused by terrorist groups, such as ISIS'.[123]

4.2 Incitement in the digital age

Since ancient times, these acts of deliberate destruction of cultural heritage were designed to demoralise the enemy and civilian populations into submission. As noted earlier, this is a strategy condemned and prohibited by the international community since the late nineteenth century. However, what distinguishes the intentional acts of destruction by groups from the Buddhas of Bamiyan to the various World Heritage listed sites in Syria is that they are not necessarily affiliated in a cultural or religious affiliation with local communities. Instead, they are sites which are defined as belonging to the cultural heritage of all humanity. Equally, their destruction is not simply directed to combatants in the conflict on the ground as was traditionally the case. Rather, the Security Council has acknowledged that cultural heritage has another significant potential for these groups. The deliberate destruction of historic sites for propaganda value had successfully garnered worldwide attention through social and traditional media. The Parliamentary Assembly of the Council of Europe had observed in 2004 that culture and its manifestations was 'increasingly the target of terrorism'. It maintained that globalisation and our information society not only enable unprecedented cultural interaction but 'potentially foster terrorism and the ideologies that encourage it ... leading to a new form of international terrorism with an "a-territorial" and "a-cultural" dimension'.[124] A decade later the Security Council, in SC Res.2170(2014), defined the 'need for Member States to act cooperatively to prevent terrorists from exploiting technology, communications and resources to incite support for terrorist acts, while respecting human rights and fundamental freedoms'.[125]

The deliberate destruction of cultural and religious monuments, including those listed as World Heritage sites in Syria and Iraq have been broadcast by ISIL through social media and the Internet. The General Assembly observed that 'attacks on cultural heritage are used as a tactic of war in order to spread terror and hatred' and it called on 'community leaders to stand up and reaffirm

---

122 Statement of the Chairperson on behalf of the Committee for the Protection of Cultural Heritage in the Event of Armed Conflict established by the Second Protocol to the 1954 Hague Convention, Statement, 4 September 2015.
123 Ibid.
124 CE Parliamentary Assembly Recommendation 1687 (2004) Combating Terrorism through Culture.
125 SC Res.2170(2014), PP12 and 13.

unambiguously that there is no justification for the destruction of humanity's cultural heritage'.[126] The UN Analytical Support and Sanctions Monitoring Team noted that '[t]he extremist, violent ideology of the Al-Qaida movement relies on propaganda' but that the transnational nature of social media meant that any collective, multilateral response is complicated because 'social media providers operate across borders.'[127] It noted that prosecutions for incitement in domestic jurisdictions, where this is possible, serve as a deterrent.[128] In SC Res.2199(2015), the Security Council 'express[ed] concern at the increased use … by terrorists and their supporters, of new information and communication technologies, in particular the Internet, to facilitate terrorist acts, as well as their use to incite, recruit, fund or plan terrorist acts'. In mid-2015, the UN Analytical Support and Sanctions Monitoring Team again referred to the need to address the 'growth of high-definition digital terror', and recommended that Internet and social media brief the Team on their strategies in responding to the 'exploitation of their services' by these terrorist organisations.[129]

4.3 Criminalisation and cooperation

These recent Security Council resolutions covering deliberate destruction of cultural heritage have repeatedly called on States to cooperate to ensure that perpetrators are held criminally responsible for such crimes. The 2003 UNESCO Declaration is an important reference point because it provides for State and individual responsibility for intentional destruction of cultural heritage (Articles VI and VII) and outlines the obligation to cooperate in respect of protecting cultural heritage against intentional destruction (Article VIII). It calls on States to establish jurisdiction and effective criminal sanctions against individuals who commit or order others to commit such acts. It requests States to cooperate with one another and UNESCO including through information sharing; consultation in cases of actual or impeding destruction; assisting in respect of educational, awareness-raising and capacity-building programmes for prevention and repression; and assisting judicial and administrative processes. States are also encouraged to establish jurisdiction and effective criminal sanctions against individuals 'who have committed or have ordered to be committed acts referred to [individual criminal responsibility] and who are found present on its territory, regardless of their nationality and the place where such act occurred' (para.VIII(2)). The Declaration requires States to recognise 'international rules related to the criminalization of gross violations of

---

126 GA Res.69/281(2015), paras 2 and 8.
127 Sixteenth Report of the Analytical Support and Sanctions Monitoring Team submitted pursuant to resolution 2161 (2014) concerning Al-Qaida and associated individuals and entities, 29 October 2014, UN Doc.S/2014/770, paras 17 and 21.
128 UN Doc.S/2014/770, para. 22.
129 Seventeenth report of the Analytical Support and Sanctions Monitoring Team submitted pursuant to resolution 2161(2014) concerning Al-Qaida and associated individuals and entities, 16 June 2015, UN Doc.S/2015/441, para. 44.

human rights and international humanitarian law, in particular, when intentional destruction of cultural heritage is linked to those violations'.[130] Like the ICTY jurisprudence, this link had been highlighted by the Human Rights Council in 2007 which recognised that 'intentional destruction of cultural heritage may constitute advocacy and incitement to national, racial or religious hatred and thereby violates fundamental principles of international human rights law' and that States bore primary responsibility to 'prohibit, prevent, stop and punish' such acts.[131]

Intergovernmental bodies, such as the Council of Europe and the United Nations, have instruments that cover unlawful acts against cultural heritage and provide guidance to States Parties on how these obligations can be translated into domestic law and cooperation between them to achieve these objectives. The Council of Europe Recommendation No.R(96)6 on the protection of Cultural Heritage against unlawful acts emphasises that it is preventative in purpose and it is primarily focused on identifying and managing risks to cultural property through unlawful acts or negligence. It preamble states: '[P]revention should be primarily concerned with educating and informing owners, professionals and the public about conservation and respect for cultural heritage and with encouraging a multidisciplinary approach to prevention, using all available human, physical and electronic means'.[132] The European Convention on Offences relating to Cultural Property adopted by the Council of Europe in 1985 is primarily geared towards curbing the illicit trade in cultural objects.[133] It covers acts including 'appropriating cultural property through violence or menace', and States Parties may choose to extend its application to 'destruction or damaging of cultural property of another person'.[134] A State Party is obliged to establish jurisdiction to prosecute offences committed on its territory, outside its territory by a national or resident, or outside its territory against its own property or that of a national or original located in its territory (Article 13). Likewise, the International Guidelines for Crime Prevention and Criminal Justice Responses with Respect to Trafficking in Cultural Property and Other Related Offences provide detailed strategies in respect of crime prevention, criminal justice policies, and international cooperation to facilitate national and international efforts for the protection of cultural heritage but are largely centred on the illicit traffic of cultural objects.[135]

---

130 Intentional Destruction Declaration, para. IX.
131 HRC Res.6/11 on Protection of cultural heritage as an important component of the promotion and protection of cultural rights, 28 September 2007.
132 Recommendation No. R(96)6, PP12.
133 European Convention on Offences relating to Cultural Property, 23 June 1985, not entered into force, CETS No. 119.
134 European Convention on Offences relating to Cultural Property, Appendix III, paras 1 and 2.
135 International Guidelines for Crime Prevention and Criminal Justice Responses with Respect to Trafficking in Cultural Property and Other Related Offences, GA Res.69/196 of 26 January 2015, UN Doc.A/RES/69/196.

5 Conclusion

The Arch of Triumph which formed part of the 2,000-year-old Roman city of Palmyra was destroyed in mid-2015 by ISIL forces which circulated video and photographs of these acts on social media and the Internet. The organisation had already destroyed the Lion of Al-lāt, the Temple of Bel and Temple of Baal Shamin (Figure 12.2) in the World Heritage listed Syrian city. Like the Taliban before it in 2001, it has ordered the deliberate destruction of Islamic and non-Islamic monuments, shrines and statutes on Syrian and Iraqi territories under its control, justified on the basis on their interpretation of religious teachings. These monuments and sites which have been destroyed in Palmyra evidenced how cosmopolitan and culturally diverse this city has been throughout its long history. The intended impact of ISIL's visual recording of their acts of destruction and broadcasting globally via the Internet and social media goes beyond these occupied territories. Instead, they are addressed to a global audience. Both the perpetrators and the intended audience of these images understand these sites and monuments to be of universal significance to humanity as a whole. It is for this reason that these actions have repeatedly elicited international condemnation and calls in international fora such as the Security Council and UNESCO for the perpetrators to be held criminally responsible.

In various multilateral instruments since the mid-nineteenth century, the international community had repeatedly and consistently confirmed its prohibition of

Figure 12.2 The Temple of Baal Shamin, Palmyra, Syria
Source: iStock.

the deliberate destruction of cultural and religious sites and the requirement that violations be subject to legal proceedings. The nature of international law has invariably meant that the obligation for holding perpetrators criminally responsible has primarily fallen to the territorial State where the acts occurred or the State of nationality of the offender. However, States have often been unable to fulfil these obligations for a variety of reasons including the lack of control over their territory and its inhabitants or the violation of international humanitarian law and human rights law by the government itself. The obligation then falls to the international community through intergovernmental organisations such as the UN Security Council and international tribunals such as the International Criminal Court. Recent acts of intentional destruction of monuments at World Heritage sites have engaged both the Security Council and the ICC which have called upon all Member States to cooperate in bringing the perpetrators of these international crimes to justice. New technologies will prove vital in the evidence-gathering and reconstruction processes.[136] Yet history shows that such actions have met with limited success and are by definition reactive. Significantly, multilateral instruments which have included the criminalisation of deliberate acts of destruction against cultural property have consistently incorporated preventative and punitive obligations. Accordingly, existing preventative measures such as those contained in the 1954 Hague Convention and its Protocols and the initiative to extend the mandate of UN peacekeepers so that they can be deployed to protect World Heritage sites have a potentially significant, proactive impact.[137] The urgency of these avenues of international cooperation were recognized in Security Council Resolution 2347 of 2017, the first resolution specifically dedicated to condemnation of the deliberate destruction of cultural heritage and recognizing it as a threat to international peace and security.

Bibliography

Agreement by the Governments of the United Kingdom, the United States of America, the Provisional Government of the French Republic and USSR for the Prosecution and Punishment of the Major War Criminals of the European Axis, signed and entered into force 8 August 1945, 82 UNTS 279.

Agreement Between the United Nations and the Royal Government of Cambodia Concerning the Prosecution under Cambodian Law of Crimes Committed During the Period of Democratic Kampuchea, GA Res 57/228B of 22 May 2003, UN Doc.A/RES/57/228B (2003) Annex.

---

136 See for example, UNITAR/UNOSAT, *Satellite-based Damage Assessment to Cultural Heritage Sites in Syria*, (Geneva: UNITAR, 2015).

137 Anon, 'UN to deploy peacekeepers to protect world heritage sites', *The Guardian* (18 October 2015), available at www.theguardian.com/world/2015/oct/17/un-peacekeepers-protect-world-heritage-sites-isis (accessed 19 January 2017).

Boylan, P.J. (1993). Review of the Convention for the Protection of Cultural Property in the Event of Armed Conflict (The Hague Convention of 1954), UNESCO Doc.CLT-93/WS/12, p. 17.

Bories, C. (2005). *Les bombardements serbes sur la vieille ville de Dubrovnik: La protection internationale des biens culturels*. Paris: Pedone.

Charter of the International Military Tribunal, Nuremberg annexed to the Agreement by United Kingdom, United States, France and USSR for the Prosecution and Punishment of the Major War Criminals of the European Axis, 8 August 1945, 82 UNTS 279.

Clemen, P. (1919). *Protection of Art during War*. Leipzig: E.A. Seeman.

Committee of Ministers of the Council of Europe, The Namur Call, 23–24 April 2015.

Council of Europe, Parliamentary Assembly Recommendation 1687 (2004), Combating Terrorism Through Culture.

Committee on the Progressive Development of International Law and its Codification 'Draft Convention for the Prevention and Punishment of Genocide', 6 June 1947, UN Doc.A/AC. 10/42.

Convention (II) with Respect to the Laws and Customs of War on Land and Annex, 29 July 1899, in force 4 September 1900, *American Journal of International Law* (1907), vol. 1 (supp.), p. 129.

Convention (IV) respecting the Laws and Customs of War on Land, and Annex, 18 October 1907, in force 26 January 1910, *American Journal of International Law* (1907), vol. 1(supp.), p. 90.

Convention for the Protection of Cultural Property in the Event of Armed Conflict, 14 May 1954, into force 7 August 1956, 249 UNTS 240.

Convention on the Means of Prohibiting and Preventing the Illicit Import, Export and Transfer of Ownership of Cultural Property, 14 November 1970, in force 24 April 1972, 823 UNTS 231.

Convention on the Prevention and Punishment of the Crime of Genocide, UNGA Res 260A(III), 9 December 1948, in force 12 January 1951, 78 UNTS 277.

Convention concerning the Protection of the World Cultural and Natural Heritage, 16 November 1972, into force 17 December 1975, 1037 UNTS 151.

Coulibaly, M. (2012). Referral under Article 14 ICC Statute from Malian Minister for Justice to ICC Prosecutor, 13 July 2012. Available at www.icc-cpi.int/NR/rdon lyres/A245A47F-BFD1-45B6-891C-3BCB5B173F57/0/ReferralLetterMali130712.pdf (accessed 17 January 2017).

Council of Europe, Recommendation No. R(96)R of the Committee of Ministers to Members States on the Protection of Cultural Heritage against Unlawful Acts, adopted 19 June 1996.

Declaration of the Four Nations on General Security (Moscow Declaration), 30 October 1943, *American Journal of International Law* (1944) vol. 38 (supp.), pp. 7–8.

De Visscher, C. (1949, June). International Protection of Works of Art and Historic Monuments. In Department of State Publication 3590, International Information and Cultural Series 8, reprinted in *Documents and State Papers*, pp. 821–828.

Draft Code of Crimes Against the Peace and Security of Mankind, 51 UN GAOR Supp. (No 10) at p. 14, UN Doc.A/CN.4/L.532, corr.1, corr.3 (1996).

European Convention on Offences Relating to Cultural Property, 23 June 1985, not entered into force, CETS No. 119.

Frulli, M. (2005). Advancing the protection of cultural property through the implementation of individual criminal responsibility: The case-law of the International Criminal Tribunal for the former Yugoslavia. *Italian Yearbook of International Law*, 15, 195–197.
Grotius, H. (1925). *De jure belli ac pacis. Libri tres*. J.B. Scott (ed.) and F.W. Kelsey (trans.). Oxford: Clarendon Press.
Horne, J., and Kramer, A. (2001). *German Atrocities 1914: A History of Denial*. New Haven, CT: Yale University Press.
Huber, M. (1913). La propriété publique en cas de guerre sur terre. *Revue Générale de Droit International Public*, p. 657.
Human Rights Council Res.6/11 on Protection of cultural heritage as an important component of the promotion and protection of cultural rights, 28 September 2007.
Human Rights Council Resolution S-22/1 of 1 September 2014, UN Doc.A/HRC/RES/ 2- 22/1, PP6.
International Committee of the Red Cross. (2013). *The Domestic Implementation of International Humanitarian Law. A Manual*. Geneva: ICRC, Annex XVIII.
International Criminal Court, Prosecutor's Statement on Mali, 1 July 2012, OTP Briefing, Issue#126, 20 June–3 July 2012.
International Criminal Court (2015, 26 September). Press Release: Situation in Mali, Ahmad Al Faqi Al Mahdi surrendered to the ICC on charges of war crimes regarding the destruction of historical and religious monuments in Timbuktu, Doc.ICC-CPI-2015926-PR1154.
International Criminal Court Prosecutor (ICCP), Situation in Mali Article 53(1), Report, 16 January 2013.
International Declaration concerning the Laws and Customs of War, 27 August 1874, not ratified, 1 *American Journal of International Law* (1907) vol. 1 (supp.), p. 96.
International Law Commission, Report of the International Law Commission on the Work of its Forty-Third Session, UN Doc.A/46/10/supp.10 (1991) at p. 268.
International Military Tribunal, Nuremberg. (1947). 'Judgment'. *American Journal of International Law*, 41, p. 172, at pp. 248–249.
Kéba M'Baye, M. (1992). Final Report of the United Nations Commission of Experts Established Pursuant to SC Res.780, UN Doc. S/1994 674 (27 May 1994) Annex XI: Destruction of Cultural Property Report.
Ki-moon, B. (2012, 8 August). Secretary-General's Remarks to the Security Council on Mali. Speech delivered at the UN Security Council. Available at www.un.org/sg/statements/index.asp?nid=6232 (accessed 19 January 2017).
Ki-moon, B. (2012, 28 November). Report of the Secretary-General on the situation in Mali, UN Doc. S/2012/894.
Nicholas. L. (1994). *The Rape of Europa: The Fate of Europe's Treasures in the Third Reich and the Second World War*. London: Papermac.
Protocol for the Protection of Cultural Property in the Event of Armed Conflict (First Hague Protocol), 14 May 1954, into force 7 August 1956, 249 UNTS 358.
Protocol Additional to the Geneva Conventions of 12 August 1949 and Relating to the Protection of Victims of Non-International Armed Conflicts, 8 June 1977, entered into force 7 December 1978, 125 UNTS 609.
Rolin-Jaequemyns, G. (1871). Essai complémentaire sur la guerre franco-allemande dans ses rapports avec le droit international. *Revue de droit international*, 2, 288, at 302.
Trial of the Major War Criminals before the International Military Tribunal, Nuremberg, 14 November 1945–1 October 1946, (42 vols, Nuremberg: [s.n.], 1947–1949), vol. 1 and vol. IV.

Report on the obligations of the Parties to implement Chapter 4 (Criminal Responsibility and Jurisdiction) of the Second Protocol to the 1954 Hague Convention, March 2012.

Rome Statute of the International Criminal Court, 17 July 1998, into force 1 July 2002, 2187 UNTS 90.

Schwelb, E. (1946). Crimes against humanity. *British Yearbook of International Law*, 23, 178.

Second Protocol to the Hague Convention for the Protection of Cultural Property in the Event of Armed Conflict (1999 Hague Protocol) 26 March 1999, into force 9 March 2004, 2253 UNTS 212.

Statute for the International Criminal Tribunal for Rwanda SC Res.955 of 8 November 1994, UN Doc.S/RES/ 955(1994).

Statute of the Special Court for Sierra Leone, 16 January 2002, into force 12 April 2002, 2178 UNTS 138.

UNESCO. (1957). Recommendation on International Principles Applicable to Archaeological Excavations, in UNESCO, 1956, Records of the General Conference, Ninth Session, New Delhi 1956: Resolutions. Paris: UNESCO.

UNESCO. (2012, 22 March). Guidelines for the Implementation of the 1999 Second Protocol to the Hague Convention of 1954 for the Protection of Cultural Property in the Event of Armed Conflict, 22UNESCO Doc.CLT-09/CONF/219/3 REV.4, p. 28.

UNESCO. (2014). Executive Board Item 31 Protection of Iraqi Heritage, Explanatory Note, 1 October 2014, UNESCO Doc.195EX/31.

UNESCO. (2015). Executive Board decision 196EX/29, Culture in conflict areas: A Humanitarian Concern and A Safety Issue. UNESCO's role and responsibilities, 22 May 2015.

UNESCO. (2003). Declaration concerning the Intentional Destruction of Cultural Heritage, adopted by the General Conference of UNESCO at its 31st session, 17 October 2003.

UNESCO. (2001). Resolution on Acts constituting a crime against the common heritage of humanity, 31C/Res.26 of 2 November 2001.

UN General Assembly, Res.69.281 on Saving the Cultural Heritage of Iraq, 28 May 2015, UN Doc.A/RES/ 69/281.

UN General Assembly, Res.55/243 on the Destruction of Relics and Monuments in Afghanistan, 9 March 2001, UN Doc.A/RES/55/243.

UN General Assembly, International Guidelines for Crime Prevention and Criminal Justice Responses with Respect to Trafficking in Cultural Property and Other Related Offences, GA Res.69/196 of 26 January 2015, UN Doc.A/RES/69/196.

UN Secretary-General, Report of the Secretary-General on the situation in Mali, 22 September 2015, UN Doc.S/2015/732.

UN Secretary-General's Bulletin on the Observance by UN Forces of International Humanitarian Law, 6 August 1999, UN Doc.ST/SGB/ 1999/13.

UN Security Council, Secretary-General to the President of the UN Security Council, Report annexing the Interim Report of the Commission of Experts Established Pursuant to SC Res.780(1992), UN Doc.S/1993/25274 (9 February 1993).

UN Security Council Resolution No. 2056 on Peace and Security in Africa, 5 July 2012, UN Doc.S/RES/2056(2012).

UN Security Council Resolution No. 2071 of 12 October 2012, UN Doc.S/RES/2071 (2012).

UN Security Council Resolution No. 2085 of 20 December 2012, UN Doc.S/RES/2085 (2012).

UN Security Council Resolution No. 2139 of 22 February 2014, UN Doc.S/RES/2139 (2014), PP8.
UN Security Council Resolution No. 2164 of 25 July 2014, UN Doc.S/RES/2164(2014).
UN Security Council Resolution No. 2170 of 15 August 2014, UN Doc.S/RES/2170 (2014).
UN Security Council Resolution No. 2199 of 14 November 2014, UN Doc.S/2014/815, OP15.
UN Security Council Resolution No. 2227 of 29 June 2015, UN Doc.S/RES/2227(2015).
UN Security Council Report. (2015, September). Monthly forecast: Mali. Available at www.securitycouncilreport.org/monthly-forecast/2015-09/mali_18.php?print=true (accessed 5 October 2015).
UN Security Council, Sixteenth Report of the Analytical Support and Sanctions Monitoring Team submitted pursuant to resolution 2161 (2014) concerning Al-Qaida and associated individuals and entities, 29 October 2014, UN Doc.S/2014/770, paras 17 and 21.
UN Security Council, Seventeenth report of the Analytical Support and Sanctions Monitoring Team submitted pursuant to resolution 2161 (2014) concerning Al-Qaida and associated individuals and entities, 16 June 2015, UN Doc.S/2015/441, para.44.
Committee for the Protection of Cultural Heritage in the Event of Armed Conflict established by the Second Protocol to the 1954 Hague Convention, Statement of the Chairperson on behalf of the Committee on the Syrian site of Palmyra, 4 September 2015. Available at www.unesco.org/new/fileadmin/MULTIMEDIA/HQ/CLT/pdf/Statement-Chairperson-Palmyra_03.pdf (accessed 19 January 2017).
UNITAR/UNOSAT. (2015). *Satellite-based Damage Assessment to Cultural Heritage Sites in Syria*. Geneva: UNITAR.
Anon. (2015, 18 October). UN to deploy peacekeepers to protect World Heritage sites. *The Guardian*. Available at www.theguardian.com/world/2015/oct/17/un-peacekeepers-protect-world-heritage-sites-isis (accessed 19 January 2017).

Court cases

International Court of Justice, Application of the Convention for the Prevention and Punishment of the Crime of Genocide (Bosnia and Herzegovina v Serbia and Montenegro), ICJ, Judgment of 26 February 2007, at p. 344.
International Court of Justice, Application of the Convention for the Prevention and Punishment of the Crime of Genocide (Croatia v. Serbia), ICJ, Judgment of 3 February 2015, para. 389.
Trial of Karl Lingenfelder, French Permanent Military Tribunal, Metz (judgment of 11 March 1947), in UNWCC, *Law Reports of Trials of War Criminals* (London: HMSO, 1949), vol. 9, p. 67.
Prosecutor v Duško Tadić, Interlocutory Appeal on Jurisdiction Judgment, No IT-94-1-A, Appeals Chamber, ICTY, (2 October 1995) at 98 and 127.
Prosecutor v Zoran Kupreškić and Others, Trial Judgment, Case No IT-95-16-T, Trial Chamber, ICTY (14 January 2000) at 544; and Prosecutor v Tihomir Blaškić, Trial Judgment, Case No IT-95-14-T, Trial Chamber, ICTY (30 March 2000) at 207.
Prosecutor v Duško Tadić, Opinion Trial Judgment, No IT-94-1-T, Trial Chamber, ICTY (7 May 1997) at 644.

Prosecutor v Radislav Krstić, Appeals Judgment, Case No IT-98-33-A (19 April 2004) at 25.
Prosecutor v Dario Kordić and Mario Čerdez, Trial Judgment, No IT-95-14/2-T (26 February 2001) at 207.
Prosecutor v Pavle Strugar, Appeals Judgment, No IT-01-42-A, Appeals Chamber, ICTY (17 July 2008) at 277–278.
Prosecutor v Miodrag Jokić, Judgment on Sentencing Appeal, No IT-01-42/1-A, Appeals Chamber, ICTY (30 August 2005).
Prosecutor v Duško Tadić, Appeal Judgment, No IT-94-1-A, Appeals Chamber, ICTY (2 October 1995) at 66–70.
Prosecutor v Pavle Strugar, Rule 98bis Motion, No IT-01-42-T, Trial Chamber II, ICTY (21 June 2004), at 80–81.
Prosecutor v Miodrag Jokić, Trial Judgment, No IT-01-42/1-S, Trial Chamber I, ICTY (18 March 2004) at 49 and 51.
Prosecutor v Pavle Strugar, Trial Judgment, Chamber II, ICTY, No IT-01-42-T (31 January 2005) at 310.
Prosecutor v Radoslav Brđanin, Trial Judgment, Case No IT-99-36-T, Trial Chamber II, ICTY (1 September 2004).

Chapter 13

Concluding thoughts: towards a socio-legal research and policy agenda on environmental crimes

Tiffany Bergin and Emanuela Orlando

Increasing global concern about environmental and natural resource protection has prompted new efforts to understand the characteristics and causes of environmental harms. This book contributes to such efforts by bringing together legal and social science perspectives on environmental crimes, with the aim of fostering greater dialogue among policymakers, academics from different disciplines, representatives from international organisations, activists and concerned citizens around the world. Given the complex nature of many environmental offences, and the dearth of current knowledge about some aspects of these crimes, it is not surprising that *interdisciplinary* environmental research has recently gained greater prominence. Indeed, scholars have argued that a combination of disciplinary perspectives and types of expertise is essential for achieving a more comprehensive understanding of environmental harms, and for developing appropriate strategies to respond to such offences.[1] In particular, as this edited collection demonstrates, an exchange and integration of knowledge among legal scholars and social scientists could improve our understanding of, and responses to, environmental crimes.

Since the control and prevention of environmental crimes are often highly regulated by law and legal principles, social scientists (such as green criminologists) could benefit from greater familiarity with legal analysis.[2] At the same time, legal scholars and lawyers could benefit from the broader understanding of environmental harms endorsed by many green criminologists. This broader understanding of environmental harms focuses not only on those actions expressly defined as illegal in the law, but also on those actions that may not be strictly defined as illegal yet which cause significant environmental damage. Adopting a broader conceptualisation of environmental harms and crimes may facilitate the discovery of appropriate strategies to tackle and prevent environmental offences; this conceptualisation would, in turn, also encourage scholars to think beyond just

---

1 E.D. Roy *et al.*, 'The elusive pursuit of interdisciplinarity at the human-environment interface', *Bioscience* (2013), Vol. 63, Issue 9, 745.
2 In this sense, see M. Hall, 'The role and use of law in green criminology', *International Journal for Crime, Justice and Social Democracy* (2014), Vol. 3, Issue 2, 97–110.

criminal or civil/administrative sanctions to also consider the potential value of extra-legal strategies and soft regulatory approaches.

By presenting the perspectives of lawyers and social scientists (including, primarily, green criminologists), this book's chapters illustrate the insights that a cross-disciplinary approach can bring to the study of environmental harms. To this end, the book's three parts present legal and social science perspectives on three respective themes: (i) conceptualising and defining environmental harms and crimes; (ii) critically evaluating the limitations of current approaches to prevent, or respond to, environmental harms; (iii) and identifying potential paths forward. For each of these themes, the interaction between legal and social science disciplinary perspectives permits us to better appraise the perspectives' methodological and analytical differences, as well as the perspectives' commonalities and points of intersection. We contend that such commonalities could form the basis for an innovative, integrated approach to environmental harms that is fundamentally *socio-legal* in its orientation. Building on the themes discussed above, we will now explore in greater depth several of the main areas of convergence and contention across the book's various chapters.

1 Defining the subject matter of interest

One of the main areas of contention to emerge in this volume is how to define the subject matter of interest, an issue that we briefly addressed in the introduction. Now, at the end of the book, the question underlining this issue seems clearer: Should we focus solely on those environmental harms that are criminalised in the law, or should we also consider those actions that may not be expressly illegal but are harmful to the environment? While the former definition is typically employed by legal scholars, some social scientists have adopted the latter, broader definition.[3] However, this divide in definitions is not always as clear-cut as it may appear at first glance; as this book's chapters illustrate, within both law and social science, different scholars have employed diverse definitions. For example, South's chapter and McKie and colleagues' chapter demonstrate that even within a single sub-discipline – that of green criminology – divisions exist regarding terminology used to describe the actions of interest. South's chapter also illustrates that social scientists do not necessarily deny the relevance of a strong criminal framework, as the discussion of ecocide makes clear. But even within legal scholarship it is possible to draw a distinction between a 'legalistic' understanding of environmental crimes – which confines the subject of interest to those harms and behaviours

---

3 See Chapter 2 by South in this volume, which explains how green criminology encompasses the study of environmental *harms*; South's chapter illustrates how this broader approach allows researchers to tackle those environmentally harmful activities that skirt the boundaries between legality and illegality. A similar point is made in Chapter 3 by McKie *et al.*, which discusses the important implications of such an expansive focus for the development of a notion of social harms.

which are specifically proscribed by criminal law – and the 'socio-legal' approach which emphasises that crime itself is a socially constructed, subjective concept; accordingly, socio-legal definitions also include in the spectrum of analysis civil and regulatory violations.[4]

These questions about definitions have important practical ramifications for preventing or responding to environmental harms. Specifically, such questions force us to consider the extent to which *criminal* penalties should be used to sanction environmental harms, as such penalties can only be employed against actions that are expressly illegal. Relatedly, we must also consider the broader question of which kinds of conduct should trigger the imposition of criminal sanctions; should criminal sanctions be applied to mere violations of legal or administrative provisions, or must actual damage to the environment occur? This complex issue has been the object of a lively scholarly debate within the legal literature,[5] and it is possible to discern different scholarly approaches for examining the added value of criminal law as compared with other types of responses, such as administrative fines or civil sanctions. In this volume, such debate is reflected in the chapter by Faure, which presents a law and economics approach to analysing the most appropriate responses to environmental pollution. Performing an economic analysis of environmental crimes allows a broader range of factors – such as the level of detection, the prosecution rate, the expected amount of sanction, the level of legal certainty ensured by criminal prosecution as well as its economic costs compared with administrative or civil penalties – to be considered when determining whether, and to what extent, criminal liability is the preferred option to maximise compliance. The discussion of criminal liability versus civil sanctions is also partly reflected from a national law perspective in the chapter by Brosnan. Specifically, Brosnan discusses the important revision of the UK system of environmental law enforcement brought about by the 2008 Regulatory Enforcement and Sanctions Act[6] from the more practice-oriented perspective of the Environment Agency. Focusing in particular on the introduction of civil sanctions and the new

---

4 See N. Lacey, 'Legal constructions of crime', in *The Oxford Handbook of Criminology*, 4th Edition (Oxford University Press, 2007), 179; see also C. Gibbs *et al.* 'Introducing conservation criminology', *British Journal of Criminology* (2010),Vol. 50, Issue 1, 124–144.
5 Among others, M. Faure and M. Visser, 'How to punish environmental pollution? Some reflections on various models of criminalisation of environmental harm', *European Journal of Crime, Criminal Law and Criminal Justice* (1995), Vol. 4, 316–368; A. Ogus and C. Abbot, 'Sanctions for pollution: Do we have the right regime?', *Journal of Environmental Law* (2002), Vol. 14, Issue 3, 283–298; M. Woods and R. Macrory, *Environmental Civil Penalties: A More Proportionate Response to Regulatory Breach* (University College London, 2003). See also the introductory chapter 'Forging a socio-legal approach to environmental harms', in this volume.
6 For details of the Act and associated debates, see Regulatory Enforcement and Sanctions Act 2008, BERR, Department for Business Enterprise & Regulatory Reform, July 2008, available at: http://webarchive.nationalarchives.gov.uk/+/http:/www.berr.gov.uk/files/file47135.pdf

discretionary powers conferred on the Environment Agency, the author discusses the principles and factors guiding the Environment Agency's decision about whether to start criminal prosecution. On the other hand, Kramer's contribution on the European Union approach to environmental crimes illustrates how, at least at the EU level, criminal law still retains an important role in the context of environmental protection strategies, and as a tool for the enforcement of environmental legislation. Yet, through his critical analysis of the EU Directive on the protection of the environment through criminal law, he also argues that a weak and limited criminal framework is insufficient and that a more rigorous and extensive application of criminal sanctions is needed if we are to achieve an effective prevention of environmental offences. This argument finds support in the chapters by Razzaque and by Jacobs and Varella, which, by offering examples from international and domestic legal perspectives, illustrate how many serious environmental offences could be prevented with appropriate legal and institutional frameworks of monitoring, supervision and enforcement. In particular, Razzaque's chapter looks at the international law framework applicable to the unlawful movement of toxic waste and underlines how, in this context, the application and effectiveness of international norms is severely undermined by several regulatory failures, including the lack of tough compliance mechanisms at the international level, weak remedies, and the lack of sanctioning provisions for non-compliance with international obligations.

A further point that emerges from the book is how, also from a legal perspective, the notion of environmental crimes, and the consequent application of criminal sanctions, can be ultimately influenced by other factors which are 'external' to a purely legalistic definition. For example, Brosnan's contribution highlights the role that socio-legal considerations related to the determination of the existence of a public interest play in the Environment Agency's decision whether to prosecute. On the other hand, the chapter by Vrdoljak on the criminalisation of the intentional destruction of cultural heritage extends the scope of analysis to include the cultural and spiritual dimensions of the territorial space and of the environment, as embedded in the concept of cultural heritage and, more specifically, of cultural landscapes. The author traces the historical evolution of the international law responses to intentional attacks against cultural property and shows how those crimes often reflect specific historical and political settings. In particular, she examines how acts of targeted destruction of cultural property have evolved over time from being perpetrated in the specific and more traditional context of war crimes, to become part of violent crimes against humanity and genocide and, most recently, to symbolically represent an act of terrorism against cultural values that are of universal significance to humanity as a whole. In this context, she suggests that, in certain circumstances, the material act of intentionally destroying monuments, artefacts and heritage sites may also entail profound social and human implications, and *de facto* amount to a violation of the human rights of the population living in those territories who bear an established spiritual link to those sites.

2 The value of alternative strategies

A second key theme that emerges in multiple chapters is the need to consider alternative strategies to respond to environmental offences in addition to purely legal approaches. The need for alternative strategies is evident in several of the social science chapters. For example, Wyatt's chapter, 'The legal and social context of wildlife trafficking', shows that strictly legal responses to wildlife trafficking – in particular, outright bans – fail to account for the role of animal products in many communities' cultural practices and traditional economies; as a result, such bans are likely to be undermined. Instead, according to Wyatt, a more rounded, socio-legal approach is needed, which also includes 'alternative livelihood programs, educational campaigns about the environmental consequences of wildlife consumption or limitations rather than bans' (Wyatt, Chapter 10, this volume). In other words, a broader, more community-focused response is more likely to prove effective.

This need for broader strategies is echoed in South's chapter, which argues for 'more suitable and potent legal mechanisms, as well as more conscientious individual choices' to target these harms (South, Chapter 2, this volume). McKie and colleagues' chapter identifies 'the structural limits that prevent the law from slowing rates of ecological destruction', a similar acknowledgement that legal strategies alone are not enough to combat these harms. These complexities are also evident in Rothe and Collins' analysis of the role of international financial institutions (IFIs). Rothe and Collins (Chapter 6, this volume) ultimately argue that 'changes within the organizational structures' of the IFIs themselves are needed in order to reduce the environmental harms they describe – a policy reform that would stretch beyond traditional, regulatory approaches to environmental harms.

Finally, Walters' work reminds us not to forget the important role of environmental activism in any strategy to address environmental harms. Specifically, Walters' work highlights how environmental activists can play a role 'in environmental law enforcement' but can also be 'a threat to corporate and governing elites that seek power and profit through the exploitation of natural resources' (Walters, Chapter 11, this volume). Walters' work underscores the idea that many actors are involved in these issues and contribute to their complexity. Such complications may be difficult to combat through a single, exclusively legal approach to these crimes.

The idea that additional strategies may be needed to complement criminal sanctions and traditional enforcement strategies is – perhaps surprisingly – echoed in several of the book's law chapters. In particular, Razzaque argues that, while criminal law may represent an important and valuable tool to address the illegal movement of toxic ships and hazardous waste, it nevertheless needs to be combined with other 'complementary mechanisms'; these may include funding to incentivise the ship-breaking industries to properly dismantle the ship in an environmentally sound manner, provided that this funding is linked to, and conditional upon, socially responsible conduct by the company. A similar line of arguments is found in the chapter by Jacobs and Varella. Examining the causes and consequences of major environmental disasters arising in relation to the off-shore exploration of oil, the authors emphasise the importance of a robust criminal legal framework, while at the same time stressing the need to complement it with an appropriate institutional apparatus. This institutional apparatus must be capable of effectively monitoring the application and enforcement of the law, as well as 'alternative' strategies aimed at enhancing compliance and the sustainable behaviour of the industry sector. Finally, in her contribution on the intentional destruction of cultural heritage, Vrdoljak acknowledges the central role that criminal law still retains at the international level in punishing attacks to cultural property, but recognises the difficulties often encountered by territorial states in enforcing the international criminal responsibility of perpetrators of those crimes, as well as the limitations of a reactive approach based solely on criminalisation. Accordingly, she argues that, especially where the destruction of cultural heritage signifies a terrorist attack to universal cultural values of the humanity as a whole, a more comprehensive approach is need. Such an approach should include a broader involvement of the international community through the actions of international organisations and tribunals, the use of new technologies in evidence-gathering and reconstruction processes, and a combination of criminal sanctions and preventive measures.

3 International complexities

Environmental harms often cross international borders, and the global nature and consequences of these offences is a third key theme that emerges in multiple chapters. South, for example, argues that 'an international law of ecocide' and 'an international court' to deal with environmental crimes are reforms that merit consideration, given the serious global consequences of environmental devastation (South, Chapter 2, this volume). On the other hand, McKie and colleagues adopt a sceptical view of international approaches to environmental harms, weighing both the advantages and disadvantages of 'multinational environmental agreements (or MEAs)' (McKie *et al.*, Chapter 3, this volume). Walters' chapter highlights not only the globalised nature of environmental offences, but also the ways in which global inequalities can affect the distribution – and response to – these offences. Specifically, Walters makes the following important observation: 'The green activists protecting rainforests in their native South American countries ... are protecting natural resources that are often illegally pirated and sold "legally" in markets in the UK, Australia, and the US' (Walters, Chapter 11, this volume). This observation highlights the links between developed and developing countries on environmental crime issues. Similarly, it is clear in Wyatt's analysis of wildlife crime that communities around the world have different cultural traditions and economic needs, which must be accounted for, but which may not be reflected in broad-based, international frameworks. In particular, both Wyatt's chapter and McKie and colleagues' chapter highlight limitations of the Convention on International Trade in Endangered Species (CITES). While Wyatt's critique focuses on the issues outlined in the previous paragraph, McKie and colleagues point out the additional problem that 'treaties like CITES are only effective when the problem is addressed by all countries and not just a few', meaning that, to ensure effectiveness, efforts must also be made to 'create new pro-environmental domestic laws in countries where those laws do not yet exist' (McKie and colleagues, Chapter 3, this volume).

The transnational and global dimension of those crimes is gaining increasing attention at the international level where multiple efforts are taking place to devise the most appropriate strategies to prevent and combat those offences. From an international law perspective, the relevance of those crimes relates primarily to the presence of cross-border flows of illegally sourced goods or illegal services, often with the involvement of organised criminal networks. The emergence and proliferation of transnational organised crime has become an increasingly pressing issue in the environmental field. The vast financial profits and the low detection and prosecution rates are a significant incentive for criminal networks and organised groups. At the same time, the transnational dimension and global reach of those crimes transcend the controlling and policing capacity of single nation-states, posing new and important challenges for regulators and law enforcement agencies. International bodies and organisations such as the UN Environment Programme, the European Union, and the UN Interregional Crime and Justice Research Institute recognise five broad areas of transnational environmental offences, namely: the illegal trade in wildlife and protected species; the illegal trade in ozone-depleting substances; dumping and illegal transport of various kinds of hazardous waste; illegal, unregulated and unreported fishing; and illegal logging and trade in timber.[7] In all of these cases, environmental harm is the result of acts or activities in contravention of international conventions or national laws, such as in the case of the illegal movement of toxic shipwrecks in contravention of existing international conventions that prohibit the illegal trade of hazardous waste, discussed in Chapter 8 by Razzaque, or in the case of the illegal wildlife trade in contravention of CITES, discussed in Chapter 10 by Wyatt.

There is, however, another category of environmental harms that exhibits international relevance. This is the case when the object of the offence is regarded as of universal value, and thus requires concerted action by the international community as a whole. The analysis by South on the need to establish an

---

7 There are, however, other environmental offences which share similar features, including: biopiracy and transport of biological and genetically modified material; illegal dumping of oil in ocean waters; trade in hazardous chemicals and pesticides in contravention to the 1998 Rotterdam Convention on the Prior Informed Consent Procedure for Certain Hazardous Chemicals and Pesticides in International Trade (for further discussion, see: G. Hayman and D. Brack, *International Environmental Crime: The Nature and Control of Environmental Black Markets*, Royal Institute of International Affairs, 2002); and other emerging crimes including carbon trade-related and water management crime (UNEP Global Environmental Alert Services (GEAS) – January 2013, available at www.unep.org/geas).

international crime of ecocide in the case of severe environmental violations reflects such an understanding. A similar approach emerges in Vrdoljak's analysis of harms to those parts of cultural and natural heritage that are of outstanding universal value and therefore merit the interest and concern of the international community.

Linked with globalisation and rapid developments in communication and information technologies, a further issue of concern is the role of digitalisation in facilitating criminal offences. While technological achievements (such as satellite images, database management software, etc.) are increasingly employed in the detection, investigation and prosecution of offences, they can also provide terrorists and criminal groups with new means to disguise the illicit proceeds of crimes, or facilitate their efforts to solicit funding and recruit new members from a global audience.[8] The impact of such technology-enabled crimes in the context of natural resources and cultural heritage is explored by Vrdoljak. Specifically, she discusses how digitalisation through the internet and social media has facilitated terrorist groups' efforts to recruit new members, plan terrorist attacks against cultural heritage sites and spread terror and hatred.

Finally, there is a further layer to the international dimension of environmental harms and crimes. As discussed in the chapters by South, McKie *et al.*, and Rothe and Collins, threats against the environment are not confined to specific identifiable sources but, increasingly, they are spread globally and committed by diverse actors. Atmospheric pollution, climate change, the depletion of natural resources and biodiversity are just a few examples of the severe environmental toll imposed by the unsustainable production and consumption processes which characterise current societal models and patterns of economic growth.

Given the complexities associated with the transnational and global dimension of environmental offences, the diversity of factors and motivations driving those crimes, and the linkages of transnational organised crime with other offences – such as fraud, corruption and money-laundering – an interdisciplinary approach that brings together different types of expertise appears necessary. Several chapters in this book have noted the limitations of solely relying on law enforcement and criminal justice systems to deal effectively with environmental offences. Those limits become more accentuated in relation to harms and crimes whose reach and impact extends beyond the single nation-state; here, the persistent weaknesses of international law enforcement procedures pose an important obstacle to effective action against environmental offences.[9] Moreover, while criminal sanctions and strict enforcement procedures may be employed to address violations of environmental law, they are not suited to other forms of environmental harms which are the products of legitimate activities at the global scale; moreover, international

---

8 Kim-Kwang Raymond Choo *et al.*, 'The future of technology-enabled crime in Australia', *Trends and Issues in Crime and Criminal Justice* 341, 2007 (Australian Institute of Criminology, July 2007).
9 See Chapter 8 by Razzaque and Chapter 10 by Wyatt in this book.

criminal law is not sufficient against the insidious threats posed by terrorist groups (see Chapter 12 by Vrdoljak in this volume). Therefore, while the need for further development of legal and institutional frameworks for international collaboration and cooperation in the detection and prosecution of criminal offences cannot be overstated, an effective framework to prevent, control and combat those crimes necessitates combining the legalistic and reactive nature of criminal justice approaches with broader and more forward-looking strategies that focus on the drivers of environmental offences. In this sense, the integration of social science expertise can help to shift the focus away from a purely law enforcement-oriented approach towards a more strategic way of thinking which attaches greater consideration to the underlying conditions that produce environmental crimes. Indeed, as is illustrated in the chapters by McKie and colleagues and by South, the green criminology perspective highlights the criminogenic effects of present-day lifestyles and socio-economic models; an approach that takes into account the green criminology perspective will thereby extend the scope of analysis to address behaviours and activities which traditionally escape the radar of law and regulation. Ultimately, we contend that a better understanding of the individual and societal drivers of environmental offences can help efforts to frame more specific and appropriate responses to the environmental challenges examined in this volume.

4 Forging a 'socio-legal' approach

The overarching goal of this book is to forge a socio-legal approach to environmental harms that draws upon the contributions and perspectives of both legal and social science research to respond to – and, ultimately, prevent – environmental harms. This goal of bringing together legal and social science perspectives is opportune, as sociological considerations are gradually penetrating further into legal analysis. For example, Faure combines a law and economic analysis with a 'socio-legal' perspective on the causes and responses to environmental crimes. This author acknowledges that firms do not always act according to a mere cost–benefit calculation and that there may be different reasons, other than the threat of criminal sanctions, which induce companies to comply with environmental norms. Hence he argues for further empirical research on the actual reasons behind business non-compliance in order to adjust the reactions to environmental offences to the specificities of the situation at hand. As he explains: 'For those perpetrators who violate because of a lack of information, information strategies based on a cooperation model, gently guiding the perpetrator towards compliance, may be appropriate. For the calculating polluter, rationally saving, for example, on investments in pollution prevention technologies, a dissuasive approach based on deterrent sanctions may be indicated' (Faure, Chapter 5, this volume).

Furthermore, Brosnan's chapter illustrates how, in the UK regulatory system, socio-legal considerations about the public interest element at stake and the ultimate goals that the criminal process seeks to achieve play an important role in determining the appropriate enforcement action against environmental offences – that is, whether by means of criminal prosecution or administrative or civil sanctions – and the eventual sentencing decision. It is also interesting to note that both a law and economics approach and a socio-legal perspective inspired Macrory's review of the previous regulatory enforcement system which provided the basis for the current UK Regulatory Enforcement and Sanctions Act of 2008.[10]

By forging a socio-legal approach to environmental harms, this book's ultimate goal is to improve current strategies for responding to – and preventing – such offences. To that end, based on the research contained in the book's chapters, we can identify three specific suggestions to shape future research and policy in this area. These suggestions are: critically investigating the concept of environmental harm itself; examining the motives of offenders and the preconditions that facilitate certain environmentally harmful practices; and exploring the effectiveness of alternative strategies.

The first suggestion, which is perhaps the most fundamental, relates to the concept of *environmental harm* itself, including its origins, definition and assessment. Throughout this book, these issues have emerged repeatedly. What is the subject of interest for our research? Are we interested merely in those actions that are expressly criminalised in the law, or are we interested more broadly in harmful actions, regardless of whether they are illegal in a particular context? What type of impacts needs to be addressed through legal and/or policy instruments? Confronting these questions is essential for any in-depth analysis of environmental offences and will likely resurface in future interdisciplinary efforts to study environmental harm. One of the main conclusions emerging from this book is that it is critical *not* to assume that all researchers define and approach the subject of interest in the same way.[11] Instead, such diversity of definitions and approaches has important consequences for how we conceptualise both the problem and the problem's potential policy solutions.

The second suggestion that emerges from this book is the need to carefully investigate the motives of offenders, as well as the macro- and micro-level drivers of environmental offences in order to improve prevention efforts. The importance of prevention – that is, reducing the likelihood that environmental offences will be committed in the first place – is central to both law and social science perspectives. Within the legal perspective, prevention is typically emphasised through the deterrent effect of criminal sanctions. However, criminal sanctions are usually directed at specific criminal behaviours, often without considering the broader picture of the 'external' factors and conditions which can help drive those crimes. Thus, an effective strategy to combat environmental crimes requires us to consider other mechanisms for prevention that tackle these offences' root causes and conditions. Social science scholarship, by clarifying political, economic, societal

---

10 Cit. above n. 6
11 See discussion in introductory chapter 'Forging a socio-legal approach to environmental harms', particularly section 2.

and other root causes, could therefore play a critical role in helping expand our range of prevention approaches. For example, empirical research on the causes of transnational environmental crimes (including those considered in this book, such as trade in endangered species and the transboundary transfer of hazardous waste) reveals that the effectiveness of traditional enforcement approaches to dispel those criminal activities can be limited by their failure to tackle the underlying market forces that favour illicit trade.[12] Similarly, both Rothe and Collins' chapter and McKie and colleagues' chapter in this volume illustrate the complex political and economic forces that can help drive certain environmental offences. Therefore, prevention approaches may need to incorporate political and economic components in order to be most effective, and prevention represents one area in which both law and policy could benefit from insights from social science research.

The third, and final, suggestion we propose emerges out of the book's larger conclusion that alternative strategies – beyond just legal approaches – are needed to respond to environmental harms. The limitations of law enforcement as a means for controlling and addressing the harmful practices considered in this book have been noted in several contributions. However, whereas some scholars (see, for example, the chapters in this volume by Kramer, or Razzaque, or Jacobs and Varella) attribute these limitations to the poor formulation of law and its enforcement, others emphasise the need to address the broader conditions which facilitate those harmful behaviours. Various chapters also stress the potential of 'alternative' or 'complementary' strategies to address these offences, including community-based responses (Wyatt, Chapter 10); the combination of 'hard' and 'soft' legal tools (Razzaque, Chapter 8); and international cooperation and a reliance on international institutions (Vrdoljak, Chapter 12). Given the potential utility of alternative strategies, future research should explore the effectiveness of such strategies in greater detail, examining *which* specific alternative strategies are most effective for dealing with different types of environmental offences. Interdisciplinary research that draws upon various types of social science and legal knowledge could be particularly helpful for illuminating creative approaches. (Such approaches may not be apparent when researching environmental harms from the perspective of a single discipline.) In addition to the criminological scholarship emphasised in this book, other social disciplines – including economics and geography – also hold great potential value. We hope that future researchers can build on the interdisciplinary perspective contained in this volume by including even more disciplines in future work. Such a broad perspective may uncover further creative insights into environmental harms – and, in particular, strategies for their prevention.

Overall, this volume has endeavoured to lay the groundwork for an innovative, socio-legal approach to environmental harms that draws upon the strengths of

---

12 G. Hayman and D. Brack, *International Environmental Crime: The Nature and Control of Environmental Black Markets*, Workshop Report (2002, Royal Institute of International Affairs).

both legal and social science perspectives. The chapters by legal scholars, practitioners and social scientists demonstrate how different disciplinary perspectives and types of expertise can all help illuminate the problem of environmental harms. At the same time this collection has also revealed how appropriate and effective responses to environmental harms and crimes can benefit from a cross-disciplinary dialogue and collaboration. Through the interface of the different disciplinary approaches, the book has tried to identify the main differences, but also to acknowledge that there are points of contact and areas where there is a penetration of their respective approaches (that is, criminologists acknowledge the importance of criminal law, and legal scholars are increasingly inclined to consider the value of extra-legal responses), demonstrating how there is still scope for mutual learning and a sharing of expertise. Ultimately, we hope that this work – and, in particular, the thoughtful chapters by the contributors to this volume – will encourage future research and interdisciplinary efforts to study these harmful offences.

Bibliography

Choo, K.-K.R., Smith, R. G., and McCusker, R. (2007, July). The future of technology-enabled crime in Australia. *Trends and Issues in Crime and Criminal Justice, 341*. Canberra: Australian Institute of Criminology. Available atwww.aic.gov.au/publications/current%20series/tandi/341-360/tandi341.html (accessed 6 February 2017).

Faure, M., and Visser, M. (1995). How to punish environmental pollution? Some reflections on various models of criminalisation of environmental harm. *European Journal of Crime, Criminal Law and Criminal Justice*, 4, 316–368.

Gibbs, C., Gore, M.L., McGarrell, E., and Rivers III, L. (2010). Introducing conservation criminology. *British Journal of Criminology*, 50(1), 124–144.

Hall, M. (2014). The role and use of law in green criminology. *International Journal for Crime, Justice and Social Democracy*, 3(2), 97–110.

Hayman, G., and Brack, D. (2002). *International Environmental Crime: The Nature and Control of Environmental Black Markets*. Workshop Report. London: Royal Institute of International Affairs. Available at http://ec.europa.eu/environment/archives/docum/pdf/02544_environmental_crime_workshop.pdf (accessed 6 February 2017).

Lacey, N. (2007). Legal constructions of crime. In M. Maguire, R. Morgan, and R. Reiner (eds), *The Oxford Handbook of Criminology* (4th edn) (pp. 179–200). London: Oxford University Press.

Ogus, A., and Abbot, C. (2002). Sanctions for pollution: Do we have the right regime? *Journal of Environmental Law*, 14(3), 283–298.

Regulatory Enforcement and Sanctions Act 2008. BERR, Department for Business Enterprise & Regulatory Reform, July 2008. Available at http://webarchive.nationalarchives.gov.uk/+/http://www.berr.gov.uk/files/file47135.pdf (accessed 6 February 2017).

Roy, E.D., Morzillo, A.T., Seijo, F., Reddy, S.M.W., Rhemtulla, J.M., Milder, J.C., Kuemmerle, T., and Martin, S.L. (2013). The elusive pursuit of interdisciplinarity at the human-environment interface. *Bioscience*, 63(9), 745–753.

Woods, M., and Macrory, R. (2003). *Environmental Civil Penalties: A More Proportionate Response to Regulatory Breach*. London: Centre for Law and the Environment, University College London.

Index

Abbot, Carolyn 8–9, 82, 92, 94
activism, environmental *or* green 15, 220–236, 271
  criminalization of 230–231
  impacts of 224–225
  involvement of citizens in 220
  relationship to environmental crime prevention 222–224, 231
  risks of involvement in 221, 232, 233
administrative law 66–7, 79, 81–2, 87
  administrative penal law 82, 83, 88
administrative enforcement *or* proceedings 41, 82, 83
administrative sanctions 64, 73, 75, 82, 83, 97, 100, 185, 196, 202, 269
Afghanistan 127, 254, 255
Africa 111, 113, 157, 210
African Elephant Conservation Act 43
Agent Orange 30
agriculture 25, 72, 233
  EU directives or regulations related to 61
  global restructuring of 111
  jobs related to 207
  see also food
air pollution 22, 50, 61 (note 11), 68–70
  from vehicles 69–70
  see also Clean Air Act
Amazon rainforest 23
animals 205, 212–213, 232, 271
  abuse *or* mistreatment of 24
  attribution of rights to 26
  experimentation on 230, 231
  international trade in 43
  listed in CITES 206
  smuggling of 24
  welfare of 26, 111, 206, 210, 211–213, 216
  see also wildlife

Asia 111, 232, 156, 158–160, 165, 210, 224, 232
  South Asia 155–156, 157, 159, 160–161, 165, 170, 173
  Southeast 209, 210
Australia 8, 232, 272

Bahamas 120, 170
Bamako Convention on the Ban of the Import to Africa and the Control of Transboundary Movement and Management of Hazardous Wastes within Africa 157, 160
Bangladesh 155–156, 158–159, 161, 175–176
Basel Action Network (BAN) 44–45, 155 (note 4)
Basel Convention on the Control of Transboundary Movements of Hazardous Waste and their Disposal 42, 43, 44–45, 154–160, 161, 162–164, 165, 167, 168, 172, 175
bears 210
  bile of 209–210, 212
  polar 206, 209
Becker, Gary 8, 79, 84, 89, 95, 96
behavioural law and economics 78
Belgium 158, 80, 94, 119
Belize 207
biodiversity 116, 137
  crimes against 62
  International Year of Biodiversity 223
  loss of 20, 33, 74, 207, 231, 274
"bio-piracy" 23, 273 (note 7)
biosphere 42, 48–50, 51
birds 117, 193, 213
  smuggling of 213
  see also wildlife

Black Act of 1723 11
Bosnia and Herzegovina 253,
Brazil 132–141, 146, 149–151
bushmeat 210, 212

Canada 158,
capitalism 38, 40, 48, 51, 221
carbon dioxide 42, 48–49
Cartagena Protocol on Biosafety to the Convention on Biological Diversity 43
China 42, 122, 156, 158, 171, 206, 209, 210
civil liability 68, 80, 143, 144
civil penalties 8, 21–22, 41, 46, 68, 80, 139, 185, 188–190, 197–198, 203, 211, 268, 269, 276
   under the Regulatory Enforcement and Sanctions Act 196–197
civil society 47, 123
Clean Air Act 47
Clean Water Act 25, 28, 47
climate change 20, 22, 23, 24, 31–32, 40, 42, 48, 73, 135, 186, 274
"climate crisis" 120
Clinton, Bill 46
Clyde River 221, 225, 226, 229
Code for Crown Prosecutors 190–1, 197
common-but-differentiated responsibilities principle 154, 160
colonialism 110
"compassionate conservation" 26–27
complementary mechanisms 174, 271
Comprehensive Environmental Response, Compensation, and Liability Act 47
"conservation criminology" 21
consumer demand 7, 209
   for exotic foods 210
   for gold 122–123
consumerism 122
continental shelf 132–134, 140
Convention of Biological Diversity 43
Convention on the Conservation of Migratory Species of Wild Animals 43
Convention on International Trade in Endangered Species of World Fauna and Flora (CITES) 42–44, 80, 205, 207–208, 216, 272–273
   appendices to 206
   classification of countries related to 207
   Conference of the Parties for 206
   founding of 205
   Management Authorities within member countries 205, 211
   relationship to animal welfare 211–212
   species monitored by 206
Convention on Civil Liability for Oil Pollution Damage 136
Convention on the Prevention of Marine Pollution by Dumping of Wastes and Other Matter 43
Convention for the Prevention of Pollution from Ships 136
Convention for the Protection of Cultural Property in the Event of Armed Conflict 241–246, 254, 267–268, 273
Convention for the Protection of World Cultural and Natural Endangered Species 43
Convention on Wetlands of International Importance especially as Waterfowl Habitat 43
Convention concerning the World Cultural and Natural Heritage 244, 255–6
Council of Europe 58, 256, 257, 259
   Convention on the Protection of the Environment through Criminal Law 58, 63
Court of Justice of the European Union 59, 70, 71
corporate crime 86, 99, 100–101
corporations 45, 47, 48, 50, 78, 95, 109, 111
corruption 20, 60, 89, 111, 140, 161, 176, 177, 232, 274
cost-benefit analysis 9, 78, 84, 91, 195, 275
crime, corporate *see* corporate crime
crime, environmental *see* environmental crime(s)
crime, white-collar *see* white-collar crime
criminal liability 58, 63–64, 67–68, 72, 74, 79, 97, 269
   expressive function of 8
   fault-based 164
   of legal persons *or* entities 58, 63, 64, 74, 100
   of officials 67, 72
   strict application of 11, 29, 74, 88, 163, 164, 192
criminal penalties *or* sanctions 7, 11, 13, 26, 46, 59–60, 68, 139, 144, 172–173, 190, 211, 258, 268–269, 271, 274–275
   adverse reputational consequences of 10

Index 281

deterrent effect of 276
for air pollution 22
symbolic role of 8
criminal prosecution 5, 9, 11, 22, 28, 32, 67, 89, 91, 94, 96–98, 157, 171–2, 174, 188–194, 198–99, 203, 222, 223, 224
rate of 9
criminologists 4–7, 13, 21, 24, 38–44, 46, 48–51, 94, 110, 232, 267–268, 278
see also criminology
see also green criminology
criminology 4, 6, 9, 14, 16, 20–22, 38–42, 46–47, 50, 221–222, 229, 268, 275
see also criminologists
see also green criminology
culpability 191, 192, 200
of States 253
cultural heritage 16, 223, 239, 241, 243, 245, 250, 255-6
destruction of 237, 253–4, 257–9
World heritage 16, 237–8, 244, 247, 254–5, 257, 260, 261

death penalty 11
deforestation 22, 24, 74, 109, 135
see also illegal logging
Democratic Republic of Congo 111
Demolishcon 178
Denmark 58, 89, 158, 172, 206
deregulation
Deregulation Act
detection 220, 222, 233
probability of 80–1, 83, 84–6, 91, 94, 96, 100;
detection rate 89, 94, 95
deterrence 10–12, 47–50, 80–86, 88–91, 94–96, 98–100, 144, 150, 188, 190, 201
theory *or* approach 11, 12, 48–50, 88, 89–90, 100
general 47
law-and-economic theory of 9
Optimal 81, 82
specific 48
developing countries 41, 45, 47, 110–112, 118, 154–156, 158, 160, 162–163, 167–171, 173–174, 179, 231, 267, 272
Direct Action Committee against Nuclear War 226
Directive 2008/99 8, 17 (note 52), 58–76, 100, 174 (note 136)
discourse 39–40, 42, 113, 122–123, 220, 222, 233

"earth jurisprudence" 20, 26
Earth Summit 29
ecocide 20, 22, 26, 29–33, 74, 268, 272, 274
"eco-crime" 221–222, 224, 230–233
"ecological footprint" 48–50
"ecomafia" 223
economics 8, 9, 14, 48, 78, 233, 269, 276, 277
"eco-terrorism" 229–230
economic development 41, 113–114, 118, 121–123, 132, 136
see also economic growth
see also sustainable development
economic growth 121, 160, 187, 233, 274
see also economic development
endangered species 7, 24, 43, 66, 206, 214, 216, 277
Endangered Species Act 43
energy independence
enforcement strategy 12, 88–90
cooperative enforcement or strategy 45, 46, 88–9, 90, 91, 92
deterrent strategy or reasoning *see also* deterrence theory
information strategy 91
enforcement of environmental law, 46–7, 79
private enforcement 79–80
public enforcement 80
Enforcement and Sanctions statement (ESS) 187–88
Enforcement and Sanctions Guidance (ESG) 187, 189
Enforcement Undertaking (EU) 197–8
England 11, 174, 185–186, 196, 200, 226, 229
see also United Kingdom
Environment Agency *see* UK Environment Agency
environmental activism *see* activism, environmental
environmental crime(s) 3–17, 20–22, 26–28, 33, 38–42, 45–51, 75–76, 78, 84–88, 91–94, 98–100, 109, 113, 123–124, 143–144, 157–158, 171–175, 193, 195, 220–224, 230–232, 267–270, 272, 275–277
definitions of 5–6, 21, 61
interdisciplinary approaches to 3–5, 7, 275
motivations for 3, 6, 10–11, 16–17, 123, 254, 274

transnational examples of 21, 173, 224, 231–232, 273–274, 277
environmental harm(s) 3–4, 6–7, 13–15, 17, 21, 23, 30, 39–40, 42, 46, 50, 80–82, 92, 109, 112–118, 123, 222, 224–225, 230, 233, 267–269, 271–278
environmental impact assessment 145, 175
environmental justice 27–28, 41, 46–47, 50
environmentally sound management 155, 162–163, 171, 271
environmental sustainability *see* sustainability
Environmental Protection Agency (EPA) *see* US Environmental Protection Agency (EPA)
Equator Principles
Ethiopia 114
Europe 8, 24, 64, 73–74, 93–94, 96, 101, 154, 159, 167–171, 212, 232, 241, 256–257, 259
European Commission 59, 60, 63, 64, 68, 72–3, 155–6, 169, 171
European Union 8, 44–45, 58–61, 64, 100–101, 155–156, 167–171, 270, 273
Network for the Implementation and Enforcement of Environmental Law 44, 156 (note 11)
EU Regulation on Shipment of Waste 155, 168
EU Regulation on Ship Recycling 155, 160, 167–170, 174
Europol 222
Exxon Valdez 25, 97 (footnote 89)

Faslane Peace Camp 221, 225–229
Federal Bureau of Investigation (FBI) 230
Financial Action Taskforce 224
fly-tipping 10
food security 23
fossil fuels 22, 74, 120
see also oil
Foucault, Michel 220–221
free trade 220, 230, 232
Friends of the Earth 27

gas(es) 22, 42, 54, 121, 127–131, 133–134, 136, 145, 148, 211
genocide 23, 29–31, 41, 74, 110, 238, 249, 251–254, 270
Ghana 113, 115–117, 121–122
Global Witness 220–221
globalization 109–113, 117, 123, 257, 274
crimes of 109–113, 117, 123

gold 114–117, 121–123
Green Climate Fund 118
"green crime" 39–42, 50–51
see also environmental crime
see also green criminology
green criminology 4–6, 14, 20–21, 38–42, 46–47, 50, 221–222, 229, 268, 275
see also "green crime"
see also criminology
Greenland 206
Guinea 114
Gulf of Mexico 25, 132–133, 141, 146, 148

Habermas, Jürgen 220
Hampton, Philip 12, 188
Harrington paradox 94–5, 96, 100
hazardous waste *see* waste, hazardous
HIV infection 111
human rights 40, 109–111, 161, 167, 173, 177–178, 197, 238, 249–251, 256–261, 270
hunting *see* wildlife, hunting of
hydrocarbon 113, 145
Hong Kong Convention for the Safe and Environmentally Sound Recycling of Ships 155, 158, 160, 161, 164–9

Illegality 5
illegal logging 3, 23, 109, 230, 273
see also deforestation
illegal trade in wildlife 3, 21, 24, 65, 205, 207, 211–2
illegal trade in waste 74 *see also* toxic trade
incapacitation 150
India 42, 122, 155–156, 158–159, 172, 175, 208
India's Supreme Court 172, 175
indigenous peoples 23, 25, 109–110, 113–118, 209, 232
Indonesia 111, 128, 232
intent 26, 28, 30, 74, 88, 189, 192, 252, 253,
intentionality 11, 22, 30
intergenerational equity 29
International Convention for the Regulation of Whaling 43
International Court of Justice 253
International Criminal Court 29, 31–32, 74, 238, 246–248, 261

International Criminal Tribunal for the Former Yugoslavia (ICTY) 238, 243, 250–253, 259
International Environmental Court 28
International Finance Corporation (IFC) 113–118, 121–123
international financial institutions (IFIs) 15, 109–117, 123, 271
International Labour Organization 161
International Law Commission 30, 250
International Maritime Organization 161
International Monetary Fund 109–112, 118
International Treaty on Plant Genetic Resources for Food and Agriculture 43
International Year of Biodiversity 223
Interpol 3, 24, 44, 157–158, 222–223, 232
   Environmental Crimes Committee 222–223
   General Assembly 223
Iraq 119, 128, 134, 254–257, 260
ISIL 255–257, 260,
Italy 71, 223
ivory 44, 210, 214
   see also poaching of elephants

Japan 206
Jubilee South Asia-Pacific Movement on Debt and Development 120

Kuznets curve 41
Kyoto Protocol to the United Nations Framework Convention on Climate Change 43

Lacey Act 43
Le Joola, capsizing of the 110
legal certainty 7, 269
Legambiente 223–224
Liberia 129, 170
Liechtenstein 163
livestock 72, 209, 211, 216
   see also wildlife, captive breeding of
logging, illegal see illegal logging
Louisiana 25, 146
Lusaka Agreement on Co-operative Enforcement Operations Directed at Illegal Trade in Wild Fauna and Flora 224

Macrory Penalty Principles 188, 195
Macrory Review 196
Macrory, Richard 12

Malawi 208
Mali 129, 247–248
Markey, Ed 144
mens rea 31, 88, 251, 253
Mexico 158
Migratory Bird Treaty Act 25
Minerals Management Service (MMS) 144
mining, open-pit 109, 113–117
   definition of 114
mode of production see production, mode of
Mongolia 114
Montenegro 253
Montreal Protocol on Substances that Deplete the Ozone Layer 43
multinational environmental agreements (MEAs) 38, 42–45, 47, 272

Namibia 213–216
naming and shaming see shaming approach
National Wildlife Crime Unit 44
Natural Environment and Rural Communities Act 43–44
natural resources 8, 29, 111–113, 116, 123, 140, 164, 213–214, 221, 232, 271–274
negligence 11, 22, 28, 30, 60, 64–65, 67, 69, 91, 140–143, 164, 189, 192, 195, 259
neo-liberal policies 111, 113, 123–124, 177, 230
New Zealand 208
Nigeria 25
nitrates 72–3, 115
non-governmental organizations (NGOs) 13, 44, 47, 123, 171, 175, 211, 221–224, 214, 230
non-monetary sanctions 82–3, 86–7, 95
North-South 178
Nuremberg Tribunal 237, 239, 240–241, 243
Nuremberg judgment 239, 241, 250–251

Obama, Barack 25, 141
OECD 155–156, 163, 176,
Ogus, Anthony 8–9, 82, 92, 94
oil 24–26, 28, 74, 99, 121, 127–131, 132–151, 158, 166, 200, 230–231, 272
open-pit mining see mining, open pit
optimal sanctions 83, 85–6, 92,
organizational theory 121
organised crime 20, 39, 42, 60, 158, 172, 220, 222–4, 231–2, 273,
ozone depletion 21–22, 33, 62, 65, 273–4

Pak Mun Dam 109–110
Pakistan 120, 155, 156, 158, 159, 175,
Panama 170, 120
pangolins 210, 212
persecution 249–252
Peru 232
pigs, farming of 211
plants 43, 109–110, 206, 209, 211
poaching 41, 44, 207, 210, 212, 214–215
  of elephants *see also* ivory trade
  of rhinos 212
polar bears *see* bears, polar
policymakers 222, 267
political economy 38, 50, 112, 117, 123, 233
polluter pays principle 155, 170, 174
pollution 16, 20–21, 22, 25, 41, 68–70, 78–82, 84, 87–88, 90, 100, 154, 157–159, 185, 195, 203, 222–223, 269, 275
  in air 33, 68–70, 274
  in water 31, 75, 116, 136–137, 193
  laws related to 6–7, 132, 136–137
poverty 111–114, 117, 121–123, 151
precautionary principle 154, 162
prior informed consent procedure 162 *see also* Rotterdam Convention on prior informed consent
privatization 112–113
Proposal for an EU Directive on the protection of the environment through criminal law 59–60, 63
proportionality 187, 188, 191, 194–5
prosecution *see* criminal prosecution
protests 220–222, 226–232
  see also activism, environmental
Protocol on Liability and Compensation to the Basel Convention 163–4
proximity principle 162
public-private collaborations 113

rainforest 23, 232, 272
  see also Amazon rainforest
radioactive waste *see* waste
raptors, smuggling of 213
rational-choice theory 9, 78
rationality 9–11, 48–50, 78, 81, 91, 100, 275
refugees 231
Refuse Act 25
Reiman, Jeffrey 221–222
Regulatory Enforcement and Sanctions Act 196

Regulatory position statement 190
Regulators' Code 186–188
reputation
  loss of 9–10, 98–100 *see also* reputational sanctions
reputational sanctions 98–99
Resource Conservation and Recovery Act 47
resources *see* natural resources
restorative justice 27–28, 31
rhinos 206, 210, 214
  poaching of 212
risk aversion 96
Rome Statute 29–32, 247–248, 253, 255–256
Rotterdam Convention on the Prior Informed Consent Procedure for Certain Hazardous Chemicals and Pesticides in International Trade 43, 161, 273 (note 7)
Rwanda 110–111, 253

Safe Drinking Water Act 47
Scotland 221, 225–229
  see also United Kingdom
Scottish National Party 225
Security Council
self-policing 45–46, 146
self-regulation 13, 91, 176, 178–9
Senegal 110
sentencing 158, 192, 198
  considerations 200
  guidelines 92–3
  policy 92–3, 95
Sentencing Council of England and Wales Guidelines 200–202
Serbia 253–254
seriousness 200, 202
  of a case *or* matter 192, 197, 198
  of offence 191, 195, 201
shaming approach 98–99
shark fin soup 206
sharks, killing of 212
ship-breaking 154, 155,158, 159, 160
social harm 39–40, 42, 50, 83, 222, 268 (note 3),
social justice 214, 222
social media 16, 237, 254, 257–258, 260
social science 3–4, 7–8, 10–17, 267–268, 271, 275–278
social responsibility of companies 176
socio-legal approaches 4, 12–16, 21, 185, 188, 213, 269, 275–277

sociology 8–9, 20, 39, 222, 275
"soft power" 231
South America 210, 232, 272
South Asia *see* Asia, South
Southeast Asia *see* Asia, Southeast
"species justice" 233
"speciesism" 24
starvation 112, 124
  see also food
state-corporate crime 109
Stockholm Convention on Persistent Organic Pollutants 43, 161
street crime 39
Structural Adjustment Programs (SAPs) 110, 112
sturgeon, fishing of 208
Summers, Lawrence 50
Supreme Court of Spain 67
sustainability 23, 42, 48, 114, 122, 132, 205
  see also sustainable development
sustainable development 29, 113, 123, 186
  see also sustainability
Syria 120, 254–257, 260,

Thailand 109
timber *see* logging
Timor-Leste 111
toxic trade 154–5, 157, 160–1,171–2
toxic waste 21, 23, 39, 154, 156, 172–179, 214, 270
traditional medicine *see* wildlife, use of in traditional medicine
transnational organised crime *see also* organised crime 231, 273–4,
"treadmill of crime" 50
"treadmill of production" 38, 48, 50
Trinidad and Tobago 112
turtles, importation of 80–81, 212–213
Turkey 156,158,
Tuvalu 42

Uganda 111
United Kingdom 43, 68–69, 132, 212
  see also England; Scotland; Wales
UK Border Force 44
UK Environment Agency 9, 15, 174, 185–198, 203, 269–270
UK Ministry of Defence 226, 228–229
UNESCO 238, 241, 248, 254–256, 260
UNESCO Declaration concerning the Intentional Destruction of Cultural Heritage 254, 256, 258

United Nations 242, 244, 250, 254, 259
  Convention to Combat Desertification
  Convention Against Transnational Organised Crime 172, 256
  Convention on the Law of the Seas 43, 134 (note 8), 139
  Convention on the Rights of the Child 194
  Environment Programme 207, 231
  for Italy 223
  Framework Convention on Climate Change 43, 118
  Interregional Crime and Justice Institute 42
  Millennium Development Goals 43, 223–224
universal jurisdiction 246
UN Human Rights Council 161
UN Security Council 238, 247, 248, 255, 257, 258, 260–261
  resolutions of 248, 254, 256, 258
United States 8, 30, 42–43, 45–49, 132–133, 138, 143, 149–150, 208, 224, 232
US Environmental Protection Agency (EPA) 46, 137
US Fish and Wildlife Services 43
US Department of Justice 43, 48–49
US State Department 232

victim(s) 24, 26–28, 40, 80–81, 111, 156, 160, 191, 193, 202–203, 211, 221, 230
Vienna Convention for the Protection of the Ozone Layer 43
Vietnam 30

Wales 174, 196, 200
  see also United Kingdom
war crimes 270, 30, 31, 238, 240, 243–245, 247, 248, 256
waste 41–43, 44–45, 61, 114–116, 154–179
  electronic *or* e- 42, 45
  illegal disposal of 39, 65–66, 75, 97
  hazardous 5 (note 7), 23, 40–45, 62, 154–179, 193, 271, 273, 277
  radioactive 25, 62, 65, 67, 71
  toxic *see* toxic waste
  illegal trade of 155 *see also* toxic trade
  shipment of 45, 61, 155, 174
water 70–71
water 20, 24–29, 65, 67, 69, 114–115, 133, 137, 141–142, 146, 148, 149–151, 185–186, 198

quality of 70, 116, 186
nitrates in 72–73, 115
pollution in 24, 31, 75, 94, 110, 115–117, 193
waste 70–71
white-collar crime 39, 78, 109
Wild Bird Conservation Act 43
wildlife 3, 10–11, 15, 21, 24, 41–44, 145, 205–217, 224, 230, 232, 271–273
captive breeding of 211
see also livestock, farming of
consumption of the meat of 208–212
cultural meaning of 209–211
endangered species of 7, 43, 66, 216, 277
hunting of 206, 208–210, 212–216
legal trade in 207
smuggling of *see* wildlife, trafficking of
trafficking of 205, 207, 210–217
use of in traditional medicines 209–210
Wildlife and Countryside Act 43
Wildlife Conservation Society 232
World Bank 50, 109–113, 118, 120, 122, 127, 223
World Trade Organization 112
World Customs Organization 44
World Wildlife Fund 211
World Heritage List 244–5, 248
World Heritage site 237, 247, 254–255, 257, 261

Yugoslavia 120, 238, 243, 253